Socioeconomic Profile of Pharmacists in South Florida

Who They Are
What They Do
How Much They Like It

Manuel J. Carvajal
Graciela M. Armayor
Patrick C. Hardigan

VOLUME 1

College of Pharmacy Monograph Series
Nova Southeastern University

Printed in the United States of America

ISBN: 978-0-692-01143-0

http://pharmacy.nova.edu
www.nova.edu

ABOUT THE AUTHORS

MANUEL J. CARVAJAL, Ph.D. in Economics (University of Florida, 1974), is Professor and Chairperson of Sociobehavioral and Administrative Pharmacy at Nova Southeastern University. He is the author/editor of seven books and over 100 journal articles and technical reports on various areas of human capital, including pharmacist workforce, fertility, poverty, gender and ethnic differences, and discrimination. His work involves applied econometrics geared to problem solving and policy recommendations. He has served as a consultant to the U.S. Agency for International Development, the U.S. Department of Agriculture, the World Bank, the Library of Congress, and other organizations.

GRACIELA M. ARMAYOR, Pharm.D. (University of Florida, 1987) and M.S. in Health Professions Education (Nova Southeastern University, 2006), is an assistant professor of Sociobehavioral and Administrative Pharmacy at Nova Southeastern University. She is a Board-certified pharmacotherapist specialist and has practiced in several clinical settings in Florida and Georgia as a clinical pharmacist and clinical coordinator. Her research interests include development and evaluation of innovative delivery and assessment methods for healthcare education and the impact of race, ethnicity, and culture on healthcare outcomes.

PATRICK C. HARDIGAN, Ph.D. in Psychometrics (University of Wyoming, 1996), is the Executive Director for Research at Nova Southeastern University's Health Professions Division. He has published over 50 articles in refereed journals and has provided numerous professional presentations. His research interests include personality type and career choice, latent class modeling of turnover, and item-response-theory approaches to job satisfaction.

FOREWORD

The evolution of the practice of pharmacy in the U.S. over the last half century has gained much relevance in patient care. Today's pharmacists play significant and multifaceted roles in the provision of health care, which enable them to lead fundamental initiatives toward healthcare reform. Their contribution, however, is conditioned by the availability and diversity of qualified practitioners. In light of the currently strong demand for pharmacy services, an in-depth assessment of factors that influence the supply of such services is of the essence. Of course, an assessment of the pharmacist workforce must pay close attention to the past and present state of our national and local healthcare systems; the social, economic, and political environments of a specific area; public as well as private financing opportunities; administrative constraints that affect the costs and benefits of alternative courses of action; and the size, composition, and growth of the population.

The mission of the Nova Southeastern University College of Pharmacy is to address society's pharmacy-related needs. This is largely attained by conducting innovative research and other forms of scholarship. With that in mind, plus the challenges facing the profession in the future, the authors of this book have launched an effort to identify and describe trends within the South Florida pharmacist workforce. Our College of Pharmacy views research oriented toward the discovery of pharmacy trends, as well as the prediction and early detection of future needs, to be vital to the implementation of an educational program that provides the necessary knowledge-based components and skills-development activities to allow our students to become outstanding providers of pharmacy services and leaders in continuing efforts to improve and reform our healthcare system. Therefore, we gladly support this research endeavor.

With the work by Drs. Carvajal, Armayor, and Hardigan, the College of Pharmacy is proud to establish its monograph series. This monograph series is intended to provide a peer-reviewed forum for worldwide scholars' high-quality manuscripts dealing with pharmacy-related original research not published or under consideration for publication elsewhere. The first volume provides a clear and far-reaching overview of the pharmacist workforce in South Florida, with implications for future shifts. Readers have the opportunity to appreciate the authors' extraordinary presentation of empirical evidence within the context of various theoretical frameworks in an extensive review of the literature. Gender, ethnic identification, and age interact with one another in the analysis of demographic characteristics; their convergence on what pharmacists do while practicing their profession and determination of labor market outcomes; and job-related perceptions, attitudes, and opinions that influence the way pharmacists practice their profession. The authors' insightful interpretation and arguments presage the success of this first volume. It seems only logical that work of this caliber be continued in forthcoming volumes.

Andrés Malavé, Ph.D., Dean
College of Pharmacy
Nova Southeastern University

CONTENTS

PREFACE

Explorations into the size, nature, and composition of the pharmacist workforce are an important component of the search for means to enhance pharmacy practice, improve clinical and economic outcomes of medication use, and enrich quality of life for both practitioners and healthcare consumers. Attaining and maintaining an adequate supply of pharmacists, in terms of both volume of practitioners and quality of training, are critical to the provision of timely and accurate pharmaceutical care. This is particularly relevant in light of the growing demand for pharmacy services, as well as the diversification of pharmacists' roles experienced in the last few decades as the focus of the profession has transitioned from product-centered to patient-centered.

Both the quantity and type of professional services rendered by pharmacists are strongly influenced by factors associated with the gender, ethnic group, and age of practitioners. Thus, analyzing the workforce composition by gender, ethnic group, and age is essential to understanding the dynamics involved. Men and women tend to think differently, perceive different kinds of rewards and obstacles in identical situations, and consequently, are prone to follow different courses of action. Decisions made regarding one's professional life are made within the context of the decision maker's unique set of household conditions and constraints; since men and women play different household roles, which are largely dictated by society, a study of the gender composition of the workforce is of utmost significance to the provision of pharmacy services.

Similarly, the ethnic composition is relevant in determining who receives, or rather, does not receive, healthcare services. Insofar as ethnic minority populations seem to draw more services from minority practitioners with whom they are easily able to identify, an ethnically mixed workforce is pivotal to increasing both the quantity and quality of services rendered to ethnic minorities, whose presence in our society is increasingly visible due to growing immigration flows. In addition, of course, decisions regarding one's professional life are made within the context of the norms and mores of the decision maker's ethnic identification group.

Age considerations are consequential, too. The forthcoming retirement and/or reduction in the amount of labor supplied by many baby-boom pharmacists and their replacement by younger practitioners with a different outlook on work and life are bringing substantial changes into the workforce. Therefore, both the quantity and the quality of pharmacy services available to satisfy society's needs are affected.

This exploration focuses on variables that can be grouped along three paths of inquiry into the pharmacist workforce: who they are, what they do, and how much they like what they do. Demographic variables determine who pharmacists are. They include marital status, the presence of children in the household, schooling, investments in human capital beyond schooling, and professional experience. Gender, ethnic group, and age greatly influence these variables. For example, women often have to make choices between housework and marketwork that men generally are not forced to make; more often than not, their marital status and number, as well as ages of progeny, are likely to affect their schooling, their undertaking of postgraduate training, and their labor force participation to a greater extent than they affect men's. Minorities may experience different marriage and/or offspring patterns than do non-minorities, and because of income and wealth disparities may encounter fewer schooling and postgraduate training opportunities available to them or may exhibit different patterns of labor force attachment. Age is an important determinant of demographic variables not only because of its effect on marital status and presence of children, but also because it sets the time horizons over which individuals may accrue returns from their schooling and postgraduate training investments as well as their work experience.

Who pharmacists are governs what they do. What pharmacists do while practicing their profession is captured in this book under the heading of situation variables. These indicators address labor market outcomes that result from the interaction of demographic indicators, preferences, and market conditions. The situation outcomes examined in this book include employment longevity, choice of practice setting, whether pharmacists primarily serve a specific population, type of pharmacy activities, urban-rural location of practice setting, distance to work and commuting time, amount of labor supplied, pharmacy earnings, wage rate, household income, and whether or not the pharmacist's spouse works. Once again, gender, ethnic group, and age are responsible for outcome differentials. One of the purposes of this research endeavor is to discover the nature and intensity of these differentials.

Who pharmacists are also governs their job-related perceptions, attitudes, and opinions. Furthermore, perceptions, attitudes, and opinions influence, and are influenced by, what pharmacists do while practicing their profession in such a way that the three paths of inquiry–demographic, situation, and opinion variables—are intimately intertwined through a symbiotic relationship affected by gender, ethnic group, and age. Opinion indicators are intended to focus on how much pharmacists like what they do in terms of the perception of their role in the healthcare delivery system, their individual working conditions, and other components of job and career satisfaction. The job-related opinion variables probed in this book are satisfaction with current job and with the profession, workload, stress, advancement opportunities, job security, autonomy, fairness in the workplace, supervisor's performance in providing help and support, job atmosphere, flexibility, coworkers' professional quality, and coworkers' willingness to render help and support.

The exploration takes place in South Florida, which is defined as comprising Broward, Miami-Dade, and Palm Beach—the three larger counties on the Atlantic coast; Collier, Hendry, Lee, and Monroe—the four smaller, contiguous counties on the Gulf coast or inland; and Martin and Pasco counties—located on the periphery, to detect possible contrasts. The location is ideal for this kind of study for several reasons. It encompasses a relatively small area, approximately 11,400 square miles, in such a way that exogenous forces such as climate, topography, physical accessibility, state laws and taxes, etc. may be held constant. Yet the nine counties included in the study are quite heterogeneous. Broward, Miami-Dade, and Palm Beach are highly urbanized, while the other counties are generally more rural. Minorities comprise a substantial portion of the population, and more importantly, a substantial portion of practicing pharmacists are members of a minority ethnic group. In addition, all relevant age groups are represented; there is not only a heavy geriatric presence in the general population of the area, but also in the South Florida pharmacist workforce, since many practitioners opt to continue working past their 70th birthday. Thus, South Florida constitutes a desirable social science laboratory because of its overall diversity and ethnic mix.

The behavior of the demographic, situation, and opinion indicators is reported in 90 detailed tables presented at the end of Chapters 3, 4, 5, and 6. Most of these tables are arranged into two sets of headings: a) county of residence, gender, and ethnic group; and b) county of residence, gender, and age group. In order to protect respondents' anonymity, the data for the four smaller counties (Collier, Hendry, Lee, and Monroe) are aggregated into one category, and the same procedure is applied to Martin and Pasco, the periphery counties.

While the study is empirically oriented, it contains extensive discussions of the arguments and contentions commonly found in the literature in examining each variable. Since no specific hypotheses are tested throughout the book—please bear in mind that this is an exploration—the authors refrain from espousing any line of reasoning or opposing side. Rather, a variety of arguments are presented to provide a theoretical context within which to interpret and assess the behavior of each indicator.

Finally, the variety theme extends into the methodological approach followed from the beginning. The book is written by an economist, a pharmacist, and a behavioral scientist. Considerations regarding supply and demand, the provision of pharmaceutical care, and the power of perception and interpretation are combined throughout the text in an attempt to complement one another. The authors hope this combination will contribute to a better understanding of the variables affecting pharmacist workforce dynamics in South Florida and elsewhere as well as highlighting the relevance of this research field within the realm of social and administrative pharmacy.

ACKNOWLEDGMENTS

The authors wish to express their gratitude to Nova Southeastern University's Health Professions Division for its financial support of this project. They extend their appreciation to Dr. Andrés Malavé for selecting this book as the first volume of the newly created Nova Southeastern University College of Pharmacy Monograph Series. Thanks also are due to Dr. Leanne Lai for obtaining the names and addresses of registered South Florida pharmacists, to Drs. Sari H. Turchan and Hiroko Ouchi for their diligent work as student research assistants, and to Ms. Kathleen P. Hagen and Ms. Kymberly Robinson for editing various versions of the manuscript. Most importantly, the authors thank the hundreds of practitioners throughout South Florida who gave of their precious time to reply to the survey questionnaire. Without their responses, this profile would not have been possible.

LIST OF TABLES

Tables—Chapter 2

Tables—Chapter 3

Tables—Chapter 4

Tables—Chapter 5

Tables—Chapter 6

1 INTRODUCTION

The composition of the U.S. labor force has changed dramatically over the past few decades. Women have emerged as a substantial component, minority workers have grown in relative importance, and labor force participants have aged. Gender, ethnic, and age diversity today are the rule rather than the exception in virtually every occupation [DiCecio *et al.*, 2008; Mau and Kopischke, 2001; Nguyen, 2008; Pitts, 2009; Toossi, 2007]. Pharmacy is no exception. A profession once dominated by men has become increasingly attractive to women. Since 1985, the majority of pharmacy school graduates nationwide have been female—currently over two-thirds of graduates are women—with consequent gains in composition, from 31 percent in 1990 to 43 percent in 2000 and about half at the present time [Brown *et al.*, 2006; Gardner and Stowe, 2007; Johnson, 2008; Kenreigh and Wagner, 2006; Mott, 2000; Rix, 2006; Shih, 2000; Walton and Cooksey, 2001].

Gains by minorities are less noticeable. A recent Report of the American Society of Hospital Pharmacists (ASHP) Task Force on Pharmacy's Changing Demographics [2007] points out that in the 2003–2004 academic year, Asian Americans received 23 percent of pharmacy degrees, while the shares of Non-Hispanic Blacks and Hispanics were 7.7 percent and 3.7 percent, respectively. (The percentage of Non-Hispanic Blacks shows a modest increase from 4.3 percent in 1985, but the percentage of Hispanics has remained constant.) Thus, both affected minorities continue to be underrepresented in the profession [Manasse and Speedie, 2007]. At the same time, a steady flow of immigrants has caused the foreign-born share of the U.S. population to increase from 4.8 percent in 1970 to 11.1 percent in 2000. Most new immigrants come from Asia and Latin America [Blau and Khan, 2005], that is, two of the most salient ethnic minority groups.

Age diversity is important in light of the inevitable, forthcoming retirement prospects of the baby-boom generation. Yet baby boomers seem to be postponing retirement plans. The number of older pharmacists is increasing, as well as their median age; in fact, the growth of the older workforce in the next decade is projected to be much greater than the workforce growth of the other age groups [Mott *et al.*, 2006; Toossi, 2007]. But as more baby boomers reach 55 years of age or older, and their labor supply declines because they opt for either part-time work or retirement, overall labor force participation rates are bound to decrease [Mahrous and Maziarz, 2008]. Nonetheless, Knapp and Cultice [2007] estimate that continued and even increased work force participation by older pharmacists who remain active in the profession will boost the supply of pharmacy services in the next few years.

If these general trends that drive the U.S. labor force, the health sector, and pharmacy toward greater gender, ethnic, and age diversity were absent, our socioeconomic system would lack the capability to fulfill the healthcare and other needs of all Americans. Increasing diversity among healthcare professionals is important because diversity leads to more widespread and effective coverage of specific groups, especially ethnic minorities, which have a long history of inaccessibility to, and underutilization of, healthcare services. As a point of illustration, consider that African Americans have a greater probability than Non-Hispanic Whites to die from stroke, cancer, or diabetes *mellitus*, and experience higher infant mortality rates. Non-Hispanic Blacks and Hispanics also have higher rates of HIV infection than do non-minorities, and are more likely to die from homicide [Kingston *et al.*, 2001]. A landmark report by the Institute of Medicine [Smedley *et al.*, 2003] has found that, in addition to exhibiting poor health status, minorities are less likely than non-minorities to receive health care services, including clinically necessary procedures, even when controlling for insurance availability, patient income, and other access-related factors. Despite recent improvements in absolute numbers, the issue of ethnic disparities in health and health care continues to be very relevant [Cohen *et al.*, 2002]. The evidence suggests that provider stereotyping, bias, and uncertainty during the clinical encounter contribute to the disparate treatment of minorities. The report points out that one approach to remedying disparities in health care due to provider factors is to increase the diversity of the healthcare workforce. In the long run, improving the quality of health care in the U.S. requires the elimination of ethnic disparities in health [Bierman *et al.*, 2002].

African American, Hispanic, and female practitioners are more likely to provide care to the poor and to patients on Medicaid than are their non-minority, male counterparts [Cantor *et al.*, 1996; Smedley *et al.*, 2004; Weeks and Wallace, 2006a, 2006b, 2006c]. Increasing diversity among healthcare professionals also is conducive to improved patient options, better communication with patients, more choices for practitioners, and greater levels of patient and professional satisfaction [Report of the ASHP *Ad Hoc* Committee, 2005]. Diversity of healthcare professionals promotes cultural competency, which seems to affect clinical outcomes significantly.

Cultural competency rests on the awareness of one's cultural beliefs, opinions, attitudes, and practices; the realization that they are influenced strongly by one's own gender, ethnic group, and age, among other factors; and the recognition that people from other groups may not share the same beliefs, opinions, attitudes, and practices. It dictates that healthcare practitioners be sensitive, understanding, and respectful in dealing with patients whose cultural outlook is different, no matter how deviant their ideas might seem, and that they act in a nonjudgmental, flexible way for the sake of the patient while not demeaning him/her in any way. According to Cohen *et al.* [2002], cultural competency enables healthcare practitioners to understand how patients perceive and experience illnesses, seek medical advice, comply with prescribed regimens, and respond to therapy within the context of their biases, belief systems, socioeconomic position in society, personal experiences, and myriad culturally defined factors that are manifested in everyday occurrences such as language barriers; taboos; or preference for unorthodox, alternative remedies, among others. Such awareness and sensitivity are unlikely to be transmitted through books, lectures, or discussion groups; they must be acquired by exposure. Only by encountering and interacting with individuals of different backgrounds can the young understand the world of the old, Non-Hispanic Whites grasp the home environments of ethnic minorities, and everybody realize that the massive entry of women into a traditionally predominantly male profession does not necessarily mean that expectations and career paths will be identical, or even similar, for both genders.

DEMAND FOR PHARMACISTS

Labor market outcomes are determined by the interaction of supply and demand forces. Labor supply is shaped by individual-specific preferences that yield choices between work and nonmarket activity in response to available opportunities. These opportunities arise out of employment decisions implemented by business firms and the public sector. Understanding the structure of the demand for labor requires knowledge of the ongoing relationships among organizational environments, forms, and structures as these organizations respond to their customers' demand for goods and services within existing social expectations and institutional constraints. More specifically, labor demand is a derived demand influenced by employer-established job requirements such as skills, experience, and productivity [Gabriel and Schmitz, 2007; Sørensen, 2007].

The demand for pharmacists is intimately related to the demand for pharmaceuticals and pharmacist-provided patient care services. It has risen in the recent past and is likely to continue rising rapidly in the foreseeable future [Okunade, 2006]. The overall growth of the population and the sustained increase in life expectancy and, consequently, aging of the population are major factors pushing up the demand for pharmacists. Individuals 65 years of age and older consume twice as many prescription medications as the rest of the country; they also purchase 40 percent of all nonprescription drugs, even though they comprise less than 15 percent of the population. Furthermore, 85 percent of them suffer from at least one chronic condition (*i.e.*, heart disease, cancer, stroke, musculoskeletal disorders, or Alzheimer's disease) that requires continuous treatment, and more than half use regularly three or more prescription medications [Manasse and Speedie, 2007; Report of the ASHP Task Force on Pharmacy's Changing Demographics, 2007]. Between 2000 and 2030 the U.S. population is projected to grow by an estimated 82 million people, or 29 percent [U.S. Census Bureau, 2005]. During the same time period, the population of individuals 65 years of age and older will more than double [U.S. Census Bureau, 2005, 2008b], and the U.S. Bureau of Health Professions [2008] projects that demographic changes alone will increase the number of new prescriptions generated through physician offices and hospital visits by approximately 44 percent between 2005 and 2030. As the population continues to expand and the 65-year-and-older segment increases in both absolute numbers and relative importance, the demand for pharmacy services also will continue to go up. A rapid growth in the demand for pharmacists and other healthcare occupations reflects three basic phenomena—an aging population in need of more health care, a wealthier population that can afford it, and advances in medical technology that continue to reduce morbidity and mortality.

Another important factor influencing the growth of prescription medication use has been the expansion of prescription drug coverage by third-party payers in both the private and the public sectors. Throughout the 20th century, prescription coverage increased dramatically due to the provision of such benefits by private health insurance and managed care plans [U.S. Bureau of Health Professions, 2000]. In 2003, the Medicare Prescription Drug Improvement and Modernization Act (MMA), which created Medicare Part D, was enacted. The MMA marked the first time the Federal Government provided comprehensive prescription drug coverage for seniors and other Medicare recipients. Following its full implementation in 2006, Medicare Part D was estimated to provide prescription drug coverage to about 11 million people who had no previous prescription coverage. As a result of the increase in coverage, it is estimated that the volume will amount to an additional 14 to 30 million prescriptions per month [Manasse and Speedy, 2007; U.S. Bureau of Health Professions, 2008]. As more individuals acquire prescription drug coverage through third-party payers, the demand for pharmacist services will increase further.

Pharmacists' expanding range of responsibilities also has been a contributing factor to the rapidly growing demand for their services. In a succinct, yet revealing, synopsis of pharmacists' roles in the last 100 years, Manasse and Speedie [2007] show how primary responsibilities have broadened from preparing reliable medications and distributing them to patients in the early 20th century to distributing medications manufactured by large-scale production facilities in midcentury; moving into clinical roles, especially in hospital settings, in the 1960s, which involved interacting with physicians and nurses, providing drug information, monitoring drug therapy, and occasionally adjusting doses based on pharmacokinetic data; and counseling patients in the 1970s about their prescription drugs and the best way to use them. The sequel to this process was the passage of the Omnibus Reconciliation Act of 1990, which requires pharmacists to review patients' prescriptions and provide proper counseling as integral components of their professional responsibilities.

With the adoption of pharmaceutical care as the profession's mission, the pharmacist's role continued to expand from a product-centered to a patient-centered focus in the latter part of the 20th century. Under pharmaceutical care the profession embraced the obligation to meet the medication-use needs of society [American Society of Hospital Pharmacists, 1993; Hepler and Strand, 1990; Penna, 1990]. As a result, pharmacists engaged in efforts to improve the quality of the medication-use process and identify ways to reduce medication errors in all practice settings. Today, in addition to their dispensing functions, pharmacists deliver an increasing number of patient-related services that include providing drug information; patient education; therapeutic drug monitoring; consulting on drug utilization programs; providing formulary management services; coordinating care with other healthcare professionals; conducting research; and furthering public health initiatives such as smoking cessation programs, diabetes education, and immunizations [Cooksey *et al.*, 2002; Oh *et al.*, 2002; Pedersen *et al.*, 2001; U.S. Bureau of Health Professions, 2000]. These services are provided in a wide variety of sites encompassing not only community and hospital, but also industry, long-term care, home health, and other venues. In addition, new jobs are emerging in the insurance/managed-care industry; in an attempt to improve preventative care and cut costs, insurers use pharmacists to analyze trends and patterns in medication use, sales and marketing, and pharmacy informatics (*i.e.*, the use of information technology to improve patient care). Moreover, passage of the MMA and its recognition of the need for medication therapy management services is expected to expand further the role of pharmacists as providers of disease and drug therapy management services [Alexander and Gatewood, 2008; Martin and McSpadden, 2008]. These requirements, added through time to the practice of pharmacy, have exerted additional pressure on the quantity and quality of services demanded.

Other factors accounting for a rapidly expanding labor demand for pharmacists are advances in medical technology that allow a greater array of health problems to be treated more aggressively, along with the development of pharmaceuticals designed to treat conditions previously considered untreatable; direct-to-customer advertising; greater acceptance by society of the use of pharmaceuticals to treat illnesses; higher levels of national income, which allow people to buy more and better healthcare goods and services; greater administrative requirements for handling third-party payments; and market expansions in the chain pharmacy industry [Cline, 2003; Gershon *et al.*, 2000; Kenreigh and Wagner, 2006; Teeter, 2004; Walton and Cooksey, 2001]. Competition in the community pharmacy marketplace has led to the replacement of independently owned retail pharmacies by chain drugstores. The shift from independent pharmacies to chain pharmacies has created a demand for more practitioners. Unlike independent pharmacies, chain drugstores require a larger staffing level because their pharmacists tend to work fewer hours, thus requiring more practitioners to staff each store. In addition, the opening of new chain pharmacies and expansion of hours of operation, with some increasing to 24 hours per day, has further raised the demand for pharmacists in this setting [U.S. Bureau of Health Professions, 2000]. Finally, the demand for pharmacists also is influenced by the use of technology and/or support personnel, who may serve as substitutes for pharmacists or increase their productivity in certain aspects of their jobs. Walton *et al.* [2004a] point out that throughout the U.S., pharmacists and pharmacy technicians and aides relate to one another as complements rather than substitutes. In the future, the projected demand for pharmacists is likely to change according to changes in government policies and programs, the shift to centralized distribution nuclei by chain drugstore companies, advances in biotechnology and their impact on individualized drug therapy, and the level of economic conditions [Thompson, 2009; U.S. Bureau of Health Professions, 2008].

SUPPLY OF PHARMACISTS

The demand for pharmacy services by a dynamic healthcare environment requires an adequate supply of pharmacists. The current pharmacy workforce is estimated to be between 230,000 and 250,000 practitioners nationwide, which makes pharmacy the third largest professional healthcare group in the United States after nurses and physicians [Knapp and Cultice, 2007; U.S. Bureau of Labor Statistics, 2009]. Accounting for approximately 55 percent of the workforce, men constitute a slight majority in spite of the massive entrance of women into the profession in the last few decades, and with the exception of Asian Americans, ethnic minorities are underrepresented [U.S. Bureau of Health Professions, 2008]. About 22 percent of pharmacists have earned a Pharm.D. degree, a fraction which will increase in the future with new generations of graduates as the traditional bachelor of science degree was phased out in 2004.

Affected by new graduates annually, net migration, and occupational separation, the size of the pharmacist workforce is changing constantly. Graduates include students who fulfill the academic requirements of domestic colleges and schools of pharmacy and subsequent licensure, as well as graduates from foreign institutions who become licensed to practice the profession in the United States. An average of 600 foreign-trained pharmacists are estimated to enter the workforce every year, and they comprise less than 6 percent of the active pharmacist workforce [Knapp and Cultice, 2007; U.S. Bureau of Health Professions, 2000, 2008]. The annual number of U.S. graduates has fluctuated historically. It increased rapidly from 3,360 to 8,011 between 1960 and 1977, but during the 1980s and 1990s there were periods of decline followed by periods of rapid growth and subsequent periods of decline. Since 2004, a sustained growth has been recorded in the number of U.S. graduates entering the workforce, with an all-time high of about 10,500 new entrants in 2008 [American Association of Colleges of Pharmacy, 2009].

In pharmacy, as in other healthcare professions, there has been a shortage of practitioners for over a decade [Cline and Mott, 2000; Johnson, 2008; Kahaleh and Gaither, 2005; Kenreigh and Wagner, 2006; Knapp and Livesey, 2002]. In 2000, the Pharmacy Workforce Study reported a shortage of pharmacists in the U.S. that was believed to have started as early as 1998 [U.S. Bureau of Health Professions, 2000]. More recent findings, however, provide evidence to support an easing of this shortage, as indicated by a drop in the pharmacy vacancy rate from 8 percent in 2000 to approximately 5 percent in 2004. This amounts to a shortage of about 10,400 pharmacists nationwide [Knapp and Cultice, 2007; Thompson, 2009; U.S. Bureau of Health Professions, 2008]. While the low supply of licensed pharmacists has contributed to the shortage, it has not been the primary force; rather, demand issues such as the rapid growth in medication use and the expanding array of pharmacist services have been the main causes [Cooksey *et al.*, 2002; Mahrous and Maziarz, 2008]. Yet the increasing number of pharmacists entering the workforce has helped to ease the pressure. This trend has been conditioned by the opening of new colleges and schools throughout the United States, the use of distance learning models in pharmacy education, and a decrease in the separation rates from the profession.

The 21st century is witnessing so far an explosion in the number of colleges and schools of pharmacy established all around the country. The number of colleges and schools with fully accredited professional degree programs rose from 82 in 2000 to 93 in 2009, with 18 additional programs receiving candidate status and another five being granted pre-candidate status [Accreditation Council for Pharmacy Education, 2009]. More of these colleges and schools are moving to increase class size via adoption of distance learning models that use both satellite campuses and the Internet. Consequently, the number of professional degrees conferred is expected to increase by 100 degrees per year over the next ten years [Knapp and Cultice, 2007].

Separation from the workforce may result from death, retirement, or leaving practice. Most pharmacists remain active in the profession for at least 35 years; by 55 years of age, 85 percent of practitioners are estimated to continue working, and this fraction drops to slightly below half by age 65 [U.S. Bureau of Health Professions, 2008]. Gender conditions the activity rate. Women 30–39 years old are less likely than men of the same age to be active, probably due to engaging in childrearing and household work, while women are more likely than men to be active in the 40–60-year-old bracket. This latter trend reveals a preference for early retirement by male pharmacists. Higher wages in response to the labor shortage have drawn some pharmacists back into the workforce and have motivated others to postpone retirement [Thompson, 2009]. As a result, separation rates from the workforce have declined recently [Knapp and Cultice, 2007]. The aggregate effect of the growth in the number of new U.S. graduates and the drop in the separation rate from the profession has increased the supply of pharmacists in the labor market beyond the predictions of the Pharmacy Workforce Study of 2000 [Knapp and Cultice, 2007; U.S. Bureau of Health Professions, 2000, 2008].

The pharmacist's role in the future will be heavily influenced by the adequacy of labor supply. By the year 2020, the workforce is projected to reach 305,000 practitioners. This workforce will be 62 percent female, 68 percent will be practicing with a Pharm.D. degree, and will be about four years younger than the current workforce. The ratio of pharmacists per 100,000 population is expected to rise, although the ratio of pharmacists per 100,000 population 65 years and older will go down as more baby boomers move into their senior years. Current projections estimate that the number of pharmacists in the workforce of the future will be sufficient to meet the demands of a growing and aging population only if the use of prescription drugs remains at current levels. This is not likely to be the case, however, because the adoption of new curative technology continuously expands the range of diseases that may be treated, new preventive medications prove to be successful in reducing morbidity and mortality rates, and previously uninsured individuals obtain insurance coverage through proposed healthcare reform programs, all three of which tend to increase the use of prescription drugs [Knapp and Cultice, 2007; Thompson, 2009; U.S. Bureau of Health Professions, 2008]. If this is the case, the supply of pharmacists would need to increase beyond what is currently projected to meet the demand generated by the growth in per capita consumption of pharmaceuticals. Other factors such as the desire to work fewer hours and changes in retirement patterns also may alter future supply projections.

LABOR-LEISURE DECISIONS

Why do pharmacists, or, for that matter, other individuals work? Neoclassical economic theory holds that people work in response to their valuation of market goods, leisure, and other pursuits in an attempt to optimize utility [Carvajal and Hardigan, 2007; Hotchkiss, 2006; Mott, 2001; Pettit and Hook, 2005]. This involves a tradeoff among wage rates, job characteristics, and nonwork activities, including leisure. When the wage rate goes up, an hour of work is more attractive to pharmacists due to the increase in cost for an hour of leisure; a rise in the wage rate increases the opportunity cost of leisure (*i.e.*, consumption of nonmarket activities) as the marginal utility of consuming more goods and services increases, thus triggering a tendency to substitute out of leisure time into labor time, that is, a substitution effect, to take advantage of the inducement, work more hours, and consume additional amounts of market goods and services.

But rising wage rates cannot lead indefinitely to more hours of work; eventually one would run out of leisure time. As leisure becomes relatively scarce because of the substitution effect, the marginal utility of nonmarket activities is likely to rise, which in turn increases the opportunity cost of work and market goods and services that may be purchased with additional income. In other words, with more income, the pharmacist is able to buy additional amounts of goods and services, but he/she needs more time to consume them. Since the pharmacist is better off financially due to the wage rate increase, he/she can afford to consume more leisure time along with goods and services, and reduce the amount of time spent working. This mechanism is known as the income effect.

Different wage rates carry with them opposite substitution and income effects based on pharmacists' valuation of leisure, appreciation of job characteristics, and other factors. The outcome will depend on whether the positive substitution effect prevails over the negative income effect, the negative income effect outweighs the positive substitution effect, or they merely cancel each other. Obviously, pharmacists' valuation of leisure, appreciation of job characteristics, and response to other factors are highly subjective. For example, other factors may include one's marital status or the presence of children in the household, self-worth perceptions, life-cycle stage, cultural background, and myriad personal characteristics and situations influenced by gender, ethnic group, and age.

The interplay of supply of and demand for labor does not take place in a vacuum. Oftentimes structural conditions of labor markets affect decisions to work as well as employment outcomes. These conditions may be stirred by prejudice, bias, or outright hostility against certain groups, ranging from disguised barriers to open discrimination. Ultimately, these groups may self-select out of a profession or trade because they perceive few advancement opportunities or project that they have to surmount onerous obstacles compared to other groups. Some populations may even become clustered in enclaves characterized by severe isolation, high crime rates, or other unpalatable working conditions [Dickerson, 2007; Leggon, 2006].

In a competitive market, discrimination, aside from its legal implications, leads to an economic penalty on the perpetrator. When an employer discriminates against workers on the basis of anything other than productivity differences, he/she/it pays a premium vis-à-vis nondiscriminating employers who are willing to hire more workers from the affected groups. The demand for affected groups' workers tends to mitigate, and eventually may eliminate, any earnings effects on affected groups, but the extent to which wage differentials are reduced or eliminated depends on the intensity and extent of preferences for discrimination by employers and the interaction of these factors with the labor market structure [O'Neill and O'Neill, 2005]. Likewise, the adverse work surrounding conditions of less desirable areas may require a compensation differential in pay to offset the influence of an enclave or geographically depressed area.

Even if employers are not prejudiced against individual members of affected groups, the affected groups may suffer the consequences of statistical discrimination. If employers believe that women, ethnic minorities, or younger people in general tend to exhibit certain undesirable job-related traits such as less attachment to the labor force or greater propensity to change jobs, they may use this information (or misinformed stereotype) to refrain from hiring women, ethnic minorities, and/or the young in positions that require substantial fixed costs related to firm-paid employment and training. While statistical discrimination is likely to disappear as employers discover the benefits of obtaining more accurate and specific information about the pharmacists they intend to hire (*e.g.*, checking references from previous employers or inquiring about their work history), in the short run, statistical discrimination may cause wage and other differentials between affected and unaffected groups [Blau and DeVaro, 2007; Hersch, 2006].

SOURCES OF DIVERSITY

Diversity has been extolled repeatedly as beneficial for all groups—men and women, the various ethnic classifications, younger and older—and for society as a whole [Ash, 2008; Otto and Gurbey, 2006]. It fosters variety in thinking on issues and creates divergent processes, thus broadening the width of options to deal with problems and conflicts. It also provides advantages in terms of programming and creativity that cannot be obtained otherwise [Cox and Blake, 1991].

Since pharmacists are expected to play an increasing role in the provision of healthcare services, studying their employment-related choices, the determinants of these choices, and their impact on the labor market is important for health workforce planning and programming. Analyzing patterns of pharmacists' characteristics, perceptions, and job-related behavior is likely to reveal how they react to changes in labor demand and provide insights into the future of the pharmacist workforce. Following the central theme outlined earlier, these patterns are analyzed along gender, ethnic, and age classifications.

Gender Diversity

Differences between men and women transcend physical appearance and biological functions. As a general rule, according to Maier [1999], in striving for success men engage in competition to win, while women search for a balance in life activities and try to advance others as well as themselves; men subordinate other life activities to the pursuit of career goals, while women attempt to find an equilibrium between work and non-work activities; and men's purpose of communication is to solve problems, establish status, and convey independence, while for women it is to establish connection and attain intimacy. He also points out that men's image of leadership lies within a hierarchical setting, driven by status, while for women the concept of authority is of a more personal nature, determined by competence and expertise. This diversity of views has a profound impact on the reactions by men and women to all sorts of stimuli.

Decisions regarding whether or not to work, amount of effort, venue, etc. usually are made within the context of households' decision packages influenced by the composition of the household, constraints, and the gender-role ideology of marital partners, among other factors. Traditionally men and women fulfill different roles in the family. Regardless of level of income, men tend to assume the role of breadwinners and women tend to assume the role of homemakers [Corrigall and Konrad, 2007; Perrone *et al.*, 2005; Potucheck, 1997; Shauman and Noonan, 2007; Sinacore and Akçali, 2000]. Men and women are likely to choose heterogeneous levels of commitment in the career and home spheres of their lives due to their socially defined, differentiated involvement with child care and household responsibilities. Since personal energy levels are finite, women normally assign less importance to the centrality of market work in their lives than do men [Brown, 2002; Harpaz and Fu, 1997; Phillips and Imhoff, 1997] and end up working in the labor market fewer hours than do men, plus they show a greater propensity to work part time because they are expected to do relatively more chores at home [Carvajal and Hardigan, 2008; Cunningham, 2008; Fogli and Veldkamp, 2007; Gaither, 1999; Hojat *et al.*, 2000; Hundley, 2000; Mott, 2000; Poeschl *et al.*, 2006; Quesenberry *et al.*, 2006].

Consequently, compared to men, women experience more interruptions in their careers, which affects negatively their acquisition of special training, work experience, and other human-capital assets, all of which is reflected in lower earnings and wage rates, fewer promotions, and less accessibility to management positions [Ahituv and Tienda, 2004; Alon *et al.*, 2001; Blasius and Pae, 2005; Report of the ASHP Task Force on Pharmacy's Changing Demographics, 2007; Valentine, 2001]. According to a recent study, men's average salary is 17 percent higher than the average salary of their female counterparts [Campbell, 2007]. These factors also increase the potential for discrimination by employers who believe that women are less productive than men on account of their domestic obligations. The essence of gender discrimination lies in employers' sustained preference to hire men when faced with a choice between equally qualified men and women. Thus, gender discrimination sets a higher hurdle for women than for men, and women who are able to cross the hurdle do so because they perform better than their male peers; ironically, however, if the standards for women were lowered under the guidelines of an affirmative-action initiative in search of gender balance, the newly hired women would perform worse than their male colleagues, which would reassure discriminators that the practice of preferring men to women in the workplace is appropriate [Green *et al.*, 2007]. Obviously the same argument applies to other affected groups such as ethnic minorities, the elderly, and so on. An interesting observation is that even if women and minorities hired under affirmative action have lower readily observed qualifications, employers generally do not report significantly lower performance for these groups relative to Non-Hispanic White men [Holzer and Neumark, 2000].

While marriage and family formation probably are the variables that exert the greatest influence on men's and women's labor market outcomes (since getting married and having children increase women's household labor time and decrease their number of hours of paid work [Coltrane, 2000; Kaufman and Uhlenberg, 2000]), caring for the elderly also detracts more from women's than from men's labor force attachment. If women continue to assume more of the burden of informal caregiving as the population ages, their position in the labor force may deteriorate. Caregiving for more than ten hours per week has serious, negative consequences on female workers [Carmichael and Charles, 2003a, 2003b], although, as Lilly *et al.* [2007] point out, potential caregivers who are employed full time and are earning fairly high wages may opt not to care but to maintain or even increase their hours of paid labor in order to buy care services.

Moreover it may be argued that caregivers, especially women, tend to self-select from a pool of underemployed or labor force nonparticipants who have relatively low labor market opportunity costs; if this is the case, the negative impact of caregiving on women's working outcomes may be overestimated.

Whether women, and to a lesser extent men, interrupt their careers or work fewer hours on account of marriage, the birth of a child, caregiving, or other reasons such as personal illness, etc., they may face serious challenges when they attempt to re-enter the workforce. Barriers to career re-entry include high levels of anxiety, low self-esteem, lack of institutional support, and an absence of mentors [Mark and Gupta, 2002]. The Report of the ASHP Task Force on Pharmacy's Changing Demographics [2007] recommends that career re-entry programs be institutionalized and that they address specific personal and educational needs. Some of the features recommended are offering refresher courses, flexible work schedules, opportunities to update skills, and an effective mentoring network.

Several studies suggest that younger women are likely to experience the greatest work-family conflict challenges—Adams *et al.* [1996] and Mott *et al.* [2004] define work-family conflict as a situation in which the role pressures from work and family are mutually incompatible—and there are several reasons for this effect. One is that younger female professionals usually have a spouse with a similarly, or perhaps more, demanding professional career, whereas male professionals tend to have spouses with less demanding jobs, if at all [Bergman *et al.*, 2003; Gjerberg, 2003]. This magnifies work-family conflict for the woman insofar as society bestows on her most household responsibilities and family obligations, even when she works as many hours as her spouse [Jovic *et al.*, 2006]. More often than not, women hold different work and family values and interests from those held by men, which lead them to search for and choose jobs that minimize work-family conflict. Work-family conflict is detrimental to both work and family life [Perrone *et al.*, 2006], as it has been linked to psychological distress, marital discord, and reduced work and life satisfaction [Allen *et al.*, 2000; Bruck *et al.*, 2002; Chiu, 1998; Grant-Vallone and Donaldson, 2001; Perrewe and Hochwarter, 2001].

Another reason for the special predicament of many women, especially younger women, is the perception by themselves, as well as others, of their jobs as a secondary income source. Notwithstanding the dramatic long-term increase in female labor force participation of the last 60 years, much of which can be attributed to the work of married women, the participation of men is more procyclical than the participation of women [Mosisa and Hipple, 2006]. (Procyclical labor force participation means that the rate increases during economic expansions, when more people join the workforce because jobs are easier to find, and falls during economic downturns as individuals drop out of the labor force in response to fewer opportunities available.) This relationship evinces the so called added-worker effect, whereby women enter the labor force, or work more hours, to offset their spouses' job losses. As men become unemployed or are forced to work fewer hours during a downturn of the business cycle, women move in to compensate for the loss of household income. The fact that female labor force participation is almost three times more volatile than the participation of men reflects society's general view that women are primarily homemakers and secondarily income earners [DiCecio *et al.*, 2008].

Still another instance that manifests the relatively greater burden of younger women regarding work-home conflict can be found in the distribution of costs and benefits of family migration due to gender asymmetries. Wives are less likely than are husbands to initiate moves because wives' gains from migration usually are exceeded by their husbands' losses [Shauman and Noonan, 2007]. They also are less likely to resist moves initiated by their husbands (*i.e.*, job-related relocation, search for new opportunities, etc.) because, as secondary income earners, their income loss resulting from family migration often is exceeded by their husbands' expected earnings gains. Thus, when compared to their men, the job longevity of younger, married women tends to be substantially less.

Notwithstanding these and other gender asymmetries, over the last 60 years female labor force participation has gone up steadily, while the percentage of men participating in the workforce has declined [Blank and Shierholz, 2006; Hartmann, 2001; Hotchkiss, 2005]. The two trends have occurred in spite of men's continuously limited participation in household chores [Poeschl, 2000; Stohs, 1995]. Quesenberry *et al.* [2006] illustrate this point using data from the National Council for Women's Organization stating that, on average, women devote 35.1 hours per week to household duties while men devote, on average, 17.4 hours per week. Fernández *et al.* [2004] argue that the initial factor that pushed up female labor force participation can be traced to the higher proportion of children brought up by working mothers during World War II. The mobilization of men on account of the war, according to them, provided a powerful exogenous shock to women's labor supply and the acceptance by subsequent generations that women belong in the labor market. This was followed by a period of rapid growth of female-dominated occupations in the post-war era [Pettit and Hook, 2005] and the elimination of legal barriers to gender-based employment and pay discrimination [Luce and Brenner, 2006]. Afterwards, three major developments accelerated the trend: One was the expansion of household technologies (*i.e.*, dishwasher, clothes washer and dryer, microwave oven, vacuum cleaner, etc.), which have eased the burden of household production, affording women more time to devote to educational attainment and the pursuit of market jobs without a drop in the consumption of home-produced goods. Second, improved medical knowledge and obstetric practices have reduced the time and cost associated with women's reproductive role, and the introduction of infant formula has reduced women's comparative advantage in child care by providing an effective breast milk substitute. And third, progressively more effective means of contraception have provided women with more control over the number and timing of childbearing outcomes [Albanesi and Olivetti, 2007; Falcao and Soares, 2007; Goldin and Katz, 2002; Greenwood *et al.*, 2005; Hotchkiss, 2006].

Fogli and Veldkamp [2007], however, contend that focusing on the availability of technology misses the fact that a woman's beliefs are an important determinant of her labor participation decision. Departing from the assumption that a woman's choice to work is affected by the expected effect of employment on her children, they argue that women pass down beliefs about the importance of nurturing to their children and each generation updates these beliefs depending on the children's outcomes. Initially, very few women participated in the labor market, but eventually the effects of workforce participation became less uncertain and participation rates rose. Supporting this view, Goldin [1990] argues that shifts in demand toward the service sector, reduced work hours, and rising real wages have encouraged women's workforce participation. In any event, men and women constantly redefine their gender roles, and this process often requires new ways to balance work and family roles [Coltrane, 2000; Coltrane and Adams, 2001; Kroska, 2004; Nock, 2001; Robinson and Hunter, 2008; Tsuya and Bumpass, 2004]. In a relatively recent study of younger and older couples, younger wives report a higher incidence of participation in the workforce and contribute a greater fraction of total household income, while their husbands are more likely to engage in housework, compared to older couples [Rogers and Amato, 2000]. Since labor supply decisions usually are made within a household context involving other choices, the increase in family income from more wives participating in the job market may have provided an income effect for husbands to decrease their work effort.

Ethnic Diversity

Citing various sources, the Report of the ASHP *Ad Hoc* Committee on Ethnic Diversity and Cultural Competency [2005] points out that between 1980 and 2000 the Black population in the United States increased by 28 percent. During the same period, the Hispanic population grew by 122 percent and the Asian population expanded by 190 percent. These ethnic minorities are expected to comprise approximately 37 percent of the general population in 2025 and account for 90 percent of nationwide population growth between now and 2050.

The analysis of race/ethnic relations has a tortuous history. Its origin goes back to the 17th century, but it was not until the 19th century that it became widespread in Europe and the United States to explain human differences [Miles, 1993]. Phenotypes (*i.e.*, physical traits such as skin color, facial characteristics, etc.) were believed by social scientists of the time to distinguish groups or races not only in terms of visible attributes but also, more importantly, in terms of corporeal and intellectual capabilities. Cultural development was commonly viewed as a product of biological differences, and arguments revolving around "biology as destiny" led to the representation of Blacks as inferior. These arguments often contained religious overtones—outside the White race there was no favor from God; therefore, there should be neither honor nor respect from man—and provided a convenient justification for slavery, imperialism, and anti-immigration policies in many countries [Barkan, 1992; Bissell *et al.*, 2003].

At the time of emancipation, most Americans, including influential politicians, rejected the notion that Blacks could ever prosper as free men and women. Consider the following quote regarding Blacks found in Franklin [2005, p. 123]: "Free them, and make them politically and socially our equals? My own feelings [will] not admit of this; and if mine would, we well know that those of the great mass of White people will not. Whether this feeling accords with justice and sound judgment, is not the sole question, if indeed, it is any part of it. A universal feeling, whether well or ill founded, cannot be safely disregarded. We cannot, then, make them equals." These words were uttered by Abraham Lincoln in Peoria, Illinois only seven years prior to the Civil War.

During Reconstruction the status of Blacks, by that time free men and women, deteriorated steadily in American society [Franklin, 2005]. They were depicted in scientific as well as literary journals as lazy, immoral, and criminal, totally unworthy of citizenship or political participation. The concept of one great society in which race was irrelevant, largely espoused today by most Americans, was simply out of the question. Thus, several states, mostly in the South, but also in other parts of the nation, proceeded to legislate inequality. Literacy laws and understanding provisions allowed the disfranchisement of Blacks. Grandfather clauses in state constitutions permitted otherwise unqualified people to vote if their fathers or grandfathers could vote in 1866, which obviously could not apply to Blacks. Later on, at the turn of the 20th century, proponents of the so called Progressive Era economics argued that the labor force should be rid of "unfit workers," a term that included Blacks, immigrants, and women, as they were perceived to be defective in character and intellect [Leonard, 2003, 2005; Levy and Peart, 2003]. And all along, numerous statutes based on the "separate but equal" doctrine were designed to segregate the races and discriminate openly against Blacks—churches, schools, cemeteries, transportation vehicles, bars and restaurants, and all public places had separate accommodations for Whites and Blacks.

The implications of race inequalities out of scientific racism have not been the sole domain of the United States. They have emerged in other parts of the world too. Not that long ago, Nazi Germany implemented a massive drive to cleanse society of "inferior" races, which encompassed not only Jews but also Gypsies and other "undesirables" such as communists and homosexuals, with the participation and complicity of health professionals. More recently, the civil war in the former Yugoslavia was the scenario of multiple ethnic cleansing episodes, and several armed conflicts throughout Africa have resulted in systematic, widespread killing of individuals whose distinguishing characteristics were phenotypical.

Most social scientists today focus on ethnicity rather than race in their analysis of human relations. While race and physical appearance may play a substantial role in making ethnic distinctions, as is the case with Non-Hispanic Blacks, the concept of ethnicity is more comprehensive as it embodies language, religion, heritage, cultural identity, and other symbolic representations, which ultimately are arbitrary, whatever people may use to differentiate between themselves and others [Bissell *et al.*, 2003]. Focusing on ethnicity instead of race allows a more meaningful approach to appraising the behavior of economic, social, and political variables as well as their impact on the provision and use of healthcare services.

Today Non-Hispanic Blacks of different ethnic backgrounds—African Americans, Afro-Caribbeans, Africans, etc.—are highly segregated from Non-Hispanic Whites and disadvantaged compared to them. According to Logan and Deane [2003], Black immigrants possess higher levels of formal schooling and income than do native African Americans, and tend to live in different neighborhoods. Of particular interest in South Florida are Afro-Caribbeans, who are growing at a faster rate than other well-established minorities in the U.S. such as Cubans and Koreans. Over two-thirds of the Afro-Caribbean population living in the United States are foreign born. Their income and socioeconomic status are higher than those of the rest of African Americans and Hispanics, although well below those of Non-Hispanic Whites and Asian Americans.

Hispanics are the country's largest single minority. They constitute an ethnic group comprising different races. The term "Hispanic" identifies individuals sharing a cultural background who have developed, over the years, a distinct social identity marked heavily by economic features. By and large, they use the Spanish language frequently; they profess, at least nominally, Catholicism; and they have customs and traditions influenced by Spanish rule. About 55 percent of them are foreign born [Fry and Lowell, 2006]. To be sure, many of them may employ or even prefer other terms to identify themselves (*i.e.*, Latinos, Chicanos, etc.), and most individuals from some regions formerly under Spanish rule (*i.e.*, the Philippines, Morocco, and the Low Countries) do not consider themselves Hispanic. Yet, despite these caveats, Hispanic is the term of choice of the U.S. Census Bureau and other agencies [Carvajal and Alonso, 2002].

While Hispanics often are viewed by Non-Hispanics as a monolithic group, they actually form a mosaic of subgroups who have joined the larger American population in different manners and at different times, and have encountered dissimilar experiences in their socioeconomic, political, and environmental settings [Carvajal, 1997; Cattan, 1993]. Each subgroup is a composite of people who have markedly different labor force and employment characteristics.

Nearly two centuries ago Mexican Americans became a minority not by immigrating (as the other Hispanic subgroups) or being forcefully brought into the New World in slavery (as were Blacks), but by conquest. When today's areas of Arizona, California, New Mexico, and Texas were taken away from Mexico in the 1800s, their indigenous inhabitants became *de facto* second-class citizens subservient to Non-Hispanic White settlers. As time went on and wealth and income inequalities between the U.S. and Mexico intensified, massive waves of both legal and illegal migration across the border ensued. Surplus labor conditions in Mexico's primarily agricultural economy pushed Mexicans into U.S. areas capable of generating a greater demand for labor.

Puerto Rican migration also is linked to surplus labor conditions at home, although Puerto Ricans' demand for jobs is mostly in the manufacturing and service sectors. Since they are U.S. citizens by birth, there are no restrictions or illegal immigration problems with this subgroup. Puerto Ricans began migrating into the United States shortly after their island was relinquished by Spain at the end of the Spanish-American War, with the heaviest flow occurring between 1940 and 1960.

Unlike Mexicans and Puerto Ricans, whose migration flows respond primarily to economic factors, the Cuban diaspora has been politically motivated, especially at the beginning. In the 1960s and 1970s, it consisted of professionals, managers, and former government officials who would not adapt to a Marxist regime. With the advent of *Marielitos* and rafters, the latest Cuban migration waves are characterized by the migrants' younger, poorer, and less skilled nature. An important feature of this subgroup is that, until recently, Cubans have received massive amounts of government-sponsored human capital and resettlement assistance in the form of job training and placement, professional recertification, and research and training programs.

Other Hispanics, the last category recognized by the U.S. Census Bureau, consist of a potpourri of individuals who identify a wide array of places as their country of origin. They relate their birth or ancestry to El Salvador, the Dominican Republic, Spain, Colombia, Guatemala, Nicaragua, Ecuador, or Peru (the most numerous subgroups), or simply use general reference terms such as "Latino" or "Spanish." Fry and Lowell [2006] point out that while native Hispanics generally earn higher wages than do immigrants, not all groups fare the same. Some are more prosperous than others.

Each of the three major subgroups is the dominant Hispanic force in an area of the United States—Mexican Americans in the Southwest, Puerto Ricans in the New York and New Jersey metropolitan areas, and Cubans in South Florida—while being subordinate elsewhere. The vast economic, social, and political differences among these areas underscore the distinct characteristics of origin of each subgroup and contribute to shape their acculturation patterns. In South Florida, both economic development and ethnic diversity are direct consequences of Hispanic immigration. The first major wave was that of Cuban immigrants, which took place in the late 1950s and throughout the 1960s, and was characterized by predominantly White and well-educated individuals with a remarkable propensity for entrepreneurship. Since international migration often entails leaving behind family and friends, as well as adapting to a strange country with different norms, language, customs, etc. [Chowdhury and Pedace, 2007]—an experience found by many to be intimidating— early Cuban and other Latin American immigrants into South Florida sought to live and work near people with similar cultures. With subsequent immigration waves, Hispanic businesses found a growing demand for their goods and services, as well as an abundant and relatively inexpensive source of labor. Information and opportunities, both limited and costly outside the early Cuban-led network, facilitated the adaptation of, and provided the economic means to, later immigrants. This led to the formation of an enclave economy with a strong grip on construction, real estate, clothing, and entertainment. Both a sustained expansion of tourism and the proliferation of trade with Latin America and the Caribbean have contributed greatly to the South Florida boom, a boom that has established the Spanish language and Hispanic values and customs as a lifestyle. This environment has attracted numerous Hispanics, especially more Cubans, Colombians, Nicaraguans, and Puerto Ricans, who usually experience few difficulties in adapting to situations in which the meaning of their ethnicity has been established by previous Hispanic settlers.

Notwithstanding the broadly accepted benefits brought about by cultural diversity, a recent experiment illustrates the many caveats and complexities of this phenomenon. Ash [2008] configured various homogeneous and heterogeneous groups of Hispanic and Non-Hispanic White students, assigned them the same set of tasks, and measured the satisfaction scores of the groups. The experiment produced strong evidence in support of the theory of self-categorization, namely, that creating ethnically homogenous groups produces greater satisfaction with group processes. The groups with similar ethnic composition showed more satisfaction than did the groups with diverse composition, regardless of whether the groups were Hispanic or Non-Hispanic White. When a minority (Hispanic or Non-Hispanic White) person was placed into a group, the mean satisfaction score dropped significantly.

Ethnic identification has economic repercussions because the choice of cultural self-identity is closely related to the acceptance of, and acculturation into, dominant social norms. (As a general rule, different ethnic groups are assumed to hold different beliefs, values, attitudes, and expectations, and consequently are anticipated to behave differently.) If ethnicity is endogenous in certain circumstances, as is the case in South Florida with its rich ethnic mix, a cultural self-identity may or may not be used to distance oneself from a subordinate group or to improve one's chances of being accepted into the dominant group. While acculturation brings forth some degree of acceptance by the mainstream, which opens up a wider range of economic opportunities, it also carries with it an implicit cost; by adopting the norms of the dominant group (*i.e.*, language, religious affiliation, values, etc.), individuals may alienate themselves from their own ethnic communities [Bodenhorn and Ruebeck, 2003].

The effective acculturation of an ethnic group into the mainstream depends not only on the group's actions, but also on the receptiveness and willingness of the majority population to accept the minority group. The extent to which the majority opens its doors to minorities—in its residential neighborhoods, schools, businesses, jobs, social clubs, and political participation—largely determines minorities' degree of identification with their own ethnic communities. Minority group members who gain access to broader economic, social, and political opportunities are more likely to identify themselves with the mainstream, thereby reducing the attachment to their own ethnic communities for purposes of improving living conditions for themselves and their children [Alba and Nee, 2003]. Thus, believing in social mobility (*i.e.*, the attainment of higher socioeconomic status through hard work, education, and other investments in human capital) tends to reduce self-identification with one's ethnic group, while the presence of ethnic-related economic and social barriers tends to increase minorities' self-identification with their groups, especially if they perceive that such group affiliations are responsible for the restrictions on their mobility [Chong and Kim, 2006].

The literature is replete with studies reporting all sorts of ethnic differences in self-identity and outcomes—labor force participation, unemployment, income, wealth, education, poverty, housing, discrimination, healthcare services, and others too numerous to mention. For example, Ong and Patraporn [2000] point out that, compared to African Americans, Asian Americans have achieved greater economic success and are more optimistic about their future prospects; Muhammad *et al.* [2004] report that in 2001 the typical Black household's net worth was $19,000, compared to $121,000 for Non-Hispanic Whites; and De la Garza [2004] argues that Hispanics' general socioeconomic conditions are similar to, if not worse than, the conditions faced by African Americans. One factor to consider is that many Hispanics and Asian Americans are immigrants, and immigrant households often exhibit lower female labor force participation rates both because of a relatively large number of children present and due to differences in cultural norms about working wives [Blank and Shierholz, 2006]. Within Hispanics, Mason [2004] finds strong incentives favoring acculturation among Mexican Americans and Cuban Americans, as they, and to a lesser extent Puerto Ricans, are able to increase income and wage rates by acculturating into a Non-Hispanic White ethnic identity, although neither abandonment of the Spanish language nor of a specific Hispanic self-identity is sufficient to overcome the penalties associated with having a dark complexion or Non-European phenotype.

According to Altonji *et al.* [2000], the root of all differentials between Non-Hispanic Whites and Blacks lies in the huge wealth gap that exists between both ethnic groups. This gap is much larger than the gap in earnings and influences access to capital for new businesses, is a source of social and political influence, affects the quality of housing and neighborhoods, and shapes the ability to finance higher education. Since savings are a positive function of income and Blacks generally earn lower income levels than Whites, it follows that Blacks report lower savings, which translates into less wealth. The authors argue, however, that Blacks and Whites would experience similar wealth levels if the relationship between wealth and income and the demographics for Blacks were the same as they are for Whites and if Blacks and Whites had the same distributions of income and demographic characteristics.

Royster [2007] contends that African American men seeking employment consistently are subject to stereotypes that mark them as relatively less skilled and incompetent, and Lang and Manove [2006] maintain that at least some of the wage disparities among ethnic groups reflect differential treatment in the labor market. Yet Hellerstein and Neumark [2005] point out that ethnic differences in employment, pay, etc. are not necessarily indicative of discrimination, but may be generated by segregation along skill lines. Indeed, segregated into inferior schools with fewer resources than those available to Non-Hispanic White students, Black and Hispanic youths are more likely to enter local labor markets with less and lower-quality education, which makes them less desirable to local employers and reduces substantially their chances of going to college. There is empirical evidence that segregation in the workplace remains pervasive, and it accounts for a sizable share of wage gaps between Non-Hispanic Whites and minority groups [Hellerstein *et al.*, 2007]. Would better schooling for minorities help reduce ethnic disparities in employment and income? At least one study finds no support for the contention that if Blacks and Whites lived in the same neighborhoods, their interaction via social networks would improve the employment conditions and prospects of Blacks [Dickerson, 2007]. And when ethnic group is analyzed jointly with gender, female Blacks and Hispanics seem to exhibit even more unfavorable indicators [Dickerson, 2006; Read and Cohen, 2007].

Age Diversity

Perhaps age-related disparities in beliefs, attitudes, and behavior leading to different labor and socioeconomic outcomes have not received the attention in the literature that has been granted to gender and ethnic variations. That is likely to change in the near future as the baby-boom generation, comprised of individuals born between 1946 and 1964, approaches retirement. The decline in the size of the labor force potentially brought about by baby boomers' retirement is likely to be compounded by the fact that female workforce participation has begun to drop after rising steadily for over half a century. (Male labor force participation rates have been dropping since the 1950s.) Yet this decrease in women's workforce participation has been recorded virtually in all age groups except for workers 55 years and older; in fact, the older age groups report a sharp increase [Mosisa and Hipple, 2006]. Toossi [2007] estimates that in the next decade, the older labor force will grow more than five times faster than the overall labor force. The expanding participation by older persons, however, is not enough to offset the declining participation rates of younger workers. Therefore, the labor force is expected to shrink, at least relative to the population, and it also is expected to age.

Populations, and consequently their labor force, age as a result of an increase in their life expectancy and/or a drop in their fertility rates. Both trends apply to the U.S. population. But the aging pattern is different for the major ethnic groups. The Non-Hispanic White labor force traditionally has been older than the labor force of African Americans, Hispanics, and Asian Americans, and this trend is anticipated to continue, at least over several decades, as it reflects higher birth rates of African Americans and Hispanics as well as heavy immigration flows of Hispanics and Asian Americans [Toossi, 2007].

Rix [2006] and Toossi [2007] attribute the growing workforce participation rates of senior citizens to several reasons. One is that older people are leading longer and healthier lives than did previous generations, which poses the opportunity, and sometimes the need, for greater work longevity. Second, their levels of education are higher than the levels of their predecessors, and more educated people tend to participate more often in the labor force. A third reason is that the trend away from defined benefit pension plans and toward defined contribution plans acts as an incentive for older persons to remain working, since defined contribution plans are based on an individual's contribution, the employer's contribution, and the investment returns on these contributions. A fourth reason for the growing labor force participation of senior citizens is that, starting in 2000, the full retirement age for Social Security benefits began a scheduled increase and the benefits for early retirement declined; both measures intended to encourage the continuation of labor market activity. Finally, the high cost of health insurance and a decrease in health benefits, especially at older ages, have forced many individuals to continue working, or even go back to work after retirement, to have access to job-related health insurance.

Knapp and Cultice [2007] find a trend toward more work participation by older pharmacists, many of whom remain active in the workforce on a part-time basis. The switch from full-time to part-time employment seems to occur gradually. Some pharmacists end their careers through phased retirement, reducing the number of hours or days worked, while others utilize bridge employment (*i.e.*, undertaking a project or assignment with a defined life span that involves duties different from the norm). Whatever they do, older part-time pharmacists have issues that may be of little or no concern to younger pharmacists. Some of the motivating factors for older pharmacists to seek part-time employment include earning additional income to maintain or improve a desired living standard, avoid depletion of savings, a specific purpose (*i.e.*, travel, pay off mortgage, etc.), fight boredom, validation of personal worth, and unanticipated care of dependents such as grandchildren [Teeter, 2004].

Younger versus older worker comparisons possess a deeper perspective that transcends age, namely, a perspective related to the role that work plays in people's lives. Baby boomers are described in the literature as a generation holding a solid work ethic characterized by clearly defined professional goals, drive for material success, a sense of duty, generating lots of effort and long work hours, and commitment to their employers. They consider their work as an important, if not the most important, part of their lives, and often define themselves in terms of what they do. Conversely, generation Xers, the term used to describe individuals born between 1965 and 1990, tend to exhibit a preference for autonomy and flexible work schedules, are more interested in family and close friends than in material success, organize their lives around the latest technologies, place emphasis on personal growth and creativity, view organizations with cynicism or contempt, and are more open towards diversity (Jovic *et al.*, 2006; Kennedy, 2003; Shields and Shields, 2003; Smola and Sutton, 2002; Southard and Lewis, 2004; Wah, 2000; Washburn, 2000]. The ongoing attempts by generation Xers to attain a more balanced life in terms of work and leisure often are interpreted by baby boomers as an erosion of work ethics and lack of commitment, while the younger generation criticizes baby boomers as being overly cautious, too competitive, loyal to their organizations beyond reason, and addicted to hierarchical structures.

An obvious implication of this difference in values and attitudes is that recent cohorts of women have entered, and continue entering, the labor force with different views from those held by baby boomers regarding the importance of career goals vis-à-vis family life [Crittenden, 2001]. Generation X women are having more children, at an earlier age, than did women from the baby-boom generation, and are supplying fewer hours to the labor market. Greater completed fertility and less attachment to work mean that future labor supply is likely to drop, especially when female baby boomers, now in their 40s and 50s, retire from the workforce, and a sustained decline in female labor force participation may pose a serious threat to future economic growth [Vere, 2007].

An analysis of age-based disparities would be deficient if it did not make reference to ageism, a term used to describe problems experienced due to age being a barrier to gaining initial employment, a detriment in interacting with colleagues and others, and an obstacle to promotion opportunities [Allen *et al.*, 2006]. The incidence of ageism is highest with the very young and the very old, and it seems to affect women more than men [Duncan and Loretto, 2004]. Inexperience and the absence of skills affect the young, while mandatory retirement, job dislocation, and skills obsolescence plague older workers. Age is a formidable employment barrier for the old; not only is their average duration of unemployment 35 percent longer than it is for their younger counterparts, but, upon re-employment, older workers often experience lower wages with fewer benefits compared to their younger peers [Rix, 2006].

FLORIDA AND SOUTH FLORIDA 2

This chapter seeks to explore the settings in which Florida pharmacists in general, and South Florida pharmacists in particular, work and provide their services. The first part addresses the state and local population's characteristics and major socioeconomic and labor force indicators. This is followed by an assessment of the health status of the population, including morbidity and mortality, health behavior and risk factors, ethnic disparities, access to health care, and availability of health insurance. The third part focuses on the practice of pharmacy, containing a brief history of the profession, a view of the colleges of pharmacy, and a discussion of the various types of practice sites.

POPULATION OVERVIEW

With an estimated population of 18.3 million persons in 2008, Florida is the fourth most populous state in the nation [U.S. Census Bureau, 2009d]. Since the last census in 2000, the population of Florida has increased by approximately 2.3 million people, or 14.2 percent, which yields an annual rate of growth of 1.4 percent. Florida is one of the fastest growing states, ranked third in population growth behind Texas and California. According to the University of Florida Bureau of Economic and Business Research [2009], all 67 Florida counties experienced a population increase between 1970 and 2000.

From 2000 to 2008, the population in the eight South Florida counties of Broward, Collier, Hendry, Lee, Martin, Miami-Dade, Monroe, and Palm Beach expanded by 805,398 persons, a 13.5 percent increase, to approximately 6.7 million inhabitants [The Florida Legislature, 2009c]. Seven of these eight counties report an absolute increase in population during this period. Lee, Miami-Dade, and Palm Beach are among the top five counties in the state in terms of population increase since 2000, with Miami-Dade gaining the largest number of residents of any Florida county. Monroe was the only South Florida county losing residents; its population declined by 3,508 inhabitants.

Population growth depends on two factors: natural increase, which is the difference between the number of births and the number of deaths, and net migration, which is the difference between the number of people moving in and out of a region. Unlike most other states, where population expansion is largely determined by natural increase, Florida's population growth is primarily attributed to net migration. Between 2000 and 2008, net migration accounted for 82 percent of Florida's overall population growth [The Florida Legislature, 2009b]. Migration into the state is influenced by, among other factors, the warm climate and proximity to the Caribbean and Central and South America, which make Florida an attractive destination for both domestic and international immigrants. Many people believe wrongly that most migration into Florida comes from outside the United States, but the U.S. Census Bureau [2008c] estimates that between 2000 and 2008 only about one-third of the state's net migration was international.

Although the overall growth rate slowed down in the first few years of the 21st century, and actually declined in 2008 and 2009 because of the national economic downturn, projections indicate Florida's population will continue to grow and experience a 46 percent increase by the year 2030, when it will reach 24 million residents [The Florida Legislature, 2009a]. According to these projections, between 2000 and 2030 Florida will be the third fastest growing state in the nation and will surpass New York as the third most populous state [Florida's Population, 2009]. The population expansion in the southern portion of the state also is expected to continue. With the exception of Monroe, all South Florida counties are projected to continue growing. Smith and Rayer [2009] estimate that South Florida will add about 1.2 million residents between 2008 and 2030 to reach a population of 8 million persons by 2030. Migration is expected to be the driving force of population growth over the next 20 years. Although the currently weaker housing market and the economic contraction have affected people's ability to relocate to the state, causing negative migration rates, this situation is expected to change by 2011 as a result of the anticipated economic recovery [The Florida Legislature, 2009a].

Gender, Ethnic Identification, and Age

Historically high levels of migration have made Florida's population one of the most diverse in the United States. A summary of the demographic makeup of the state and its southern counties in relation to overall U.S. levels is presented in Table 2-1. Women slightly outnumber men. Following a typical population composition spread, there are more men than women in the age brackets younger than 40 years; as the population grows older, women increasingly outnumber men, with at least three women per every two men 85 years of age or older [Florida's Population, 2009]. In 2008 the mean age of Floridians was 40.2 years, which makes Florida, tied with New Hampshire, the state with the fourth oldest population [U.S. Census Bureau, 2009d].

Floridians are a rich mix of ethnic, cultural, and linguistic backgrounds. On average, two out of every five residents belong to an ethnic minority. According to estimates of the U.S. Census Bureau [2009d], Florida's population consists of 60.3 percent Non-Hispanic Whites, 21.0 percent Hispanics, 15.9 percent Blacks, 2.3 percent Asian Americans, and the remaining 0.5 percent other minorities. Approximately 19 percent of the state's residents are foreign born [U.S. Census Bureau, 2009a]. In South Florida the presence of ethnic minorities (44 percent) is greater than in the rest of the state. In fact, minority groups outnumber Non-Hispanic Whites in three South Florida counties—Broward, Hendry, and Miami-Dade [U.S. Census Bureau, 2009d].

The composition of Florida's population has become older over the last 60 years. Between 1950 and 2000, the proportion younger than 15 years of age declined from 26.2 percent to 19.0 percent, while the proportion 65 years of age or older rose from 8.6 percent to 17.6 percent [Smith and Rayer, 2009]. In 2008, Florida had the nation's largest percentage of population 65 years of age or older [U.S. Census Bureau, 2009d]. Its relatively warm climate and leisurely style of living have made the state a retirement haven for the elderly. Over one-third of Florida residents 65 years of age or older live in the eight South Florida counties, and this age group accounts for 13.3 percent of the population of South Florida [U.S. Census Bureau, 2009f].

The senior population of Florida, like in the rest of the country, is expected to continue growing as baby boomers reach their golden years. By 2030, when all baby boomers are at least 65 years old, nearly one out of every five U.S. residents is expected to be 65 years of age or older. This age group is projected to increase to 88.5 million persons, or 20.2 percent of the U.S. population, by 2050, more than twice the size of the 38.7 million population recorded in 2008. Similarly, the 85 years or older population is expected to treble, from 5.4 million persons, or 2.3 percent, to 19 million persons, equivalent to 4.3 percent of the U.S. population [Bernstein and Edwards, 2008]. In Florida the growth of the elderly population will be even faster. By 2030, the number of individuals 65 years of age or older is expected to more than double to 7.8 million, accounting for 27 percent of the population, or more than one out of every four Floridians. The number of residents 85 years or older also will double in this time period to almost one million persons, or 3.2 percent of the state population [U.S. Census Bureau, 2009c]. Projections for the South Florida counties indicate that the number of residents 65 years or older will grow to approximately 2 million persons, or 24 percent of South Florida residents, by 2030 [Smith and Rayer, 2009].

Florida's population also has become more ethnically diverse. Minority groups have grown in relative size. In 1980, 14.7 percent of the population was classified as Non-White, compared to 17.8 percent in the year 2000 [The Florida Legislature, 2009b]. The portion of the Hispanic population increased from 6 percent in 1970 to 21 percent in 2008 [Smith and Rayer, 2009; U.S. Census Bureau, 2009d]. Hispanics are quite diverse. Included in this category are large communities of Cuban Americans in Miami and Tampa, Puerto Ricans in Tampa and Orlando, and Central and South Americans in inland West-Central and South Florida [U.S. Census Bureau, 2009a]. With 36 percent of the South Florida population, Hispanics constitute the largest single minority group in the bottom portion of the peninsula. In Miami-Dade more than half (62.4 percent) of the population is Hispanic [U.S. Census Bureau, 2009d]. Blacks, the second largest minority group, make up 18.5 percent of the population of South Florida.

Currently minority groups comprise about one-third of the U.S. population, but projections predict that minorities will continue to expand more rapidly than non-minorities, and by 2042, ironically, there will be more minorities than non-minorities in the United States [Bernstein and Edwards, 2008]. Minority groups are growing at a faster rate in Florida than in the rest of the nation. Smith and Rayer [2009] project that by 2030 minorities will comprise 45 percent of Florida's population. Hispanics are the fastest growing minority group nationally and in Florida. Throughout the country Hispanics are expected to nearly treble by 2050 to an estimated 133 million persons, or 30 percent of overall residents. In Florida, Hispanics are anticipated to grow at a significantly faster rate, largely because of high migration and birth rates. They are projected to account for one-fourth of Florida's population in 2030, with approximately 6 million persons. The South Florida Hispanic population is expected to reach 3.3 million persons, or 41.5 percent of the population, by 2030.

Distribution of the Population

Nearly 90 percent of Florida's people live in urban areas [Florida Department of Health, 2009e]. The state has 20 Metropolitan Statistical Areas (MSAs), defined by the federal government as one urbanized area of 50,000 or more population, plus adjacent territory that exhibits a high degree of social and economic integration with the core [U.S. Census Bureau, 2008a; U.S. Office of Management and Budget, 2006]. Most metropolitan areas in the state are found in coastal areas. On the east, MSAs stretch from Jacksonville to Miami and include all counties on the Atlantic coast with the exception of Monroe. On the west, MSAs stretch from the Tampa-St. Petersburg-Clearwater area in the center of the state to Naples-Marco Island in the south. The interior, northern part of the state has several MSAs which connect the east and west coasts.

The most densely populated areas are located in the southern and central regions, by the Atlantic and the Gulf of Mexico. These areas, which include a substantial portion of the eight South Florida counties, are characterized by high rates of positive net migration [U.S. Census Bureau, 2008a] and contain 35.9 percent of the state's residents. Broward, Miami-Dade, and Palm Beach are the three most populous counties, and together account for nearly one-third (29.5 percent) of the population of Florida [U.S. Census Bureau, 2009d]. Over 98 percent of individuals in these three counties live in urban areas [Florida Department of Health, 2009e]. Included in Broward and Miami-Dade is the Miami-Fort Lauderdale-Pompano Beach MSA, which is the largest in the southeastern U.S. with over 5 million people.

Socioeconomic Characteristics

Floridians' levels of schooling are comparable to the rates across the U.S. (see Table 2-2). Residents of South Florida report a slightly lower percentage of high-school graduates, but a slightly higher level of college graduates, compared to the rest of the state. People in Monroe and Palm Beach counties show the region's highest levels of schooling, whereas residents of Hendry and Miami-Dade show the lowest, which is probably affected by the relatively high immigration rates of these last two counties. Table 2-2 also shows that Florida's median household income in 2008 was $48,637, about 6.8 percent below the national median. Levels of income in the South, however, generally are lower than in the rest of the country. Three-quarters (76 percent) of households receive earned income, 19 percent receive retirement income other than Social Security, and 33 percent receive Social Security benefits [U.S. Census Bureau, 2009b]. This latter statistic is higher than the national average, which is 27 percent of households receiving Social Security benefits, and is consistent with the greater concentration of senior citizens in the state. The various indicators related to the proportion of persons living in poverty are comparable to the national rates. With the exception of Hendry and Miami-Dade residents, South Floridians compare favorably with the rest of the state. The median household income for South Florida is $51,691, but there are broad differences among counties—from a high of $56,984 in Monroe to a low of $38,736 in Hendry. In Hendry and Miami-Dade, both with large minority populations, the poverty indicators are substantially higher than for the state as a whole. In particular, the children in Hendry and the elderly in Miami-Dade are more prone to live in poverty.

Workforce Characteristics

Approximately 9 million persons, or 61.3 percent of Florida's population 16 years and older, are active in the labor force [U.S. Census Bureau, 2009b]. Florida's workforce is predominantly civilian (99 percent) and white-collar (60 percent). Most of them have jobs in the private sector, and only 12 percent are employed by the federal, state, or local governments. Between 2006 and 2008, the breakdown of occupational categories in Florida's civilian workforce is management, professional, and related occupations (32.0 percent); sales and clerical (28.4 percent); service (18.5 percent); construction, extraction, maintenance, and repair (11.0 percent); production, transportation, and material moving (9.2 percent); and others (0.9 percent). The leading industries for the employed civilian workforce are educational services, health care, and social assistance (18.9 percent); retail trade (12.9 percent); professional, scientific, management, administrative, and waste management services (11.7 percent); and arts, entertainment, recreation, accommodation, and food services (10.5 percent).

The South Florida workforce consists of approximately 5.5 million persons and represents 38 percent of the state's workforce [U.S. Census Bureau, 2009b]. It is similar to the state labor force insofar as it is primarily civilian and white-collar in nature, and works in the private sector.

The composition of leading occupations and industries employing workers in the private sector is comparable to those of the rest of the state.

HEALTH STATUS

The health status of a population is a difficult factor to assess because of the absence of an easily measured indicator that determines conclusively and effectively how healthy a group of people may be. This is why the overall health of a population often is assessed by analyzing several indicators, including life expectancy at birth, overall mortality rates, infant mortality rates, and risk factors and behaviors associated with increased mortality. Life expectancy at birth probably is the simplest measure of population health. Presumably the average number of years that members of a population are expected to live is related to their health status. Life expectancy at birth is strongly affected by infant mortality; excessive deaths among infants reduces life expectancy in a population to a greater extent than excessive deaths among adults. Populations with high infant-mortality rates tend to exhibit generally low life expectancies.

When one looks at life expectancy at birth as a measure of health, it is clear that, on average, Americans, including Floridians, improved their health status significantly throughout the 20th century [National Center for Health Statistics, 2009]. A person born in Florida in 2008 is expected to live 79.2 years, almost 33 years longer than a person born in 1900 [Griggs and Jones, 2009]. The longer life expectancies observed today can be attributed largely to improved access to health care, advances in medical knowledge and practices, healthier lifestyles, and improved public health services, all major signs of progress that have exerted a substantial impact on decreasing infant mortality rates over the last 100 years.

Today, Florida is ranked 24th in terms of life expectancy at birth [American Human Development Project, 2009]. While life expectancy in Florida is not one of the highest in the nation, it is higher than the 77.9 year life expectancy of the U.S. population [Xu *et al.*, 2009]. Floridians are expected to live approximately 1.5 years longer than the average American; however, not all Floridians share the same life expectancy. Women and Non-Hispanic Whites tend to live longer than men and members of ethnic minorities. Non-Hispanic White women exhibit the longest life expectancy in Florida, at 82.8 years, and minority men have the shortest life expectancy at 73.6 years [Griggs and Jones, 2009].

Florida compares favorably with the rest of the U.S. in terms of overall mortality rates (see Table 2-3 for United States - Florida - South Florida comparisons of this and other health indicators). Mortality, measured by the age-adjusted death rate or the number of deaths that occur in a specific population adjusted for age per year, has declined consistently since the 1970s. Florida's age-adjusted death rate in 2007 was 685 per 100,000 population, making Florida the eighth state with the lowest rate at 9.7 percent below the national average [Heron *et al.*, 2009; Xu *et al.*, 2009]. With the exception of Hendry, the mortality rate of every South Florida county is lower than the mortality rate of both the nation and the state. Variations in mortality rates are associated with several factors, including differences in socioeconomic status, ethnic composition, access to health care, and differences in risk for specific causes of death. The relatively high mortality rate in Hendry, which is 8.9 percent above the national rate, is likely affected by the characteristics of its population—poor, with a low level of schooling, high uninsured rates, and a strong presence of ethnic minorities.

The overall decline in mortality experienced in Florida and the rest of the country over the last 30 years is due largely to a significant decline in the rate of deaths related to heart disease and stroke [Florida Department of Health, 2009c; National Center for Health Statistics, 2009]. Control of risk factors, improved access to early detection, more sophisticated diagnostic procedures, and more effective medications and interventions to treat these diseases have had a profound impact on morbidity and mortality rates. Yet even with a substantial drop in the rate of deaths from heart disease, heart disease and cancer continue to be the overall leading causes of death in Florida and South Florida, as well as in the rest of the United States [Florida Department of Health, 2009d; Heron *et al.*, 2009]. Unlike the case with heart disease, cancer rates have decreased only slightly over the same period. Cancer remains the leading cause of death of Floridians 45–74 years of age, accounting for 30.9 percent of total deaths in this age range [Griggs and Jones, 2009]. In both Florida and South Florida heart disease and cancer together account for almost half of all deaths [Florida Department of Health, 2009c; Heron *et al.*, 2009].

Florida's drop in the rates of death from heart disease and cancer has been accompanied by increased death rates from chronic lower respiratory disease (109 percent), kidney disease (107 percent), and diabetes (19 percent) [Florida Department of Health, 2009c]. In South Florida chronic lower respiratory disease is one of the top five causes of death. Alzheimer's disease death rates in the state also have increased steadily since 1980 and is one of the top causes of death in both Florida and the South Florida counties [Florida Department of Health, 2009d]. The higher rate of Alzheimer's disease related deaths in Florida, compared to the nation, can be attributed in part to the greater proportion of elderly population.

Although HIV/AIDS mortality has decreased consistently since 1995, following the introduction of antiretroviral therapy, HIV/AIDS disease continues to be of concern. HIV/AIDS ranks as one of the top causes of death for Floridians 35–44 years old and is one of the leading causes of overall mortality in Broward and Monroe [Florida Department of Health, 2009c; Griggs and Jones, 2009; Xu *et al.*, 2009].

Compared to the national average, infant mortality in Florida and South Florida is high. Florida's 2008 infant mortality rate, which measures the annual number of deaths of infants under one year of age, was 7.3 per 1,000 live births [Griggs and Jones, 2009]. This rate is 9 percent higher than the national average and ranks Florida as the state with the 21st highest incidence of infant mortality in the nation [Heron *et al.*, 2009]. In 2007, six of the eight South Florida counties (not counting Pasco) reported infant mortality rates higher than the state average, and in all counties mortality rates were higher than the U.S. average. The South Florida counties with the highest incidence of infant mortality are Hendry and Martin, where the combined rate is 52 percent above the national average. Infant mortality is related to the underlying health of the mother, public health practices, socioeconomic conditions, and availability and use of appropriate health care for infants and pregnant women.

While Florida's infant mortality remains high relative to other states, the rate has declined noticeably over the past 20 years. The infant mortality rate has dropped 25 percent since 1990 and currently is about half of what it was in 1980 [Griggs and Jones, 2009]. The leading causes of death for Florida's infants in 2008 were perinatal period conditions, congenital/chromosomal anomalies, accidents, and sudden infant death syndrome. These causes account for 81.6 percent of all infant deaths and are similar to the leading causes in the rest of the U.S. [Heron *et al.*, 2009].

Health Behavior and Risk Factors

People's behavior and lifestyle have a major impact on their health. Behaviors such as smoking, consuming an unhealthy diet, insufficient physical activity, and alcohol use tend to increase the risk of developing a number of chronic conditions including heart disease, cancer, diabetes, and stroke. Over the last few decades Americans have become increasingly overweight and are leading more sedentary lives [National Center for Health Statistics, 2009; Trust for America's Health, 2009]. The proportion of American adults who are obese has doubled over the last 30 years and stands at approximately one-third of all American adults. Florida is ranked 39th among states with the highest proportion of obese residents. Yet, while high, the proportion of Floridians and South Floridians who are overweight or obese is slightly lower than the national average (see Table 2-3). In South Florida, Miami-Dade, Lee, and Hendry have the highest proportions of overweight or obese individuals, and Martin has the lowest [Florida Department of Health, 2009a; National Center for Chronic Disease Prevention and Health Promotion, 2007].

Obesity in children also has increased recently. According to the National Survey of Children's Health, one-third of U.S. children are either obese or overweight [Trust for America's Health, 2009]. In Florida, childhood obesity is estimated to affect one-third of children 10–17 years old. This makes Florida the state with the 17th highest percentage of overweight and obese children in the country. A major contributing factor to obesity is the lack of physical activity. It is estimated that 24.5 percent of all Floridians lead a sedentary life [Florida Department of Health, 2009a]. In South Florida, Hendry and Miami-Dade residents exhibit the highest proportions of individuals who lead relatively inactive lives. Thus, it is not surprising that these counties report the region's highest levels of overweight individuals. The activity level of Florida's children is not much better. According to the National Survey of Children's Health, only 34 percent of Florida's children 6–17 years of age engage in vigorous physical activity, say, 30 minutes of continuous exercise three times per week [Trust for America's Health, 2009].

Smoking is a risk factor for heart disease and lung cancer. It also is a significant risk factor for the development of chronic lung diseases, a group of illnesses showing an increased prevalence in Florida over the last 30 years [Florida Department of Health, 2009c]. Following the Surgeon General's report on smoking in 1964, the rate of cigarette smoking in the U.S. has declined consistently. However, a significant number of individuals continue to partake in this unhealthy activity [National Center for Health Statistics, 2009]. Nearly one-fifth of women and high-school students and one-quarter of men in the U.S. smoke cigarettes, a practice engaged by almost 11 percent of pregnant women [National Center for Health Statistics, 2009]. The overall proportions of Floridians and South Floridians who smoke are comparable to the proportion of smoking Americans outside Florida [Florida Department of Health, 2009a]. In South Florida smoking is less common among Miami-Dade residents and more common among Hendry and Monroe residents. While more men than women continue to report smoking, over time the fraction of men who smoke has decreased more rapidly than the proportion of smoking women. In Florida, Non-Hispanic Whites are more likely to smoke than are persons from other ethnic groups, followed by Hispanics and Blacks [National Center for Chronic Disease Prevention and Health Promotion, 2007].

Alcohol use increases the risk of developing chronic diseases. It also may contribute to increased mortality from related, unintentional injuries, including motor vehicle accidents. According to the National Center for Health Statistics [2009], 61 percent of U.S. adults currently drink alcohol. Drinking is most prevalent among adults 25–44 years old, 73.7 percent for men and 60.9 percent for women, and declines steadily beyond 45 years of age. It is most common among Non-Hispanic Whites (66 percent), followed by American Indians (53 percent), Hispanics (51 percent), Blacks (48 percent), and Asian Americans (43 percent).

While low to moderate intake of alcohol is associated with a lower risk of coronary heart disease incidence and mortality, heavy alcohol consumption, and consuming five or more drinks in one day, can have both acute and chronic detrimental effects on health [Rehm *et al.*, 2003]. Table 2-3 shows that approximately 15 percent of adults in the U.S., and 20 percent in Florida, have engaged in heavy or binge drinking in the past year [Florida Department of Health, 2009a]. Compared to the average American, Floridians in general and most South Floridians are less likely to engage in heavy alcohol use; exceptions are Hendry, Lee, and Monroe residents. In these three counties heavy or binge drinking exceeds the state average [Florida Department of Health, 2009c]. Men are twice more prone than women to engage in heavy or binge drinking. The prevalence of heavy or binge drinking also varies by ethnic group; they are most common practices among American Indians, followed by Non-Hispanic Whites, Hispanics, Blacks, and Asian Americans [National Center for Health Statistics, 2009].

A word of caution is warranted here. The behavior and risk factor profiles of Americans in general, and Floridians in particular, need improvement. Decreasing obesity, smoking, and excessive drinking continue to be major public health objectives in the United States insofar as these behaviors exert a major impact on both morbidity and mortality.

Health Disparities

The health status of minority populations in the U.S. does not compare favorably with the status of Non-Hispanic Whites. Ethnic minorities suffer disproportionate morbidity and mortality rates from chronic diseases relative to the nonminority population. Minorities exhibit more chronic illnesses and worse health status; face greater barriers to healthcare access, including less access to health insurance; and tend to receive a lower quality of health care even when controlling for insurance coverage status, patient's income, and other access-related factors [Smedley *et al.*, 2003].

In 2006 the age-adjusted death rate of the Black population was 30 percent greater than it was for Non-Hispanic Whites [Heron *et al.*, 2009]. While the U.S. life expectancy at birth has increased since the beginning of the 20th century and the gap between Blacks and Non-Hispanic Whites has narrowed, disparities in life expectancy persist [National Center for Health Statistics, 2009]. In 2006 Non-Hispanic Whites' life expectancy at birth was 78 years, a full five years longer than the life expectancy of Blacks [Harper *et al.*, 2009]. Several factors contribute to this disparity, including higher rates of infant mortality, HIV/AIDS, homicide, and heart disease in Blacks. The life expectancy gap between Blacks and Non-Hispanic Whites at age 65 is smaller but still exists [National Center for Health Statistics, 2009]. Accurate life expectancy figures are available only for Non-Hispanic Whites and Blacks. The death rates for other minority groups probably is not accurate due to underreporting of ethnicity on death certificates [Harper *et al.*, 2009]. Wide disparities also are detected among ethnic minorities in infant mortality rates. According to the National Center for Health Statistics [2009], infant mortality rates in 2005 were highest for Non-Hispanic Blacks (13.6 deaths per 1,000 live births), Puerto Ricans (8.3 deaths per 1,000 live births), and American Indians (8.1 deaths per

1,000 live births), and lowest for Cubans (4.4 deaths per 1,000 live births), Central and South Americans (4.7 deaths per 1,000 live births), and Asian Americans (4.9 deaths per 1,000 live births).

In addition, ethnic disparities occur in the prevalence of many chronic diseases. Minority Americans are much more likely than Non-Hispanic Whites to suffer from diabetes, cardiovascular diseases, asthma, and certain cancers [Mead *et al.*, 2008]. One of the most striking health disparities is the prevalence of AIDS. The case rate for Black adults and adolescents is about ten times greater than it is for non-minority adults and adolescents. AIDS cases also are more prevalent among Hispanics; compared to Non-Hispanic Whites, their likelihood of suffering from AIDS is 3.3 times greater [U.S. Department of Health and Human Services, 2009a].

Disparities are common across various risk factors for disease and disability, too. Blacks exhibit a greater probability than non-minorities to be overweight or obese, and American Indians are more prone than Non-Hispanic Whites to smoke. Both obesity and smoking are aggravating risk factors for cardiovascular diseases and cancer, the leading causes of death nationwide [Mead *et al.*, 2008; Trust for America's Health, 2009]. Conversely, African Americans, Hispanics, and Asian Americans tend to smoke less relative to non-minorities [Mead *et al.*, 2008]. Differences also are present in the practice and utilization of preventative health behaviors and services. In general, ethnic minority groups report undertaking fewer breast cancer screenings, less beta-blocker use after myocardial infarction, and fewer diabetes *mellitus* related eye examinations relative to Non-Hispanic Whites after adjusting for age, gender, and income [O'Connell *et al.*, 2007].

Many of the ethnic disparities found nationwide are replicated throughout Florida. In 2008 the life expectancy at birth of non-minority men and women in Florida was approximately three years longer than it was for minority men and women [Griggs and Jones, 2009]. While Florida has experienced an overall decline in its mortality rate over the past 40 years, along with a drop in the gap between minority and non-minority death rates, the gap still exists. Minorities exhibit substantially higher age-adjusted death rates during this period than do Non-Hispanic Whites. The mortality rate differential is associated with similar differentials in most causes of death, including diabetes, hypertension, homicide, anemia, and HIV/AIDS [Griggs and Jones, 2009]. As a point of illustration, consider the 2008 HIV/AIDS death rates in Florida: 31.9 per 100,000 population for minority men versus 5.6 per 100,000 population for non-minority men, and 17.3 per 100,000 population for minority women versus 1.3 per 100,000 population for non-minority women.

Florida's minority infant mortality rate dropped from 12.2 per 1,000 live births in 2007 to 11.8 per 1,000 live births in 2008; yet this rate is 2.3 times greater than the infant mortality rate of Non-Hispanic Whites. The infant mortality rates of minorities in South Florida counties for which data are available are two to three times greater than the infant mortality rates of non-minorities [Griggs and Jones, 2009].

Many factors such as income, education, and access to insurance contribute to health disparities, but even after adjusting for these factors, disparities often persist [Mead *et al.*, 2008]. Other disparity determinants that are more complex and involve many participants include the health system and its bureaucratic processes, healthcare providers, and patients themselves [Smedley *et al.*, 2003]. In light of the growing diversity of the nation in general, and Florida and South Florida in particular, an increasing number of minority Americans find themselves at risk of disease.

Access to Health Care

Healthcare services are provided in different settings. Changes in both the reimbursement of healthcare services and the cause-of-disease processes in the 20th century have configured where and how patients receive healthcare services today. Early in the 20th century, when acute infectious diseases still were quite prevalent, hospitals were the major site of care for most individuals [McCarthy and Schafermeyer, 2007]. However, treatment of chronic diseases, the most common today, requires more than hospital care. It requires a continuum of care which includes acute hospitalization, ambulatory care, and long-term care services.

Although the types of services provided by hospitals have changed noticeably over the last 30 years, hospitals remain the central provider of acute health services. In 2008 there were 200 hospitals in Florida, which make it the nation's fourth highest in terms of number of hospitals [Henry J. Kaiser Family Foundation, 2009c]. In Florida there are approximately 2.8 hospital beds per 1,000 residents, and in South Florida the number is greater, 3.4 hospital beds per 1,000 residents. In both instances the indicator is greater than the national average of 2.7 beds per 1,000 population [Florida Department of Health, 2009b]. This indicator varies widely among South Florida counties, from a high of 3.8 beds per 1,000 residents in Miami-Dade to a low of 0.6 beds per 1,000 residents in Hendry. Hendry is the only county in South Florida with lower hospital bed availability than the national average.

The growing representation of elderly persons in the population, increased prevalence of chronic diseases, less reimbursement for hospital services, and less care available at home have contributed to the expanding demand for long-term care support [McCarthy and Schafermeyer, 2007]. Long-term care services are provided in various settings. Skilled nursing facilities provide the most medically and therapeutically intensive services. Florida is the sixth highest state in terms of certified skilled-nursing facilities, with 671 of them reported in 2008 [Henry J. Kaiser Family Foundation, 2009g]. Florida has approximately 81,000 skilled-nursing facility beds and 29 percent are located in South Florida [Florida Department of Health, 2009b]. An occupancy rate of 88 percent suggests that the statewide availability of these facilities is adequate. However, availability in South Florida is only 3.5 beds per 1,000 population, which is lower than the state average of 4.4 beds per 1,000 population. Surprisingly, Hendry has the highest ratio of beds per residents and Broward has the lowest ratio, which is explained by the sparsely populated nature of Hendry vis-à-vis the densely populated nature of Broward.

In general, the quality of Florida's skilled-nursing facilities seems to be well above the national average. Only 9 percent of Florida's facilities have deficiencies that may lead to actual harm or jeopardy of a resident. This is much lower than the 26 percent reported for these facilities nationwide. In fact, Florida is the state with the fewest serious skilled-nursing facility deficiencies in the U.S. [Henry J. Kaiser Family Foundation, 2009g].

Residents who do not require hospitalization or care in skilled-nursing facilities usually receive health care in an ambulatory setting. The exact number of sites offering ambulatory care services in an area is difficult to assess because this type of care is provided in a variety of settings and by different practitioners including, among others, physicians, nurses, physician assistants, and therapists. Since ambulatory care services in the U.S. traditionally have been provided by primary care physicians who work in private or public non-federal settings [McCarthy and Schafermeyer, 2007], evaluating the number of these physicians in an area helps identify the availability of ambulatory care services for a population. In Florida, as well as in the rest of the country, there are 1.2 non-federal primary care physicians per 1,000 residents [Henry J. Keiser Family Foundation, 2009d]. The ratio of primary care physicians per 1,000 residents in South Florida is 1.1, slightly less than the national and state average [Florida Department of Health, 2009b]. Miami-Dade and Palm Beach share the highest ratio in South Florida with 1.2 physicians per 1,000 population, while Hendry, a rural county, has the lowest at 0.8 physicians per 1,000 persons.

Although the overall number of primary care physicians in the state and in most areas of South Florida appears to be adequate, 2.8 million Floridians, about 15 percent of the population, are estimated to live in primary care health professional shortage areas [Henry J. Kaiser Family Foundation, 2009a]. The portion of Floridians living in these areas is greater than the national average of 11.8 percent. Every South Florida county, with the exception of Miami-Dade, has selected areas suffering from a shortage of healthcare professionals [U.S. Department of Health and Human Services, 2009b]. These areas normally are located in rural and inner-city sectors of each county. The lack of adequate healthcare providers in these communities usually exerts a significant impact on the ability of individuals to access healthcare services.

Ambulatory care services also are provided by rural healthcare clinics and federally qualified healthcare centers. In Florida there are 142 rural healthcare clinics and 41 federally qualified healthcare centers [Henry J. Kaiser Family Foundation, 2009e, 2009f]. Compared to other states, Florida ranks ninth in number of rural clinics and fourth in number of federally qualified healthcare centers. These settings generally provide care to underserved populations.

Availability of Health Insurance

Access to healthcare services in the United States is largely determined by the ability to pay for such services. Healthcare coverage in most industrialized countries is universal, but in the U.S. it is a matter of choice available through a variety of sources. In 2008 the major sources of coverage for Floridians were private employer-sponsored health insurance (46.7 percent), Medicare (16.5 percent), Medicaid (10.1 percent), other public coverage (1.3 percent), and individual private health insurance (5.2 percent). One-fifth (20.2 percent) of Floridians are uninsured [Henry J. Kaiser Family Foundation, 2009b].

Unavailability of health insurance is a major obstacle to obtaining most healthcare services. According to the National Health Care Disparities Report of 2008, uninsured patients are twice as likely to leave the emergency department without being treated, compared to insured patients [U.S. Department of Health and Human Services, 2009a]. The Henry J. Kaiser Family Foundation [2009b] reports that 15.4 percent of all Americans lack healthcare coverage. The absence of health insurance is especially prominent in minority populations. On average, more than one out of every three Hispanics and American Indians nationwide do not have health insurance. These proportions are nearly three times the average of Non-Hispanic Whites. Blacks and Asian Americans also are more likely than non-minorities to lack health insurance, with nearly one out of every five members of both groups being without coverage [Mead *et al.*, 2008].

Florida in general and South Florida in particular show unusually high rates of uninsured persons. The empirical evidence of the 2008 American Community Survey reveals that 3.7 million Floridians are uninsured [Turner *et al.*, 2009]. Since Medicare covers most of the elderly and various state and federal programs are available to many children, the highest rates of uninsured persons occur in the 18–65 year old population [DeNavas-Walt *et al.*, 2009]. In 2008, 2.2 million adults in Florida reported that they did not see a doctor in the past 12 months because of cost considerations [Henry J. Kaiser Family Foundation, 2009h]. Florida's uninsured rate of 20.2 percent makes it the state with the third highest rate of uninsured persons [Henry J. Kaiser Family Foundation, 2009b]. Compared to other areas in the state, South Florida exhibits the highest rates of uninsured residents [U.S. Census Bureau, 2009e]. The uninsured rates of every South Florida county are higher than the state average and exceed the national average substantially (see Table 2-3). These high rates in South Florida respond to a combination of a large foreign-born population; a large population of Hispanics, which is the single ethnic group with the highest uninsured rate in the country; and an abundance of service-sector jobs that frequently do not provide insurance benefits [DeNavas-Walt *et al.*, 2009]. The healthcare reform initiatives passed recently by Congress are designed to address the health coverage problem faced by many South Florida communities.

Conclusion

In conclusion, Floridians are living significantly longer lives than they did in the 1970s, as evinced by a long-term upward trend in life expectancy at birth and an overall decline in age-adjusted death rates. Heart disease and cancer remain the top causes of death for individuals throughout the state as well as in South Florida. Infant mortality rates have dropped over the last 20 years, but they remain above the national average. A significant number of Floridians continue to partake in health behaviors which increase their risk of developing chronic illnesses such as heart disease, cancer, diabetes, and chronic lung diseases. While the overall health status of Floridians has improved in the last three decades, improvements have not occurred equally in all segments of the population. The health status of minorities continues to lag behind the status of Non-Hispanic Whites even though gaps in some health indicators have narrowed in recent years.

Although the availability of healthcare facilities in Florida compares favorably with other states, shortages of primary care providers are a concern in specific areas of South Florida. Florida in general and South Florida in particular have unusually high rates of uninsured persons. Uninsured rates are especially high within minority populations, most noticeably Hispanics, and there is a concern that disparities in healthcare access and outcomes may become a huge problem if minority populations continue to grow as projected. This may have a devastating impact on South Florida communities that already experience a large presence of minorities and uninsured residents.

PRACTICE OF PHARMACY IN FLORIDA

The origins of pharmacy practice can be traced to the dawn of civilization, when our ancestors began to use plants and other materials available in their surroundings to treat illnesses and injuries. Evidence of drug retailers has been found in Babylon as far back as 2111 B.C., and throughout time the use of drugs in the treatment of diseases has been a common practice. Ancient Egyptians, Greeks, Romans, and Chinese developed and applied medicinal drugs in efforts to cure numerous ailments and reduce the pain or discomfort associated with them [Posey, 2003; Sonnedecker, 1976]. In these early times practitioners often exercised jointly the responsibilities of priest, physician, and pharmacist in their practice, and reliance on the supernatural probably was as important as, if not more than, observation of the therapeutic properties of the various medicaments. The first pharmacists in Florida probably were medicine men of native tribes.

Colonization by the Spanish and French brought to Florida European pharmacy practice, which frequently was combined with Native American health remedies [Posey, 2003]. According to Grambling [1973], the first Non-Native American pharmacist in Florida, and possibly the United States, is believed to be an unnamed apothecary who was a member of Fort Caroline, an ill-fated French colony, founded in 1564 near present-day Jacksonville. He states that the first Florida drugstore was established between 1815 and 1820 in Pensacola. By 1887, the year in which the Florida Pharmaceutical Association, now the Florida Pharmacists Association, was founded, there were 163 drugstores in the state.

Around the time of the American Revolution, colonists who supported the British often were dispossessed of their land and slaves. Many moved south of Georgia to the northern edge of what would become the state of Florida, hoping that they would be able to return to their homes after the British defeated the revolutionaries. The displaced British sympathizers settled almost exclusively in the northern portion of the peninsula, creating the only economic development experienced in the area. Obviously the American experiment with democracy did not fail, the exiled colonists never returned, and the newly settled areas in Florida continued to flourish while the rest of the state remained in wilderness for over a century. Thus, it is not surprising that most drugstores in the late 1800s were located in the northern and western parts of the state, as far south as Tampa, in areas to which railroad transportation had been extended. What is considered South Florida today was mostly frontier even at the turn of the 20th century. It was not until 1896 that the Flagler railroad reached Miami, effectively opening South Florida to the rest of the state and the nation. In 1905 Key West became the first South Florida city to have an established drugstore.

As a result of the Florida Pharmaceutical Association's efforts to regulate the training and practice of the profession in the state, the Florida Board of Pharmacy was established in 1889 [Grambling, 1973]. By 1896 there were 576 registered Florida pharmacists. These practitioners entered the 20th century performing the social role of the apothecary, preparing and selling medicinal drugs from their drugstores. By the middle of the 20th century, the healthcare role of pharmacists had expanded to include hospital care. Although the demand for hospital pharmacists grew rapidly as more hospitals were built, thanks to increased funding provided by the Hill-Burton Act, competent hospital pharmacists were extremely scarce at the time [Higby, 1997; Magalian, 1993]. In 1947 the Florida Hospital Pharmacists Association, now known as the Florida Society of Health-System Pharmacists, was founded. The original purpose of the society was to increase both the quantity and quality of hospital pharmacists to improve patient care and safety. In the latter part of the 20th century, clinical pharmacy and subsequently pharmaceutical care, as discussed previously, became important movements that redefined the profession.

By the year 2000 both the state and the practice of pharmacy had changed considerably. Florida was no longer part of the frontier, but had evolved into a populous state with a sophisticated population living primarily in urban areas [Florida Department of Health, 2009e; U.S. Census Bureau, 2008c]. South Florida, until recently considered primitive, rural, and isolated, had become the portion of the state with the greatest population concentration. The practice of pharmacy had been transformed from the traditional apothecary model, based mainly on the drug product, into the current practice of pharmaceutical care, which focuses on the patient's total care rather than the product itself [Higby, 1997; Posey, 2003]. The number of practicing pharmacists had increased dramatically and the services provided by pharmacists had expanded well beyond the apothecary. In 2010 there are slightly over 23,000 pharmacists living in the state with active pharmacy licenses, most of them working within the profession; of these, 36 percent live in South Florida. Needless to say, the number of pharmacists in the state is expected to continue growing [Florida Department of Health, 2010b].

Table 2–1. Selected demographic characteristics of South Florida counties, Florida, and the United States in July 2008.

Demographic Characteristics	United States	Florida	South Florida Counties		
			Broward	Collier	Hendry
Population (persons)	304,059,724	18,328,340	1,751,234	315,258	39,453
Male population (percent)	49.3	49.1	48.7	50.6	56.4
Median age (years)	36.8	40.2	40.2	44.9	30.8
Age distribution (percent)	100.0	100.0	100.0	100.0	100.0
Under 5 years	6.9	6.2	6.3	6.3	8.8
5–19 years	20.3	18.1	19.3	15.8	22.9
20–44 years	34.4	32.4	32.2	28.1	37.6
45–64 years	25.7	25.9	27.7	23.4	19.0
65–84 years	10.9	14.5	11.5	22.5	10.3
85 years and older	1.9	2.8	3.0	4.0	1.4
Ethnic distribution (percent)	100.0	100.0	100.0	100.0	100.0
Non-Hispanic White	65.6	60.3	47.3	67.5	37.4
Non-Hispanic Black	12.8	15.9	25.5	5.7	13.4
Hispanic	15.4	21.0	24.0	25.5	47.9
Asian American	4.5	2.3	3.1	1.1	0.7
Other	1.7	0.5	0.1	0.2	0.6

Table 2–1. Selected demographic characteristics of South Florida counties, Florida, and the United States in July 2008 (continued).

Demographic Characteristics	South Florida Counties				
	Lee	Martin	Miami-Dade	Monroe	Palm Beach
Population (persons)	593,136	138,660	2,398,245	72,243	1,265,293
Male population (percent)	49.4	49.5	48.5	53.2	48.8
Median age (years)	42.8	47.5	39.2	48.2	43.5
Age distribution (percent)	100.0	100.0	100.0	100.0	100.0
Under 5 years	6.2	4.8	6.4	4.5	5.9
5–19 years	16.3	15.2	18.9	12.8	17.1
20–44 years	30.3	26.5	33.8	26.9	29.3
45–64 years	24.3	27.1	25.6	39.9	25.6
65–84 years	19.3	21.3	13.1	14.4	17.4
85 years and older	3.6	5.1	2.3	1.4	4.7
Ethnic distribution (percent)	100.0	100.0	100.0	100.0	100.0
Non-Hispanic White	72.7	81.3	17.8	73.6	63.3
Non-Hispanic Black	8.0	5.9	19.5	5.4	16.5
Hispanic	17.5	10.4	61.0	18.9	17.8
Asian American	1.3	1.0	1.6	1.3	2.2
Other	0.5	1.4	0.1	0.8	0.2

Source: U.S. Census Bureau (2009), "2008 Population Estimates Program," http://www.factfinder.census.gov/home/en/official_estimates_ 2008.html. Accessed September 25, 2009.

Table 2–2. Selected socioeconomic characteristics of South Florida counties, Florida, and the United States in 2008.

Socioeconomic Characteristics	United States	Florida	South Florida Counties		
			Broward	Collier	Hendry
Schooling of persons 25 years and older					
High school graduates or higher (percent)	84.5	84.9	86.8	84.2	59.1
College graduates or higher (percent)	27.4	25.7	29.0	30.5	6.2
Median household income (dollars)	52,175	48,637	53,236	60,133	38,736
Group below poverty level					
Population (percent)	13.2	12.6	11.5	10.2	26.6
Under 18 years of age (percent)	18.2	17.6	15.5	18.1	28.1
65 years and older (percent)	9.8	10.0	12.0	5.6	6.4
Families (percent)	9.6	9.0	8.3	6.7	17.6
Female head of household (percent)	28.2	24.6	19.5	23.6	28.5

Socioeconomic Characteristics	South Florida Counties				
	Lee	Martin	Miami-Dade	Monroe	Palm Beach
Schooling of persons 25 years and older					
High school graduates or higher (percent)	86.6	88.7	76.8	90.4	86.5
College graduates or higher (percent)	25.0	29.3	26.8	30.0	31.5
Median household income (dollars)	51,599	54,182	44,364	56,984	54,301
Group below poverty level					
Population (percent)	9.9	9.3	16.1	10.3	10.8
Under 18 years of age (percent)	15.3	17.1	20.4	10.7	15.8
65 years and older (percent)	6.5	5.8	21.7	9.9	7.6
Families (percent)	6.8	5.2	12.6	6.5	7.3
Female head of household (percent)	22.1	18.8	24.3	22.6	21.9

Source: U.S. Census Bureau (2009), "Fact finder: American Community Survey 2008 data profile," http://www.factfinder.census.gov/servlet/DatasetMainPageServlet?_program=ACS&_submenuld=datasets_2&_lang-en. Accessed November 9, 2009.

Table 2–3. Selected health characteristics of South Florida counties, Florida, and the United States in 2008.

Health Characteristics		United States	Florida	South Florida Counties		
				Broward	Collier	Hendry
Age-adjusted deaths per 100,000 population		760	686	665	495	826
Infant death rate per 1,000 births		6.7	7.3	7.7	7.5	10.1
Leading causes of death (percentage of all causes)	1	Heart disease (25.0)	Heart disease (24.6)	Heart disease (26.4)	Cancer (27.3)	Heart disease (25.1)
	2	Cancer (23.0)	Cancer (23.8)	Cancer (22.9)	Heart disease (22.5)	Cancer (19.8)
	3	Cerebrovascular diseases (5.5)	Chronic lower respiratory diseases (6.0)	Cerebrovascular diseases (5.6)	Accidents (6.4)	Accidents (11.3)
	4	Chronic lower respiratory diseases (5.3)	Accidents (5.2)	Accidents (5.2)	Cerebrovascular diseases (5.4)	Chronic lower respiratory diseases (5.7)
	5	Accidents (4.8)	Cerebrovascular diseases (5.0)	Chronic lower respiratory diseases (4.9)	Chronic lower respiratory diseases (5.3)	Diabetes *mellitus* (2.8)

Table 2–3. Selected health characteristics of South Florida counties, Florida, and the United States in 2008 (continued).

<table>
<tr><th colspan="2" rowspan="2">Health Characteristics</th><th colspan="5">South Florida Counties</th></tr>
<tr><th>Lee</th><th>Martin</th><th>Miami-Dade</th><th>Monroe</th><th>Palm Beach</th></tr>
<tr><td colspan="2">Age-adjusted deaths per 100,000 population</td><td>549</td><td>588</td><td>641</td><td>650</td><td>601</td></tr>
<tr><td colspan="2">Infant death rate per 1,000 births</td><td>7.0</td><td>10.2</td><td>7.4</td><td>7.0</td><td>6.9</td></tr>
<tr><td rowspan="5">Leading causes of death (percentage of all causes)</td><td>1</td><td>Heart disease (25.2)</td><td>Cancer (27.2)</td><td>Heart disease (28.4)</td><td>Cancer (23.3)</td><td>Heart disease (26.7)</td></tr>
<tr><td>2</td><td>Cancer (24.7)</td><td>Heart disease (23.7)</td><td>Cancer (21.9)</td><td>Heart disease (22.7)</td><td>Cancer (23.6)</td></tr>
<tr><td>3</td><td>Chronic lower respiratory diseases (5.9)</td><td>Chronic lower respiratory diseases (6.4)</td><td>Cerebrovascular diseases (5.0)</td><td>Accidents (10.0)</td><td>Cerebrovascular diseases (4.9)</td></tr>
<tr><td>4</td><td>Accidents (5.4)</td><td>Cerebrovascular diseases (6.3)</td><td>Chronic lower respiratory diseases (4.4)</td><td>Chronic lower respiratory diseases (5.4)</td><td>Accidents (4.8)</td></tr>
<tr><td>5</td><td>Cerebrovascular diseases (4.8)</td><td>Accidents (4.8)</td><td>Accidents (4.1)</td><td>Cerebrovascular diseases (4.0)</td><td>Chronic lower respiratory diseases (4.8)</td></tr>
</table>

Table 2–3. **Selected health characteristics of South Florida counties, Florida, and the United States in 2008 (continued).**

Health Characteristics		United States	Florida	South Florida Counties		
				Broward	Collier	Hendry
Leading causes of death (percentage of all causes)	6	Alzheimer's disease (3.1)	Diabetes *mellitus* (3.0)	Diabetes *mellitus* (2.5)	Alzheimer's disease (3.9)	Cerebrovascular diseases (4.9)
	7	Diabetes *mellitus* (2.9)	Alzheimer's disease (2.8)	Alzheimer's disease (2.2)	Diabetes *mellitus* (2.5)	Suicide (1.8)
	8	Influenza and pneumonia (2.2)	Suicide (1.6)	Suicide (1.6)	Chronic liver diseases and cirrhosis (1.7)	Chronic liver diseases and cirrhosis (1.4)
	9	Kidney disease (1.9)	Chronic liver diseases and cirrhosis (1.4)	HIV/AIDS (1.5)	Suicide (1.6)	Alzheimer's disease (1.4)
	10	Septicemia (1.4)	Influenza and pneumonia (1.3)	Chronic liver diseases and cirrhosis (1.5)	Influenza and pneumonia (1.1)	Influenza and pneumonia (0.7)
Adult overweight or obesity (%)		66.9	62.1	57.3	59.6	62.3
Adult smokers (%)		19.9	19.3	18.1	17.4	21.6
Heavy or binge drinking (%)		20.6	16.2	13.3	16.1	19.1
Uninsured persons under 65 (%)		15.4	20.2	27.1	34.1	33.6

Table 2–3. **Selected health characteristics of South Florida counties, Florida, and the United States in 2008 (continued).**

Health Characteristics		South Florida Counties				
		Lee	Martin	Miami-Dade	Monroe	Palm Beach
Leading causes of death (percentage of all causes)	6	Diabetes *mellitus* (2.8)	Alzheimer's disease (3.1)	Diabetes *mellitus* (3.6)	Chronic liver diseases and cirrhosis (3.2)	Alzheimer's disease (3.3)
	7	Alzheimer's disease (2.4)	Suicide (1.6)	Alzheimer's disease (2.8)	Suicide (2.5)	Diabetes *mellitus* (2.1)
	8	Chronic liver diseases and cirrhosis (1.7)	Chronic liver diseases and cirrhosis (1.5)	HIV/AIDS (2.0)	Alzheimer's disease (2.3)	Suicide (1.4)
	9	Suicide (1.7)	Diabetes *mellitus* (1.5)	Homicide (1.4)	HIV/AIDS (1.5)	Influenza and pneumonia (1.0)
	10	Influenza and pneumonia (1.3)	Influenza and pneumonia (0.7)	Influenza and pneumonia (1.4)	Influenza and pneumonia (1.5)	Chronic liver diseases and cirrhosis (0.9)
Adult overweight or obesity (%)		63.7	54.9	64.9	52.0	57.6
Adult smokers (%)		19.6	16.9	15.4	22.3	17.5
Heavy or binge drinking (%)		18.9	16.8	15.0	22.3	14.6
Uninsured persons under 65 (%)		27.4	27.7	30.9	30.8	27.1

METHODOLOGY 3

The aim of this chapter is to explain the methodology used in developing the socioeconomic profile of South Florida pharmacists. First, the geographical boundaries are described, along with the source of the universe or complete set of pharmacists. Then the questionnaire used in the study is presented. This is followed by a discussion of the distributions of pharmacists responding to the questionnaire by county of residence and county of work, gender, ethnic group, and age group. The next section of the chapter addresses the two mailings of the questionnaire and the response to each mailing by county of residence, gender, ethnic group, and age group, and the last section presents the distribution of responses, aggregately and in each county, by all three classifications viewed simultaneously.

BOUNDARIES

For purposes of this study South Florida comprises Broward, Miami-Dade, and Palm Beach, the three larger counties on the Atlantic coast; Collier, Hendry, Lee, and Monroe, the four smaller, contiguous counties on the Gulf coast or inland; and Martin and Pasco counties, located on the periphery, to detect possible contrasts. A list of all 6,175 pharmacists licensed in Florida with addresses in these nine counties, obtained from the Florida Department of Health in September 2006, constitutes the universe for the survey and portrays the distribution appearing in the right column.

County	Number of Licensed Pharmacists
Broward	1,976
Collier	220
Hendry	10
Lee	488
Martin	136
Miami-Dade	1,665
Monroe	64
Palm Beach	1,287
Pasco	329
All nine counties	6,175

Broward, Miami-Dade, and Palm Beach counties are the listed places of residence for four-fifths (79.8 percent) of licensed pharmacists in the universe. Hendry and Monroe counties together are the home of a minute 1.2 percent, and Martin and Pasco, the periphery counties, account for 7.5 percent of the list of licensed practitioners provided by the Florida Department of Health.

SURVEY QUESTIONNAIRE

A two-page (front and back) survey questionnaire specifically designed to obtain data for the construction of this profile (see Appendix 3-1) was mailed to every pharmacist whose name appears in the universe list. In this questionnaire potential respondents are informed that the survey is intended solely for academic research purposes, that both the identity of the respondents and the answers provided by them remain anonymous at all times, and that the results would be published only aggregately. The questionnaire consists of 24 questions in the front page and 13 questions in the back page.

The front page contains questions pertaining to who the pharmacist is and what he/she does at work. A summary of the topics that these questions address; the type of their expected response (open-ended or close-ended); the range of expected responses for close-ended questions; the units in which the response is expected for open-ended questions (in parentheses), if applicable; and in the case of close-ended questions, whether the response should be limited to one choice or may embrace two or more choices, can be seen in table format in Appendix 3-2. The back page of the questionnaire includes questions probing pharmacists' perceptions and opinions related to various aspects of their job. They are measured along zero-to-ten intensity scales, ten showing the greatest intensity, and include the following work-related aspects: Career and job satisfaction, workload, stress, advancement opportunities, job security, autonomy, fairness in the workplace, help and support from supervisor, job atmosphere, scheduling flexibility, and perception of coworkers' professional quality and willingness to provide help and support.

Question 14, which refers to primary role as a pharmacist, was designed originally to elicit a single-choice response. However, after several pharmacists indicated in their reply that they engage in more than one "primary" role, the question was changed to the multiple-choice response category. In the tables pertaining to variables with multiple-choice responses, the value for the totals and subtotals may be smaller than the sum of their parts; conversely, in the tables pertaining to variables with an expected single response, the values of the totals and subtotals are exactly the same as the sum of their parts.

Responses reported by pharmacists in decimals are entered into the data set and computed as such. For example, a pharmacist may respond that he/she works 42.5 hours per week or that he/she earns $51.70 per hour. Similarly, in reporting the level of stress experienced at work, a pharmacist may circle two numbers or the space between two numbers. In these instances, the middle value is entered and computed.

DISTRIBUTION OF PHARMACISTS IN THE SAMPLE

Of the 6,175 questionnaires mailed to licensed pharmacists living in the nine counties, according to the Florida Department of Health, 148 questionnaires were returned unfilled because of various reasons—the pharmacist moved without leaving a forwarding address, passed away, was no longer working, etc. A total of 1,539 pharmacists mailed their questionnaire properly filled for a response rate of 25.5 percent. The number of observations and the rate of response compare favorably with those reported by similar studies [Desselle, 2005; Jacobson *et al.*, 2004b; Kahaleh and Gaither, 2005; Lapane and Hughes, 2006; Lin *et al.*, 2007; LoBuono, 2003; Mott, 2001; Mott *et al.*, 2004; Weeks and Wallace, 2007a, 2007b; Weeks *et al.*, 2007; Yutzie *et al.*, 2005].

Table 3-1 shows the distribution of pharmacists in the sample by county of residence, gender, and ethnic group. Almost four-fifths (77.8 percent) of respondents declare that they live in Broward, Miami-Dade, or Palm Beach counties, which is very similar to the distribution of the population of practitioners and lends credence to the contention that the sample indeed is representative of the universe from which it is drawn. Men slightly outnumber women (52.3 percent and 47.7 percent, respectively), and the relationship holds for every county except Miami-Dade, where women outnumber men. Non-Hispanic Whites account for 62.3 percent of the sample, followed by Hispanics (20.7 percent), Non-Hispanic Blacks (7.7 percent), Asian Americans (5.6 percent), and others (3.7 percent). The ethnic composition varies substantially by county. In Collier, Lee, and Martin, Non-Hispanic Whites represent over nine-tenths (90.3 percent) of the sample, whereas in Broward, Miami-Dade, and Palm Beach Non-Hispanic White pharmacists represent only 57.1 percent. In Miami-Dade, the most ethnically diverse county in South Florida, more than half (55.3 percent) of responding pharmacists are Hispanic, followed by 28.6 percent Non-Hispanic White, 9.1 percent Black, 4.1 percent Asian American, and 2.9 percent other.

The gender composition is mediated by ethnic group. While most (62.9 percent) Non-Hispanic White practitioners are men, women outnumber men by a nearly 2 to 1 ratio (65.2 percent to 34.8 percent) in all other ethnic groups combined; 67.1 percent of Hispanic pharmacists, 65.5 percent of Black pharmacists, and 59.3 percent of Asian American pharmacists are women.

The distribution of pharmacists in the sample by county of residence, age group, and gender can be observed in Table 3-2. The 30–39 and 40–49 year-old groups are the most numerous, and the number of respondents declines steadily with every subsequent age category. Yet almost one out of every four (23.0 percent) pharmacy practitioners who report their age is 60 years or older. By far the greatest concentration of older pharmacists is found in Palm Beach county, where one-third (33.7 percent) of pharmacists who declare their age report to be 60 years or older.

The gender composition also is mediated by age. The fraction of female pharmacists is highest (76.3 percent) for the group under 30 years of age and lowest (15.0 percent) among practitioners 60 years or older, which is consistent with the reportedly recent entry of women into the profession [Brown *et al.*, 2006; Gardner and Stowe, 2007; Mott, 2000; Walton and Cooksey, 2001]. In fact, if one partitions the sample into two segments, respondents under 50 years of age and respondents 50 years and older, two heterogeneous gender compositions are observed—women outnumber men on an almost 2 to 1 ratio among the younger, whereas men outnumber women almost 3 to 1 among the older.

A somewhat different perspective of the distribution of pharmacists who completed the survey questionnaire is presented in Tables 3-3 and 3-4. These tables show the distribution of respondents by county of work instead of county of residence. With the exception of Miami-Dade, more pharmacists live than work in every county represented in the study. Broward and Palm Beach report modest differences (8.9 percent and 11.2 percent fewer practitioners, respectively), but in Martin and Pasco, the periphery counties, the difference is substantial (42.7 percent fewer practitioners working than residing). Conversely, 17.8 percent more pharmacists report working than living in Miami-Dade. It should be noted that 1.8 percent of respondents throughout the sample do not disclose their county of work, so the numbers by county of work are expected to be slightly smaller vis-à-vis county of residence.

Gender, ethnic group, and age differences become evident in the relationship between county of residence and county of work, although each county seems to possess its own set of characteristics. In Miami-Dade and Palm Beach men are more prone to cross county boundaries than are women, but in Broward the opposite seems to be the case. Ethnic patterns are less consistent. In Miami-Dade Non-Hispanic White and Black pharmacists cross boundaries more often than do Asian American and Hispanic pharmacists, while in Palm Beach minority practitioners are less active in this respect than are non-minorities, and in Broward relatively more Black and Hispanic pharmacists report residence-worksite disparities relative to Non-Hispanic White and Asian American pharmacists. Curiously, pharmacists 50 years or older are more mobile across counties in Miami-Dade and Palm Beach compared to pharmacists under 50 years of age, but in Broward age does not seem to be a relevant factor.

MAILING OF QUESTIONNAIRES

Two identical mailings of questionnaires took place. The first went out on October 20, 2006 and the second mailing was sent on January 25, 2007. The purpose of the second mailing was to urge South Florida pharmacists who had not responded after the first mailing to fill out and return their survey questionnaire. Of the 1,539 total responses, more than two-thirds (70.7 percent) submitted their completed questionnaire before the second mailing went out (see Tables 3-5 and 3-6). The response percentages before the second mailing are very similar for all South Florida counties, but somewhat lower for pharmacists living outside South Florida. Perhaps their relatively delayed response might be attributed to factors related to mail forwarding.

Neither gender nor ethnic differences appear in the percentage of practitioners returning their questionnaire prior to the second mailing, except that the Asian American pharmacists' percentage is slightly lower than the percentage of the other ethnic groups. In general, pharmacists younger than 40 years of age were more responsive to the first mailing than were their 40 years or older peers, although the difference is not a major one. Therefore, the two distributions of responses, before and after the second mailing, seem to be homogeneous and the observation units contained in them may be merged into one sample.

INTERACTION BETWEEN ETHNIC GROUP AND AGE GROUP

The tables generated for the socioeconomic profile of South Florida pharmacists throughout the rest of this book depict demographic, situation, and opinion indicators arranged into two sets of classifications: county of residence, gender, and ethnic group and county of residence, gender, and age group. Only in Tables 3-7 and 3-8 do ethnic group and age group interact with each other. In order to protect respondents' anonymity, the data for the four smaller, contiguous counties (Collier, Hendry, Lee, and Monroe) are aggregated into one category. The same procedure is applied to Martin and Pasco, the periphery counties.

One can observe in Table 3-7 that ethnic identification and age show a clear relationship, which reveals that the incorporation of minorities, especially Blacks and Asian Americans, into the South Florida pharmacist workforce is a recent phenomenon. Less than one-half (44.2 percent) of pharmacists younger than 40 years of age are Non-Hispanic White. In this age bracket Hispanics constitute 28.0 percent, Blacks account for 12.1 percent, and Asian Americans comprise 10.3 percent of practitioners. Middle-aged pharmacists, 40–59 years old, exhibit a greater concentration (63.8 percent) of Non-Hispanic Whites and relatively fewer minorities: 19.6 percent Hispanics, 8.1 percent Blacks, and 4.9 percent Asian Americans. Pharmacists 60 years and older are predominantly non-minority (83.5 percent), with few Hispanics (12.4 percent), and even fewer Blacks (1.7 percent) and Asian Americans (0.9 percent).

The trend evinced by these percentages is corroborated by the median age values of the various ethnic groups, presented in Table 3-8. Non-Hispanic Whites, the longest established group, show the highest median age value, followed by Hispanics, Blacks, and Asian Americans, in that order.

ORDERING OF REFERENCE LIST

A note on the sequencing of items in the reference list. First, items are arranged alphabetically by the primary author's surname. In instances where the primary author has written more than one item in the reference list, the items are ordered by year of publication, earliest first. Single-author entries precede two-author entries beginning with the same surname, and two-author entries precede multiple-author entries beginning with the same surname. Items with three or more authors are ordered alphabetically by the primary author's surname, then chronologically by year of publication, earliest first.

Table 3–1. **Number of pharmacists who completed the survey questionnaire by county of residence, ethnic group, and gender.**

County of Residence	Gender	Number of Pharmacists					
		All Ethnic Groups	Non-Hispanic			Hispanic	Other
			White	Black	Asian		
All counties	Both genders	1,539	958	119	86	319	57
	Men	805	603	41	35	105	21
	Women	734	355	78	51	214	36
Broward	Both genders	508	316	55	35	70	32
	Men	270	199	22	11	26	12
	Women	238	117	33	24	44	20
Collier	Both genders	65	58	1	-	6	-
	Men	40	35	1	-	4	-
	Women	25	23	-	-	2	-
Hendry	Both genders	2	2	-	-	-	-
	Men	1	1	-	-	-	-
	Women	1	1	-	-	-	-
Lee	Both genders	117	106	3	5	3	-
	Men	59	54	1	3	1	-
	Women	58	52	2	2	2	-
Martin	Both genders	35	32	1	-	1	1
	Men	18	18	-	-	-	-
	Women	17	14	1	-	1	1
Miami-Dade	Both genders	342	98	31	14	189	10
	Men	140	69	9	7	54	1
	Women	202	29	22	7	135	9
Monroe	Both genders	18	15	-	-	3	-
	Men	11	9	-	-	2	-
	Women	7	6	-	-	1	-
Palm Beach	Both genders	348	270	21	20	28	9
	Men	206	179	6	6	10	5
	Women	142	91	15	14	18	4
Pasco	Both genders	61	44	3	6	4	4
	Men	39	28	-	5	3	3
	Women	22	16	3	1	1	1
Other	Both genders	43	17	4	6	15	1
	Men	21	11	2	3	5	-
	Women	22	6	2	3	10	1

Table 3–2. Number of pharmacists who completed the survey questionnaire by county of residence, age group, and gender.

County of Residence	Gender	Number of Pharmacists							
		All Age Groups	Less than 30	30-39	40-49	50-59	60-69	70 and Older	Not Known
All counties	Both genders	1,539	97	367	364	329	192	154	36
	Men	805	23	108	157	204	166	128	19
	Women	734	74	259	207	125	26	26	17
Broward	Both genders	508	25	124	136	110	60	40	13
	Men	270	4	36	70	69	51	34	6
	Women	238	21	88	66	41	9	6	7
Collier	Both genders	65	5	10	14	16	11	7	2
	Men	40	2	5	3	12	9	7	2
	Women	25	3	5	11	4	2	-	-
Hendry	Both genders	2	-	-	1	1	-	-	-
	Men	1	-	-	-	1	-	-	-
	Women	1	-	-	1	-	-	-	-
Lee	Both genders	117	10	29	28	33	9	6	2
	Men	59	3	8	14	20	8	5	1
	Women	58	7	21	14	13	1	1	1
Martin	Both genders	35	1	4	10	13	4	3	-
	Men	18	-	2	2	7	4	3	-
	Women	17	1	2	8	6	-	-	-
Miami-Dade	Both genders	342	21	94	86	63	35	34	9
	Men	140	7	25	32	28	26	19	3
	Women	202	14	69	54	35	9	15	6
Monroe	Both genders	18	1	1	6	8	2	-	-
	Men	11	-	-	3	6	2	-	-
	Women	7	1	1	3	2	-	-	-
Palm Beach	Both genders	348	24	74	65	63	60	55	7
	Men	206	4	18	26	45	57	52	4
	Women	142	20	56	39	18	3	3	3
Pasco	Both genders	61	5	14	13	16	8	4	1
	Men	39	2	6	5	14	7	4	1
	Women	22	3	8	8	2	1	-	-
Other	Both genders	43	5	17	5	6	3	5	2
	Men	21	1	8	2	2	2	4	2
	Women	22	4	9	3	4	1	1	-

Table 3–3. Number of pharmacists who completed the survey questionnaire by county of work, ethnic group, and gender.

County of Work	Gender	Number of Pharmacists					
		All Ethnic Groups	Non-Hispanic			Hispanic	Other
			White	Black	Asian		
All counties	Both genders	1,539	958	119	86	319	57
	Men	805	603	41	35	105	21
	Women	734	355	78	51	214	36
Broward	Both genders	463	305	42	32	59	25
	Men	255	202	12	10	21	10
	Women	208	103	30	22	38	15
Collier	Both genders	63	58	-	-	5	-
	Men	37	34	-	-	3	-
	Women	26	24	-	-	2	-
Hendry	Both genders	1	1	-	-	-	-
	Men	1	1	-	-	-	-
	Women	-	-	-	-	-	-
Lee	Both genders	112	99	4	5	4	-
	Men	58	51	2	3	2	-
	Women	54	48	2	2	2	-
Martin	Both genders	20	18	1	-	1	-
	Men	11	11	-	-	-	-
	Women	9	7	1	-	1	-
Miami-Dade	Both genders	403	132	43	15	198	15
	Men	181	91	19	8	59	4
	Women	222	41	24	7	139	11
Monroe	Both genders	16	13	-	1	2	-
	Men	9	8	-	-	1	-
	Women	7	5	-	1	1	-
Palm Beach	Both genders	309	230	21	21	27	10
	Men	170	144	6	6	11	3
	Women	139	86	15	15	16	7
Pasco	Both genders	35	27	2	3	3	-
	Men	22	18	-	2	2	-
	Women	13	9	2	1	1	-
Other	Both genders	89	53	5	9	17	5
	Men	46	29	2	6	6	3
	Women	43	24	3	3	11	2
Not Reported	Both genders	28	22	1	-	3	2
	Men	15	14	-	-	-	1
	Women	13	8	1	-	3	1

Table 3–4. **Number of pharmacists who completed the survey questionnaire by county of work, age group, and gender.**

County of Work	Gender	Number of Pharmacists							
		All Age Groups	Less than 30	30-39	40-49	50-59	60-69	70 and Older	Not Known
All counties	Both genders	1,539	97	367	364	329	192	154	36
	Men	805	23	108	157	204	166	128	19
	Women	734	74	259	207	125	26	26	17
Broward	Both genders	463	22	119	119	92	59	43	9
	Men	255	5	36	57	61	52	39	5
	Women	208	17	83	62	31	7	4	4
Collier	Both genders	63	5	11	14	14	10	7	2
	Men	37	2	6	3	9	8	7	2
	Women	26	3	5	11	5	2	-	-
Hendry	Both genders	1	-	-	-	1	-	-	-
	Men	1	-	-	-	1	-	-	-
	Women	-	-	-	-	-	-	-	-
Lee	Both genders	112	10	26	28	33	7	6	2
	Men	58	3	7	14	22	6	5	1
	Women	54	7	19	14	11	1	1	1
Martin	Both genders	20	1	1	6	8	3	1	-
	Men	11	-	1	1	5	3	1	-
	Women	9	1	-	5	3	-	-	-
Miami-Dade	Both genders	403	24	94	106	78	45	43	13
	Men	181	6	26	46	39	33	26	5
	Women	222	18	68	60	39	12	17	8
Monroe	Both genders	16	1	2	5	6	2	-	-
	Men	9	-	-	3	4	2	-	-
	Women	7	1	2	2	2	-	-	-
Palm Beach	Both genders	309	24	70	60	62	50	38	5
	Men	170	4	14	22	43	48	37	2
	Women	139	20	56	38	19	2	1	3
Pasco	Both genders	35	1	8	7	12	5	1	1
	Men	22	1	4	2	9	4	1	1
	Women	13	-	4	5	3	1	-	-
Other	Both genders	89	9	32	17	15	7	7	2
	Men	46	2	13	8	8	7	6	2
	Women	43	7	19	9	7	-	1	-
Not Reported	Both genders	28	-	4	2	8	4	8	2
	Men	15	-	1	1	3	3	6	1
	Women	13	-	3	1	5	1	2	1

Table 3–5. **Number of pharmacists who completed the survey questionnaire by county of residence, whether they responded after the first or second mailing, ethnic group, and gender.**

County of Residence	Time of Response	Gender	Number of Pharmacists					
			All Ethnic Groups	Non-Hispanic			Hispanic	Other
				White	Black	Asian		
All counties	All respondents	Both genders	1,539	958	119	86	319	57
		Men	805	603	41	35	105	21
		Women	734	355	78	51	214	36
	After first mailing	Both genders	1,088	696	79	52	219	42
		Men	572	441	24	22	71	14
		Women	516	255	55	30	148	28
	After second mailing	Both genders	451	262	40	34	100	15
		Men	233	162	17	13	34	7
		Women	218	100	23	21	66	8
Broward	All respondents	Both genders	508	316	55	35	70	32
		Men	270	199	22	11	26	12
		Women	238	117	33	24	44	20
	After first mailing	Both genders	373	241	36	25	50	21
		Men	205	155	14	8	21	7
		Women	168	86	22	17	29	14
	After second mailing	Both genders	135	75	19	10	20	11
		Men	65	44	8	3	5	5
		Women	70	31	11	7	15	6
Collier, Hendry, Lee, and Monroe	All respondents	Both genders	202	181	4	5	12	-
		Men	111	99	2	3	7	-
		Women	91	82	2	2	5	-
	After first mailing	Both genders	143	129	3	2	9	-
		Men	77	70	1	1	5	-
		Women	66	59	2	1	4	-
	After second mailing	Both genders	59	52	1	3	3	-
		Men	34	29	1	2	2	-
		Women	25	23	-	1	1	-
Martin and Pasco	All respondents	Both genders	96	76	4	6	5	5
		Men	57	46	-	5	3	3
		Women	39	30	4	1	2	2
	After first mailing	Both genders	67	55	3	3	3	3
		Men	39	32	-	3	2	2
		Women	28	23	3	-	1	1
	After second mailing	Both genders	29	21	1	3	2	2
		Men	18	14	-	2	1	1
		Women	11	7	1	1	1	1

Table 3–5. Number of pharmacists who completed the survey questionnaire by county of residence, whether they responded after the first or second mailing, ethnic group, and gender (continued).

County of Residence	Time of Response	Gender	Number of Pharmacists					
			All Ethnic Groups	Non-Hispanic			Hispanic	Other
				White	Black	Asian		
Miami-Dade	All respondents	Both genders	342	98	31	14	189	10
		Men	140	69	9	7	54	1
		Women	202	29	22	7	135	9
	After first mailing	Both genders	238	70	21	9	129	9
		Men	96	51	7	5	32	1
		Women	142	19	14	4	97	8
	After second mailing	Both genders	104	28	10	5	60	1
		Men	44	18	2	2	22	-
		Women	60	10	8	3	38	1
Palm Beach	All respondents	Both genders	348	270	21	20	28	9
		Men	206	179	6	6	10	5
		Women	142	91	15	14	18	4
	After first mailing	Both genders	242	188	15	11	20	8
		Men	142	125	2	4	7	4
		Women	100	63	13	7	13	4
	After second mailing	Both genders	106	82	6	9	8	1
		Men	64	54	4	2	3	1
		Women	42	28	2	7	5	-
Other	All respondents	Both genders	43	17	4	6	15	1
		Men	21	11	2	3	5	-
		Women	22	6	2	3	10	1
	After first mailing	Both genders	25	13	1	2	8	1
		Men	13	8	-	1	4	-
		Women	12	5	1	1	4	1
	After second mailing	Both genders	18	4	3	4	7	-
		Men	8	3	2	2	1	-
		Women	10	1	1	2	6	-

Table 3–6. Number of pharmacists who completed the survey questionnaire by county of residence, whether they responded after the first or second mailing, age group, and gender.

County of Residence	Time of Response	Gender	Number of Pharmacists							
			All Age Groups	Less than 30	30-39	40-49	50-59	60-69	70 and Older	Not Known
All counties	All respondents	Both genders	1,539	97	367	364	329	192	154	36
		Men	805	23	108	157	204	166	128	19
		Women	734	74	259	207	125	26	26	17
	After first mailing	Both genders	1,088	76	272	250	224	137	101	28
		Men	572	19	79	106	137	122	92	17
		Women	516	57	193	144	87	15	9	11
	After second mailing	Both genders	451	21	95	114	105	55	53	8
		Men	233	4	29	51	67	44	36	2
		Women	218	17	66	63	38	11	17	6
Broward	All respondents	Both genders	508	25	124	136	110	60	40	13
		Men	270	4	36	70	69	51	34	6
		Women	238	21	88	66	41	9	6	7
	After first mailing	Both genders	373	19	99	99	76	43	28	9
		Men	205	4	30	50	51	39	25	6
		Women	168	15	69	49	25	4	3	3
	After second mailing	Both genders	135	6	25	37	34	17	12	4
		Men	65	-	6	20	18	12	9	-
		Women	70	6	19	17	16	5	3	4
Collier, Hendry, Lee, and Monroe	All respondents	Both genders	202	16	40	49	58	22	13	4
		Men	111	5	13	20	39	19	12	3
		Women	91	11	27	29	19	3	1	1
	After first mailing	Both genders	143	12	30	33	40	18	7	3
		Men	77	4	9	12	25	17	7	3
		Women	66	8	21	21	15	1	-	-
	After second mailing	Both genders	59	4	10	16	18	4	6	1
		Men	34	1	4	8	14	2	5	-
		Women	25	3	6	8	4	2	1	1
Martin and Pasco	All respondents	Both genders	96	6	18	23	29	12	7	1
		Men	57	2	8	7	21	11	7	1
		Women	39	4	10	16	8	1	-	-
	After first mailing	Both genders	67	5	15	16	17	8	5	1
		Men	39	2	7	4	13	7	5	1
		Women	28	3	8	12	4	1	-	-
	After second mailing	Both genders	29	1	3	7	12	4	2	-
		Men	18	-	1	3	8	4	2	-
		Women	11	1	2	4	4	-	-	-

Table 3–6. Number of pharmacists who completed the survey questionnaire by county of residence, whether they responded after the first or second mailing, age group, and gender (continued).

County of Residence	Time of Response	Gender	Number of Pharmacists							
			All Age Groups	Less than 30	30-39	40-49	50-59	60-69	70 and Older	Not Known
Miami-Dade	All respondents	Both genders	342	21	94	86	63	35	34	9
		Men	140	7	25	32	28	26	19	3
		Women	202	14	69	54	35	9	15	6
	After first mailing	Both genders	238	16	67	55	46	28	18	8
		Men	96	5	17	22	16	21	13	2
		Women	142	11	50	33	30	7	5	6
	After second mailing	Both genders	104	5	27	31	17	7	16	1
		Men	44	2	8	10	12	5	6	1
		Women	60	3	19	21	5	2	10	-
Palm Beach	All respondents	Both genders	348	24	74	65	63	60	55	7
		Men	206	4	18	26	45	57	52	4
		Women	142	20	56	39	18	3	3	3
	After first mailing	Both genders	242	20	52	44	43	38	40	5
		Men	142	3	13	17	31	36	39	3
		Women	100	17	39	27	12	2	1	2
	After second mailing	Both genders	106	4	22	21	20	22	15	2
		Men	64	1	5	9	14	21	13	1
		Women	42	3	17	12	6	1	2	1
Other	All respondents	Both genders	43	5	17	5	6	3	5	2
		Men	21	1	8	2	2	2	4	2
		Women	22	4	9	3	4	1	1	-
	After first mailing	Both genders	25	4	9	3	2	2	3	2
		Men	13	1	3	1	1	2	3	2
		Women	12	3	6	2	1	-	-	-
	After second mailing	Both genders	18	1	8	2	4	1	2	-
		Men	8	-	5	1	1	-	1	-
		Women	10	1	3	1	3	1	1	-

Table 3–7. **Number of pharmacists who completed the survey questionnaire by county of residence, age group, ethnic group, and gender.**

County of Residence	Age Group (years)	Gender	Number of Pharmacists					
			All Ethnic Groups	Non-Hispanic			Hispanic	Other
				White	Black	Asian		
All counties	All groups	Both genders	1,539	958	119	86	319	57
		Men	805	603	41	35	105	21
		Women	734	355	78	51	214	36
	Less than 30	Both genders	97	48	11	9	25	4
		Men	23	13	1	2	7	-
		Women	74	35	10	7	18	4
	30 - 39	Both genders	367	157	45	39	105	21
		Men	108	48	14	11	28	7
		Women	259	109	31	28	77	14
	40 - 49	Both genders	364	214	32	18	85	15
		Men	157	103	10	8	31	5
		Women	207	111	22	10	54	10
	50 - 59	Both genders	329	228	24	16	51	10
		Men	204	155	11	12	20	6
		Women	125	73	13	4	31	4
	60 - 69	Both genders	192	160	6	3	19	4
		Men	166	145	5	2	12	2
		Women	26	15	1	1	7	2
	70 and older	Both genders	154	129	-	-	24	1
		Men	128	122	-	-	6	-
		Women	26	7	-	-	18	1
	Not reported	Both genders	36	22	1	1	10	2
		Men	19	17	-	-	1	1
		Women	17	5	1	1	9	1
Broward	All groups	Both genders	508	316	55	35	70	32
		Men	270	199	22	11	26	12
		Women	238	117	33	24	44	20
	Less than 30	Both genders	25	8	4	3	8	2
		Men	4	1	-	1	2	-
		Women	21	7	4	2	6	2
	30 - 39	Both genders	124	53	22	15	22	12
		Men	36	17	7	2	7	3
		Women	88	36	15	13	15	9
	40 - 49	Both genders	136	88	12	9	19	8
		Men	70	47	5	4	10	4
		Women	66	41	7	5	9	4
	50 - 59	Both genders	110	73	13	6	11	7
		Men	69	50	7	3	5	4
		Women	41	23	6	3	6	3
	60 - 69	Both genders	60	53	4	1	2	-
		Men	51	46	3	1	1	-
		Women	9	7	1	-	1	-
	70 and older	Both genders	40	36	-	-	3	1
		Men	34	34	-	-	-	-
		Women	6	2	-	-	3	1
	Not reported	Both genders	13	5	-	1	5	2
		Men	6	4	-	-	1	1
		Women	7	1	-	1	4	1

Table 3–7. Number of pharmacists who completed the survey questionnaire by county of residence, age group, ethnic group, and gender (continued).

County of Residence	Age Group (years)	Gender	Number of Pharmacists					
			All Ethnic Groups	Non-Hispanic			Hispanic	Other
				White	Black	Asian		
Collier, Hendry, Lee, and Monroe	All groups	Both genders	202	181	4	5	12	-
		Men	111	99	2	3	7	-
		Women	91	82	2	2	5	-
	Less than 30	Both genders	16	14	1	-	1	-
		Men	5	4	-	-	1	-
		Women	11	10	1	-	-	-
	30 - 39	Both genders	40	36	-	1	3	-
		Men	13	12	-	-	1	-
		Women	27	24	-	1	2	-
	40 - 49	Both genders	49	41	2	2	4	-
		Men	20	17	1	1	1	-
		Women	29	24	1	1	3	-
	50 - 59	Both genders	58	51	1	2	4	-
		Men	39	32	1	2	4	-
		Women	19	19	-	-	-	-
	60 - 69	Both genders	22	22	-	-	-	-
		Men	19	19	-	-	-	-
		Women	3	3	-	-	-	-
	70 and older	Both genders	13	13	-	-	-	-
		Men	12	12	-	-	-	-
		Women	1	1	-	-	-	-
	Not reported	Both genders	4	4	-	-	-	-
		Men	3	3	-	-	-	-
		Women	1	1	-	-	-	-
Martin and Pasco	All groups	Both genders	96	76	4	6	5	5
		Men	57	46	-	5	3	3
		Women	39	30	4	1	2	2
	Less than 30	Both genders	6	5	-	-	-	1
		Men	2	2	-	-	-	-
		Women	4	3	-	-	-	1
	30 - 39	Both genders	18	10	2	3	2	1
		Men	8	4	-	2	1	1
		Women	10	6	2	1	1	-
	40 - 49	Both genders	23	18	2	1	1	1
		Men	7	6	-	1	-	-
		Women	16	12	2	-	1	1
	50 - 59	Both genders	29	26	-	2	-	1
		Men	21	18	-	2	-	1
		Women	8	8	-	-	-	-
	60 - 69	Both genders	12	9	-	-	2	1
		Men	11	8	-	-	2	1
		Women	1	1	-	-	-	-
	70 and older	Both genders	7	7	-	-	-	-
		Men	7	7	-	-	-	-
		Women	-	-	-	-	-	-
	Not reported	Both genders	1	1	-	-	-	-
		Men	1	1	-	-	-	-
		Women	-	-	-	-	-	-

Table 3–7. Number of pharmacists who completed the survey questionnaire by county of residence, age group, ethnic group, and gender (continued).

County of Residence	Age Group (years)	Gender	Number of Pharmacists					
			All Ethnic Groups	Non-Hispanic			Hispanic	Other
				White	Black	Asian		
Miami-Dade	All groups	Both genders	342	98	31	14	189	10
		Men	140	69	9	7	54	1
		Women	202	29	22	7	135	9
	Less than 30	Both genders	21	6	2	-	12	1
		Men	7	3	-	-	4	-
		Women	14	3	2	-	8	1
	30 - 39	Both genders	94	15	10	4	62	3
		Men	25	4	4	2	14	1
		Women	69	11	6	2	48	2
	40 - 49	Both genders	86	18	8	6	51	3
		Men	32	13	1	2	16	-
		Women	54	5	7	4	35	3
	50 - 59	Both genders	63	21	8	3	30	1
		Men	28	14	2	3	9	-
		Women	35	7	6	-	21	1
	60 - 69	Both genders	35	18	2	1	12	2
		Men	26	17	2	-	7	-
		Women	9	1	-	1	5	2
	70 and older	Both genders	34	17	-	-	17	-
		Men	19	15	-	-	4	-
		Women	15	2	-	-	13	-
	Not reported	Both genders	9	3	1	-	5	-
		Men	3	3	-	-	-	-
		Women	6	-	1	-	5	-
Palm Beach	All groups	Both genders	348	270	21	20	28	9
		Men	206	179	6	6	10	5
		Women	142	91	15	14	18	4
	Less than 30	Both genders	24	12	3	6	3	-
		Men	4	2	1	1	-	-
		Women	20	10	2	5	3	-
	30 - 39	Both genders	74	39	10	11	9	5
		Men	18	9	2	2	3	2
		Women	56	30	8	9	6	3
	40 - 49	Both genders	65	47	6	-	10	2
		Men	26	19	2	-	4	1
		Women	39	28	4	-	6	1
	50 - 59	Both genders	63	54	2	2	4	1
		Men	45	39	1	2	2	1
		Women	18	15	1	-	2	-
	60 - 69	Both genders	60	57	-	1	1	1
		Men	57	54	-	1	1	1
		Women	3	3	-	-	-	-
	70 and older	Both genders	55	54	-	-	1	-
		Men	52	52	-	-	-	-
		Women	3	2	-	-	1	-
	Not reported	Both genders	7	7	-	-	-	-
		Men	4	4	-	-	-	-
		Women	3	3	-	-	-	-

Table 3–7. Number of pharmacists who completed the survey questionnaire by county of residence, age group, ethnic group, and gender (continued).

County of Residence	Age Group (years)	Gender	Number of Pharmacists					
			All Ethnic Groups	Non-Hispanic			Hispanic	Other
				White	Black	Asian		
Other	All groups	Both genders	43	17	4	6	15	1
		Men	21	11	2	3	5	-
		Women	22	6	2	3	10	1
	Less than 30	Both genders	5	3	1	-	1	-
		Men	1	1	-	-	-	-
		Women	4	2	1	-	1	-
	30 - 39	Both genders	17	4	1	5	7	-
		Men	8	2	1	3	2	-
		Women	9	2	-	2	5	-
	40 - 49	Both genders	5	2	2	-	-	1
		Men	2	1	1	-	-	-
		Women	3	1	1	-	-	1
	50 - 59	Both genders	6	3	-	1	2	-
		Men	2	2	-	-	-	-
		Women	4	1	-	1	2	-
	60 - 69	Both genders	3	1	-	-	2	-
		Men	2	1	-	-	1	-
		Women	1	-	-	-	1	-
	70 and older	Both genders	5	2	-	-	3	-
		Men	4	2	-	-	2	-
		Women	1	-	-	-	1	-
	Not reported	Both genders	2	2	-	-	-	-
		Men	2	2	-	-	-	-
		Women	-	-	-	-	-	-

Table 3–8. **Median age of pharmacists who completed the survey questionnaire by county of residence, ethnic group, and gender.**

County of Residence	Gender	Median Age					
		All Ethnic Groups	Non-Hispanic			Hispanic	Other
			White	Black	Asian		
All counties	Both genders	47.0	51.0	40.0	37.0	43.0	41.0
	Men	54.0	58.0	43.0	47.0	46.0	44.0
	Women	40.0	42.0	39.0	35.0	40.0	39.0
Broward	Both genders	46.0	50.0	40.0	37.5	43.0	40.5
	Men	53.0	54.0	44.5	47.0	44.0	44.0
	Women	40.0	43.0	38.0	35.0	39.0	36.0
Collier, Hendry, Lee, and Monroe	Both genders	48.5	49.0	44.0	43.0	45.0	-
	Men	55.0	55.0	49.0	50.0	52.0	-
	Women	41.5	42.0	32.5	36.5	41.0	-
Martin and Pasco	Both genders	50.0	51.0	41.0	43.0	49.0	44.0
	Men	54.0	54.0	-	49.0	62.0	53.0
	Women	42.0	42.5	41.0	33.0	39.5	36.0
Miami-Dade	Both genders	45.0	51.0	44.5	44.0	42.0	42.0
	Men	50.0	59.0	46.0	48.0	46.0	38.0
	Women	42.0	44.0	44.0	43.0	41.5	44.0
Palm Beach	Both genders	51.0	55.0	39.0	34.0	43.5	39.0
	Men	61.0	64.0	40.0	44.0	46.5	42.0
	Women	38.0	41.5	36.0	33.5	38.0	37.0
Other	Both genders	39.0	40.0	35.5	36.5	39.0	48.0
	Men	42.0	59.0	37.0	37.0	67.0	-
	Women	38.5	38.5	34.0	36.0	37.0	48.0

Appendix 3-1. Questionnaire used in the survey of South Florida pharmacists.

This is a survey of all pharmacists in South Florida intended only for academic research purposes. You and your answers will remain anonymous at all times. Results will be reported only aggregately. Please answer all questions honestly and thank-you for your participation.

1. **Gender:**
   [] Male
   [] Female

3. **Age:** ________ **years old**

4. **Marital status (choose one):**
   [] Never married
   [] Married
   [] Separated, divorced, or widowed

6. **Number of children:** ____________________

7. **What academic degree(s) do you hold?**
   [] B.S.
   [] Pharm.D.
   [] Other: ____________________

10. **Where did you get your pharmacy degree(s)?**
    [] Florida A & M University
    [] Nova Southeastern University
    [] University of Florida
    [] In the U.S. outside Florida ____________
    [] Outside the U.S. ____________

11. **Have you completed a residency or fellowship?**
    [] No
    [] Yes. Specify: ____________________

12. **Do you hold any special Board certification(s)?**
    [] No
    [] Yes. Area: ____________________

17. **How long have you been a registered pharmacist?** ____________ years

18. **How long have you worked at your primary site?** ____________ years

21. **Distance from home to work:** ____________________ miles

22. **Average one-way time commute to work:** ____________ minutes

2. **Primary ethnic group (choose one):**
   [] Non-Hispanic White
   [] Non-Hispanic Black (African American)
   [] Non-Hispanic Asian
   [] Hispanic
   [] Other

5. **If married, does your spouse work?**
   [] Yes
   [] No

8. **County where you live:** ____________________

9. **County where you work:** ____________________

13. **Type of primary practice site (choose one):**
    [] Retail community/independent
    [] Retail chain
    [] Hospital
    [] Other: ____________________

14. **Primary role as a pharmacist (choose one):**
    [] Clinical
    [] Dispensing
    [] Administrative
    [] Other

15. **Location of your primary practice site (choose one):**
    [] Large city
    [] Suburb/small city
    [] Town/rural area

16. **Do you serve primarily a patient population (*i.e.*, elderly, minority, etc.)?**
    [] No
    [] Yes. Which? ____________________

19. **Average work week:** ________ hours per week

20. **Wage rate: $** ____________________ per hour

23. **Annual income from working as a pharmacist: $** ____________ per year

24. **Annual household income: $** ________ per year

1. **On a scale of 0–10, how satisfied are you with the profession of pharmacy?**

0 1 2 3 4 5 6 7 8 9 10
Not satisfied — Extremely satisfied

2. **On a scale of 0–10, how satisfied are you with your current job?**

0 1 2 3 4 5 6 7 8 9 10
Not satisfied — Extremely satisfied

3. **On a scale of 0–10, please rate the amount of work you do in relation to other workers in your place of work.**

0 1 2 3 4 5 6 7 8 9 10
Least amount — Greatest amount

4. **On a scale of 0–10, please rate the amount of stress you experience in your job in relation to other workers.**

0 1 2 3 4 5 6 7 8 9 10
Least stress — Greatest stress

5. **On a scale of 0–10, please rate the availability of advancement opportunities for you in your place of work.**

0 1 2 3 4 5 6 7 8 9 10
Not available — Most available

6. **On a scale of 0–10, please rate your job security.**

0 1 2 3 4 5 6 7 8 9 10
Least secure — Most secure

7. **On a scale of 0–10, please rate autonomy in your job.**

0 1 2 3 4 5 6 7 8 9 10
Least autonomous — Most autonomous

8. **On a scale of 0–10, please rate overall fairness in your place of work.**

0 1 2 3 4 5 6 7 8 9 10
Not fair — Very fair

9. **On a scale of 0–10, please rate the performance of your supervisor in helping and supporting you in your job.**

0 1 2 3 4 5 6 7 8 9 10
Not at all — Most helpful

10. **On a scale of 0–10, please rate the job atmosphere in your place of work.**

0 1 2 3 4 5 6 7 8 9 10
Least pleasant — Most pleasant

11. **On a scale of 0–10, please rate scheduling flexibility in your place of work.**

0 1 2 3 4 5 6 7 8 9 10
Not flexible — Most flexible

12. **On a scale of 0–10, please rate the overall professional quality of your coworkers (*i.e.*, pharmacists, techs, etc.).**

0 1 2 3 4 5 6 7 8 9 10
Lowest quality — Highest quality

13. **On a scale of 0–10, please rate your coworkers' willingness to help you and support you in your job.**

0 1 2 3 4 5 6 7 8 9 10
Not at all — Most helpful

Appendix 3-2. Summary of questions contained in the front page of the survey questionnaire.

Question	Topic	Type of Response	If Close-Ended, Expected Response	Single/ Multiple Choices
1	Gender	Close-ended	Male Female	Single
2	Ethnic group	Close-ended	Non-Hispanic White Non-Hispanic Black Non-Hispanic Asian Hispanic Other	Single
3	Age	Open-ended	(Years)	
4	Marital status	Close-ended	Never married Married Separated/divorced/ widowed	Single
5	(If married), spouse works	Close-ended	Yes No	Single
6	Number of children	Open-ended		
7	Academic degrees	Close-ended	B.S. Pharm.D. Other	Multiple
8	County of residence	Open-ended		
9	County of work	Open-ended		
10	University granting degree	Close-ended	Florida A & M University Nova Southeastern University University of Florida In the U.S. outside Florida Outside the U.S.	Multiple
11	Completed a residency or a fellowship	Close-ended	Yes No	Single
12	Specialty Board certifification	Close-ended	Yes No	Single

Question	Topic	Type of Response	If Close-Ended, Expected Response	Single/ Multiple Choices
13	Type of primary practice site	Close-ended	Retail community/ independent Retail chain Hospital Other	Single
14	Primary role as pharmacist	Close-ended	Clinical Dispensing Administrative Other	Multiple
15	Location of primary practice site	Close-ended	Large city Suburb or small city Town or rural area	Single
16	Serving primarily a patient population	Close-ended	Yes No	Single
17	Experience as a registered pharmacist	Open-ended	(Years)	
18	Longevity in current job	Open-ended	(Years)	
19	Average work week	Open-ended	(Hours)	
20	Wage rate per hour	Open-ended	(Dollars)	
21	Distance from home to work	Open-ended	(Miles)	
22	Average one-way commute time to work	Open-ended	(Minutes)	
23	Annual income from working as a pharmacist	Open-ended	(Dollars)	
24	Annual household income	Open-ended	(Dollars)	

4 DEMOGRAPHIC VARIABLES

Economic and sociobehavioral theories suggest that demographic characteristics linked to gender, ethnic identification, and age influence labor outcomes such as workforce participation, earnings, and variables associated with job satisfaction. Perhaps the main distinguishing feature of the labor market is that the item being exchanged is embodied in people. Labor is inseparable from the person providing it, so many of the decisions affecting supply and demand are taken within a social context involving specific individuals whose gender, ethnic group, age, and other indicators such as sexual orientation, household conditions, professional skills, experience, etc. are part of who they are and what they have to offer.

The great diversity in the characteristics of both workers and jobs, even within a profession, is responsible for a wide array of non-wage factors differentiating workers and jobs from one another. Workers do not rank the desirability of jobs solely on the basis of pay and benefits, but also take into account preferences and constraints that in turn are influenced by who these workers are. Consequently, in the labor market buyers, as well as sellers, invest a great deal of time and effort in evaluating myriad features that differentiate each worker and each job. If men and women play different social roles and are subjected to different social pressures, as Costa *et al.* [2001] contend, a consideration that may be extended to the various ethnic groups, such disparities may generate differences in the acquisition of skills and communication techniques affecting labor outcomes. Along these lines, Nolen-Hoeksema *et al.* [1999] suggest that women are more likely than men to suffer failures in the early stages of their lives because they experience relatively lower social status and less power. Hence, women tend to feel they have little control over their destiny, which conditions the nature and extent to which they are willing to invest in themselves.

The variables analyzed in this chapter for South Florida pharmacists are marital status, the presence of children in the household, academic degree(s) attained, additional investments in human capital beyond schooling, and professional experience. Many of these considerations are examined from a human-capital perspective. People invest in themselves in the form of education, acquisition of special skills, experience, and so on to become more productive, get more palatable jobs, and earn higher incomes. Once acquired, human capital cannot be traded away or owned by somebody else, in the way non-human resources can be. Thus, human capital is a non-negotiable asset for which no collateral can be offered, which can pose serious financial difficulties in the private market. It also is surrounded by uncertainty insofar as the productivity of investments in human resources tends to decrease as age increases. As a result, in an attempt to increase the chances that returns may accrue over a longer time, the investment often is undertaken at an early age, when volition is immature, preferences are not definitive, and information is incomplete. Furthermore, while investments in non-human resources largely are determined by relatively constant patterns of tastes and preferences, this assumption usually is not valid for human-capital decision making because tastes and preferences not only determine investment in human resources but also are determined by these investments. For example, students develop new tastes and preferences as they go to college, graduate, and get their first job.

Implicit in this process is the expectation that workers who invest in themselves will be paid the marginal product of their more productive labor, which may not always be the case. If labor is not paid its marginal product because of workers' tastes and preferences or institutional constraints such as discrimination, human-capital investments break down as an efficient resource allocation mechanism. Some of those arguments are addressed under situation variables in Chapter 5.

MARITAL STATUS

Since the 1970s the United States has experienced a decline in the propensity to get married; a rise in the age of first marriage; and an increase in the participation of married women, especially those with children, in the labor force. Cohabitation has become more common, divorce rates have remained stable, and non-marital childbearing no longer carries the stigma it once did. These trends can be found in all major ethnic groups, although the dynamics vary substantially from one group to another [Brusentsev, 2006; Casper and Bianchi, 2002; DiCecio *et al.*, 2008; Marsh *et al.*, 2007; Pettit and Hook, 2005].

For many people, especially women, decisions to remain single, get married, or dissolve a marriage are intertwined with decisions pertaining to whether or not to work, how much to work, and where to work. Therefore, there is a growing consensus that family and career choices should not be considered exogenous to each other [Sheran, 2007]. Marriage may increase or decrease wage rates via its effect on workers' time horizon, investment in human capital, motivation, or by virtue of creating a compensating differential between regular, pleasant jobs that yield satisfaction and unpleasant but better paying jobs. These marriage-induced effects on wages may lead to greater work commitment by men and different tradeoffs for women. Ahituv and Lerman [2007] estimate that one added year of continuing marriage (as opposed to a divorce) leads to an increase of 110 hours worked per year, and divorce lowers wage rates relative to marriage but leaves them higher than they would be in a never-married state.

The impact of marital status on professional life may or may not be gender specific. For example, Napari [2006] finds that in Finland women suffer substantially stronger wage losses on account of marriage than men and Tebaldi and Elmslie [2006] accept as a common platitude that, compared to non-married women, married women participate less in the labor force, and when they do participate, they supply considerably less labor. In the Czech Republic, where unemployment rates are higher for women than for men, unemployment is higher for single workers than they are for married workers; however, the gender gap is not as large between single men and women as it is between married men and women [Lauerová and Terrell, 2007].

In a national survey of U.S. private-practice physicians, the empirical evidence reveals that marital status has no effect on the number of hours worked by male practitioners, but married female physicians work fewer hours than their single counterparts [Mitchell, 1984]. A more recent study of dermatologists concludes that gender alone bears no significant impact on the number of hours worked [Jacobson *et al.*, 2004a]. Compared to single women, however, married women may find it necessary to devote more time to housework, which may interfere with marketwork. Bryan and Sevilla Sanz [2007] argue that the type and timing of household activities are as important determinants of female labor supply and wages as is the actual amount of time devoted to housework, and a woman's specialization in certain household activities upon marrying, rather than her increase in the time devoted to housework, is the main cause of the negative effect of housework on married women's labor supply and earnings. Whatever the mechanism, there is evidence pointing toward an increase in women's household labor time and a decline in men's household labor time with the advent of marriage [Coltrane, 2000; Corrigal and Konrad, 2007]. Interestingly as well, the likelihood of marriage for men seems to go up along with their earnings potential, an association which is not significant for women [Xie *et al.*, 2003].

Sexual orientation also has an impact on professional outcomes. While it is reasonable to expect that bias and discrimination may prevent homosexual men and women from getting certain jobs, which obviously tends to reduce their labor supply, same-sex couples have no apparent gender differences by which to specialize in, or allocate within themselves, housework versus marketwork [Badgett, 2001]. At least one study finds that gay men are less likely to participate in the labor market, and less likely to seek full-time jobs, than are heterosexual men, whereas lesbian women's labor force participation is greater, and they hold full-time jobs more often, compared to heterosexual, married women [Tebaldi and Elmslie, 2006].

Differences by ethnic group are commonplace, too. Marriage does not seem to affect Cuban or Puerto Rican women's workforce participation rates, but it is a restrictive factor for Asian Indian and Arab women, and to a lesser extent Mexican and Chinese women [Read and Cohen, 2007]. Black women are less likely than White women to marry and stay married, and divorce rates are higher for Blacks than for Whites [Cherlin, 1992; Sweeney and Phillips, 2004]. Graefe and Lichter [2002] point out that this differential has been attributed by various researchers to Black men's poor employment prospects; greater economic independence by Black women, relative to women of other races, brought about by workforce participation; the receipt of welfare benefits; cultural preferences against marriage; and cultural adaptation to social and economic oppression. The traditionally high marriage rates of Hispanics has suffered in recent years by growing divorce trends, as many Hispanics have adopted mainstream American cultural patterns. For all ethnic groups non-marital childbearing is associated with reduced marriage rates, although the effects of non-marital childbearing are stronger for Blacks and Hispanics than they are for Non-Hispanic Whites. Stigma and social disapproval of non-marital childbearing for Non-Hispanic Whites, and to a lesser extent Hispanics, increase the emotional and financial costs of raising a child alone and are likely to burden unwed mothers by making them less desirable marital partners and forcing them to make marriage choices with a greater likelihood of marital instability and divorce [Graefe and Lichter, 2002].

Bedard and Deschênes [2003] contend that estimating a causal relationship between divorce and women's economic status is complicated because the factors that increase marital instability also may affect women's labor market outcomes. They report an economic disadvantage for divorced women in terms of higher poverty rates and less household income. But they suggest that the marked reduction in women's economic status after marital dissolution can be attributed primarily to the negative selection of women into divorce. Once selection is accounted for, they find little evidence of lower income levels due to the stronger labor market attachment and higher wages reported by divorced women. Along these lines, Kesselring and Bremmer [2006] find that as women experience greater levels of success in the labor market, they also tend to experience higher divorce rates, the same conclusion shared separately by Lombard [1999] for the entire population and by No *et al.* [2007] for African American women. They argue that not only does greater financial independence on the part of women make their decision to seek dissolution of marriage easier by virtue of being less dependent on their husbands for support, but women's economic success itself may cause friction within the family, thus leading to divorce.

Almost three out of every four (72.8 percent) South Florida pharmacists are married; 14.6 percent never have been married; and the remaining 12.6 percent classify themselves as separated, divorced, or widowed (see Tables 4-1 and 4-2). The highest fractions of married pharmacists are recorded in Martin and Pasco (80.2 percent) and Palm Beach (78.4 percent), while the lowest proportions occur in Miami-Dade (64.6 percent) and among pharmacists living outside the South Florida area (67.4 percent). Relatively more men than women are married, while more women than men report being in the non-married categories throughout virtually all age groups. The incidence of married pharmacists is greater for Non-Hispanic Whites than for Blacks, Hispanics, and Asians. Gender-ethnic interactions are evident, as the percentage of married Non-Hispanic White men is the highest and the percentage of married Non-Hispanic Black women is the lowest.

Variations by age group are revealing. The percentage of pharmacists who never have been married decreases steadily as age increases. The percentage of separated, divorced, and widowed pharmacists increases with age until they are 59 years old; after their 60th birthday, however, the incidence of separated, divorced, and widowed pharmacists declines sharply. Pharmacists younger than 30 years of age show the lowest marriage rates, while pharmacists 60 years or older, especially men, exhibit the highest marriage rates. It seems that the support of a spouse is a significant factor in the commitment to work by older pharmacists in South Florida.

CHILDREN IN THE HOUSEHOLD

One of the most dramatic labor market developments in the United States over the last 75 years has been the rise of female workforce participation, especially of married women with young children. In 1940 only 6 percent of mothers of preschool-age children worked in the labor market; today more than 60 percent of these mothers have jobs [Brusentsev, 2006; Fogli and Veldkamp, 2007; Tocher *et al.*, 2006; Weisbard, 2003]. Yet, in spite of women with young children staying in the workforce in record numbers, the literature shows unequivocably that the presence of small children in the household exerts a substantial and negative effect on women's labor supply and earnings while sometimes it increases men's earnings and number of hours worked [Blasius and Pae, 2005; Cohany and Sok, 2007; Coltrane, 2000; Corrigal and Konrad, 2007; Enchautegui, 1992; Ginther and Kahn, 2006; Jacobson *et al.*, 2004a; Kaufman and Uhlenberg, 2000; Mosisa and Hipple, 2006; Napari, 2006; Pettit and Hook, 2005; Poeschl *et al.*, 2006; Stephan and Levin, 2005; Tebaldi and Elmslie, 2006; Walton *et al.*, 2004b]. Specifically for pharmacists, Mott [2001] estimates that, on average, each child under the age of six years reduces women's labor supply by 222 hours per year, and each child 6–10 years old reduces women's labor supply by 169 hours annually.

Women usually devote much more time than men to childcare and childrearing activities (*i.e.*, physical care, playing with children, reading to them and teaching them skills, helping with homework, transporting them, etc.) in addition to household activities (*i.e.*, cleaning, cooking, maintenance, etc.). Consequently, the presence of children in the household influences women's labor market outcomes far more than men's. Since only women bear children and, regardless of marital status, women spend more time than men doing housework, they must make choices between having a family and pursuing a professional career that men are not forced to make. Asymmetry continues to exist between men and women in their work and family roles [McElwain *et al.*, 2005]. This situation creates housework-marketwork imbalances that are responsible for a great deal of stress [Quesenberry *et al.*, 2006]. Furthermore, sometimes there are inherent conflicts in these choices. For example, on the one hand, as they substitute housework for marketwork with the advent of children, women end up reducing their labor supply; on the other hand, household income needs rise with the presence of more children, which may require additional hours of marketwork, especially if there are no earnings from a spouse or partner [Blank and Shierholz, 2006; Hersch, 2006].

Falcao and Soares [2007] suggest that changes in the role of women in society occur because of the impact of mortality drops on household decisions. According to them, greater female labor force participation is part of the process of demographic transition that brings about longer life expectancy and a reduction in family size. Lower mortality rates reduce the return from large families and increase the return to investments in human capital. Since women traditionally specialize in raising children, reduced demand for household production leads to more investment in female human capital and labor supply, which are more than proportional to the gain in longevity and translate into increased female labor force participation.

One of the outcomes of the choices made by women who are primarily responsible for housework and childrearing may be to seek jobs compatible with household responsibilities—jobs that do not penalize them for intermittent job activity, offer flexible work schedules, are closer to home or affordable childcare centers, etc. These jobs may require lower levels of competition and institutional commitment on the part of the pharmacist, and are likely to tag along compensating differentials that often translate into women earning relatively lower wages in a dual labor market [Meyer and Mukerjee, 2007; Niederle and Vesterlund, 2005]. Of course, an alternative explanation to having and rearing children for why, compared to men, women earn lower income levels, receive fewer promotions, and so on could be that less productive women self-select into childbearing. This selection may result from some unobserved heterogeneity between mothers and non-mothers due to a negative correlation among career-orientation, motivation, and drive vis-à-vis a desire to have children [Hersch, 2006].

The intensity of the negative effect that the presence of children in the household exerts on female labor supply is mediated by age. Apps and Reese [2005] point out that, in the younger age groups, women without children tend to work a greater number of hours than women with children. Bloom *et al.* [2007] find that while the greatest negative effect of children on labor supply occurs during the fertile years (20–39 years old), the negative effect continues throughout women's careers, in such a way that higher total fertility leads to less participation by women in the workforce. They estimate that, with each additional child, female labor force participation decreases by 10–15 percentage points for 25–39 year old women and 5–10 percentage points for 40–49 year old women. These projections are equivalent to a reduction of approximately four years of paid work for each birth over the average woman's lifetime.

At the other end of the age spectrum, Wang and Marcotte [2007] report that workforce participation rates change in different ways for grandfathers and grandmothers who take in a grandchild. Labor force participation declines less rapidly for grandfathers than grandmothers, maybe because grandfathers in this position simply postpone retirement, whereas grandmothers, who are most likely to assume the primary responsibility for child care, adjust their participation in the labor market accordingly. There is no significant relationship for grandfathers between number of hours worked and caring for grandchildren; grandmothers, however, behave differently depending on whether or not they are married. If they are not married, taking in a grandchild leads them to work, on average, 257 fewer hours per year, but if they have a spouse in the home, they end up working an average of 420 more hours per year than their unmarried peers.

How soon after giving birth mothers return to work is especially important and conflicting arguments emerge. Obviously, if returning to work brings psychological benefits to the mother and income to the household, mothers and children are better off from an increase in the consumption of market goods and services, as well as from spending greater quality time together. Recent studies conclude that short maternity leaves and full-time maternal employment during the first year after giving birth are deleterious to children's health and long-term cognitive outcomes such as school readiness, verbal ability, and test scores [Baum, 2003; Berger *et al.*, 2005; Brooks-Gunn *et al.*, 2002; James-Burdumy, 2005; Ruhm, 2004; Waldfogel *et al.*, 2002]. Han *et al.* [2001] point out, however, that the effects of early maternal employment vary by ethnic group. They find no cognitive outcomes for African American children, which suggests that the context in which early maternal employment occurs may be influenced by cultural factors. Other studies report that longer maternity leaves are associated with reductions in mothers' depressive symptoms, earlier breast feeding initiation, and an improvement in overall health status [Chatterji and Markowitz, 2005, 2008].

It is estimated that since 1986 more than half of women with a child younger than one year of age are in the labor force [Cohany and Sok, 2007], although the timing of returning to work after childbirth varies across different groups of mothers. Han *et al.* [2008] report that African American and non-minority mothers exhibit the highest proportion working at nine months, considerably higher than the percentage of Hispanic and Asian American women. These disparities may reflect differences in economic needs as well as cultural norms, beliefs, or attitudes among the various ethnic groups. Women with relatively more resources—married, college education, and 30 years of age or older—tend to return to work later than women with fewer resources, possibly because they can rely on savings and/or spouse's income, and also have access to maternity leave. However, while an increasing number of employers currently offer maternity and family leave as part of their benefit packages, there is evidence indicating that women, particularly professional women, often are economically penalized for taking advantage of those programs [Luce and Brenner, 2006]. In the final analysis, the net effect on maternal and child health of the mother's return to work depends on a combination of factors such as the conditions of the leave, the relative time intensity of child health and maternal health production, the substitutability of market goods versus time in producing maternal and child health and wellbeing, and the availability of affordable child care.

Several studies show that women's labor supply is sensitive to the geographic supply of child care. Both an increase in the availability of neighborhoods' family-based childcare slots or subsidies and a decrease in the cost of child care are strongly associated with rising levels of female labor supply [Black *et al.*, 2007; Herbst and Barnow, 2008; Meyer and Mukerjee, 2007; Pettit and Hook, 2005; Sheran, 2007]. Not only does the provision of publicly funded child care foster women's employment, but in the private sector there seem to be tangible benefits, too. Brandon and Temple [2007] report that workplaces with on-site childcare facilities experience lower levels of absenteeism and greater worker productivity than do workplaces without on-site childcare facilities. Besides the tax advantages, employer-based child care seems to improve employee morale, cut recruitment costs, enhance corporate image, account for better industrial relations, and reduce maternity leave.

Almost five out of every six (82.5 percent) pharmacists in the survey who report being married, separated, divorced, or widowed also report having children (see Tables 4-3 and 4-4), with two children in the household being the mode. Relatively more female than male pharmacists are childless, which is consistent with the greater percentage of unmarried women than men, as well as their younger age, reported earlier. This comparison also supports the view that working and having children are more difficult to balance for women than for men, so women tend to sacrifice family life for the sake of their careers. While there seems to be no major ethnic differences in the incidence of practitioners without children, this incidence declines rapidly with age.

The distribution of South Florida pharmacists' average number of children, presented in Tables 4-5 and 4-6, shows a similar picture. Men have more children than women in every ethnic group and every age group. Hispanic and Asian American pharmacists, relatively younger, report fewer children than Non-Hispanic White and Black pharmacists, and the mean values decline steadily with age. If practitioners 50 years of age and older are taken as a group, completed fertility is estimated to be 2.20 children per pharmacist, 2.28 children per male pharmacist and 1.96 children per female pharmacist.

ACADEMIC DEGREE

Human-capital economists and other sociobehavioral scientists view formal education and training as ways in which people invest in themselves to increase the present value of their lifetime earnings. Human capital refers to the stock of knowledge, information, skills, and abilities that individuals acquire and that can be exchanged in the labor market for returns such as less unemployment, more appealing jobs, higher salaries and benefits, and so on. With more education and training, workers become more productive and are capable of performing tasks that others, without proper training, cannot perform, thus making their human-capital stock more exclusive and, consequently, better paid. More education and training are designed to expand one's flexibility and adaptability to new situations, which raises one's marginal productivity, employment prospects, and wages. Employers value employees with the right type and amount of human capital and usually are willing to pay for it [Cline, 2003]. According to a recent survey, workers who have received an associate's degree (*i.e.*, two years of college) earn, on average, 22 percent higher incomes than workers with only a high-school diploma. A baccalaureate degree is worth a 19 percent increase in average income over individuals whose highest level of schooling is an associate's degree, and workers who have acquired a master's degree and/or a Ph.D. degree earn, on average, 14 percent and 37 percent more, respectively, than workers whose highest level of schooling is a baccalaureate degree [Campbell, 2007]. Pursuing different forms of formal education in the U.S. is particularly important to immigrants, who frequently experience occupational downgrading when they first arrive from overseas, especially from regions that differ linguistically and culturally from ours [Akresh, 2007; Chiswick *et al.*, 2003].

Individuals who decide to invest in their post-secondary education have many options. Which one they end up choosing depends on aptitude, tastes and preferences, expected benefits, and opportunities, among other factors that configure, over time, the supply of and demand for graduates in the different academic disciplines. In the 1990s Mott and Kreling [1994] and Mott *et al.* [1995] compared the expected lifetime earnings of full-time pharmacists with the earnings of all other college graduates and found that the internal rate of return to pharmacy education was approximately 15.5 percent, much higher than the 9.5 percent estimated for general college education. As a form of human-capital investment, therefore, pursuing a degree in pharmacy seems to be a sound decision. But gaining admission into pharmacy school is not easy. Currently there are about seven applicants for every available slot in the nation's 111 or so colleges of pharmacy either fully accredited or pending accreditation [Association of Academic Health Centers, 2006; Johnson, 2008], and the number of colleges is growing rapidly. In response to recent clinical demands on practitioners, the traditional bachelor of science degree was eliminated in 2004. The Pharm.D., a doctorate, is the new required degree for pharmacists entering the profession and calls for one and one-half more years of school work. On average in the United States, pharmacists with a Pharm.D. degree are estimated to earn approximately 3.0–5.5 percent higher incomes than their colleagues with a baccalaureate degree, although the gap does not control for place of work, years of experience, or other variables [Levy, 2008; Ukens, 2007].

In pharmacy and many other fields, women outnumber men attending and graduating from college [Cohany and Sok, 2007; Knapp and Cultice, 2007; Mott *et al.*, 2006; Spalter-Roth and Erskine, 2005]. Specifically in pharmacy Brown *et al.* [2006] indicate that the fraction of female graduates has risen from 13 percent in 1960 to 53 percent in 1984 and 67 percent in 2006. Goldin *et al.* [2006] identify two major transformations in the post-WWII era that accounted for a rise in the monetary return to women's higher education and made possible the surge in female college attendance after the 1960s. The first was an expansion in life-cycle labor force participation, brought about with rapidly changing expectations among young women, but with little change in occupational diversity. The second transformation was an additional expansion in labor force participation along with a major shift out of the most traditionally defined female occupations. An increase in age at first marriage, widespread means of birth control, the emergence of feminism, and assurances by the government that gender discrimination would not be tolerated have empowered women to be more serious about earning a college degree and less concerned about depending on a man to be represented properly.

Empirical studies generally point in the same direction: More education leads to greater workforce participation and higher levels of income [Ahituv and Tienda, 2004; Akresh, 2007; Brusentsev, 2006; Han *et al.*, 2008; Hotz *et al.*, 2002; Mosisa and Hipple, 2006; Read and Cohen, 2007; Tebaldi and Elmslie, 2006]. Greater formal education and training lead to higher wages, which translate into a greater opportunity cost of nonmarket activities. In fact, differences in human-capital stock, especially schooling, often are used to explain why Blacks and Hispanics participate less in the labor force, earn lower income levels, and experience higher unemployment rates than Non-Hispanic Whites [Levy, 2006; Nguyen *et al.*, 2005].

Yet some evidence indicates that more formal education does not necessarily bring forth proportional income growth for all groups; specifically, compared to non-minority men, Blacks, Hispanics, and women experience a slower rise in the payoff to a high school or college diploma [Antecol and Bedard, 2002; Bradbury, 2002; Fry and Lowell, 2006; Lang and Manove, 2006]. This means that more formal education and training probably will be insufficient to erase gender and ethnic wage gaps. Moreover, an endogeneity issue arises insofar as education explanatory variables (*i.e.*, test scores, years of schooling, etc.) in empirical models of income determination are themselves affected by labor market discrimination against women and minorities. If the lower scores of women, and especially minorities, may justifiably be attributed, at least in part, to their anticipation that they will earn a lower return on their human capital investment because of discrimination in the labor market, estimates obtained by expressing earnings as a function of educational attainment to explain gender and/ or ethnic gaps underestimate the effects of labor market discrimination on earnings because some of the affected groups' lower attainment is itself due to labor market discrimination [O'Neill and O'Neill, 2005].

A methodological issue raised by Barrow and Rouse [2006] suggests that the relationship between education and income may not be causal in nature. Education and income may be positively correlated to the extent that individuals with greater ability both complete more schooling and would likely earn higher wages even if they had not received the additional schooling. If this were the case, empirical estimates of the return to schooling would be overestimated and increasing coverage of educational programs for the disadvantaged will not succeed in raising income levels, since schooling cannot change people's innate abilities. Furthermore, if minorities regularly attend schools of poorer quality compared to the predominantly non-minority schools, then minority students who succeed in attaining more schooling, say, going to college, may have demonstrated unusually high ability, which implies the existence of a substantial selection bias within minority groups and a severely upward bias in their estimated returns to schooling.

About two-thirds (68.5 percent) of South Florida pharmacists in the survey hold a baccalaureate degree, one-third (35.3 percent) have earned a Pharm.D., and 12.2 percent report having received at least one degree other than the B.S. or the Pharm.D. (see Tables 4-7 and 4-8). The values do not add up to 100 percent because 14.5 percent of respondents have earned more than one academic degree (see Tables 4-9 and 4-10). Inter-county differences are evident. Miami-Dade and Broward show greater than average concentration of pharmacists with a Pharm.D. degree (43.0 percent and 38.4 percent, respectively). Pharmacists living outside South Florida also report a relatively high concentration of Pharm.D. degrees (39.5 percent). At the other extreme, Palm Beach reports the lowest concentration (27.0 percent), followed by the periphery (30.2 percent), and the four smaller (30.7 percent) counties.

The incidence of women and all three minority groups with a Pharm.D. degree is substantially greater than the Pharm.D. fraction of Non-Hispanic White men, which suggests that in recent years relatively more female and minority pharmacists working in South Florida have been graduated compared to their non-minority male counterparts. By the same token, Pharm.D. degree holders are much younger than persons with a B.S. degree in pharmacy. No major differences are detected in the attainment of multiple degrees; if at all, Hispanic and younger pharmacists are slightly behind the other groups. This is somewhat surprising for one would expect that younger professionals are more likely than their older peers to invest in their education human capital stock, given their longer time horizon to recoup their investment. Instead, it seems that some South Florida pharmacists opt for returning to school later in life, after they have worked for a while, to broaden their formal education.

Tables 4-11 and 4-12 show the breakdown of pharmacists by university granting pharmacy degree. (Again, the values do not add up to 100 percent because of multiple-degree recipients.) More than half (54.3 percent) of the degrees have been granted by U.S. universities outside Florida; followed by Nova Southeastern University (20.5 percent), an institution with local South Florida headquarters; and the University of Florida (15.3 percent). Surprisingly, one out of eleven (9.1 percent) pharmacists holds a pharmacy degree from a university outside the United States. Interesting patterns emerge. Graduates from U.S. universities outside Florida and, to a lesser extent, from the University of Florida, are predominantly older, Non-Hispanic White men; while Florida A & M and Nova Southeastern graduates are primarily younger, women, and members of an ethnic minority group. These results are not surprising when one considers the location of the Florida schools of pharmacy and the populations which they serve. The University of Florida, located in North Florida, draws students from all over the state, which is less ethnically diverse than South Florida. Nova Southeastern University students are primarily from South Florida, while Florida A & M is a traditionally Black college. In any event, the differences shown in the survey highlight the contributions of Florida A & M University and Nova Southeastern University to the gender, ethnic, and age diversity of pharmacists in the region.

Inter-county patterns are detected as well. The four smaller counties (71.8 percent), the periphery counties (68.8 percent), and Palm Beach (68.1 percent) show a much greater concentration of pharmacists with U.S. degrees outside Florida, compared to Miami-Dade (36.8 percent) and pharmacists living outside South Florida (34.9 percent). But the opposite is the case for practitioners with degrees from foreign institutions—greater representation in Miami-Dade (14.6 percent) and outside South Florida (34.9 percent) than in the four smaller counties (3.5 percent), Palm Beach (5.2 percent), and Martin and Pasco (6.2 percent).

ADDITIONAL INVESTMENTS IN HUMAN CAPITAL

Sometimes pharmacists enhance their human-capital endowment by pursuing a residency, a fellowship, or other supervised form of on-the-job training. A residency is a postgraduate, one- or two-year program that allows practitioners to expand their professional knowledge through clinical application and research. The first year of residency training enriches general competencies in managing medication-use systems and supports optimal medication therapy outcomes for patients with a broad range of disease states; while the second year, if chosen, dwells on a specific area of practice. A residency provides experience in integrating pharmacy services with the comprehensive needs of individual practice settings, offers expertise leading to advanced practice skills and knowledge, and helps develop the ability to conceptualize new and improved pharmacy services. A fellowship is a directed, individualized, postgraduate training program intended to prepare participants to become independent researchers. It generally follows a residency and focuses on a specialty area. Both a residency and a fellowship are means of acquiring a competitive advantage in the job market, as employers increasingly recognize the value of their training. They also contribute to expand participants' network of professional contacts as well as enable them to gain a clearer picture of the type of practice most suitable for them.

The distribution of respondents, shown in Tables 4-13 and 4-14, reveals that only 11.2 percent of South Florida pharmacists have completed a residency or a fellowship, so this is far from a widespread practice. Pharmacists who have completed a residency or fellowship are distributed evenly throughout the South Florida counties, although they are disproportionately concentrated in the group living outside the South Florida area. Residencies and fellowships are slightly more common among women than men practitioners and are acquired more often by minority than by non-minority pharmacists. Apparently women and minorities in South Florida perceive undertaking a residency or a fellowship as a worthwhile investment likely to make them more competitive in the labor market relative to their male Non-Hispanic White peers.

The percentage of pharmacists who have completed a residency or a fellowship also is sensitive to age. It decreases steadily as age increases. About one out of every five (20.6 percent) practitioners under age 30 has a residency or fellowship, but only 3.2 percent of pharmacists 70 years or older have one. This makes sense insofar as younger persons not only have a broader time horizon than do their older counterparts over which they may accrue returns from their investment, but also are more prone to take advantage of training opportunities which were not so readily available to previous generations of pharmacists.

Another alternative available to pharmacists who wish to invest in their stock of human capital is to gain a specialty Board certification. Board certification is a way of demonstrating that a person possesses knowledge, skills, and experience in a defined area of practice beyond what is expected from a general practitioner. The agency in charge of establishing credentials is the Board of Pharmaceutical Specialties, which is an autonomous division of the American Pharmacists Association. Currently the Board recognizes five specialty practice areas (the number in parentheses is the year in which the specialty became recognized): Nuclear Pharmacy (1978), Nutrition Support Pharmacy (1988), Pharmacotherapy (1988), Psychiatric Pharmacy (1992), and Oncology Pharmacy (1996). In addition to improved feelings of self-worth and professional competence, Board certified pharmacists report a competitive edge in job hiring and retention, special recognition by employers, and occasional salary raises upon becoming certified. As of January 2009, the Board has granted over 5,500 certifications, with more than two-thirds of those certifications in Pharmacotherapy [American College of Clinical Pharmacy, 2009].

Judging by the information presented in Tables 4-15 and 4-16, this option is even less popular in South Florida, as only 10.5 percent of respondents report holding a specialty Board certification. The percentage is similar for all counties and virtually identical for male and female pharmacists. Proportionately more minority practitioners have engaged in this form of investment in themselves compared to Non-Hispanic Whites. Age does not seem to be a relevant factor, as minor random fluctuations are detected throughout the various age groups.

EXPERIENCE

Labor market experience, the last of the demographic indicators reported in this chapter, is a key determinant of labor market outcomes. It is associated in various studies with higher earnings [Akresh, 2007; Cline, 2003; Keaveny *et al.*, 2007; LoBuono, 2003], greater labor supply [Mott, 2001; Tebaldi and Elmslie, 2006], and job attitudes [Mott *et al.*, 2004]. It also is associated with explaining gender and ethnic differences in wages and employment [Graham and Smith, 2005; Levy, 2006; Napari, 2006; Reyes, 2007]. In at least one survey, however, independent pharmacists with fewer than eleven years of experience report earning higher salaries than their colleagues with more experience [Cardinale, 2005].

Experience is measured in the South Florida pharmacists study using the number of years passed since respondents became registered pharmacists. This is a potential experience indicator that is not accurate for individuals exhibiting discontinuous attachment to the labor force. To the extent that women and minorities tend to endure more unemployment and out-of-workforce episodes than non-minority men, potential experience systematically overestimates actual experience for women and minorities [Antecol and Bedard, 2002].

Even with this bias, female South Florida pharmacists possess substantially less experience compared to their male counterparts. One can easily infer from Tables 4-17 and 4-18 that the percentage of women declines as the number of years spent as a registered pharmacist increases—from 70.4 percent in the less than 5 years category to 29.8 percent for pharmacists with 20 plus years of experience—which reflects the recent, massive entry of women into the profession. As would be expected, the number of years of experience varies directly with age.

Ethnic variations emerge, too. Non-Hispanic Whites show their traditional control over the profession, with almost two-thirds (64.6 percent) of them with 20 or more years of experience. Conversely, minorities exhibit much lower percentages—37.0 percent of Hispanics, 28.6 percent of Blacks, and 21.4 percent of Asian Americans possess 20 or more years of experience, which tends to confirm their addition to pharmacy in the last few years.

These trends become even more obvious when one assesses variations in the median number of years spent as a registered pharmacist (see Tables 4-19 and 4-20). Compared to women, men possess over twice as many years of experience. Similarly, compared to all minorities combined, Non-Hispanic Whites show twice as much experience. The median values also increase with the age group and are much lower in Miami-Dade and outside the South Florida area than in Palm Beach, the periphery counties, and the four smaller counties.

Table 4–1. Number of pharmacists who completed the survey questionnaire by county of residence, marital status, ethnic group, and gender.

County of Residence	Marital Status	Gender	Number of Pharmacists					
			All Ethnic Groups	Non-Hispanic			Hispanic	Other
				White	Black	Asian		
All counties	All groups	Both genders	1,539	958	119	86	319	57
		Men	805	603	41	35	105	21
		Women	734	355	78	51	214	36
	Never married	Both genders	225	114	27	20	56	8
		Men	97	65	5	9	17	1
		Women	128	49	22	11	39	7
	Married	Both genders	1,120	728	79	55	218	40
		Men	635	483	32	23	79	18
		Women	485	245	47	32	139	22
	Separated, divorced, or widowed	Both genders	194	116	13	11	45	9
		Men	73	55	4	3	9	2
		Women	121	61	9	8	36	7
Broward	All groups	Both genders	508	316	55	35	70	32
		Men	270	199	22	11	26	12
		Women	238	117	33	24	44	20
	Never married	Both genders	76	39	13	8	12	4
		Men	38	24	2	4	7	1
		Women	38	15	11	4	5	3
	Married	Both genders	369	240	33	23	49	24
		Men	207	157	17	6	18	9
		Women	162	83	16	17	31	15
	Separated, divorced, or widowed	Both genders	63	37	9	4	9	4
		Men	25	18	3	1	1	2
		Women	38	19	6	3	8	2
Collier, Hendry, Lee, and Monroe	All groups	Both genders	202	181	4	5	12	-
		Men	111	99	2	3	7	-
		Women	91	82	2	2	5	-
	Never married	Both genders	25	23	-	1	1	-
		Men	12	11	-	-	1	-
		Women	13	12	-	1	-	-
	Married	Both genders	151	134	4	3	10	-
		Men	89	80	2	2	5	-
		Women	62	54	2	1	5	-
	Separated, divorced, or widowed	Both genders	26	24	-	1	1	-
		Men	10	8	-	1	1	-
		Women	16	16	-	-	-	-
Martin and Pasco	All groups	Both genders	96	76	4	6	5	5
		Men	57	46	-	5	3	3
		Women	39	30	4	1	2	2
	Never married	Both genders	11	8	-	2	-	1
		Men	7	5	-	2	-	-
		Women	4	3	-	-	-	1
	Married	Both genders	77	62	3	4	5	3
		Men	48	39	-	3	3	3
		Women	29	23	3	1	2	-
	Separated, divorced, or widowed	Both genders	8	6	1	-	-	1
		Men	2	2	-	-	-	-
		Women	6	4	1	-	-	1

Table 4–1. Number of pharmacists who completed the survey questionnaire by county of residence, marital status, ethnic group, and gender (continued).

County of Residence	Marital Status	Gender	Number of Pharmacists					
			All Ethnic Groups	Non-Hispanic			Hispanic	Other
				White	Black	Asian		
Miami-Dade	All groups	Both genders	342	98	31	14	189	10
		Men	140	69	9	7	54	1
		Women	202	29	22	7	135	9
	Never married	Both genders	75	23	10	3	36	3
		Men	27	15	2	2	8	-
		Women	48	8	8	1	28	3
	Married	Both genders	221	65	18	9	124	5
		Men	100	47	6	5	41	1
		Women	121	18	12	4	83	4
	Separated, divorced, or widowed	Both genders	46	10	3	2	29	2
		Men	13	7	1	-	5	-
		Women	33	3	2	2	24	2
Palm Beach	All groups	Both genders	348	270	21	20	28	9
		Men	206	179	6	6	10	5
		Women	142	91	15	14	18	4
	Never married	Both genders	30	18	3	6	3	-
		Men	9	7	-	1	1	-
		Women	21	11	3	5	2	-
	Married	Both genders	273	216	18	11	21	7
		Men	178	155	6	4	8	5
		Women	95	61	12	7	13	2
	Separated, divorced, or widowed	Both genders	45	36	-	3	4	2
		Men	19	17	-	1	1	-
		Women	26	19	-	2	3	2
Other	All groups	Both genders	43	17	4	6	15	1
		Men	21	11	2	3	5	-
		Women	22	6	2	3	10	1
	Never married	Both genders	8	3	1	-	4	-
		Men	4	3	1	-	-	-
		Women	4	-	-	-	4	-
	Married	Both genders	29	11	3	5	9	1
		Men	13	5	1	3	4	-
		Women	16	6	2	2	5	1
	Separated, divorced, or widowed	Both genders	6	3	-	1	2	-
		Men	4	3	-	-	1	-
		Women	2	-	-	1	1	-

Two unrelated, Non-Hispanic White men living in Broward County, who indicated they have a domestic partner, have been classified as married.

Table 4–2. Number of pharmacists who completed the survey questionnaire by county of residence, marital status, age group, and gender.

County of Residence	Marital Status	Gender	Number of Pharmacists: All Age Groups	Less than 30	30-39	40-49	50-59	60-69	70 and Older	Not Known
All counties	All groups	Both genders	1,539	97	367	364	329	192	154	36
		Men	805	23	108	157	204	166	128	19
		Women	734	74	259	207	125	26	26	17
	Never married	Both genders	225	43	78	54	31	9	6	4
		Men	97	10	29	27	21	6	2	2
		Women	128	33	49	27	10	3	4	2
	Married	Both genders	1,120	53	265	261	234	157	123	27
		Men	635	13	75	115	154	146	115	17
		Women	485	40	190	146	80	11	8	10
	Separated, divorced, or widowed	Both genders	194	1	24	49	64	26	25	5
		Men	73	-	4	15	29	14	11	-
		Women	121	1	20	34	35	12	14	5
Broward	All groups	Both genders	508	25	124	136	110	60	40	13
		Men	270	4	36	70	69	51	34	6
		Women	238	21	88	66	41	9	6	7
	Never married	Both genders	76	8	30	20	13	3	1	1
		Men	38	1	11	13	10	1	1	1
		Women	38	7	19	7	3	2	-	-
	Married	Both genders	369	16	90	97	74	49	33	10
		Men	207	3	23	50	48	46	32	5
		Women	162	13	67	47	26	3	1	5
	Separated, divorced, or widowed	Both genders	63	1	4	19	23	8	6	2
		Men	25	-	2	7	11	4	1	-
		Women	38	1	2	12	12	4	5	2
Collier, Hendry, Lee, and Monroe	All groups	Both genders	202	16	40	49	58	22	13	4
		Men	111	5	13	20	39	19	12	3
		Women	91	11	27	29	19	3	1	1
	Never married	Both genders	25	7	7	5	4	1	1	-
		Men	12	2	3	2	4	1	-	-
		Women	13	5	4	3	-	-	1	-
	Married	Both genders	151	9	30	38	40	18	12	4
		Men	89	3	10	16	28	17	12	3
		Women	62	6	20	22	12	1	-	1
	Separated, divorced, or widowed	Both genders	26	-	3	6	14	3	-	-
		Men	10	-	-	2	7	1	-	-
		Women	16	-	3	4	7	2	-	-
Martin and Pasco	All groups	Both genders	96	6	18	23	29	12	7	1
		Men	57	2	8	7	21	11	7	1
		Women	39	4	10	16	8	1	-	-
	Never married	Both genders	11	4	3	1	3	-	-	-
		Men	7	1	3	1	2	-	-	-
		Women	4	3	-	-	1	-	-	-
	Married	Both genders	77	2	14	18	24	12	6	1
		Men	48	1	5	6	18	11	6	1
		Women	29	1	9	12	6	1	-	-
	Separated, divorced, or widowed	Both genders	8	-	1	4	2	-	1	-
		Men	2	-	-	-	1	-	1	-
		Women	6	-	1	4	1	-	-	-

Table 4–2. **Number of pharmacists who completed the survey questionnaire by county of residence, marital status, age group, and gender (continued).**

County of Residence	Marital Status	Gender	Number of Pharmacists							
			All Age Groups	Less than 30	30-39	40-49	50-59	60-69	70 and Older	Not Known
Miami-Dade	All groups	Both genders	342	21	94	86	63	35	34	9
		Men	140	7	25	32	28	26	19	3
		Women	202	14	69	54	35	9	15	6
	Never married	Both genders	75	14	23	24	7	2	3	2
		Men	27	5	8	10	3	1	-	-
		Women	48	9	15	14	4	1	3	2
	Married	Both genders	221	7	61	58	46	22	22	5
		Men	100	2	16	20	23	20	16	3
		Women	121	5	45	38	23	2	6	2
	Separated, divorced, or widowed	Both genders	46	-	10	4	10	11	9	2
		Men	13	-	1	2	2	5	3	-
		Women	33	-	9	2	8	6	6	2
Palm Beach	All groups	Both genders	348	24	74	65	63	60	55	7
		Men	206	4	18	26	45	57	52	4
		Women	142	20	56	39	18	3	3	3
	Never married	Both genders	30	8	11	3	4	3	1	-
		Men	9	-	3	-	2	3	1	-
		Women	21	8	8	3	2	-	-	-
	Married	Both genders	273	16	58	46	48	53	46	6
		Men	178	4	15	22	37	50	46	4
		Women	95	12	43	24	11	3	-	2
	Separated, divorced, or widowed	Both genders	45	-	5	16	11	4	8	1
		Men	19	-	-	4	6	4	5	-
		Women	26	-	5	12	5	-	3	1
Other	All groups	Both genders	43	5	17	5	6	3	5	2
		Men	21	1	8	2	2	2	4	2
		Women	22	4	9	3	4	1	1	-
	Never married	Both genders	8	2	4	1	-	-	-	1
		Men	4	1	1	1	-	-	-	1
		Women	4	1	3	-	-	-	-	-
	Married	Both genders	29	3	12	4	2	3	4	1
		Men	13	-	6	1	-	2	3	1
		Women	16	3	6	3	2	1	1	-
	Separated, divorced, or widowed	Both genders	6	-	1	-	4	-	1	-
		Men	4	-	1	-	2	-	1	-
		Women	2	-	-	-	2	-	-	-

Two unrelated, 40-49 year-old men living in Broward County, who indicated they have a domestic partner, have been classified as married.

Table 4–3. Number of pharmacists who completed the survey questionnaire and reported being married, separated, widowed, or divorced by county of residence, number of children, ethnic group, and gender.

County of Residence	Number of Children	Gender	Number of Married, Separated, Widowed, or Divorced Pharmacists					
			All Ethnic Groups	Non-Hispanic			Hispanic	Other
				White	Black	Asian		
All counties	All groups	Both genders	1,314	844	92	66	263	49
		Men	708	538	36	26	88	20
		Women	606	306	56	40	175	29
	None	Both genders	215	137	13	9	49	7
		Men	74	51	7	3	11	2
		Women	141	86	6	6	38	5
	One	Both genders	225	124	22	20	52	7
		Men	100	64	6	6	22	2
		Women	125	60	16	14	30	5
	Two	Both genders	476	318	28	26	86	18
		Men	270	218	6	13	25	8
		Women	206	100	22	13	61	10
	Three	Both genders	226	149	16	3	50	8
		Men	147	112	11	1	20	3
		Women	79	37	5	2	30	5
	Four or more	Both genders	88	65	7	2	12	2
		Men	62	54	4	-	4	-
		Women	26	11	3	2	8	2
	No response	Both genders	84	51	6	6	14	7
		Men	55	39	2	3	6	5
		Women	29	12	4	3	8	2
Broward	All groups	Both genders	432	277	42	27	58	28
		Men	232	175	20	7	19	11
		Women	200	102	22	20	39	17
	None	Both genders	66	44	7	2	10	3
		Men	22	15	5	-	2	-
		Women	44	29	2	2	8	3
	One	Both genders	71	35	7	8	16	5
		Men	26	16	1	1	7	1
		Women	45	19	6	7	9	4
	Two	Both genders	167	115	11	11	21	9
		Men	99	81	2	5	7	4
		Women	68	34	9	6	14	5
	Three	Both genders	75	51	9	3	8	4
		Men	47	35	7	1	2	2
		Women	28	16	2	2	6	2
	Four or more	Both genders	23	16	4	-	1	2
		Men	18	15	3	-	-	-
		Women	5	1	1	-	1	2
	No response	Both genders	30	16	4	3	2	5
		Men	20	13	2	-	1	4
		Women	10	3	2	3	1	1

Table 4–3. **Number of pharmacists who completed the survey questionnaire and reported being married, separated, widowed, or divorced by county of residence, number of children, ethnic group, and gender (continued).**

County of Residence	Number of Children	Gender	Number of Married, Separated, Widowed, or Divorced Pharmacists					
			All Ethnic Groups	Non-Hispanic			Hispanic	Other
				White	Black	Asian		
Collier, Hendry, Lee, and Monroe	All groups	Both genders	177	158	4	4	11	-
		Men	99	88	2	3	6	-
		Women	78	70	2	1	5	-
	None	Both genders	40	36	-	-	4	-
		Men	12	11	-	-	1	-
		Women	28	25	-	-	3	-
	One	Both genders	36	31	2	1	2	-
		Men	18	15	1	1	1	-
		Women	18	16	1	-	1	-
	Two	Both genders	54	49	2	2	1	-
		Men	33	30	1	1	1	-
		Women	21	19	1	1	-	-
	Three	Both genders	22	19	-	-	3	-
		Men	17	15	-	-	2	-
		Women	5	4	-	-	1	-
	Four or more	Both genders	16	15	-	-	1	-
		Men	14	13	-	-	1	-
		Women	2	2	-	-	-	-
	No response	Both genders	9	8	-	1	-	-
		Men	5	4	-	1	-	-
		Women	4	4	-	-	-	-
Martin and Pasco	All groups	Both genders	85	68	4	4	5	4
		Men	50	41	-	3	3	3
		Women	35	27	4	1	2	1
	None	Both genders	18	15	-	-	1	2
		Men	7	6	-	-	-	1
		Women	11	9	-	-	1	1
	One	Both genders	16	13	1	1	1	-
		Men	8	7	-	-	1	-
		Women	8	6	1	1	-	-
	Two	Both genders	30	23	3	1	2	1
		Men	16	13	-	1	1	1
		Women	14	10	3	-	1	-
	Three	Both genders	13	11	-	-	1	1
		Men	12	10	-	-	1	1
		Women	1	1	-	-	-	-
	Four or more	Both genders	4	4	-	-	-	-
		Men	3	3	-	-	-	-
		Women	1	1	-	-	-	-
	No response	Both genders	4	2	-	2	-	-
		Men	4	2	-	2	-	-
		Women	-	-	-	-	-	-

Table 4–3. **Number of pharmacists who completed the survey questionnaire and reported being married, separated, widowed, or divorced by county of residence, number of children, ethnic group, and gender (continued).**

County of Residence	Number of Children	Gender	Number of Married, Separated, Widowed, or Divorced Pharmacists					
			All Ethnic Groups	Non-Hispanic			Hispanic	Other
				White	Black	Asian		
Miami-Dade	All groups	Both genders	267	75	21	11	153	7
		Men	113	54	7	5	46	1
		Women	154	21	14	6	107	6
	None	Both genders	42	12	1	2	26	1
		Men	12	6	-	1	5	-
		Women	30	6	1	1	21	1
	One	Both genders	47	9	6	3	28	1
		Men	20	6	2	2	10	-
		Women	27	3	4	1	18	1
	Two	Both genders	86	24	6	6	47	3
		Men	35	18	2	2	12	1
		Women	51	6	4	4	35	2
	Three	Both genders	55	18	3	-	33	1
		Men	30	15	2	-	13	-
		Women	25	3	1	-	20	1
	Four or more	Both genders	19	7	3	-	9	-
		Men	9	5	1	-	3	-
		Women	10	2	2	-	6	-
	No response	Both genders	18	5	2	-	10	1
		Men	7	4	-	-	3	-
		Women	11	1	2	-	7	1
Palm Beach	All groups	Both genders	318	252	18	14	25	9
		Men	197	172	6	5	9	5
		Women	121	80	12	9	16	4
	None	Both genders	43	29	3	4	6	1
		Men	19	13	1	2	2	1
		Women	24	16	2	2	4	-
	One	Both genders	47	34	5	4	3	1
		Men	25	19	2	1	2	1
		Women	22	15	3	3	1	-
	Two	Both genders	129	102	6	4	12	5
		Men	82	74	1	2	3	2
		Women	47	28	5	2	9	3
	Three	Both genders	55	48	4	-	2	1
		Men	38	35	2	-	1	-
		Women	17	13	2	-	1	1
	Four or more	Both genders	22	19	-	2	1	-
		Men	15	15	-	-	-	-
		Women	7	4	-	2	1	-
	No response	Both genders	22	20	-	-	1	1
		Men	18	16	-	-	1	1
		Women	4	4	-	-	-	-

Table 4–3. Number of pharmacists who completed the survey questionnaire and reported being married, separated, widowed, or divorced by county of residence, number of children, ethnic group, and gender (continued).

County of Residence	Number of Children	Gender	Number of Married, Separated, Widowed, or Divorced Pharmacists					
			All Ethnic Groups	Non-Hispanic			Hispanic	Other
				White	Black	Asian		
Other	All groups	Both genders	35	14	3	6	11	1
		Men	17	8	1	3	5	-
		Women	18	6	2	3	6	1
	None	Both genders	6	1	2	1	2	-
		Men	2	-	1	-	1	-
		Women	4	1	1	1	1	-
	One	Both genders	8	2	1	3	2	-
		Men	3	1	-	1	1	-
		Women	5	1	1	2	1	-
	Two	Both genders	10	5	-	2	3	-
		Men	5	2	-	2	1	-
		Women	5	3	-	-	2	-
	Three	Both genders	6	2	-	-	3	1
		Men	3	2	-	-	1	-
		Women	3	-	-	-	2	1
	Four or more	Both genders	4	4	-	-	-	-
		Men	3	3	-	-	-	-
		Women	1	1	-	-	-	-
	No response	Both genders	1	-	-	-	1	-
		Men	1	-	-	-	1	-
		Women	-	-	-	-	-	-

Two unrelated, Non-Hispanic White men living in Broward County, who indicated they have a domestic partner, have been classified as married.

Table 4–4. Number of pharmacists who completed the survey questionnaire and reported being married, separated, widowed, or divorced by county of residence, number of children, age group, and gender.

County of Residence	Number of Children	Gender	Number of Married, Separated, Widowed, or Divorced Pharmacists							
			All Age Groups	Less than 30	30-39	40-49	50-59	60-69	70 and Older	Not Known
All counties	All groups	Both genders	1,314	54	289	310	298	183	147	33
		Men	708	13	79	130	183	160	125	18
		Women	606	41	210	180	115	23	22	15
	None	Both genders	215	32	75	53	38	10	7	-
		Men	74	8	19	15	23	6	3	-
		Women	141	24	56	38	15	4	4	-
	One	Both genders	225	14	79	42	55	23	9	3
		Men	100	4	24	15	34	16	7	-
		Women	125	10	55	27	21	7	2	3
	Two	Both genders	476	5	97	125	110	79	50	10
		Men	270	-	26	55	65	73	46	5
		Women	206	5	71	70	45	6	4	5
	Three	Both genders	226	1	21	64	51	37	40	12
		Men	147	1	6	32	30	34	36	8
		Women	79	-	15	32	21	3	4	4
	Four or more	Both genders	88	-	5	12	23	21	24	3
		Men	62	-	2	5	16	18	19	2
		Women	26	-	3	7	7	3	5	1
	No response	Both genders	84	2	12	14	21	13	17	5
		Men	55	-	2	8	15	13	14	3
		Women	29	2	10	6	6	-	3	2
Broward	All groups	Both genders	432	17	94	116	97	57	39	12
		Men	232	3	25	57	59	50	33	5
		Women	200	14	69	59	38	7	6	7
	None	Both genders	66	10	24	20	11	-	1	-
		Men	22	1	7	6	7	-	1	-
		Women	44	9	17	14	4	-	-	-
	One	Both genders	71	3	24	17	18	6	2	1
		Men	26	1	6	4	10	3	2	-
		Women	45	2	18	13	8	3	-	1
	Two	Both genders	167	2	34	47	38	30	11	5
		Men	99	-	8	28	24	28	10	1
		Women	68	2	26	19	14	2	1	4
	Three	Both genders	75	1	6	24	16	11	14	3
		Men	47	1	2	13	8	11	10	2
		Women	28	-	4	11	8	-	4	1
	Four or more	Both genders	23	-	-	2	8	7	5	1
		Men	18	-	-	1	6	5	5	1
		Women	5	-	-	1	2	2	-	-
	No response	Both genders	30	1	6	6	6	3	6	2
		Men	20	-	2	5	4	3	5	1
		Women	10	1	4	1	2	-	1	1

Table 4–4. Number of pharmacists who completed the survey questionnaire and reported being married, separated, widowed, or divorced by county of residence, number of children, age group, and gender (continued).

County of Residence	Number of Children	Gender	Number of Married, Separated, Widowed, or Divorced Pharmacists							
			All Age Groups	Less than 30	30-39	40-49	50-59	60-69	70 and Older	Not Known
Collier, Hendry, Lee, and Monroe	All groups	Both genders	177	9	33	44	54	21	12	4
		Men	99	3	10	18	35	18	12	3
		Women	78	6	23	26	19	3	-	1
	None	Both genders	40	5	12	10	10	2	1	-
		Men	12	3	1	2	4	1	1	-
		Women	28	2	11	8	6	1	-	-
	One	Both genders	36	2	9	9	12	3	-	1
		Men	18	-	3	4	8	3	-	-
		Women	18	2	6	5	4	-	-	1
	Two	Both genders	54	2	8	15	11	8	8	2
		Men	33	-	4	6	6	7	8	2
		Women	21	2	4	9	5	1	-	-
	Three	Both genders	22	-	2	5	10	3	1	1
		Men	17	-	1	2	9	3	1	1
		Women	5	-	1	3	1	-	-	-
	Four or more	Both genders	16	-	1	3	6	4	2	-
		Men	14	-	1	3	5	3	2	-
		Women	2	-	-	-	1	1	-	-
	No response	Both genders	9	-	1	2	5	1	-	-
		Men	5	-	-	1	3	1	-	-
		Women	4	-	1	1	2	-	-	-
Martin and Pasco	All groups	Both genders	85	2	15	22	26	12	7	1
		Men	50	1	5	6	19	11	7	1
		Women	35	1	10	16	7	1	-	-
	None	Both genders	18	1	6	6	3	1	1	-
		Men	7	-	3	-	2	1	1	-
		Women	11	1	3	6	1	-	-	-
	One	Both genders	16	1	4	3	6	2	-	-
		Men	8	1	-	1	4	2	-	-
		Women	8	-	4	2	2	-	-	-
	Two	Both genders	30	-	5	7	11	4	2	1
		Men	16	-	2	-	8	3	2	1
		Women	14	-	3	7	3	1	-	-
	Three	Both genders	13	-	-	3	4	4	2	-
		Men	12	-	-	3	3	4	2	-
		Women	1	-	-	-	1	-	-	-
	Four or more	Both genders	4	-	-	2	-	-	2	-
		Men	3	-	-	1	-	-	2	-
		Women	1	-	-	1	-	-	-	-
	No response	Both genders	4	-	-	1	2	1	-	-
		Men	4	-	-	1	2	1	-	-
		Women	-	-	-	-	-	-	-	-

Table 4–4. Number of pharmacists who completed the survey questionnaire and reported being married, separated, widowed, or divorced by county of residence, number of children, age group, and gender (continued).

County of Residence	Number of Children	Gender	Number of Married, Separated, Widowed, or Divorced Pharmacists							
			All Age Groups	Less than 30	30-39	40-49	50-59	60-69	70 and Older	Not Known
Miami-Dade	All groups	Both genders	267	7	71	62	56	33	31	7
		Men	113	2	17	22	25	25	19	3
		Women	154	5	54	40	31	8	12	4
	None	Both genders	42	6	20	4	5	3	4	-
		Men	12	2	3	2	4	1	-	-
		Women	30	4	17	2	1	2	4	-
	One	Both genders	47	-	17	8	13	6	2	1
		Men	20	-	5	4	6	4	1	-
		Women	27	-	12	4	7	2	1	1
	Two	Both genders	86	-	22	27	19	11	7	-
		Men	35	-	6	7	7	10	5	-
		Women	51	-	16	20	12	1	2	-
	Three	Both genders	55	-	8	17	10	7	10	3
		Men	30	-	3	8	3	4	10	2
		Women	25	-	5	9	7	3	-	1
	Four or more	Both genders	19	-	1	3	5	4	5	1
		Men	9	-	-	-	3	4	2	-
		Women	10	-	1	3	2	-	3	1
	No response	Both genders	18	1	3	3	4	2	3	2
		Men	7	-	-	1	2	2	1	1
		Women	11	1	3	2	2	-	2	1
Palm Beach	All groups	Both genders	318	16	63	62	59	57	54	7
		Men	197	4	15	26	43	54	51	4
		Women	121	12	48	36	16	3	3	3
	None	Both genders	43	10	9	12	8	4	-	-
		Men	19	2	3	5	6	3	-	-
		Women	24	8	6	7	2	1	-	-
	One	Both genders	47	6	21	5	6	6	3	-
		Men	25	2	8	2	6	4	3	-
		Women	22	4	13	3	-	2	-	-
	Two	Both genders	129	-	23	27	31	25	21	2
		Men	82	-	3	13	20	25	20	1
		Women	47	-	20	14	11	-	1	1
	Three	Both genders	55	-	5	14	8	11	13	4
		Men	38	-	-	6	6	11	13	2
		Women	17	-	5	8	2	-	-	2
	Four or more	Both genders	22	-	3	2	2	5	10	-
		Men	15	-	1	-	1	5	8	-
		Women	7	-	2	2	1	-	2	-
	No response	Both genders	22	-	2	2	4	6	7	1
		Men	18	-	-	-	4	6	7	1
		Women	4	-	2	2	-	-	-	-

Table 4–4. Number of pharmacists who completed the survey questionnaire and reported being married, separated, widowed, or divorced by county of residence, number of children, age group, and gender (continued).

County of Residence	Number of Children	Gender	Number of Married, Separated, Widowed, or Divorced Pharmacists							
			All Age Groups	Less than 30	30-39	40-49	50-59	60-69	70 and Older	Not Known
Other	All groups	Both genders	35	3	13	4	6	3	4	2
		Men	17	-	7	1	2	2	3	2
		Women	18	3	6	3	4	1	1	-
	None	Both genders	6	-	4	1	1	-	-	-
		Men	2	-	2	-	-	-	-	-
		Women	4	-	2	1	1	-	-	-
	One	Both genders	8	2	4	-	-	-	2	-
		Men	3	-	2	-	-	-	1	-
		Women	5	2	2	-	-	-	1	-
	Two	Both genders	10	1	5	2	-	1	1	-
		Men	5	-	3	1	-	-	1	-
		Women	5	1	2	1	-	1	-	-
	Three	Both genders	6	-	-	1	3	1	-	1
		Men	3	-	-	-	1	1	-	1
		Women	3	-	-	1	2	-	-	-
	Four or more	Both genders	4	-	-	-	2	1	-	1
		Men	3	-	-	-	1	1	-	1
		Women	1	-	-	-	1	-	-	-
	No response	Both genders	1	-	-	-	-	-	1	-
		Men	1	-	-	-	-	-	1	-
		Women	-	-	-	-	-	-	-	-

Two unrelated, 40-49 year-old men living in Broward County, who indicated they have a domestic partner, have been classified as married.

Table 4–5. Average number of children of pharmacists who completed the survey questionnaire; reported being married, separated, widowed, or divorced; and reported number of children, by county of residence, ethnic group, and gender.

County of Residence	Gender	Average Number of Children					
		All Ethnic Groups	Non-Hispanic			Hispanic	Other
			White	Black	Asian		
All counties	Both genders	1.84	1.91	1.83	1.48	1.70	1.79
	Men	2.09	2.18	2.06	1.52	1.80	1.80
	Women	1.55	1.46	1.67	1.46	1.65	1.79
Broward	Both genders	1.82	1.89	1.92	1.62	1.54	1.87
	Men	2.11	2.18	2.17	2.00	4.50	2.14
	Women	1.50	1.40	1.70	1.47	1.55	1.75
Collier, Hendry, Lee, and Monroe	Both genders	1.68	1.69	1.50	1.67	0.70	-
	Men	2.12	2.14	1.50	1.50	2.17	-
	Women	1.12	1.12	1.50	2.00	0.80	-
Martin and Pasco	Both genders	1.68	1.71	1.75	1.50	1.60	1.25
	Men	1.98	2.00	-	2.00	2.00	1.67
	Women	1.29	1.30	1.75	1.00	1.00	0.00
Miami-Dade	Both genders	1.91	2.14	2.16	1.36	1.81	1.67
	Men	2.09	2.22	2.57	1.20	1.98	2.00
	Women	1.77	1.95	1.92	1.50	1.74	1.60
Palm Beach	Both genders	1.93	2.03	1.61	1.43	1.54	1.75
	Men	2.08	2.19	1.67	1.00	1.38	1.25
	Women	1.69	1.70	1.58	1.67	1.62	2.25
Other	Both genders	1.94	2.71	0.33	1.17	1.70	3.00
	Men	2.19	3.00	0.00	1.67	1.50	-
	Women	1.72	2.33	0.50	0.67	1.83	3.00

Two unrelated, Non-Hispanic White men living in Broward County, who indicated they have a domestic partner, have been classified as married.

Table 4–6. Average number of children of pharmacists who completed the survey questionnaire; reported being married, separated, widowed, or divorced; and reported number of children, by county of residence, age group, and gender.

County of Residence	Gender	Average Number of Children							
		All Age Groups	Less than 30	30-39	40-49	50-59	60-69	70 and Older	Not Known
All counties	Both genders	1.84	0.52	1.29	1.83	1.95	2.27	2.60	2.59
	Men	2.09	0.54	1.32	2.00	1.96	2.35	2.66	2.93
	Women	1.55	0.51	1.27	1.71	1.94	1.74	2.26	2.23
Broward	Both genders	1.82	0.62	1.25	1.75	1.92	2.46	2.67	2.50
	Men	2.11	1.33	1.22	2.00	1.95	2.51	2.64	3.25
	Women	1.50	0.46	1.26	1.52	1.89	2.14	2.80	2.00
Collier, Hendry, Lee, and Monroe	Both genders	1.68	0.67	1.09	1.57	1.92	2.20	2.42	2.00
	Men	2.12	0.00	1.80	2.00	2.28	2.24	2.42	2.33
	Women	1.12	1.00	0.77	1.28	1.24	2.00	-	1.00
Martin and Pasco	Both genders	1.68	0.50	0.93	1.81	1.67	2.00	2.71	2.00
	Men	1.98	1.00	0.80	3.20	1.71	2.00	2.71	2.00
	Women	1.29	0.00	0.91	1.38	1.57	2.00	-	-
Miami-Dade	Both genders	1.91	0.00	1.31	2.14	2.13	2.10	2.50	2.80
	Men	2.09	0.00	1.53	2.00	1.91	2.26	2.89	2.00
	Women	1.77	0.00	1.24	2.21	2.31	1.62	1.80	2.67
Palm Beach	Both genders	1.93	0.38	1.54	1.87	1.84	2.22	2.72	2.67
	Men	2.08	0.50	1.20	1.77	1.77	2.31	2.68	2.67
	Women	1.69	0.33	1.65	1.94	2.00	0.67	3.33	2.67
Other	Both genders	1.94	1.33	1.08	1.75	3.33	3.00	1.75	5.00
	Men	2.19	-	1.14	2.00	3.50	3.50	2.00	5.00
	Women	1.72	1.33	1.00	1.67	3.25	2.00	1.00	-

Two unrelated, 40-49 year-old men living in Broward County, who indicated they have a domestic partner, have been classified as married.

Table 4–7. Number of pharmacists who completed the survey questionnaire by county of residence, academic degree attained, ethnic group, and gender.

County of Residence	Academic Degree	Gender	Number of Pharmacists					
			All Ethnic Groups	Non-Hispanic			Hispanic	Other
				White	Black	Asian		
All counties	All groups	Both genders	1,539	958	119	86	319	57
		Men	805	603	41	35	105	21
		Women	734	355	78	51	214	36
	B.S.	Both genders	1,054	741	60	48	165	40
		Men	638	511	23	22	64	18
		Women	416	230	37	26	101	22
	Pharm.D.	Both genders	544	261	67	35	157	24
		Men	194	109	20	11	47	7
		Women	350	152	47	24	110	17
	Other	Both genders	188	119	11	16	31	11
		Men	121	91	3	11	10	6
		Women	67	28	8	5	21	5
Broward	All groups	Both genders	508	316	55	35	70	32
		Men	270	199	22	11	26	12
		Women	238	117	33	24	44	20
	B.S.	Both genders	333	231	32	17	31	22
		Men	208	163	14	6	14	11
		Women	125	68	18	11	17	11
	Pharm.D.	Both genders	195	99	25	17	41	13
		Men	74	43	8	5	15	3
		Women	121	56	17	12	26	10
	Other	Both genders	67	43	3	7	6	8
		Men	43	32	2	4	2	3
		Women	24	11	1	3	4	5
Collier, Hendry, Lee, and Monroe	All groups	Both genders	202	181	4	5	12	-
		Men	111	99	2	3	7	-
		Women	91	82	2	2	5	-
	B.S.	Both genders	158	144	2	4	8	-
		Men	95	85	1	3	6	-
		Women	63	59	1	1	2	-
	Pharm.D.	Both genders	62	54	3	1	4	-
		Men	24	22	1	-	1	-
		Women	38	32	2	1	3	-
	Other	Both genders	19	19	-	-	-	-
		Men	12	12	-	-	-	-
		Women	7	7	-	-	-	-
Martin and Pasco	All groups	Both genders	96	76	4	6	5	5
		Men	57	46	-	5	3	3
		Women	39	30	4	1	2	2
	B.S.	Both genders	68	56	3	3	2	4
		Men	44	37	-	3	1	3
		Women	24	19	3	-	1	1
	Pharm.D.	Both genders	29	18	2	3	2	4
		Men	11	6	-	2	1	2
		Women	18	12	2	1	1	2
	Other	Both genders	14	8	1	3	1	1
		Men	11	7	-	2	1	1
		Women	3	1	1	1	-	-

Table 4–7. Number of pharmacists who completed the survey questionnaire by county of residence, academic degree attained, ethnic group, and gender (continued).

County of Residence	Academic Degree	Gender	Number of Pharmacists: All Ethnic Groups	Non-Hispanic: White	Non-Hispanic: Black	Non-Hispanic: Asian	Hispanic	Other
Miami-Dade	All groups	Both genders	342	98	31	14	189	10
		Men	140	69	9	7	54	1
		Women	202	29	22	7	135	9
	B.S.	Both genders	200	72	14	10	98	6
		Men	101	55	5	5	35	1
		Women	99	17	9	5	63	5
	Pharm.D.	Both genders	147	29	20	4	90	4
		Men	44	15	5	2	22	-
		Women	103	14	15	2	68	4
	Other	Both genders	40	10	6	2	21	1
		Men	18	8	1	2	6	1
		Women	22	2	5	-	15	-
Palm Beach	All groups	Both genders	348	270	21	20	28	9
		Men	206	179	6	6	10	5
		Women	142	91	15	14	18	4
	B.S.	Both genders	267	227	6	9	18	7
		Men	176	163	1	3	6	3
		Women	91	64	5	6	12	4
	Pharm.D.	Both genders	94	54	15	10	12	3
		Men	34	20	5	2	5	2
		Women	60	34	10	8	7	1
	Other	Both genders	45	37	1	3	3	1
		Men	35	31	-	2	1	1
		Women	10	6	1	1	2	-
Other	All groups	Both genders	43	17	4	6	15	1
		Men	21	11	2	3	5	-
		Women	22	6	2	3	10	1
	B.S.	Both genders	28	11	3	5	8	1
		Men	14	8	2	2	2	-
		Women	14	3	1	3	6	1
	Pharm.D.	Both genders	17	7	2	-	8	-
		Men	7	3	1	-	3	-
		Women	10	4	1	-	5	-
	Other	Both genders	3	2	-	1	-	-
		Men	2	1	-	1	-	-
		Women	1	1	1	-	-	-

Both an Hispanic man and an Hispanic woman living in Miami-Dade County, who did not respond to the academic-degree question, have been classified as having a B.S. degree.

Table 4–8. Number of pharmacists who completed the survey questionnaire by county of residence, academic degree attained, age group, and gender.

County of Residence	Academic Degree	Gender	Number of Pharmacists							
			All Age Groups	Less than 30	30-39	40-49	50-59	60-69	70 and Older	Not Known
All counties	All groups	Both genders	1,539	97	367	364	329	192	154	36
		Men	805	23	108	157	204	166	128	19
		Women	734	74	259	207	125	26	26	17
	B.S.	Both genders	1,054	16	152	260	278	179	142	27
		Men	638	4	46	119	177	154	122	16
		Women	416	12	106	141	101	25	20	11
	Pharm.D.	Both genders	544	88	234	130	61	10	11	10
		Men	194	21	69	48	32	9	10	5
		Women	350	67	165	82	29	1	1	5
	Other	Both genders	188	4	23	36	61	35	24	5
		Men	121	1	8	16	43	32	17	4
		Women	67	3	15	20	18	3	7	1
Broward	All groups	Both genders	508	25	124	136	110	60	40	13
		Men	270	4	36	70	69	51	34	6
		Women	238	21	88	66	41	9	6	7
	B.S.	Both genders	333	2	41	97	88	56	39	10
		Men	208	-	12	53	58	47	33	5
		Women	125	2	29	44	30	9	6	5
	Pharm.D.	Both genders	195	24	92	45	25	3	2	4
		Men	74	4	27	21	15	3	2	2
		Women	121	20	65	24	10	-	-	2
	Other	Both genders	67	2	11	16	21	10	6	1
		Men	43	1	3	10	13	10	5	1
		Women	24	1	8	6	8	-	1	-
Collier, Hendry, Lee, and Monroe	All groups	Both genders	202	16	40	49	58	22	13	4
		Men	111	5	13	20	39	19	12	3
		Women	91	11	27	29	19	3	1	1
	B.S.	Both genders	158	3	28	37	52	21	13	4
		Men	95	1	10	16	35	18	12	3
		Women	63	2	18	21	17	3	1	1
	Pharm.D.	Both genders	62	13	17	20	8	3	-	1
		Men	24	4	6	5	5	3	-	1
		Women	38	9	11	15	3	-	-	-
	Other	Both genders	19	1	2	3	5	5	2	1
		Men	12	-	-	-	4	5	2	1
		Women	7	1	2	3	1	-	-	-
Martin and Pasco	All groups	Both genders	96	6	18	23	29	12	7	1
		Men	57	2	8	7	21	11	7	1
		Women	39	4	10	16	8	1	-	-
	B.S.	Both genders	68	1	8	16	24	11	7	1
		Men	44	-	4	5	17	10	7	1
		Women	24	1	4	11	7	1	-	-
	Pharm.D.	Both genders	29	5	10	10	3	1	-	-
		Men	11	2	4	2	2	1	-	-
		Women	18	3	6	8	1	-	-	-
	Other	Both genders	14	-	2	2	8	1	1	-
		Men	11	-	-	1	8	1	1	-
		Women	3	-	2	1	-	-	-	-

Table 4–8. Number of pharmacists who completed the survey questionnaire by county of residence, academic degree attained, age group, and gender (continued).

County of Residence	Academic Degree	Gender	Number of Pharmacists							
			All Age Groups	Less than 30	30-39	40-49	50-59	60-69	70 and Older	Not Known
Miami-Dade	All groups	Both genders	342	21	94	86	63	35	34	9
		Men	140	7	25	32	28	26	19	3
		Women	202	14	69	54	35	9	15	6
	B.S.	Both genders	200	2	31	50	51	33	27	6
		Men	101	1	9	22	23	25	18	3
		Women	99	1	22	28	28	8	9	3
	Pharm.D.	Both genders	147	21	67	38	12	1	6	2
		Men	44	7	17	12	2	1	5	-
		Women	103	14	50	26	10	-	1	2
	Other	Both genders	40	-	5	8	14	6	5	2
		Men	18	-	4	3	7	3	-	1
		Women	22	-	1	5	7	3	5	1
Palm Beach	All groups	Both genders	348	24	74	65	63	60	55	7
		Men	206	4	18	26	45	57	52	4
		Women	142	20	56	39	18	3	3	3
	B.S.	Both genders	267	6	35	56	57	55	53	5
		Men	176	2	5	22	42	52	50	3
		Women	91	4	30	34	15	3	3	2
	Pharm.D.	Both genders	94	20	40	16	13	2	1	2
		Men	34	3	13	7	8	1	1	1
		Women	60	17	27	9	5	1	-	1
	Other	Both genders	45	1	2	7	12	13	10	-
		Men	35	-	-	2	11	13	9	-
		Women	10	1	2	5	1	-	1	-
Other	All groups	Both genders	43	5	17	5	6	3	5	2
		Men	21	1	8	2	2	2	4	2
		Women	22	4	9	3	4	1	1	-
	B.S.	Both genders	28	2	9	4	6	3	3	1
		Men	14	-	6	1	2	2	2	1
		Women	14	2	3	3	4	1	1	-
	Pharm.D.	Both genders	17	5	8	1	-	-	2	1
		Men	7	1	2	1	-	-	2	1
		Women	10	4	6	-	-	-	-	-
	Other	Both genders	3	-	1	-	1	-	-	1
		Men	2	-	1	-	-	-	-	1
		Women	1	-	-	-	1	-	-	-

Both a 50-59 year-old man and a 50-59 year-old woman living in Miami-Dade County, who did not respond to the academic-degree question, have been classified as having a B.S. degree.

Table 4–9. Number of pharmacists who completed the survey questionnaire by county of residence, number of academic degrees attained, ethnic group, and gender.

County of Residence	Number of Academic Degrees	Gender	Number of Pharmacists					
			All Ethnic Groups	Non-Hispanic			Hispanic	Other
				White	Black	Asian		
All counties	All groups	Both genders	1,539	958	119	86	319	57
		Men	805	603	41	35	105	21
		Women	734	355	78	51	214	36
	One	Both genders	1,316	807	103	74	289	43
		Men	671	503	37	27	91	13
		Women	645	304	66	47	198	30
	More than one	Both genders	223	151	16	12	30	14
		Men	134	100	4	8	14	8
		Women	89	51	12	4	16	6
Broward	All groups	Both genders	508	316	55	35	70	32
		Men	270	199	22	11	26	12
		Women	238	117	33	24	44	20
	One	Both genders	430	264	50	30	62	24
		Men	220	163	20	8	21	8
		Women	210	101	30	22	41	16
	More than one	Both genders	78	52	5	5	8	8
		Men	50	36	2	3	5	4
		Women	28	16	3	2	3	4
Collier, Hendry, Lee, and Monroe	All groups	Both genders	202	181	4	5	12	-
		Men	111	99	2	3	7	-
		Women	91	82	2	2	5	-
	One	Both genders	168	148	3	5	12	-
		Men	93	81	2	3	7	-
		Women	75	67	1	2	5	-
	More than one	Both genders	34	33	1	-	-	-
		Men	18	18	-	-	-	-
		Women	16	15	1	-	-	-
Martin and Pasco	All groups	Both genders	96	76	4	6	5	5
		Men	57	46	-	5	3	3
		Women	39	30	4	1	2	2
	One	Both genders	83	70	3	3	5	2
		Men	49	42	-	3	3	1
		Women	34	28	3	-	2	1
	More than one	Both genders	13	6	1	3	-	3
		Men	8	4	-	2	-	2
		Women	5	2	1	1	-	1

Table 4–9. **Number of pharmacists who completed the survey questionnaire by county of residence, number of academic degrees attained, ethnic group, and gender (continued).**

County of Residence	Number of Academic Degrees	Gender	Number of Pharmacists					
			All Ethnic Groups	Non-Hispanic			Hispanic	Other
				White	Black	Asian		
Miami-Dade	All groups	Both genders	342	98	31	14	189	10
		Men	140	69	9	7	54	1
		Women	202	29	22	7	135	9
	One	Both genders	302	86	24	12	171	9
		Men	120	61	8	5	46	-
		Women	182	25	16	7	125	9
	More than one	Both genders	40	12	7	2	18	1
		Men	20	8	1	2	8	1
		Women	20	4	6	-	10	-
Palm Beach	All groups	Both genders	348	270	21	20	28	9
		Men	206	179	6	6	10	5
		Women	142	91	15	14	18	4
	One	Both genders	295	225	20	18	25	7
		Men	170	146	6	5	9	4
		Women	125	79	14	13	16	3
	More than one	Both genders	53	45	1	2	3	2
		Men	36	33	-	1	1	1
		Women	17	12	1	1	2	1
Other	All groups	Both genders	43	17	4	6	15	1
		Men	21	11	2	3	5	-
		Women	22	6	2	3	10	1
	One	Both genders	38	14	3	6	14	1
		Men	19	10	1	3	5	-
		Women	19	4	2	3	9	1
	More than one	Both genders	5	3	1	-	1	-
		Men	2	1	1	-	-	-
		Women	3	2	-	-	1	-

Both an Hispanic man and an Hispanic woman living in Miami-Dade County, who did not respond to the academic-degree question, have been classified as having a B.S. degree.

Table 4–10. Number of pharmacists who completed the survey questionnaire by county of residence, number of academic degrees attained, age group, and gender.

County of Residence	Academic Degree	Gender	Number of Pharmacists							
			All Age Groups	Less than 30	30-39	40-49	50-59	60-69	70 and Older	Not Known
All counties	All groups	Both genders	1,539	97	367	364	329	192	154	36
		Men	805	23	108	157	204	166	128	19
		Women	734	74	259	207	125	26	26	17
	One	Both genders	1,316	86	328	309	266	165	131	31
		Men	671	20	94	133	161	142	107	14
		Women	645	66	234	176	105	23	24	17
	More than one	Both genders	223	11	39	55	63	27	23	5
		Men	134	3	14	24	43	24	21	5
		Women	89	8	25	31	20	3	2	-
Broward	All groups	Both genders	508	25	124	136	110	60	40	13
		Men	270	4	36	70	69	51	34	6
		Women	238	21	88	66	41	9	6	7
	One	Both genders	430	22	107	117	86	53	33	12
		Men	220	3	31	57	52	44	28	5
		Women	210	19	76	60	34	9	5	7
	More than one	Both genders	78	3	17	19	24	7	7	1
		Men	50	1	5	13	17	7	6	1
		Women	28	2	12	6	7	-	1	-
Collier, Hendry, Lee, and Monroe	All groups	Both genders	202	16	40	49	58	22	13	4
		Men	111	5	13	20	39	19	12	3
		Women	91	11	27	29	19	3	1	1
	One	Both genders	168	15	33	39	51	17	11	2
		Men	93	5	10	19	34	14	10	1
		Women	75	10	23	20	17	3	1	1
	More than one	Both genders	34	1	7	10	7	5	2	2
		Men	18	-	3	1	5	5	2	2
		Women	16	1	4	9	2	-	-	-
Martin and Pasco	All groups	Both genders	96	6	18	23	29	12	7	1
		Men	57	2	8	7	21	11	7	1
		Women	39	4	10	16	8	1	-	-
	One	Both genders	83	6	16	19	24	11	6	1
		Men	49	2	8	6	16	10	6	1
		Women	34	4	8	13	8	1	-	-
	More than one	Both genders	13	-	2	4	5	1	1	-
		Men	8	-	-	1	5	1	1	-
		Women	5	-	2	3	-	-	-	-

Table 4–10. Number of pharmacists who completed the survey questionnaire by county of residence, number of academic degrees attained, age group, and gender (continued).

County of Residence	Academic Degree	Gender	Number of Pharmacists							
			All Age Groups	Less than 30	30-39	40-49	50-59	60-69	70 and Older	Not Known
Miami-Dade	All groups	Both genders	342	21	94	86	63	35	34	9
		Men	140	7	25	32	28	26	19	3
		Women	202	14	69	54	35	9	15	6
	One	Both genders	302	19	85	77	52	31	30	8
		Men	120	6	20	28	25	24	15	2
		Women	182	13	65	49	27	7	15	6
	More than one	Both genders	40	2	9	9	11	4	4	1
		Men	20	1	5	4	3	2	4	1
		Women	20	1	4	5	8	2	-	-
Palm Beach	All groups	Both genders	348	24	74	65	63	60	55	7
		Men	206	4	18	26	45	57	52	4
		Women	142	20	56	39	18	3	3	3
	One	Both genders	295	21	71	52	48	50	46	7
		Men	170	3	18	21	32	48	44	4
		Women	125	18	53	31	16	2	2	3
	More than one	Both genders	53	3	3	13	15	10	9	-
		Men	36	1	-	5	13	9	8	-
		Women	17	2	3	8	2	1	1	-
Other	All groups	Both genders	43	5	17	5	6	3	5	2
		Men	21	1	8	2	2	2	4	2
		Women	22	4	9	3	4	1	1	-
	One	Both genders	38	3	16	5	5	3	5	1
		Men	19	1	7	2	2	2	4	1
		Women	19	2	9	3	3	1	1	-
	More than one	Both genders	5	2	1	-	1	-	-	1
		Men	2	-	1	-	-	-	-	1
		Women	3	2	-	-	1	-	-	-

Both a 50-59 year-old man and a 50-59 year-old woman living in Miami-Dade County who did not respond to the academic-degree question have been classified as having a B.S. degree.

Table 4–11. **Number of pharmacists who completed the survey questionnaire by county of residence, university granting pharmacy degree(s), ethnic group, and gender.**

County of Residence	University Granting Pharmacy Degree	Gender	Number of Pharmacists					
			All Ethnic Groups	Non-Hispanic			Hispanic	Other
				White	Black	Asian		
All counties	All groups	Both genders	1,539	958	119	86	319	57
		Men	805	603	41	35	105	21
		Women	734	355	78	51	214	36
	Florida A & M University	Both genders	86	11	46	1	22	6
		Men	32	8	14	1	9	-
		Women	54	3	32	-	13	6
	Nova Southeastern University	Both genders	315	155	21	20	110	9
		Men	98	53	8	5	29	3
		Women	217	102	13	15	81	6
	University of Florida	Both genders	235	156	11	7	53	8
		Men	125	94	1	2	25	3
		Women	110	62	10	5	28	5
	In the U.S. outside Florida	Both genders	836	641	40	32	97	26
		Men	528	453	14	16	35	10
		Women	308	188	26	16	62	16
	Outside the U.S.	Both genders	140	31	9	25	56	19
		Men	48	10	8	11	11	8
		Women	92	21	1	14	45	11
Broward	All groups	Both genders	508	316	55	35	70	32
		Men	270	199	22	11	26	12
		Women	238	117	33	24	44	20
	Florida A & M University	Both genders	34	3	21	1	5	4
		Men	13	2	8	1	2	-
		Women	21	1	13	-	3	4
	Nova Southeastern University	Both genders	130	77	8	11	30	4
		Men	48	30	2	3	11	2
		Women	82	47	6	8	19	2
	University of Florida	Both genders	82	56	5	3	12	6
		Men	41	33	-	1	5	2
		Women	41	23	5	2	7	4
	In the U.S. outside Florida	Both genders	247	186	17	12	20	12
		Men	162	138	7	4	9	4
		Women	85	48	10	8	11	8
	Outside the U.S.	Both genders	47	7	8	9	10	13
		Men	19	3	7	3	1	5
		Women	28	4	1	6	9	8

Table 4–11. Number of pharmacists who completed the survey questionnaire by county of residence, university granting pharmacy degree(s), ethnic group, and gender (continued).

County of Residence	University Granting Pharmacy Degree	Gender	Number of Pharmacists: All Ethnic Groups	Non-Hispanic: White	Non-Hispanic: Black	Non-Hispanic: Asian	Hispanic	Other
Collier, Hendry, Lee, and Monroe	All groups	Both genders	202	181	4	5	12	-
		Men	111	99	2	3	7	-
		Women	91	82	2	2	5	-
	Florida A & M University	Both genders	3	1	2	-	-	-
		Men	-	-	-	-	-	-
		Women	3	1	2	-	-	-
	Nova Southeastern University	Both genders	22	19	1	1	1	-
		Men	4	4	-	-	-	-
		Women	18	15	1	1	1	-
	University of Florida	Both genders	34	32	-	-	2	-
		Men	23	22	-	-	1	-
		Women	11	10	-	-	1	-
	In the U.S. outside Florida	Both genders	145	132	2	2	9	-
		Men	85	75	2	2	6	-
		Women	60	57	-	-	3	-
	Outside the U.S.	Both genders	7	4	-	2	1	-
		Men	2	1	-	1	-	-
		Women	5	3	-	1	1	-
Martin and Pasco	All groups	Both genders	96	76	4	6	5	5
		Men	57	46	-	5	3	3
		Women	39	30	4	1	2	2
	Florida A & M University	Both genders	2	-	1	-	-	1
		Men	-	-	-	-	-	-
		Women	2	-	1	-	-	1
	Nova Southeastern University	Both genders	6	5	-	1	-	-
		Men	1	1	-	-	-	-
		Women	5	4	-	1	-	-
	University of Florida	Both genders	17	12	2	-	3	-
		Men	9	6	-	-	3	-
		Women	8	6	2	-	-	-
	In the U.S. outside Florida	Both genders	66	57	1	4	1	3
		Men	45	39	-	4	-	2
		Women	21	18	1	-	1	1
	Outside the U.S.	Both genders	6	2	-	1	1	2
		Men	3	-	-	1	-	2
		Women	3	2	-	-	1	-

Table 4–11. Number of pharmacists who completed the survey questionnaire by county of residence, university granting pharmacy degree(s), ethnic group, and gender (continued).

County of Residence	University Granting Pharmacy Degree	Gender	Number of Pharmacists					
			All Ethnic Groups	Non-Hispanic			Hispanic	Other
				White	Black	Asian		
Miami-Dade	All groups	Both genders	342	98	31	14	189	10
		Men	140	69	9	7	54	1
		Women	202	29	22	7	135	9
	Florida A & M University	Both genders	36	4	15	-	16	1
		Men	15	3	5	-	7	-
		Women	21	1	10	-	9	1
	Nova Southeastern University	Both genders	92	16	4	3	65	4
		Men	23	8	1	1	13	-
		Women	69	8	3	2	52	4
	University of Florida	Both genders	61	26	3	1	30	1
		Men	30	15	1	1	13	-
		Women	31	11	2	-	17	1
	In the U.S. outside Florida	Both genders	126	51	11	7	53	4
		Men	68	43	3	5	16	1
		Women	58	8	8	2	37	3
	Outside the U.S.	Both genders	50	7	1	3	37	2
		Men	9	1	1	-	7	-
		Women	41	6	-	3	30	2
Palm Beach	All groups	Both genders	348	270	21	20	28	9
		Men	206	179	6	6	10	5
		Women	142	91	15	14	18	4
	Florida A & M University	Both genders	9	2	6	-	1	-
		Men	3	2	1	-	-	-
		Women	6	-	5	-	1	-
	Nova Southeastern University	Both genders	53	35	6	4	7	1
		Men	17	9	3	1	3	1
		Women	36	26	3	3	4	-
	University of Florida	Both genders	39	30	1	2	5	1
		Men	22	18	-	-	3	1
		Women	17	12	1	2	2	-
	In the U.S. outside Florida	Both genders	237	206	8	6	11	6
		Men	159	151	2	-	3	3
		Women	78	55	6	6	8	3
	Outside the U.S.	Both genders	18	8	-	6	2	2
		Men	10	4	-	4	1	1
		Women	8	4	-	2	1	1

Table 4–11. Number of pharmacists who completed the survey questionnaire by county of residence, university granting pharmacy degree(s), ethnic group, and gender (continued).

County of Residence	University Granting Pharmacy Degree	Gender	Number of Pharmacists					
			All Ethnic Groups	Non-Hispanic			Hispanic	Other
				White	Black	Asian		
Other	All groups	Both genders	43	17	4	6	15	1
		Men	21	11	2	3	5	-
		Women	22	6	2	3	10	1
	Florida A & M University	Both genders	2	1	1	-	-	-
		Men	1	1	-	-	-	-
		Women	1	-	1	-	-	-
	Nova Southeastern University	Both genders	12	3	2	-	7	-
		Men	5	1	2	-	2	-
		Women	7	2	-	-	5	-
	University of Florida	Both genders	2	-	-	1	1	-
		Men	-	-	-	-	-	-
		Women	2	-	-	1	1	-
	In the U.S. outside Florida	Both genders	15	9	1	1	3	1
		Men	9	7	-	1	1	-
		Women	6	2	1	-	2	1
	Outside the U.S.	Both genders	12	3	-	4	5	-
		Men	5	1	-	2	2	-
		Women	7	2	-	2	3	-

In Miami-Dade County one Hispanic man reported being graduated from Palm Beach Atlantic University and one Hispanic man did not respond.

In Palm Beach County one Non-Hispanic White man, one Non-Hispanic White woman, one Asian man, one Asian woman, and two Hispanic women reported being graduated from Palm Beach Atlantic University and one Hispanic man did not respond.

In the "other" county category one Non-Hispanic White man and one Non-Hispanic White woman reported being graduated from Palm Beach Atlantic University.

Table 4–12. Number of pharmacists who completed the survey questionnaire by county of residence, university granting pharmacy degree(s), age group, and gender.

County of Residence	University Granting Pharmacy Degree	Gender	Number of Pharmacists							
			All Age Groups	Less than 30	30-39	40-49	50-59	60-69	70 and Older	Not Known
All counties	All groups	Both genders	1,539	97	367	364	329	192	154	36
		Men	805	23	108	157	204	166	128	19
		Women	734	74	259	207	125	26	26	17
	Florida A & M University	Both genders	86	8	20	18	22	8	7	3
		Men	32	1	5	7	11	6	1	1
		Women	54	7	15	11	11	2	6	2
	Nova Southeastern University	Both genders	315	39	157	76	30	2	2	9
		Men	98	7	42	29	15	1	2	2
		Women	217	32	115	47	15	1	-	7
	University of Florida	Both genders	235	15	42	66	54	36	18	4
		Men	125	4	11	34	32	30	11	3
		Women	110	11	31	32	22	6	7	1
	In the U.S. outside Florida	Both genders	836	23	120	201	210	142	122	18
		Men	528	7	35	89	142	128	114	13
		Women	308	16	85	112	68	14	8	5
	Outside the U.S.	Both genders	140	6	39	29	35	12	15	4
		Men	48	1	13	8	14	7	4	1
		Women	92	5	26	21	21	5	11	3
Broward	All groups	Both genders	508	25	124	136	110	60	40	13
		Men	270	4	36	70	69	51	34	6
		Women	238	21	88	66	41	9	6	7
	Florida A & M University	Both genders	34	1	12	5	11	3	1	1
		Men	13	-	3	2	6	2	-	-
		Women	21	1	9	3	5	1	1	1
	Nova Southeastern University	Both genders	130	17	63	28	17	1	-	4
		Men	48	2	21	14	9	1	-	1
		Women	82	15	42	14	8	-	-	3
	University of Florida	Both genders	82	4	15	29	20	9	4	1
		Men	41	2	2	14	13	7	2	1
		Women	41	2	13	15	7	2	2	-
	In the U.S. outside Florida	Both genders	247	1	28	73	57	48	33	7
		Men	162	-	6	41	36	42	32	5
		Women	85	1	22	32	21	6	1	2
	Outside the U.S.	Both genders	47	2	14	10	15	1	3	2
		Men	19	-	4	4	10	1	-	-
		Women	28	2	10	6	5	-	3	2

Table 4–12. Number of pharmacists who completed the survey questionnaire by county of residence, university granting pharmacy degree(s), age group, and gender (continued).

County of Residence	University Granting Pharmacy Degree	Gender	Number of Pharmacists: All Age Groups	Less than 30	30-39	40-49	50-59	60-69	70 and Older	Not Known
Collier, Hendry, Lee, and Monroe	All groups	Both genders	202	16	40	49	58	22	13	4
		Men	111	5	13	20	39	19	12	3
		Women	91	11	27	29	19	3	1	1
	Florida A & M University	Both genders	3	1	-	1	1	-	-	-
		Men	-	-	-	-	-	-	-	-
		Women	3	1	-	1	1	-	-	-
	Nova Southeastern University	Both genders	22	3	10	7	2	-	-	-
		Men	4	-	2	1	1	-	-	-
		Women	18	3	8	6	1	-	-	-
	University of Florida	Both genders	34	-	6	13	8	6	1	-
		Men	23	-	2	10	4	6	1	-
		Women	11	-	4	3	4	-	-	-
	In the U.S. outside Florida	Both genders	145	11	21	33	48	16	12	4
		Men	85	5	8	10	35	13	11	3
		Women	60	6	13	23	13	3	1	1
	Outside the U.S.	Both genders	7	1	3	3	-	-	-	-
		Men	2	-	1	1	-	-	-	-
		Women	5	1	2	2	-	-	-	-
Martin and Pasco	All groups	Both genders	96	6	18	23	29	12	7	1
		Men	57	2	8	7	21	11	7	1
		Women	39	4	10	16	8	1	-	-
	Florida A & M University	Both genders	2	1	-	1	-	-	-	-
		Men	-	-	-	-	-	-	-	-
		Women	2	1	-	1	-	-	-	-
	Nova Southeastern University	Both genders	6	-	4	2	-	-	-	-
		Men	1	-	1	-	-	-	-	-
		Women	5	-	3	2	-	-	-	-
	University of Florida	Both genders	17	2	5	4	3	2	1	-
		Men	9	1	2	-	3	2	1	-
		Women	8	1	3	4	-	-	-	-
	In the U.S. outside Florida	Both genders	66	3	7	15	24	10	6	1
		Men	45	1	3	7	18	9	6	1
		Women	21	2	4	8	6	1	-	-
	Outside the U.S.	Both genders	6	-	2	1	2	1	-	-
		Men	3	-	2	-	-	1	-	-
		Women	3	-	-	1	2	-	-	-

Table 4–12. Number of pharmacists who completed the survey questionnaire by county of residence, university granting pharmacy degree(s), age group, and gender (continued).

County of Residence	University Granting Pharmacy Degree	Gender	Number of Pharmacists: All Age Groups	Less than 30	30-39	40-49	50-59	60-69	70 and Older	Not Known
Miami-Dade	All groups	Both genders	342	21	94	86	63	35	34	9
		Men	140	7	25	32	28	26	19	3
		Women	202	14	69	54	35	9	15	6
	Florida A & M University	Both genders	36	3	5	7	9	5	6	1
		Men	15	1	2	3	4	4	1	-
		Women	21	2	3	4	5	1	5	1
	Nova Southeastern University	Both genders	92	10	49	26	4	-	1	2
		Men	23	3	11	8	-	-	1	-
		Women	69	7	38	18	4	-	-	2
	University of Florida	Both genders	61	5	7	12	12	12	11	2
		Men	30	1	1	5	5	10	6	2
		Women	31	4	6	7	7	2	5	-
	In the U.S. outside Florida	Both genders	126	2	26	35	31	15	14	3
		Men	68	1	9	16	16	13	12	1
		Women	58	1	17	19	15	2	2	2
	Outside the U.S.	Both genders	50	-	10	12	13	5	9	1
		Men	9	-	2	2	3	-	2	-
		Women	41	-	8	10	10	5	7	1
Palm Beach	All groups	Both genders	348	24	74	65	63	60	55	7
		Men	206	4	18	26	45	57	52	4
		Women	142	20	56	39	18	3	3	3
	Florida A & M University	Both genders	9	1	3	4	1	-	-	-
		Men	3	-	-	2	1	-	-	-
		Women	6	1	3	2	-	-	-	-
	Nova Southeastern University	Both genders	53	8	22	11	7	1	1	3
		Men	17	2	4	4	5	-	1	1
		Women	36	6	18	7	2	1	-	2
	University of Florida	Both genders	39	4	9	8	10	6	1	1
		Men	22	-	4	5	7	5	1	-
		Women	17	4	5	3	3	1	-	1
	In the U.S. outside Florida	Both genders	237	5	35	42	48	52	53	2
		Men	159	-	7	15	35	50	50	2
		Women	78	5	28	27	13	2	3	-
	Outside the U.S.	Both genders	18	3	4	3	2	4	1	1
		Men	10	1	1	1	1	4	1	1
		Women	8	2	3	2	1	-	-	-

Table 4–12. Number of pharmacists who completed the survey questionnaire by county of residence, university granting pharmacy degree(s), age group, and gender (continued).

County of Residence	University Granting Pharmacy Degree	Gender	Number of Pharmacists							
			All Age Groups	Less than 30	30-39	40-49	50-59	60-69	70 and Older	Not Known
Other	All groups	Both genders	43	5	17	5	6	3	5	2
		Men	21	1	8	2	2	2	4	2
		Women	22	4	9	3	4	1	1	-
	Florida A & M University	Both genders	2	1	-	-	-	-	-	1
		Men	1	-	-	-	-	-	-	1
		Women	1	1	-	-	-	-	-	-
	Nova Southeastern University	Both genders	12	1	9	2	-	-	-	-
		Men	5	-	3	2	-	-	-	-
		Women	7	1	6	-	-	-	-	-
	University of Florida	Both genders	2	-	-	-	1	1	-	-
		Men	-	-	-	-	-	-	-	-
		Women	2	-	-	-	1	1	-	-
	In the U.S. outside Florida	Both genders	15	1	3	3	2	1	4	1
		Men	9	-	2	-	2	1	3	1
		Women	6	1	1	3	-	-	1	-
	Outside the U.S.	Both genders	12	-	6	-	3	1	2	-
		Men	5	-	3	-	-	1	1	-
		Women	7	-	3	-	3	-	1	-

In Miami-Dade County one 20-29 year-old man reported being graduated from Palm Beach Atlantic University and one 30-39 year-old man did not respond.

In Palm Beach County one 20-29 year-old man, two 20-29 year-old women, one 30-39 year-old man, one 30-39 year-old woman, and one 50-59 year-old woman reported being graduated from Palm Beach Atlantic University and one 30-39 year-old man did not respond.

In the "other" county category one 20-29 year-old man and one 20-29 year-old woman reported being graduated from Palm Beach Atlantic University.

Table 4–13. **Number of pharmacists who completed the survey questionnaire by county of residence, whether or not they have completed a residency or fellowship, ethnic group, and gender.**

County of Residence	Have Completed a Residency or Fellowship	Gender	Number of Pharmacists					
			All Ethnic Groups	Non-Hispanic			Hispanic	Other
				White	Black	Asian		
All counties	All groups	Both genders	1,539	958	119	86	319	57
		Men	805	603	41	35	105	21
		Women	734	355	78	51	214	36
	Yes	Both genders	173	87	19	13	48	6
		Men	73	46	8	5	13	1
		Women	100	41	11	8	35	5
	No	Both genders	1,366	871	100	73	271	51
		Men	732	557	33	30	92	20
		Women	634	314	67	43	179	31
Broward	All groups	Both genders	508	316	55	35	70	32
		Men	270	199	22	11	26	12
		Women	238	117	33	24	44	20
	Yes	Both genders	52	32	8	3	7	2
		Men	24	18	4	1	1	-
		Women	28	14	4	2	6	2
	No	Both genders	456	284	47	32	63	30
		Men	246	181	18	10	25	12
		Women	210	103	29	22	38	18
Collier, Hendry, Lee, and Monroe	All groups	Both genders	202	181	4	5	12	-
		Men	111	99	2	3	7	-
		Women	91	82	2	2	5	-
	Yes	Both genders	21	17	1	1	2	-
		Men	8	8	-	-	-	-
		Women	13	9	1	1	2	-
	No	Both genders	181	164	3	4	10	-
		Men	103	91	2	3	7	-
		Women	78	73	1	1	3	-
Martin and Pasco	All groups	Both genders	96	76	4	6	5	5
		Men	57	46	-	5	3	3
		Women	39	30	4	1	2	2
	Yes	Both genders	10	7	-	2	-	1
		Men	7	6	-	1	-	-
		Women	3	1	-	1	-	1
	No	Both genders	86	69	4	4	5	4
		Men	50	40	-	4	3	3
		Women	36	29	4	-	2	1

Table 4–13. **Number of pharmacists who completed the survey questionnaire by county of residence, whether or not they have completed a residency or fellowship, ethnic group, and gender (continued).**

County of Residence	Have Completed a Residency or Fellowship	Gender	Number of Pharmacists					
			All Ethnic Groups	Non-Hispanic			Hispanic	Other
				White	Black	Asian		
Miami-Dade	All groups	Both genders	342	98	31	14	189	10
		Men	140	69	9	7	54	1
		Women	202	29	22	7	135	9
	Yes	Both genders	47	11	4	1	0	1
		Men	14	5	1	-	8	-
		Women	33	6	3	1	22	1
	No	Both genders	295	87	27	13	159	9
		Men	126	64	8	7	46	1
		Women	169	23	19	6	113	8
Palm Beach	All groups	Both genders	348	270	21	20	28	9
		Men	206	179	6	6	10	5
		Women	142	91	15	14	18	4
	Yes	Both genders	32	18	5	4	3	2
		Men	14	9	2	1	1	1
		Women	18	9	3	3	2	1
	No	Both genders	316	252	16	16	25	7
		Men	192	170	4	5	9	4
		Women	124	82	12	11	16	3
Other	All groups	Both genders	43	17	4	6	15	1
		Men	21	11	2	3	5	-
		Women	22	6	2	3	10	1
	Yes	Both genders	11	2	1	2	6	-
		Men	6	-	1	2	3	-
		Women	5	2	-	-	3	-
	No	Both genders	32	15	3	4	9	1
		Men	15	11	1	1	2	-
		Women	17	4	2	3	7	1

Table 4–14. Number of pharmacists who completed the survey questionnaire by county of residence, whether or not they have completed a residency or fellowship, age group, and gender.

County of Residence	Have Completed a Residency or Fellowship	Gender	Number of Pharmacists							
			All Age Groups	Less than 30	30-39	40-49	50-59	60-69	70 and Older	Not Known
All counties	All groups	Both genders	1,539	97	367	364	329	192	154	36
		Men	805	23	108	157	204	166	128	19
		Women	734	74	259	207	125	26	26	17
	Yes	Both genders	173	20	61	38	27	16	5	6
		Men	73	3	20	15	15	14	3	3
		Women	100	17	41	23	12	2	2	3
	No	Both genders	1,366	77	306	326	302	176	149	30
		Men	732	20	88	142	189	152	125	16
		Women	634	57	218	184	113	24	24	14
Broward	All groups	Both genders	508	25	124	136	110	60	40	13
		Men	270	4	36	70	69	51	34	6
		Women	238	21	88	66	41	9	6	7
	Yes	Both genders	52	4	22	8	10	6	-	2
		Men	24	-	5	6	7	5	-	1
		Women	28	4	17	2	3	1	-	1
	No	Both genders	456	21	102	128	100	54	40	11
		Men	246	4	31	64	62	46	34	5
		Women	210	17	71	64	38	8	6	6
Collier, Hendry, Lee, and Monroe	All groups	Both genders	202	16	40	49	58	22	13	4
		Men	111	5	13	20	39	19	12	3
		Women	91	11	27	29	19	3	1	1
	Yes	Both genders	21	-	6	7	6	1	-	1
		Men	8	-	3	-	3	1	-	1
		Women	13	-	3	7	3	-	-	-
	No	Both genders	181	16	34	42	52	21	13	3
		Men	103	5	10	20	36	18	12	2
		Women	78	11	24	22	16	3	1	1
Martin and Pasco	All groups	Both genders	96	6	18	23	29	12	7	1
		Men	57	2	8	7	21	11	7	1
		Women	39	4	10	16	8	1	-	-
	Yes	Both genders	10	3	2	1	3	-	-	1
		Men	7	1	1	1	3	-	-	1
		Women	3	2	1	-	-	-	-	-
	No	Both genders	86	3	16	22	26	12	7	-
		Men	50	1	7	6	18	11	7	-
		Women	36	2	9	16	8	1	-	-

Table 4–14. Number of pharmacists who completed the survey questionnaire by county of residence, whether or not they have completed a residency or fellowship, age group, and gender (continued).

County of Residence	Have Completed a Residency or Fellowship	Gender	Number of Pharmacists							
			All Age Groups	Less than 30	30-39	40-49	50-59	60-69	70 and Older	Not Known
Miami-Dade	All groups	Both genders	342	21	94	86	63	35	34	9
		Men	140	7	25	32	28	26	19	3
		Women	202	14	69	54	35	9	15	6
	Yes	Both genders	47	6	19	12	3	3	2	2
		Men	14	1	7	3	1	2	-	-
		Women	33	5	12	9	2	1	2	2
	No	Both genders	295	15	75	74	60	32	32	7
		Men	126	6	18	29	27	24	19	3
		Women	169	9	57	45	33	8	13	4
Palm Beach	All groups	Both genders	348	24	74	65	63	60	55	7
		Men	206	4	18	26	45	57	52	4
		Women	142	20	56	39	18	3	3	3
	Yes	Both genders	32	7	6	10	3	5	1	-
		Men	14	1	1	5	1	5	1	-
		Women	18	6	5	5	2	-	-	-
	No	Both genders	316	17	68	55	60	55	54	7
		Men	192	3	17	21	44	52	51	4
		Women	124	14	51	34	16	3	3	3
Other	All groups	Both genders	43	5	17	5	6	3	5	2
		Men	21	1	8	2	2	2	4	2
		Women	22	4	9	3	4	1	1	-
	Yes	Both genders	11	-	6	-	2	1	2	-
		Men	6	-	3	-	-	1	2	-
		Women	5	-	3	-	2	-	-	-
	No	Both genders	32	5	11	5	4	2	3	2
		Men	15	1	5	2	2	1	2	2
		Women	17	4	6	3	2	1	1	-

Table 4–15. Number of pharmacists who completed the survey questionnaire by county of residence, whether or not they hold a specialty Board certification, ethnic group, and gender.

County of Residence	Hold Specialty Board Certification	Gender	Number of Pharmacists					
			All Ethnic Groups	Non-Hispanic			Hispanic	Other
				White	Black	Asian		
All counties	All groups	Both genders	1,539	958	119	86	319	57
		Men	805	603	41	35	105	21
		Women	734	355	78	51	214	36
	Yes	Both genders	162	81	15	13	49	4
		Men	83	51	6	7	17	2
		Women	79	30	9	6	32	2
	No	Both genders	1,377	877	104	73	270	53
		Men	722	552	35	28	88	19
		Women	655	325	69	45	182	34
Broward	All groups	Both genders	508	316	55	35	70	32
		Men	270	199	22	11	26	12
		Women	238	117	33	24	44	20
	Yes	Both genders	59	35	8	6	9	1
		Men	35	25	3	2	4	1
		Women	24	10	5	4	5	-
	No	Both genders	449	281	47	29	61	31
		Men	235	174	19	9	22	11
		Women	214	107	28	20	39	20
Collier, Hendry, Lee, and Monroe	All groups	Both genders	202	181	4	5	12	-
		Men	111	99	2	3	7	-
		Women	91	82	2	2	5	-
	Yes	Both genders	20	16	1	1	2	-
		Men	12	9	1	1	1	-
		Women	8	7	-	-	1	-
	No	Both genders	182	165	3	4	10	-
		Men	99	90	1	2	6	-
		Women	83	75	2	2	4	-
Martin and Pasco	All groups	Both genders	96	76	4	6	5	5
		Men	57	46	-	5	3	3
		Women	39	30	4	1	2	2
	Yes	Both genders	11	9	-	-	1	1
		Men	8	7	-	-	-	1
		Women	3	2	-	-	1	-
	No	Both genders	85	67	4	6	4	4
		Men	49	39	-	5	3	2
		Women	36	28	4	1	1	2

Table 4–15. Number of pharmacists who completed the survey questionnaire by county of residence, whether or not they hold a specialty Board certification, ethnic group, and gender (continued).

County of Residence	Hold Specialty Board Certification	Gender	Number of Pharmacists					
			All Ethnic Groups	Non-Hispanic			Hispanic	Other
				White	Black	Asian		
Miami-Dade	All groups	Both genders	342	98	31	14	189	10
		Men	140	69	9	7	54	1
		Women	202	29	22	7	135	9
	Yes	Both genders	41	8	1	3	28	1
		Men	13	3	-	2	8	-
		Women	28	5	1	1	20	1
	No	Both genders	301	90	30	11	161	9
		Men	127	66	9	5	46	1
		Women	174	24	21	6	115	8
Palm Beach	All groups	Both genders	348	270	21	20	28	9
		Men	206	179	6	6	10	5
		Women	142	91	15	14	18	4
	Yes	Both genders	28	13	5	3	6	1
		Men	13	7	2	2	2	-
		Women	15	6	3	1	4	1
	No	Both genders	320	257	16	17	22	8
		Men	193	172	4	4	8	5
		Women	127	85	12	13	14	3
Other	All groups	Both genders	43	17	4	6	15	1
		Men	21	11	2	3	5	-
		Women	22	6	2	3	10	1
	Yes	Both genders	3	-	-	-	3	-
		Men	2	-	-	-	2	-
		Women	1	-	-	-	1	-
	No	Both genders	40	17	4	6	12	1
		Men	19	11	2	3	3	-
		Women	21	6	2	3	9	1

Table 4–16. Number of pharmacists who completed the survey questionnaire by county of residence, whether or not they hold a specialty Board certification, age group, and gender.

County of Residence	Hold Specialty Board Certification	Gender	Number of Pharmacists							
			All Age Groups	Less than 30	30-39	40-49	50-59	60-69	70 and Older	Not Known
All counties	All groups	Both genders	1,539	97	367	364	329	192	154	36
		Men	805	23	108	157	204	166	128	19
		Women	734	74	259	207	125	26	26	17
	Yes	Both genders	162	12	35	38	41	15	19	2
		Men	83	6	11	16	27	13	10	-
		Women	79	6	24	22	14	2	9	2
	No	Both genders	1,377	85	332	326	288	177	135	34
		Men	722	17	97	141	177	153	118	19
		Women	655	68	235	185	111	24	17	15
Broward	All groups	Both genders	508	25	124	136	110	60	40	13
		Men	270	4	36	70	69	51	34	6
		Women	238	21	88	66	41	9	6	7
	Yes	Both genders	59	6	12	13	17	5	5	1
		Men	35	3	4	7	12	5	4	-
		Women	24	3	8	6	5	-	1	1
	No	Both genders	449	19	112	123	93	55	35	12
		Men	235	1	32	63	57	46	30	6
		Women	214	18	80	60	36	9	5	6
Collier, Hendry, Lee, and Monroe	All groups	Both genders	202	16	40	49	58	22	13	4
		Men	111	5	13	20	39	19	12	3
		Women	91	11	27	29	19	3	1	1
	Yes	Both genders	20	-	4	7	5	3	1	-
		Men	12	-	3	1	5	3	-	-
		Women	8	-	1	6	-	-	1	-
	No	Both genders	182	16	36	42	53	19	12	4
		Men	99	5	10	19	34	16	12	3
		Women	83	11	26	23	19	3	-	1
Martin and Pasco	All groups	Both genders	96	6	18	23	29	12	7	1
		Men	57	2	8	7	21	11	7	1
		Women	39	4	10	16	8	1	-	-
	Yes	Both genders	11	1	1	4	4	1	-	-
		Men	8	1	1	1	4	1	-	-
		Women	3	-	-	3	-	-	-	-
	No	Both genders	85	5	17	19	25	11	7	1
		Men	49	1	7	6	17	10	7	1
		Women	36	4	10	13	8	1	-	-

Table 4–16. Number of pharmacists who completed the survey questionnaire by county of residence, whether or not they hold a specialty Board certification, age group, and gender (continued).

County of Residence	Hold Specialty Board Certification	Gender	Number of Pharmacists							
			All Age Groups	Less than 30	30-39	40-49	50-59	60-69	70 and Older	Not Known
Miami-Dade	All groups	Both genders	342	21	94	86	63	35	34	9
		Men	140	7	25	32	28	26	19	3
		Women	202	14	69	54	35	9	15	6
	Yes	Both genders	41	1	12	8	8	3	8	1
		Men	13	1	3	4	2	1	2	-
		Women	28	-	9	4	6	2	6	1
	No	Both genders	301	20	82	78	55	32	26	8
		Men	127	6	22	28	26	25	17	3
		Women	174	14	60	50	29	7	9	5
Palm Beach	All groups	Both genders	348	24	74	65	63	60	55	7
		Men	206	4	18	26	45	57	52	4
		Women	142	20	56	39	18	3	3	3
	Yes	Both genders	28	4	6	6	7	3	2	-
		Men	13	1	-	3	4	3	2	-
		Women	15	3	6	3	3	-	-	-
	No	Both genders	320	20	68	59	56	57	53	7
		Men	193	3	18	23	41	54	50	4
		Women	127	17	50	36	15	3	3	3
Other	All groups	Both genders	43	5	17	5	6	3	5	2
		Men	21	1	8	2	2	2	4	2
		Women	22	4	9	3	4	1	1	-
	Yes	Both genders	3	-	-	-	-	-	3	-
		Men	2	-	-	-	-	-	2	-
		Women	1	-	-	-	-	-	1	-
	No	Both genders	40	5	17	5	6	3	2	2
		Men	19	1	8	2	2	2	2	2
		Women	21	4	9	3	4	1	-	-

Table 4–17. **Number of pharmacists who completed the survey questionnaire by county of residence, number of years as a registered pharmacist, ethnic group, and gender.**

County of Residence	Years as a Registered Pharmacist	Gender	Number of Pharmacists					
			All Ethnic Groups	Non-Hispanic			Hispanic	Other
				White	Black	Asian		
All counties	All groups	Both genders	1,539	958	119	86	319	57
		Men	805	603	41	35	105	21
		Women	734	355	78	51	214	36
	Less than 5	Both genders	199	75	23	20	71	10
		Men	59	24	8	5	19	3
		Women	140	51	15	15	52	7
	5 - 9	Both genders	182	80	20	23	50	9
		Men	57	27	6	9	13	2
		Women	125	53	14	14	37	7
	10 - 19	Both genders	345	181	42	23	78	21
		Men	122	65	15	9	25	8
		Women	223	116	27	14	53	13
	20 and more	Both genders	799	614	34	18	117	16
		Men	561	483	12	12	47	7
		Women	238	131	22	6	70	9
	No response	Both genders	14	8	-	2	3	1
		Men	6	4	-	-	1	1
		Women	8	4	-	2	2	-
Broward	All groups	Both genders	508	316	55	35	70	32
		Men	270	199	22	11	26	12
		Women	238	117	33	24	44	20
	Less than 5	Both genders	56	17	10	7	17	5
		Men	16	3	5	1	5	2
		Women	40	14	5	6	12	3
	5 - 9	Both genders	66	26	12	12	8	8
		Men	20	10	3	3	2	2
		Women	46	16	9	9	6	6
	10 - 19	Both genders	128	71	17	9	20	11
		Men	51	29	7	3	8	4
		Women	77	42	10	6	12	7
	20 and more	Both genders	255	201	16	6	25	7
		Men	182	157	7	4	11	3
		Women	73	44	9	2	14	4
	No response	Both genders	3	1	-	1	-	1
		Men	1	-	-	-	-	1
		Women	2	1	-	1	-	-

Table 4–17. **Number of pharmacists who completed the survey questionnaire by county of residence, number of years as a registered pharmacist, ethnic group, and gender (continued).**

County of Residence	Years as a Registered Pharmacist	Gender	Number of Pharmacists					
			All Ethnic Groups	Non-Hispanic			Hispanic	Other
				White	Black	Asian		
Collier, Hendry, Lee, and Monroe	All groups	Both genders	202	181	4	5	12	-
		Men	111	99	2	3	7	-
		Women	91	82	2	2	5	-
	Less than 5	Both genders	21	17	1	1	2	-
		Men	6	5	-	-	1	-
		Women	15	12	1	1	1	-
	5 - 9	Both genders	18	17	-	1	-	-
		Men	9	8	-	1	-	-
		Women	9	9	-	-	-	-
	10 - 19	Both genders	47	39	2	1	5	-
		Men	13	10	1	-	2	-
		Women	34	29	1	1	3	-
	20 and more	Both genders	110	102	1	2	5	-
		Men	79	72	1	2	4	-
		Women	31	30	-	-	1	-
	No response	Both genders	6	6	-	-	-	-
		Men	4	4	-	-	-	-
		Women	2	2	-	-	-	-
Martin and Pasco	All groups	Both genders	96	76	4	6	5	5
		Men	57	46	-	5	3	3
		Women	39	30	4	1	2	2
	Less than 5	Both genders	7	3	-	-	2	2
		Men	4	2	-	-	1	1
		Women	3	1	-	-	1	1
	5 - 9	Both genders	11	9	-	2	-	-
		Men	4	3	-	1	-	-
		Women	7	6	-	1	-	-
	10 - 19	Both genders	20	15	3	2	-	-
		Men	5	3	-	2	-	-
		Women	15	12	3	-	-	-
	20 and more	Both genders	58	49	1	2	3	3
		Men	44	38	-	2	2	2
		Women	14	11	1	-	1	1
	No response	Both genders	-	-	-	-	-	-
		Men	-	-	-	-	-	-
		Women	-	-	-	-	-	-

Table 4–17. Number of pharmacists who completed the survey questionnaire by county of residence, number of years as a registered pharmacist, ethnic group, and gender (continued).

County of Residence	Years as a Registered Pharmacist	Gender	Number of Pharmacists					
			All Ethnic Groups	Non-Hispanic			Hispanic	Other
				White	Black	Asian		
Miami-Dade	All groups	Both genders	342	98	31	14	189	10
		Men	140	69	9	7	54	1
		Women	202	29	22	7	135	9
	Less than 5	Both genders	54	11	4	-	37	2
		Men	14	5	-	-	9	-
		Women	40	6	4	-	28	2
	5 - 9	Both genders	46	4	4	2	35	1
		Men	15	1	2	1	11	-
		Women	31	3	2	1	24	1
	10 - 19	Both genders	88	21	10	6	47	4
		Men	30	11	4	3	11	1
		Women	58	10	6	3	36	3
	20 and more	Both genders	153	62	13	6	69	3
		Men	81	52	3	3	23	-
		Women	72	10	10	3	46	3
	No response	Both genders	1	-	-	-	1	-
		Men	-	-	-	-	-	-
		Women	1	-	-	-	1	-
Palm Beach	All groups	Both genders	348	270	21	20	28	9
		Men	206	179	6	6	10	5
		Women	142	91	15	14	18	4
	Less than 5	Both genders	46	22	6	9	9	-
		Men	14	7	2	3	2	-
		Women	32	15	4	6	7	-
	5 - 9	Both genders	35	23	4	4	4	-
		Men	6	4	1	1	-	-
		Women	29	19	3	3	4	-
	10 - 19	Both genders	55	32	8	5	4	6
		Men	20	11	2	1	3	3
		Women	35	21	6	4	1	3
	20 and more	Both genders	210	192	3	1	11	3
		Men	166	157	1	1	5	2
		Women	44	35	2	-	6	1
	No response	Both genders	2	1	-	1	-	-
		Men	-	-	-	-	-	-
		Women	2	1	-	1	-	-

Table 4–17. Number of pharmacists who completed the survey questionnaire by county of residence, number of years as a registered pharmacist, ethnic group, and gender (continued).

County of Residence	Years as a Registered Pharmacist	Gender	Number of Pharmacists					
			All Ethnic Groups	Non-Hispanic			Hispanic	Other
				White	Black	Asian		
Other	All groups	Both genders	43	17	4	6	15	1
		Men	21	11	2	3	5	-
		Women	22	6	2	3	10	1
	Less than 5	Both genders	15	5	2	3	4	1
		Men	5	2	1	1	1	-
		Women	10	3	1	2	3	1
	5 - 9	Both genders	6	1	-	2	3	-
		Men	3	1	-	2	-	-
		Women	3	-	-	-	3	-
	10 - 19	Both genders	7	3	2	-	2	-
		Men	3	1	1	-	1	-
		Women	4	2	1	-	1	-
	20 and more	Both genders	13	8	-	1	4	-
		Men	9	7	-	-	2	-
		Women	4	1	-	1	2	-
	No response	Both genders	2	-	-	-	2	-
		Men	1	-	-	-	1	-
		Women	1	-	-	-	1	-

Table 4–18. Number of pharmacists who completed the survey questionnaire by county of residence, number of years as a registered pharmacist, age group, and gender.

County of Residence	Years as a Registered Pharmacist	Gender	Number of Pharmacists							
			All Age Groups	Less than 30	30-39	40-49	50-59	60-69	70 and Older	Not Known
All counties	All groups	Both genders	1,539	97	367	364	329	192	154	36
		Men	805	23	108	157	204	166	128	19
		Women	734	74	259	207	125	26	26	17
	Less than 5	Both genders	199	86	86	14	10	-	-	3
		Men	59	21	31	3	3	-	-	1
		Women	140	65	55	11	7	-	-	2
	5 - 9	Both genders	182	10	140	22	7	-	-	3
		Men	57	2	42	9	4	-	-	-
		Women	125	8	98	13	3	-	-	3
	10 - 19	Both genders	345	-	140	161	32	6	1	5
		Men	122	-	35	69	15	2	1	-
		Women	223	-	105	92	17	4	-	5
	20 and more	Both genders	799	-	-	163	277	183	151	25
		Men	561	-	-	74	180	162	127	18
		Women	238	-	-	89	97	21	24	7
	No response	Both genders	14	1	1	4	3	3	2	-
		Men	6	-	-	2	2	2	-	-
		Women	8	1	1	2	1	1	2	-
Broward	All groups	Both genders	508	25	124	136	110	60	40	13
		Men	270	4	36	70	69	51	34	6
		Women	238	21	88	66	41	9	6	7
	Less than 5	Both genders	56	21	28	1	5	-	-	1
		Men	16	3	11	1	1	-	-	-
		Women	40	18	17	-	4	-	-	1
	5 - 9	Both genders	66	4	47	12	2	-	-	1
		Men	20	1	11	6	2	-	-	-
		Women	46	3	36	6	-	-	-	1
	10 - 19	Both genders	128	-	48	61	13	2	-	4
		Men	51	-	14	29	8	-	-	-
		Women	77	-	34	32	5	2	-	4
	20 and more	Both genders	255	-	-	62	88	58	40	7
		Men	182	-	-	34	57	51	34	6
		Women	73	-	-	28	31	7	6	1
	No response	Both genders	3	-	1	-	2	-	-	-
		Men	1	-	-	-	1	-	-	-
		Women	2	-	1	-	1	-	-	-

Table 4–18. **Number of pharmacists who completed the survey questionnaire by county of residence, number of years as a registered pharmacist, age group, and gender (continued).**

County of Residence	Years as a Registered Pharmacist	Gender	Number of Pharmacists							
			All Age Groups	Less than 30	30-39	40-49	50-59	60-69	70 and Older	Not Known
Collier, Hendry, Lee, and Monroe	All groups	Both genders	202	16	40	49	58	22	13	4
		Men	111	5	13	20	39	19	12	3
		Women	91	11	27	29	19	3	1	1
	Less than 5	Both genders	21	14	7	-	-	-	-	-
		Men	6	4	2	-	-	-	-	-
		Women	15	10	5	-	-	-	-	-
	5 - 9	Both genders	18	2	13	2	1	-	-	-
		Men	9	1	7	1	-	-	-	-
		Women	9	1	6	1	1	-	-	-
	10 - 19	Both genders	47	-	20	19	7	-	1	-
		Men	13	-	4	5	3	-	1	-
		Women	34	-	16	14	4	-	-	-
	20 and more	Both genders	110	-	-	25	49	20	12	4
		Men	79	-	-	12	35	18	11	3
		Women	31	-	-	13	14	2	1	1
	No response	Both genders	6	-	-	3	1	2	-	-
		Men	4	-	-	2	1	1	-	-
		Women	2	-	-	1	-	1	-	-
Martin and Pasco	All groups	Both genders	96	6	18	23	29	12	7	1
		Men	57	2	8	7	21	11	7	1
		Women	39	4	10	16	8	1	-	-
	Less than 5	Both genders	7	3	4	-	-	-	-	-
		Men	4	2	2	-	-	-	-	-
		Women	3	1	2	-	-	-	-	-
	5 - 9	Both genders	11	3	6	1	1	-	-	-
		Men	4	-	4	-	-	-	-	-
		Women	7	3	2	1	1	-	-	-
	10 - 19	Both genders	20	-	8	11	1	-	-	-
		Men	5	-	2	3	-	-	-	-
		Women	15	-	6	8	1	-	-	-
	20 and more	Both genders	58	-	-	11	27	12	7	1
		Men	44	-	-	4	21	11	7	1
		Women	14	-	-	7	6	1	-	-
	No response	Both genders	-	-	-	-	-	-	-	-
		Men	-	-	-	-	-	-	-	-
		Women	-	-	-	-	-	-	-	-

Table 4–18. **Number of pharmacists who completed the survey questionnaire by county of residence, number of years as a registered pharmacist, age group, and gender (continued).**

County of Residence	Years as a Registered Pharmacist	Gender	Number of Pharmacists							
			All Age Groups	Less than 30	30-39	40-49	50-59	60-69	70 and Older	Not Known
Miami-Dade	All groups	Both genders	342	21	94	86	63	35	34	9
		Men	140	7	25	32	28	26	19	3
		Women	202	14	69	54	35	9	15	6
	Less than 5	Both genders	54	21	22	9	1	-	-	1
		Men	14	7	5	2	-	-	-	-
		Women	40	14	17	7	1	-	-	1
	5 - 9	Both genders	46	-	38	5	2	-	-	1
		Men	15	-	11	2	2	-	-	-
		Women	31	-	27	3	-	-	-	1
	10 - 19	Both genders	88	-	34	42	8	4	-	-
		Men	30	-	9	17	2	2	-	-
		Women	58	-	25	25	6	2	-	-
	20 and more	Both genders	153	-	-	30	52	31	33	7
		Men	81	-	-	11	24	24	19	3
		Women	72	-	-	19	28	7	14	4
	No response	Both genders	1	-	-	-	-	-	1	-
		Men	-	-	-	-	-	-	-	-
		Women	1	-	-	-	-	-	1	-
Palm Beach	All groups	Both genders	348	24	74	65	63	60	55	7
		Men	206	4	18	26	45	57	52	4
		Women	142	20	56	39	18	3	3	3
	Less than 5	Both genders	46	22	17	3	3	-	-	1
		Men	14	4	7	-	2	-	-	1
		Women	32	18	10	3	1	-	-	-
	5 - 9	Both genders	35	1	30	2	1	-	-	1
		Men	6	-	6	-	-	-	-	-
		Women	29	1	24	2	1	-	-	1
	10 - 19	Both genders	55	-	27	24	3	-	-	1
		Men	20	-	5	13	2	-	-	-
		Women	35	-	22	11	1	-	-	1
	20 and more	Both genders	210	-	-	35	56	60	55	4
		Men	166	-	-	13	41	57	52	3
		Women	44	-	-	22	15	3	3	1
	No response	Both genders	2	1	-	1	-	-	-	-
		Men	-	-	-	-	-	-	-	-
		Women	2	1	-	1	-	-	-	-

Table 4–18. Number of pharmacists who completed the survey questionnaire by county of residence, number of years as a registered pharmacist, age group, and gender (continued).

County of Residence	Years as a Registered Pharmacist	Gender	Number of Pharmacists: All Age Groups	Less than 30	30-39	40-49	50-59	60-69	70 and Older	Not Known
Other	All groups	Both genders	43	5	17	5	6	3	5	2
		Men	21	1	8	2	2	2	4	2
		Women	22	4	9	3	4	1	1	-
	Less than 5	Both genders	15	5	8	1	1	-	-	-
		Men	5	1	4	-	-	-	-	-
		Women	10	4	4	1	1	-	-	-
	5 - 9	Both genders	6	-	6	-	-	-	-	-
		Men	3	-	3	-	-	-	-	-
		Women	3	-	3	-	-	-	-	-
	10 - 19	Both genders	7	-	3	4	-	-	-	-
		Men	3	-	1	2	-	-	-	-
		Women	4	-	2	2	-	-	-	-
	20 and more	Both genders	13	-	-	-	5	2	4	2
		Men	9	-	-	-	2	1	4	2
		Women	4	-	-	-	3	1	-	-
	No response	Both genders	2	-	-	-	-	1	1	-
		Men	1	-	-	-	-	1	-	-
		Women	1	-	-	-	-	-	1	-

Table 4-19. Median number of years as a registered pharmacist of pharmacists who completed the survey questionnaire by county of residence, ethnic group, and gender.

County of Residence	Gender	Number of Pharmacists					
		All Ethnic Groups	Non-Hispanic			Hispanic	Other
			White	Black	Asian		
All counties	Both genders	20.0	26.0	12.0	9.0	15.0	13.0
	Men	29.0	33.0	12.0	11.0	17.0	14.5
	Women	13.0	15.0	12.0	7.0	12.0	11.5
Broward	Both genders	20.0	26.0	12.0	7.5	14.5	11.0
	Men	27.0	30.0	12.0	11.0	17.0	14.0
	Women	13.0	15.5	12.0	6.0	13.0	10.0
Collier, Hendry, Lee, and Monroe	Both genders	22.0	23.0	17.0	10.0	15.5	-
	Men	30.0	30.0	19.5	25.0	30.0	-
	Women	15.0	15.5	9.0	6.0	15.0	-
Martin and Pasco	Both genders	23.5	25.0	16.0	11.5	27.0	22.0
	Men	29.0	29.0	-	13.0	40.0	29.0
	Women	16.0	16.5	16.0	5.0	12.0	12.5
Miami-Dade	Both genders	17.0	26.5	16.0	12.0	15.0	14.5
	Men	24.0	32.0	12.0	12.0	16.0	10.0
	Women	15.0	16.0	17.5	12.0	13.0	15.0
Palm Beach	Both genders	25.0	30.0	10.0	7.0	10.5	14.0
	Men	36.5	41.0	9.5	6.0	21.0	18.0
	Women	10.5	15.0	10.0	7.0	8.0	13.0
Other	Both genders	7.0	16.0	7.0	4.0	7.0	3.0
	Men	12.5	35.0	7.0	6.0	26.5	-
	Women	5.0	7.5	9.0	2.0	6.0	3.0

Table 4-20. Median number of years as a registered pharmacist of pharmacists who completed the survey questionnaire by county of residence, age group, and gender.

County of Residence	Gender	Number of Pharmacists							
		All Age Groups	Less than 30	30-39	40-49	50-59	60-69	70 and Older	Not Known
All counties	Both genders	20.0	2.0	8.0	19.0	28.0	40.0	50.0	27.5
	Men	29.0	3.0	7.0	19.0	29.0	40.0	50.5	40.0
	Women	13.0	2.0	8.0	18.0	27.5	33.0	47.5	16.0
Broward	Both genders	20.0	2.5	8.0	19.0	28.5	40.0	50.0	24.0
	Men	27.0	3.0	7.0	19.0	28.5	40.0	50.0	36.0
	Women	13.0	2.0	8.0	18.0	28.5	39.0	48.0	16.0
Collier, Hendry, Lee, and Monroe	Both genders	22.0	2.0	9.5	21.0	30.0	40.0	50.0	31.0
	Men	30.0	2.5	7.5	23.5	30.0	40.0	50.0	36.0
	Women	15.0	2.0	11.0	19.0	28.0	41.5	50.0	21.0
Martin and Pasco	Both genders	23.5	4.0	7.0	19.0	29.0	39.0	51.0	53.0
	Men	29.0	2.5	6.0	21.0	29.0	39.0	51.0	53.0
	Women	16.0	5.0	10.5	19.0	27.5	39.0	-	-
Miami-Dade	Both genders	17.0	2.0	7.0	16.0	27.0	35.0	50.0	28.0
	Men	24.0	3.0	8.0	16.0	28.0	36.0	51.0	51.0
	Women	15.0	2.0	7.0	16.0	27.0	25.0	35.0	26.5
Palm Beach	Both genders	25.0	2.0	8.0	20.0	28.0	43.0	51.0	20.0
	Men	36.5	1.5	6.0	19.0	28.0	43.0	51.0	48.5
	Women	10.5	2.5	9.0	20.0	27.0	35.0	55.0	15.0
Other	Both genders	7.0	1.5	5.0	12.0	30.5	35.5	55.0	33.0
	Men	12.5	1.0	5.0	11.5	37.5	40.0	55.0	33.0
	Women	5.0	2.0	5.0	16.0	27.5	31.0	-	-

SITUATION VARIABLES 5

This chapter focuses on what pharmacists do while practicing their profession. It addresses labor market outcomes that result from the interaction of job availability, skills, preferences, and factors beyond one's control, such as bias and discrimination. The job characteristics examined here include employment longevity, choice of practice setting, whether pharmacists primarily serve a specific patient population, pharmacy activities, urban-rural location of practice setting, distance to work and commuting time, number of hours supplied, incidence of part-time work, pharmacy earnings, wage rate, household income, and whether or not the pharmacist's spouse works. Since these characteristics are viewed and valued differently according to people's demographic features, beliefs, and attitudes, they are expected to vary by gender, ethnic group, and age group.

Several studies show that men and women assign different values to the same job characteristics [Bender *et al.*, 2005; Kim, 2005; Konrad *et al.*, 2000a]. Women are less likely than men to identify earnings as the most important aspect of their job, but place a greater emphasis on social relations at work and the significance of tasks performed. This is of utmost importance to the pharmacist workforce insofar as women, compared to men, tend to work fewer hours, are more likely to work part time, and exhibit less labor force attachment [Mott, 2001; Mott *et al.*, 2002; Quiñones and Mason, 2000; Walton and Cooksey, 2001]. Men tend to compete too much and women tend to shy away from competition [Niederle and Vesterlund, 2005]. Similar patterns also may be identified for different ethnic and age groups whereby certain workers choose to spend more time pursuing non-marketwork activities [Mott *et al.*, 2006]. Moreover the analysis may be extended beyond gender, ethnicity, and age to other job characteristics such as practice setting. For instance, community pharmacists report greater levels of work enrichment and less intention to leave their current jobs compared to hospital and clinic pharmacists [Lin *et al.*, 2007].

EMPLOYMENT LONGEVITY

This variable measures experience using a different criterion than number of years since the pharmacist became licensed. Cumulative professional experience is a demographic indicator; as such, it is part of workers' human-capital stock regardless of where they have worked, what activities they have performed, etc. Conversely, current job tenure assesses the influence of acquiring knowledge and skills that may be of relatively small value outside a specific workplace. Carvajal and Hardigan [2004] and Robson and Wallace [2001] use current-job tenure in conjunction with cumulative professional experience to gain a broader view of socioeconomic determinants of labor market outcomes. Along these lines Price and Wulff [2005] find an inverse association between employment longevity and job satisfaction.

Green *et al.* [2007] argue that employment longevity is important because employers spend a considerable amount of resources to train workers into the specific requirements demanded by the jobs they offer, and they would prefer to amortize these costs over longer, rather than shorter, time horizons. They find that, compared to their male counterparts, women are 1.5 percent more likely to leave work within one year, 3.3 percent more likely to leave within two years, and 2.8 percent more likely to leave within three years. They also find that, on average, women hold their jobs for a shorter period of time than men.

Employment longevity leads to job-related plateaus, which occur when employees become bored with their jobs or with the tasks they perform [McCleese and Eby, 2006]. Bardwick [1986] identifies three types of plateaus: Structural or hierarchical plateaus, which take place when the number of positions and advancement opportunities within an organization dwindle; content plateaus, which happen when workers master their position and become bored; and life plateaus, which occur when workers are unable to find fulfillment in any area of life. All three types are related negatively to job satisfaction and favorable labor outcomes.

Cline [2003] reports that job-specific human capital has little value for pharmacists. One possible explanation for this finding, according to him, is that many pharmacy jobs within a practice setting are similar in nature, so the amount of learning is limited when a pharmacist changes jobs, especially when he/she changes jobs within a setting. Thus, there is no monetary reward for a practitioner associated with learning the specifics of a given job. An alternative explanation may be that pharmacists do not remain with the same employer long enough for employers to reap benefits from investing in their workers' job-specific human-capital stock.

The results from the South Florida pharmacists survey reveal that over one-quarter (28.8 percent) of pharmacists have worked less than three years at their current practice site (see Tables 5-1 and 5-2). Another 43.2 percent have a job longevity between three and nine years, 18.0 percent have worked between ten and 19 years, and the remaining 10.0 percent have held their current job for at least 20 years. There seem to be few differences among counties, but gender differences are obvious. Men exhibit longer longevity than women. More women than men report working in the same site less than three years, while, at the other end of the spectrum, almost twice as many men as women have worked in their current job 20 years or more. This is probably due to the relatively recent entry of women into the pharmacy workforce, as well as their discontinuous participation in it compared to men.

Some ethnic differences are apparent, too. The percentage of pharmacists working for the same employer under three years is about the same for all ethnic groups, but the fractions of Non-Hispanic White and Hispanic pharmacists working 20 years or longer in the same site are higher than the fractions of Blacks and Asian Americans. Unlike their non-minority peers, however, the incidence of Hispanic women working at least 20 years in the same job is about as high as the incidence of Hispanic men.

Age patterns are as might be expected. Over one-third (35.1 percent) of pharmacists younger than 50 years of age respond that they have held the same job for less than three years, compared to only 2.8 percent in the 20-year-plus tenure category. In the 60-years-and-older group, the same number of pharmacists have worked less than three years and 20 years or more.

PRACTICE SETTING

Although, in most instances, working in a practice setting results primarily out of a combination of subjective factors, including preferences and job opportunities, this indicator normally is associated with multiple demographic, situation, and opinion variables. For example, jobs in institutional settings offer opportunities for pharmacists to exercise their clinical skills, whereas working in a large chain pharmacy offers better salary rewards [Cardinale, 2005; Cline and Mott, 2000; Levy, 2008; Mahrous and Maziarz, 2008]. Cline [2003] argues that pharmacists' wages in large chain, mass merchandiser, and HMO settings are unrelated to human capital because the demand for pharmacists in these settings is in disequilibrium with its supply, but in independent pharmacies and other settings this is not the case. Also, the levels of role conflict and job stress are reported to be higher in chain, mass merchandiser/supermarket, and hospital pharmacies compared to independent pharmacies [Mott *et al.*, 2004; Ukens, 2004].

Various studies nationwide suggest that approximately two-thirds of pharmacists work in retail venues (traditional chain, supermarket, mass merchandiser, or independently owned); one-fourth work in hospitals and long-term care facilities; and the rest work in manufacturing and research, academia, government, managed care, pharmaceutical benefit management, and the insurance industry [Knapp and Livesey, 2002; Manasse and Speedie, 2007; Mott, 2001; Walton and Cooksey, 2001]. According to some of these studies, relatively more women than men prefer to work in a hospital setting, while relatively more men than women work in drugstores. Practitioners who choose independent pharmacies over large chains are predominantly Non-Hispanic Whites, and older pharmacists are less likely to work in hospitals than are younger pharmacists. The recent shift in the profession to a more patient-centered practice may be partly responsible for these trends. By and large younger, more ethnically mixed female pharmacists with Pharm.D. degrees prefer to work in hospitals because they are more able to apply their clinical skills in that setting. Furthermore, hospital practice generally allows for more flexible work schedules and offers more opportunities in patient-centered practice, which are particularly attractive to female practitioners.

Kahaleh and Gaither [2007] report that work setting also affects empowerment and its consequences. Pharmacists who work in independent pharmacies have more access to information pertaining to their jobs and receive more institutional support than their counterparts in hospitals or chain pharmacies. This leads to more institutional commitment and loyalty, as well as less job turnover intention, by independent-setting pharmacists. The authors conclude that, in all settings, feelings of power through access to information, ability to mobilize resources, support from supervisors, and perception of opportunities to grow in one's job engender in employees more commitment to organizational goals.

In South Florida, according to Tables 5-3 and 5-4, more than half (54.0 percent) of pharmacists who completed the survey questionnaire work in retail (15.0 percent in community/independent stores and 39.0 percent in large chains), 24.5 percent work in hospitals, 20.5 percent work in other settings, and the remaining 1.0 percent provide no response. These other venues employ, in relative terms, twice as many pharmacists in South Florida as in the rest of the country. Women prefer working in hospitals and in other settings, while men tend to concentrate in retail, especially community/independent pharmacies. Therefore, local gender preferences conform to those reported elsewhere. Ethnic variations in practice setting are imperceptible, and the only age variation worth reporting is that older (60 years plus) pharmacists work more often in retail pharmacies and less frequently in hospitals compared to younger pharmacists. Miami-Dade and the periphery counties exhibit a relatively greater concentration of practitioners in hospitals, while Palm Beach is characterized by relatively more pharmacists in retail.

Slightly less than half (45.2 percent) of the survey respondents serve primarily a specific patient population (see Tables 5-5 and 5-6). There are neither differences by county nor by gender, and the only ethnic variant that can be detected pertains to Non-Hispanic Blacks, who serve a particular patient population less often than do other ethnic groups. In terms of age, older pharmacists tend to serve specific patient populations more often relative to their younger peers.

TYPE OF PHARMACY ACTIVITIES

According to both the American Pharmacists Association [2010] and the American Society of Health-System Pharmacists [2010], the primary role of the pharmacist is to help individuals make the best use of medications. Pharmacists address medication use in different venues, and in doing so take on roles that transcend the traditional role of drug dispenser. The responsibilities of today's pharmacists are multifaceted and include, depending on the practice site and specific job description, patient care management, administrative activities, the provision of drug information services, and conducting research.

Community pharmacy practice is still considered the heart and soul of the profession [Posey, 2003]. While community pharmacists still spend most of their time dispensing medications, a major part of their job encompasses the identification, resolution, and prevention of drug therapy problems through the evaluation of medication profiles, the provision of patient education, and the assessment of drug adherence patterns. In addition, community pharmacists' managers and other administrative personnel are called upon to coordinate the services provided by the pharmacy, facilitate billing and payment for consumers participating in group health benefit plans, manage the acquisition of drug products, and handle human resources issues.

Hospital pharmacists also embrace a broad range of responsibilities. Since the pharmacy is responsible for the safe and effective use of drugs by patients in a hospital, the pharmacist's role is crucial throughout patients' hospital stay. McCarthy and Schafermeyer [2007] identify three major types of activities conducted by hospital pharmacists: drug product distribution, patient care or clinical services, and administrative duties. Distributive responsibilities are associated with the drug product and include order entry and verification, checking medication carts, supervision of technicians, and preparation of sterile products. Patient care or clinical services include ensuring the quality of drug therapy, monitoring patient progress, advocating cost-effective therapy, providing discharge patient education, managing adverse drug reaction programs, responding to drug information inquiries, and communicating with other healthcare providers. Administrative responsibilities usually range from dealing with personnel issues to managing the drug budget of the hospital, as well as serving as the pharmacy representative on a number of multidisciplinary hospital committees. The extent of participation by pharmacists in these activities largely depends on the size of each institution. In small hospitals one pharmacist may be responsible for carrying out all three types of activities, while in larger institutions these responsibilities may be spread out among various specialists.

Lapane and Hughes [2006] point out that the work of pharmacists serving long-term care patients varies according to their role, either dispensing or consulting. Dispensing pharmacists spend more of their time in activities related to dispensing medications, much like retail pharmacists do, while consultant pharmacists normally spend their time conducting federally mandated drug-regimen reviews, developing and delivering in-service education programs, traveling to nursing homes, and attending meetings [Posey, 1997]. As pharmacists' roles in clinical research, therapeutic substitution, patient assessment, and other areas expand, the sources and intensity of stress are likely to expand as well [Lapane and Hughes, 2006].

Pharmacists' workload in all venues continues to increase and more time seems to be devoted to dispensing medications and administrative responsibilities instead of counseling and clinical activities [Knapp and Cultice, 2007; Schommer *et al.*, 2006]. A somewhat recent nationwide study concludes that while 56 percent of community pharmacists' time is devoted to dispensing, 19 percent is spent on consultation, 16 percent is allocated to business management practices, and 9 percent goes to drug use management, these pharmacists would prefer to apportion more time of their professional activities to consultation and drug use management, and less time to medication dispensing and business-related activities [Schommer *et al.*, 2002].

In comparison, respondents to the survey of South Florida pharmacists, which includes practitioners from all venues, are divided along different classifications (see Tables 5-7 and 5-8). They report the following breakdown of primary pharmacy activity: 65.6 percent dispensing, 18.5 percent clinical, 12.6 percent administrative, and 7.3 percent other. (The total exceeds 100 percent because several practitioners checked more than one entry as their primary activity.) The four smaller counties show a high percentage of dispensing pharmacists and a low proportion of clinical pharmacists, whereas Martin and Pasco portray the opposite. There are relatively more men than women administrators and relatively more women than men clinicians. Some ethnic differences are apparent, too—fewer Non-Hispanic Whites performing clinical activities and fewer Asian Americans doing administrative work compared to pharmacists from the other ethnic groups—but more striking are differences by age group. Clinical work is favored by pharmacists younger than 40 years of age at the expense of administrative responsibilities, while pharmacists 60 years and older concentrate primarily on dispensing medications. Very few older pharmacists do clinical or administrative work.

URBAN-RURAL LOCATION

Assessing the differences in work characteristics of pharmacists who live in rural vis-à-vis urban settings is important because scarcity of healthcare practitioners in rural areas restricts access to health care for the rural population. Rural households usually earn lower income levels than urban households. They also have less access to employment-based health insurance. Both factors further restrict access to healthcare services [Hart *et al.*, 2002; Larson and Hill, 2005; Weeks *et al.*, 2005; West and Weeks, 2006]. Consequently, the smaller demand for rural practitioners tends to reduce their incomes. At least three studies report that rural residence exerts a negative impact on pharmacists' earnings [Carvajal and Hardigan, 2004; Levy, 2008; Meyer and Mukerjee, 2007] as well as the earnings of other healthcare professionals [Weeks and Wallace, 2008], all of which helps explain the paucity of rural healthcare providers in virtually all fields [Lindsay, 2007; Wall and Brown, 2007].

Besides lower earnings, there are other disadvantages associated with working in rural areas, such as having access to less resources and experiencing greater isolation compared to city practitioners [Arnold *et al.*, 1997]. Rural healthcare workers usually have a broader scope of practice and work more hours than their urban peers. Oftentimes they are the only ones providing a specific healthcare service, which translates into characteristically unreasonable schedules and greater difficulties in balancing the personal and professional aspects of their lives [Hart *et al.*, 2002; Incitti *et al.*, 2003; Martin, 2000]. Yet some studies report the opposite, namely, that rural practitioners are more satisfied with office location, safety on the job, job-related travel, and other extrinsic work-related considerations than their urban colleagues [Faubion *et al.*, 2001]. According to Lindsay [2007], while men are attracted by the autonomy that is commonly found in rural practices, women practicing in rural areas enjoy the personable working environment and the respect with which they are treated by colleagues and patients.

Nationwide studies have determined that female healthcare providers exhibit a lower propensity to live and work in small towns and rural areas relative to men [Walton *et al.*, 2004b; Weeks *et al.*, 2007], and the tendency by age group is not clearly apparent [Cline and Mott, 2000; Jacobson *et al.*, 2004b; Wall and Brown, 2007]. A restricted range of alternatives in certain places may force groups with limited mobility (*i.e.*, women, older workers, etc.) to accept employment in a few local, lower-paying establishments, which may give rise to wage disparities for men *versus* women, younger *versus* older, and so on even if other conditions remain the same throughout all groups.

The South Florida pharmacists survey data reveal that the region is heavily urbanized (see Tables 5-9 and 5-10). Only 4.2 percent of respondents say they practice in towns or rural areas. More than half (56.2 percent) practice in a large city setting and the remaining 39.6 percent practice in a suburb or small town. Wide variations are detected across counties. Relatively few pharmacists in the four smaller counties (23.5 percent) and the periphery counties (31.9 percent) report working in a large city, and the fraction who report working in towns or rural areas (8.0 percent and 20.2 percent, respectively) is much greater than in the other counties. Conversely, in Miami-Dade 86.6 percent of respondents indicate that they work in a large city and only 2.1 percent declare working in a town or rural area.

Gender differentials accord with results from national studies—in large cities half the pharmacists (50.0 percent) are women, but in suburbs, small towns, and rural areas women's share drops to 43.7 percent. Ethnic disparities are apparent, too: Less than half (45.4 percent) of Non-Hispanic White practitioners work in large cities, but this category accounts for substantially greater shares of minorities—53.5 percent of Asian Americans, 78.2 percent of Hispanics, and 78.8 percent of Blacks. This is probably due to the fact that ethnic minorities, especially Hispanics, live predominantly in large cities, particularly in Broward and Miami-Dade counties. When gender and ethnic group are combined, however, an interesting pattern emerges—only 34.4 percent of Non-Hispanic White pharmacists working in large cities are women, but there are actually more female than male pharmacists working in large cities within every minority group (60.9 percent Asian Americans, 61.3 percent Blacks, and 69.3 percent Hispanics).

There are also differences by age group. Pharmacists younger than 40 years of age tend to work in large cities more often than in the suburbs, small towns, or the countryside, although the difference is rather tenuous. But when age group and gender are combined, disparities become obvious: Less than three out of every ten (29.1 percent) pharmacists under 40 years of age working in large cities are men, but the proportion goes up dramatically to 78.9 percent for the male pharmacists 60 years and older.

DISTANCE TO WORK AND COMMUTING TIME

Measuring workers' proximity of residence to their job site provides another way of analyzing mobility and possible constraints. The distance a pharmacist travels to and from work, or any job-related site such as a childcare facility, represents real costs in terms of travel time and other expenditures, which condition labor force participation and affect wages, place of employment, and numerous other variables. Distance to work and commuting time may be responsible for all sorts of disparity patterns. For example, if household and childrearing responsibilities forced women to forego better-paying jobs for the sake of working more closely to home, differences in commuting time, workforce attachment, and salary across genders would be a logical consequence of market adjustment. Herbst and Barnow [2008] report that female labor supply is responsive to the geographical distribution of childcare facilities, and Black *et al.* [2007] find that married women's workforce participation rates are much lower in cities in which commuting times are longer, even after controlling for labor market conditions. They also find that women with young children are particularly sensitive to longer commutes. Along these lines, Dickerson [2007] reports that women, in general, are more likely than men to work near home.

Minorities' labor force participation, hours worked, and wages also may be sensitive to commuting distance and time, especially when minorities live in ethnic enclaves. The spatial configuration of Blacks and Hispanics relative to non-minorities in a metropolitan area tends to affect minorities' working extent and outcomes in the context of structural conditions of the local labor market, since the opportunity cost of working is an increasing function of an individual's commute time. Mechanisms associated with residential segregation limit mobility and accessibility to employment opportunities, all of which are central to spatial mismatch analysis [Dickerson, 2007; Herbst and Barnow, 2008].

Pharmacists in South Florida show a broad distribution in terms of proximity to work (see Tables 5-11 and 5-12). About one-fifth (20.4 percent) live within five miles of their job site, one-fourth (24.3 percent) live between five and nine miles, another one-fifth (20.8 percent) live between ten and 14 miles, 12.3 percent live between 15 and 19 miles, and the remaining 22.2 percent travel at least 20 miles to go to work and another 20 miles or more to return to their homes. Pharmacists residing in the four contiguous, smaller counties, a less urbanized area of South Florida, report less travel distance to and from work, and pharmacists in Martin and Pasco engage in longer distances. Men and women exhibit very similar distributions, but, ethnically, Blacks show a greater propensity to travel to work compared to Non-Hispanic Whites, which suggests the existence of residential segregation. Blacks may be traveling to jobs in predominantly Non-Hispanic White areas that pay higher wages and offer better benefit packages. If this is the case, the demand for minority pharmacists elsewhere may be responsible for pulling minority pharmacists out of serving primarily minority populations. Differences by age group are virtually nonexistent. These conclusions are supported by Tables 5-13 and 5-14, which present pharmacists' median travel distance from home to work.

Almost one-quarter (24.4 percent) of South Florida pharmacists spend less than 15 minutes going to work (see Tables 5-15 and 5-16). Another 36.9 percent, the largest single category, spend 15–29 minutes, while 25.6 percent take 30–44 minutes, and the remaining 13.1 percent report spending three-quarters of an hour or more getting to work. Probably due to travel congestion, Broward and Miami-Dade pharmacists spend more time going from home to work than practitioners residing in the other counties. Men devote slightly more time on their way to work than women, while Blacks' time spent going to work is longer, and Asian Americans' is less, compared to Non-Hispanic Whites and Hispanics. Older pharmacists (60 years of age or older) seem willing to spend more time traveling to work than younger pharmacists (younger than 40 years of age). Tables 5-17 and 5-18 indicate that overall practitioners' median one-way commute time is 20 minutes, which is very similar to the average commute to work of 22 minutes reported by Cardinale [2005] for the entire nation. The 20-minute commute median applies to both men and women; all ethnic groups except Blacks; and virtually all age groups.

LABOR SUPPLY

The individual supply of labor, often measured by the number of hours worked per period of time, is a variable of great concern in pharmacy and other healthcare fields that experience a shortage of practitioners [Buerhaus *et al.*, 2006; Cline and Mott, 2000; Johnson, 2008; Kahaleh and Gaither, 2005; Knapp and Livesey, 2002; Smith *et al.*, 2007; Walton *et al.*, 2004b; Weeks and Wallace, 2007b]. It is conditioned by workers' background, demographic characteristics, skills, perceptions, and attitudes, all of which are influenced by socioeconomic and institutional constraints. If different factors (*i.e.*, gender, ethnic identification, or age) motivate different groups of workers to trade off work and leisure, as human-capital theorists propose, heterogeneous labor supply formulations, with different explanatory variables, would apply to the different groups [Brusentsev, 2006; Gabriel and Schmitz, 2007]. In spite of the importance of this topic for the pharmacy profession, surprisingly few studies have attempted to analyze the issue, and they have focused primarily, if not exclusively, on gender [Carvajal and Hardigan, 2007; Mott, 2001].

Kenreigh and Wagner [2006] have identified several factors contributing to the pharmacist shortage. They include unprecedented increases in the volume of prescriptions; a relative growth in the population 65 years or older, which uses a disproportionately high percentage of prescription as well as non-prescription drugs; greater administrative requirements for handling third-party payments, which consume up to 20 percent of pharmacists' time; and not enough pharmacy schools in the nation to keep up with increases in the demand for pharmacists' services. Mahrous and Maziarz [2008] also point to the rise in prescription volume as the main reason for the workforce shortage, together with the long-term expansion of the economy, the development of new drugs, direct-to-consumer marketing, and an increasing number of refills. They warn that a heavier workload of prescriptions dispensed per pharmacist may lead to a rise in the occurrence of medication errors, longer working hours, and decreased quality of life for practitioners, as well as a reduction in patient safety and in the number of opportunities for pharmacists to interact with patients and perform medication management activities.

As a point of reference in another healthcare profession experiencing a practitioner shortage, registered nurses attribute their own lack of professionals to inadequate salaries and benefits, growing career options for women, undesirable working hours, and a negative work environment [Buerhaus, 2006]. Their recommendations for recruitment and retention strategies include providing tuition benefits, offering signing bonuses, allowing for flexible work schedules, and increasing current salaries. Employing foreign nurse graduates is perceived generally as an ineffective strategy by most nurses.

Conventional economic theory dictates that when quantity of labor supplied falls short of quantity of labor demanded, a rise in the wage rate should restore equilibrium. In other words, a labor shortage in the long run exists only when wages are inadequate and inflexible. In a recent article, however, Carvajal and Hardigan [2007] have found evidence of a backward-bending labor supply curve for pharmacists, whereby the income effect is stronger than the substitution effect. As their wage rate rises, and it is clear that pharmacists' wages have been rising [Levy, 2008; Mahrous and Maziarz, 2008; Walton *et al.*, 2007], pharmacists seem to respond by working fewer hours and still meet whatever target incomes that establish or maintain their earnings-leisure equilibrium. The backward-bending effect applies to both genders, although it seems to be stronger for women than it is for men. Thus, increases in the wage rate resulting from market forces are not likely to alleviate the shortage; if they affect it at all, they are likely to make it worse.

Another factor which may aggravate the pharmacist shortage is that over two-thirds of pharmacy school graduates are women, and women in general tend to work fewer hours, leave the workforce more often, and for longer periods of time, than men [Cline, 2003; Keaveny *et al.*, 2007; Kenreigh and Wagner, 2006; Sousa-Poza and Sousa-Poza, 2000a; Walton *et al.*, 2004b; Weeks and Wallace, 2007c]. This trend also is going on in other areas of health care, especially medicine. Jacobson *et al.* [2004a, p. 191] have formulated the following powerful statement regarding this trend: "If indeed women continue to enter the field of medicine in such a high proportion and continue to work fewer hours per week than men, the United States may soon have to adjust its physician workforce pool accordingly, a shift that becomes especially relevant for specialties in which women dominate." Queneau [2006] attributes the increasing feminization of the pharmacist workforce to a trend whereby pharmacies are increasingly managed by large corporations rather than by independent businesses. He claims that, historically, independent pharmacies have attracted more men than women because chain pharmacies experience more pressure to increase the representation of women and minorities in compliance with equal employment opportunity ordinances and regulations.

Searching for deeper insights into the nature of gender disparities in situation and opinion variables, Carvajal and Hardigan [2008] set an experiment to control for number of hours worked. They question whether male and female pharmacists' career- and workplace-oriented perceptions and behavior are more consistent with persons of the same gender committed to work more (in the case of women) or fewer (in the case of men) hours or they show more affinity with people exhibiting similar work input regardless of gender. They conclude that, regardless of work input, male and female pharmacists exhibit different behavior characteristics. McElwain *et al.* [2005] and Voydanoff [1988] complement this finding when they state that, because of the traditional gender-based division of labor, women are more likely to experience family demands intruding on their work life and men tend to have work demands interfering with the family aspects of their lives.

At least part of the reason why women generally work fewer hours, and exhibit less labor force attachment, than men may be attributed to the presence of children, especially younger children, in the household. Childbearing and childrearing, along with the housework they entail, are labor-intensive activities [Aanerud *et al.*, 2007]. Before children arrive, adult household members are able to supply ample labor without sacrificing much leisure. But the advent of preschool children changes drastically the household's pattern of time use, which is reflected in the time choices of its members—women who become parents work fewer hours or drop out of the labor force altogether, albeit temporarily, to devote more time to their newly acquired household and childrearing responsibilities, whereas men with children experience an increase in their marketwork hours compared with their childless counterparts, most likely to increase income to defray the additional expenditures brought about by children being added to the household [Apps and Rees, 2005; Blasius and Pae, 2005; Burda *et al.*, 2007; Jacobson *et al.*, 2004a]. In the final analysis, reducing one's marketwork hours may help alleviate work-family conflict, but it also may lead to financial problems. This generalization, however, is subject to the influence of perceptions and attitudes, such as those related to couples' housework allocation patterns. Women who hold more egalitarian attitudes toward gendered family roles and whose husbands are willing to assume a greater share of unpaid housework are more prone to work, and work more hours, relative to women with less egalitarian attitudes [Corrigall and Konrad, 2007; Cunningham, 2008].

Female labor supply often is viewed as the margin of adjustment in household responses to key policy changes (*i.e.*, taxation of household income or welfare entitlement programs), as well as events which affect the composition and/or functioning of the household, for example, having a child, suffering an illness, or caregiving [Black *et al.*, 2007]. In today's workforce fewer than 10 percent of employees are part of a traditional household in which the male partner is the sole provider [Rose, 1998]. The much needed two-income standard usually requires flexible work arrangements so that family demands may be accommodated when both parents work in the labor market. Women who live in households with sources of income other than their own work tend to respond by working fewer hours when an external shock occurs [Hotchkiss, 2005; Mitra and Singh, 2006; Mosisa and Hipple, 2006]. Similarly, married women's labor supply decreases whenever married women suffer an illness and they are covered by their husband's health insurance policy. Recently Bradley *et al.* [2005] have concluded that a health shock, such as the diagnosis of breast cancer, leads to much greater declines in the labor supply of women insured by their spouse's health policy than the labor supply of women with health insurance through their employer. And Lilly *et al.* [2007] find a strong, inverse relationship between intensity of caregiving and number of hours worked, particularly for women.

The effect of ethnic identity on labor supply seems to be conditioned by gender. Read and Cohen [2007] cite U.S. Census figures which indicate that Non-Hispanic White and Black women participate in the labor force more often than Hispanic women. In general, women and minorities experience conflicting demands on their time at greater levels than those experienced by their non-minority male peers [Gormley, 2003; Hagedorn and Sax, 2003; Turner, 2002]. Smith *et al.* [2007] find that in nursing, a profession dominated by women, Blacks show more employment stability than their Non-Hispanic White colleagues. Tebaldi and Elmslie [2006] report that, compared to Black women, Non-Hispanic White women exhibit less workforce attachment and supply less market labor, but Black men are less likely to be in the labor force, and supply less labor, than Non-Hispanic White men. Antecol and Bedard [2002] also find that Black and Mexican American men have less attachment to the labor force when compared to non-minority men. Specifically for pharmacists, Carvajal and Hardigan [2007] find no difference in the number of hours worked between minority and non-minority men, while, on average, African American and Hispanic women work 13.7 percent more hours relative to Non-Hispanic White women.

Age also is responsible for labor supply differentials, and its effect is independent of neither gender nor ethnicity. Carvajal and Hardigan [2007] point toward male pharmacists experiencing a progressively shorter workweek as they approach retirement, while female pharmacists express an increasing commitment to work later in life, after demands from childrearing ease off, a trend which is confirmed by the findings of Andrén [2003] and Gonzalez [2004]. In medicine, Cull *et al.* [2002], Dorsey *et al.* [2003], and Jacobson *et al.* [2004b] indicate that, compared to their elders, the younger generation of physicians has different lifestyle needs and practice styles, including a desire to work fewer hours. And from a broader perspective, Nguyen [2008] contends that the prospects for replacing retiring workers with younger persons possessing the same or more skills are not promising. He argues that there are not enough native-born Americans interested in, and qualified to, meet rising labor demands, and the lack of younger, skilled replacements will force employers to hire immigrants to fill the gap. In short, increases in the availability of both women and minorities, as well as the aging of baby boomers, have changed and will continue to change the profile of the U.S. workforce. Within a few decades, Non-Hispanic Whites will no longer be dominant, at least in numbers. The future U.S. labor force will not resemble the labor force of the past: it will not think, act, hold the same values, share the same experiences, pursue the same activities, or attempt to satisfy the same needs and wants, including number of hours worked [DiCecio *et al.*, 2008].

From a broader perspective, Reynolds [2003] points out that approximately 60 percent of all employees in the U.S. prefer to work a different number of hours than they actually work—some want to work more, others want to work less. He suggests that the concepts of "overwork" and "underwork" are not so much about actual work hours, an objective indicator, as they are about the mismatch between actual and preferred work hours, which is a subjective indicator. Since preferred hours are a function of personal characteristics, some of which may change over the long run, and actual hours depend largely on job demands, workers with different personal characteristics and different types of jobs may feel overworked or underworked at various points along the measurement of work hours. Mismatches often arise because employers and employees exhibit conflicting preferences in work hours [Jacobs and Gerson, 2000].

According to the survey, most pharmacists (54.4 percent) in South Florida work an average of 40–44 hours per week (see Tables 5-19 and 5-20). Less than one-fifth (18.7 percent) work 45 hours or more, 12.6 percent work 30–39 hours, 7.9 percent work 20–29 hours, and 6.4 percent work less than 20 hours. There are no appreciable differences among counties in work hour patterns and no clear indication that women work consistently fewer hours than do men, although proportionately more men than women work at least 45 hours per week. Ethnic differences, however, are apparent: Compared to Non-Hispanic White pharmacists, Black, Asian American, and Hispanic pharmacists work more hours. Also of interest are age differences in the number of hours worked, as the work effort of both men and women seems to decline with age.

Tables 5-21 and 5-22 show the median number of hours worked per week. The universal median is 40 hours, which reveals that the number of respondents with this work effort is so massive that, regardless of the values above or below it, the median is the same for all counties, both genders, all ethnic groups, and all age groups except 70 years of age or older. In comparison, Levy [2008] reports that pharmacists who responded to the *Drug Topics* survey logged an average (not median) value of 44.1 hours per week, higher than the 40.9 hours reported in 2006 and the 41.8 hours reported several years before by Walton and Cooksey [2001]. According to them, at that time men practitioners outworked women practitioners 44.1 hours to 37.2 hours per week.

PART-TIME WORK

The part-time work issue is a by-product of labor supply, but since it possesses its own characteristics and arguments, it deserves separate treatment. In pharmacy, as in many other occupations in the United States, part-time employment constitutes a growing share of the market [Teeter, 2004]. Workers may work part time to earn additional income in a secondary job, to acquire or sharpen skills that may not be required or commonly used in their primary or full-time employment, because of limited labor demand, or because their opportunity cost is so high that working a limited number of hours is enough to optimize their labor-leisure equilibrium. The focus of this section is on the last motive.

Oftentimes part-time workers are individuals who are transiting into retirement or who have family responsibilities. These family responsibilities force household members, usually women, to choose between buying goods and services from the market sector or producing them at home. In fact, several studies show higher rates of part-time employment by female than male pharmacists [Quiñones and Mason, 2000; Walton and Cooksay, 2001]. Part-time jobs provide workers with a means of attaining the optimal tradeoff between domestic and market production while maintaining, or even adding to, their human-capital stock in the form of experience for the future. They also provide a means to gain esteem from others through working while, at the same time, obtain self-esteem and social acceptance from caring for their families and their homes [Booth and van Ours, 2007]. Thus, it is not surprising to learn that, in general, part-time work increases satisfaction with work-family balance [Saltzstein *et al.*, 2001], and specifically pharmacists who work part time tend to experience lower levels of role conflict, role overload, job stress, and work-home conflict relative to pharmacists working full time [Mott *et al.*, 2004].

The part-time work issue is not unique to pharmacy. It also affects other healthcare professions. For instance, Cull *et al.* [2002] report a clear relationship between gender and part-time employment among practicing pediatricians and pediatric residents—women are more likely than men to work part time and use the extra time to care for their children. Jacobson *et al.* [2004a] arrive at similar findings using a sample of dermatology residents and Yutzie *et al.* [2005] conclude that relatively more female than male graduates of a general surgery residency program work part time, as women are driven to work less because of personal and family demands.

Teeter [2004] identifies several concerns common to pharmacists working part time. Some of the concerns are whether or not the part-time worker is expected to sign a contract for a specific period of time; whether he/she may work for a competitor while under contract; whether or not benefits, and what kind of benefits, are available; whether benefits, if available, may be refused and renegotiated for a higher wage rate; what the employer's expectations are for on-call service; and whether the worker may request not to be contacted during certain times.

If part-time employment is defined as working less than 30 hours per week, then 14.3 percent of South Florida pharmacists work part time (see Tables 5-19 and 5-20), slightly less than the 17.2 percent reported by Mott *et al.* [2004] and the 16.8 percent reported by Walton and Cooksey [2001]. (According to the Census Bureau, 17 percent of all U.S. workers worked under 35 hours per week in 2007.) Unlike similar national surveys, however, the incidence of part-time work is virtually the same for male and female pharmacists. (In fact, the rate for women, 13.8 percent, is surpassed by the 14.6 percent rate for men.) As a point of comparison, the gender disparity in part-time employment found by Walton and Cooksey [2001] is 11.4 percent for men and 27.9 percent for women. The absence of such disparity in South Florida may be explained by the fact that many older pharmacists, predominantly male, who have delayed retirement, opt for part-time work instead, and the large number of minority practitioners, most of them women, who choose to work full time. Palm Beach, with a heavy concentration of older pharmacists, exhibits a high percentage of part-time workers, whereas the four smaller counties show the lowest incidence of part-time employment in the region.

Indeed part-time employment is an option chosen by relatively few minority pharmacists—only 3.4 percent of Blacks, 8.1 percent of Asian Americans, and 12.4 percent of Hispanics work part time, compared with 17.3 percent of Non-Hispanic Whites. A closer analysis of the survey data reveals that ethnic variation is mediated by gender. If pharmacists from the three minority groups are pooled, their part-time female fraction (12.8 percent) is not much lower than the incidence of Non-Hispanic White women (15.5 percent), but the minority male proportion of part-time workers (3.9 percent) is well below the proportion of Non-Hispanic White men (18.4 percent).

When the effect of age is considered, one realizes that the fraction of part-time practitioners remains relatively low, about 8 percent, and does not change much, among groups below 60 years of age. But more than one out of every three (34.2 percent) pharmacists 60 years or older indicate that they are working under 30 hours per week. Gender exerts a strong influence here, too. Only ten male pharmacists under 60 years of age report working part time, which amounts to 2.1 percent, while the fraction of women pharmacists in the same age range is 12.2 percent. When one focuses on pharmacists 60 years of age or older, however, the incidence of part-time work is virtually identical for both genders.

PHARMACY EARNINGS

Wages and salaries are the ultimate indicator of success for the American worker. Of all the rewards offered by employers in return for their employees' contributions toward attaining organizational goals and objectives, pay is the critical variable used as an incentive for performance and retention of worthwhile workers [Gardner *et al.*, 2004; Heneman and Judge, 2000; Milkovich and Newman, 2004; Vandenberghe and Tremblay, 2008]. A relatively high income earned within a given profession or trade communicates to the world that a worker is capable of coping with the pressures of the labor market, as well as surmounting the many obstacles posed by peers, employers, clients, and a wide array of individuals and institutions interacting with one another in complex ways. So it is not surprising that this is one of the most, if not the most, sensitive variable discussed in this book.

Wages and salaries are determined by the interaction of three sets of forces: Human-capital stock, individual preferences, and employers' characteristics. All three sets are influenced by gender, ethnicity, and age. Therefore, it follows that wages and salaries for different workers are largely a direct or indirect product of gender, ethnic, and age variations. When one is confronted with the irrefutable evidence that women; ethnic minorities; and, to a lesser extent, younger, and sometimes older, persons earn consistently lower incomes than middle-aged, Non-Hispanic White men [Antecol and Bedard, 2002; Blau and Khan, 2006; Bradbury, 2002; Bryan and Sevilla Sanz, 2007; Carvajal, 2006; Fry and Lowell, 2006; Gardner and Stowe, 2007; Graham and Smith, 2005; Green *et al.*, 2007; Hersch, 2006; LoBuono, 2003; McMurray *et al.*, 2000; Srinivas, 2007; Weinberg, 2007], the underlying reasons for such differentials ought to be searched in one or more of these three sets of forces.

Variations in human-capital stock perhaps are the most frequently used line of reasoning towards explaining differences in pay among groups of workers. Skills acquired through formal education, experience, and other forms of investment are postulated to generate a stock of capital that increases workers' productivity and becomes appealing to employers. The value of human-capital stock depends on the price placed by the labor market in a given place and at a given time on these skills. As individuals sell their bundles of skills to employers at an equilibrium market price per unit of skill, their wages and salaries depend partly on the nature, quantity, and quality of skills possessed as well as the returns commanded by the skill vector within a given specialty. Wu [2007] argues that male-female income differences can be attributed primarily to gender differences in the marginal costs of human-capital production. He suggests that since men generally spend more time in the labor market and consequently gain more experience than women, they face lower marginal costs in the human-capital production process that are conducive to more human-capital accumulation and relatively greater income levels in the long run.

Insofar as men and women play different social roles and are subject to different social pressures, they vary in their distribution of personality traits, as well as their acquisition of skills and communication techniques, which give rise to disparities in employment patterns [Costa *et al.*, 2001]. In two different studies, Mueller and Plug [2006] and Semykina and Linz [2006] report that women who develop personality traits commonly found in men tend to earn higher incomes than the rest of women. Ichino and Moretti [2006] attribute part of the gender wage gap to the menstrual cycle, which they claim raises female absenteeism and detracts from women's human-capital stock.

More conventional arguments point to women's tendency to experience career interruptions more often than men [Aanerud *et al.*, 2007; Blau *et al.*, 2002; Keaveny *et al.*, 2007], which leads to findings that women suffer considerably larger wage losses attributed to marriage, children, and migration than men [Napari, 2006; Shauman and Noonan, 2007]. Whatever the nature of the human-capital disparity, there is evidence that when human capital and other variables are controlled, workers of both genders tend to exhibit approximately equal wage-and-salary outcomes [Carvajal and Hardigan, 2004; Keavenry *et al.*, 2007; Reyes, 2007].

A variation of the human-capital version is explored by Mueller and Plug [2006]. Personality, like human-capital stock, is inherent to the individual and not subject to change in the short run. They find that the five basic personality traits—extroversion *vs.* introversion, agreeableness *vs.* antagonism, conscientiousness *vs.* lack of direction, neuroticism *vs.* emotional stability, and openness *vs.* closedness to experience—have substantial, either positive or negative, earnings effects comparable to those commonly reported for cognitive ability. They also report gender differences: Major earnings advantages for men are associated with antagonism, emotional stability, and openness to experience, whereas for women earnings advantages are associated with conscientiousness and openness to experience. Semykina and Linz [2006] also find substantial gender differences in personality traits and their effect on earnings. According to them, men are more likely to exhibit an internal locus of control and need for challenge, while women are more prone to exhibit an external locus of control and need for affiliation. Women's earnings are strongly influenced by personality, while the effect of personality on earnings in men is small and not always statistically significant. An interesting research initiative would be to ascertain whether men and women exhibiting these traits tend to invest in their human-capital stock more frequently than do other men and women.

A portion of ethnic disparities in wages and salaries also may be attributed to differences in human-capital stock. Schooling and immigration status seem very relevant in explaining earnings differences between non-minorities and minorities, especially foreign-born Hispanics and Asian Americans, many of whom arrive in the U.S. with lower valued skills (*i.e.*, little U.S. education and training supplementing the formal education acquired abroad) as well as poor command of the English language [Akresh, 2006; Orrenius and Zavodny, 2007]. (As a point of reference, Fry and Lowell [2006] report that over 55 percent of the Hispanic labor force in the United States is foreign born.) O'Neill and O'Neill [2005] conclude that most wage-and-salary disparities between minorities and non-minorities are due to differences in the quantity and quality of the human-capital stock they bring into the labor market, while others, like Akresh [2007] and Mason [2004], show that recent immigrants' earnings rise rapidly when they become acculturated into the mainstream.

Age also is subject to the influence of human capital. As individuals grow older, they tend to acquire more skills, experience, and other human capital endowments. Thus, their earnings normally increase at a decreasing rate [Strayhorn, 2008; Zhang, 2005]. Specifically for pharmacists,

Carvajal and Hardigan [2004] find that the age-earnings relationship, approximated by years of experience, is mediated by gender. Their empirical results reveal a compression problem in wages for male pharmacists, probably resulting from the shortage of practitioners in many areas. The wages of older pharmacists, who are predominantly men, do not seem to keep pace with the wages at which younger practitioners, with less experience, are hired.

In addition to differences in skills, workers exhibit work-related tastes and preferences which may act as compensation differentials. Many of these tastes and preferences are shaped at the household level within a cultural context, and pertain to monetary and non-monetary characteristics of alternative job opportunities perceived as advantages or disadvantages by different groups of workers. They include factors such as benefits, job location and activities, proximity to worksite, work hours, fairness in the workplace, scheduling flexibility, stress, chances for advancement, and many others that tend to enhance or depreciate a job opening. Employment opportunities with characteristics regarded by most workers as disadvantages normally pay more than opportunities with advantages. In a mobile market, individuals choose among different job openings, based on wages and salaries plus net advantages. Thus, wage-and-salary differentials are likely to persist between homogeneous types of labor as they tend to equalize the net advantages of alternative employment opportunities. Economics does not posit that worker mobility equalizes wages; rather it asserts a tendency toward equalizing the net advantages of job opportunities available when workers are free to choose among them.

Advantages and disadvantages may be interpreted differently by different groups of people. For instance, men consider earnings and responsibility to be more important than women, while women consider good coworkers and supervisors, as well as the significance of the tasks they perform, to be more important than do men [Bradford *et al.*, 2001; Konrad *et al.*, 2000a; Tanner *et al.*, 1999]. Along these lines, Cooper and Lewis [1999] find that women equate success with developing expertise rather than climbing the organizational ladder, which is most men's view. Compared to men, women generally hold different work and family values and interests, which lead them to select specialties and jobs that facilitate, or at least are compatible with, work-family balance. Their costs and benefits of paid labor relative to other pursuits, such as household work and leisure, motivates them to choose jobs with shorter commutes, flexible schedules, and more harmonious organizational climates, while men have a propensity to engage in jobs that offer the opportunity to work overtime and upward mobility to management positions in stressful environments like chain pharmacy settings [Hersch, 2006; Hundley, 2001b; Jovic *et al.*, 2006; Mott, 2001; O'Halloran, 2003; O'Neill and O'Neill, 2005; Pettit and Hook, 2005]. Tanner *et al.* [1999] contend that the main reason why women in pharmacy earn less than men is that they have a greater propensity to remain as employees throughout their careers. Moreover, women are more willing than men to trade off income for the characteristics that they value relatively more within a given job [Bender *et al.*, 2005]. To the extent that these conditions hold true, salary-and-wage disparities arise because of differences in preferences regarding working conditions.

Compensation differentials also give rise to ethnic disparities in earnings [Levy, 2006; O'Halloran, 2003]. Compared with Non-Hispanic Whites, Blacks and Hispanics experience higher rates of workplace fatalities and injuries, and normally receive a compensation for the additional risk incurred [Leeth and Ruser, 2003; Viscusi, 2003]. A similar case may be hypothesized for individuals who work in sites located in dangerous neighborhoods, such as high crime or heavy drug-use areas. Each worker must decide if the additional wage premium on a relatively high-risk job is enough to offset the greater likelihood of injury or exposure to danger. Economic efficiency implies that, at or close to equilibrium, persons less concerned with safety end up earning relatively higher incomes while working in more perilous establishments, although the distribution of job risks across ethnic groups would be viewed as even more inequitable than it is if Blacks and Hispanics end up receiving a lower premium than Non-Hispanic Whites for accepting employment in hazardous workplaces.

The third set of forces configuring salary-and-wage levels has to do with the so called gender stratification theory, which negates the basic tenet of drive toward equality in equilibrium inherent in the human-capital approach. It focuses on employers' characteristics and identifies constraints and obstacles that impede advancement at work by women, minorities, and younger or older workers. It is based on the notion that workers' earnings depend on institutional factors rather than market forces. These factors may include seniority; collective bargaining; and others such as gender, ethnicity, and age over which the worker has no control. Whenever equally qualified individuals (*i.e.*, education, skills, labor force attachment, etc.) in a profession or trade are treated unequally on account of their gender, ethnic identification, age, or for that matter other characteristics not addressed in this book (*i.e.*, sexual orientation, religious affiliation, etc.), discrimination occurs. Thus, discrimination in the context of this discussion erects non-market, institutional barriers which hinder the hiring, retention, and advancement of specific groups of people [Ezeala-Harrison, no date; Meyer and Mukerjee, 2007; National Academy of Sciences *et al.*, 2007; Tenner *et al.*, 1999]. Oftentimes women, ethnic minorities, and younger or older individuals discover in their work life that economic achievements do not always erase gender, ethnic, or age boundaries that constrain their opportunities.

The subtleties of employers' exclusionary practices, illegal in the United States, frequently disguise them in such a way that it is difficult to detect or prevent them. Exclusionary practices cover stereotypical assumptions about women's and minorities' ability and/or willingness to perform certain jobs, their moral character and/or customs, and various forms of sexual or cultural harassment, which make women and minorities the object of social isolation, bias, and hostility in an unwelcoming environment. Cleveland *et al.* [2000] contend that stereotypes tend to magnify perceived gender differences in the workplace. They examine several cultures and find men universally described as aggressive, strong, rational, and realistic, all characteristics leading to competence, whereas women are viewed as affectionate, charming, emotional, and submissive, all of which are equated with a non-professional, less credible attitude; yet, women who portray the predominantly "male" traits tend to be perceived as bossy or pushy, thus creating a double standard [Murphy and Zorn, 1995; Price and Wulff, 2005]. Mueller and Plug [2006] report that, on average, men are substantially more antagonistic (non-agreeable) than are women, and men alone are rewarded for this trait.

Women and members of minority groups experience exclusionary practices when they encounter inflexible work hours, inadequate childcare provisions, insensitive comments and remarks, and generally unaccommodating employers whose stressors make jobs less attractive for them or, if already employed, dissuade them from staying in their jobs. Even when they meet the Non-Hispanic White male job-performance standard, many women and minorities are not rewarded as generously in terms of wages and salaries or promotion to management/supervisory positions, so gender and ethnic parity are more illusory than genuine. Moreover, minority-group women frequently are subject to dual discrimination—as women and as minorities—thus facing even more barriers to success [Belknap, 2001; Bradbury, 2002; Dickerson, 2006; Luce and Brenner, 2006; National Academy of Sciences *et al.*, 2007; Pogrebin *et al.*, 2000]. They are neither male nor Non-Hispanic White; thus, they have little in common with people on top of the workplace hierarchy, which limits their ability to build influence and advance within their organization [Griffin *et al.*, 2005].

Relevant to the analysis of institutional factors and discrimination is the concept of market segmentation, which refers to the stratification of labor markets into layers or segments maintained by institutional barriers keeping the layers apart. One of the layers, called the primary sector, is characterized by relatively high wages and salaries, handsome returns to human-capital investment, stable employment, and desirable overall working conditions. The other layer, called the secondary sector, lacks these attributes, so different salary-and-wage setting mechanisms apply to both segments. Rationing is crucial in this theoretical context for workers of the secondary sector cannot work in the primary sector due to their gender, ethnicity, age, or any other such characteristic. Thus, workers do not choose the secondary sector because it possesses characteristics palatable to certain groups of individuals; rather these groups are thrown into the secondary sector because of institutional constraints that prevent them from acceding to primary-sector employment. Taking the argument to another dimension, Llorens *et al.* [2008] point out that women and minorities frequently are driven into the public sector, where equity is monitored closely, by the relatively lower wages they earn in the private sector.

Market segmentation often is responsible for job segregation. Although originally job segregation was used in an inter-occupational sense, the concept retains its meaning when applied to different specialties, practice sites, etc. within a profession or trade. It often influences adversely the salaries and wages of women, African Americans, and Hispanics [Catanzarite, 2003]. Kmec [2003] shows that workers employed in predominantly Black jobs earn substantially less income than workers employed in comparable but predominantly White jobs. Perhaps the main danger of gender and ethnic segregation is that they tend to perpetuate themselves by reinforcing gender and ethnic stereotypes, which hamper the educational and training opportunities of women and minorities, thus constraining their career aspirations and future professional attainment [Correll, 2001; Hellerstein *et al.*, 2007; Queneau, 2006].

Nguyen *et al.* [2005] argue that gender and ethnic socioeconomic differentials are transmitted from one generation to the next. Although intergenerational income mobility is estimated to be high for both men and women, their estimated income elasticities suggest that income mobility is lower for women than for men, and this finding applies to all major ethnic groups. Hispanics may appear to be more educationally and occupationally mobile compared to Non-Hispanic Whites, but the main reason for this appearance is that they are far more likely than their parents to obtain a high-school diploma. Hispanics still lag behind non-minorities in terms of education and occupation, and Blacks lie in between. Furthermore, although inequality is associated with recent increases in poverty within all ethnic groups, it seems to have the greatest effect on Hispanics. This association, however, may be due to the concentration of Hispanics in low-skill occupations and rapid growth in the immigration of Hispanics with few skills [Iceland, 2003]. In the final analysis, the transmission of educational attainment from parent to child is much weaker for Blacks and Hispanics than it is for non-minorities.

The literature is replete with studies pointing to the effects of gender discrimination [Allen *et al.*, 2006; Blau and DeVaro, 2007; Bradbury,

2002; Kee, 2006; Leggon, 2006; Leung, 2006; Levy, 2006; Long, 2005; Luce and Brenner, 2006; National Academy of Sciences *et al.*, 2007; Tanner *et al.*, 1999; Wallace and Weeks, 2002; Weinberg, 2007] and ethnic discrimination [Altonji *et al.*, 2000; Antecol and Bedard, 2002; Carvajal, 2004; Dickerson, 2007; Hellerstein and Neumark, 2005; Lang and Manove, 2006; Strayhorn, 2008; Viscusi, 2003] in explaining income and employment disparities beyond the market forces of human-capital accumulation and workers' preferences. Chong and Kim [2006] clearly point out that African Americans have suffered the indignities of discrimination to a greater extent than other groups, although women, Hispanics, and Asian Americans also have been subjected to bias, intolerance, and rejection in many ways.

Transcending the tenets of the traditional dual labor market theory, Hudson [2007] suggests that as the practice of allocating workers to inferior jobs on the basis of gender and ethnic identity has declined because of legal sanctions and institutional pressures, employers have turned to non-standard work arrangements and immigrants to supply labor for lower-wage jobs. This may apply across the job spectrum or within a specific trade or profession. Not only are non-standard jobs more prone to pay lower wages, but they also are less likely to provide health insurance, pensions, and other benefits [Hudson, 2001; Kalleberg *et al.*, 2000]. Recent immigrants, frequently lacking access to information networks, provide ample opportunity for job stratification [Hondagneu-Sotelo, 2001].

In spite of the anonymous nature of the survey, one out of every ten practitioners (10.5 percent) in South Florida refrains from disclosing his/her annual income earned as a pharmacist (see Tables 5-23 and 5-24). This refusal evinces the sensitive and confidential nature in which this information is perceived by respondents. Of those who respond, 14.4 percent indicate that they earn under $70,000; a quarter (24.7 percent) earn $70,000–99,999; 43.0 percent earn $100,000–119,999; and 17.9 percent earn $120,000 or more. The only appreciable difference among counties is that pharmacists in Palm Beach earn lower income levels, probably because of the greater prevalence of part-time employment. Gender disparities are apparent, as more women than men report earning under $100,000 per year and men outnumber women over two to one in the $120,000 plus bracket.

Ethnic disparities can be discerned, too. Non-Hispanic Whites and Hispanics show greater concentrations than Blacks and Asian Americans in the lowest and highest wage-and-salary income brackets, while Blacks and Asian Americans abound more in the middle income ($70,000–119,999) brackets, largely influenced by their low incidence of part-time work. And when gender and ethnic classifications are combined, one may observe that minority women's earnings lag behind the earnings of minority men to a much greater extent than Non-Hispanic White women's earnings fall behind the earnings of their Non-Hispanic White male counterparts—much greater representation in the less-than-$100,000 category and lower proportional representation in the $120,000 plus income group vis-à-vis men. This is the opposite of the findings for the whole U.S. population reported by Bayard *et al.* [1999].

The percentage of pharmacists unwilling to provide information on their wages and salaries increases with age. Younger practitioners are not as apprehensive as are their seniors regarding this matter. The distribution is consistent with the classical inverted-U shape effect of age on income, with over one-third (35.5 percent) of pharmacists 60 years and older earning under $70,000, probably because of a widespread part-time practice. Gender-age interaction outcomes are noticeable as well. The gender disparity—proportionately many more women than men in the lower income brackets and more men than women in the upper income brackets—is stronger for pharmacists under 60 years old than it is for those 60 years or older.

The distribution of median annual incomes by gender, ethnic group, and age group, shown in Tables 5-25 and 5-26, confirms the relationships identified above. According to these tables, the median annual wage-and-salary income for South Florida pharmacists is $100,000, which is below the $107,143 average salary reported by Levy [2008]. There is no gender median income gap within Non-Hispanic Whites, but a substantial one exists for all three minority groups, especially Hispanics. The inverted-U age-income relationship emerges clearly, with older pharmacists exhibiting much lower median income levels. Within every age group, the men's median income level exceeds the women's median income level.

WAGE RATE

In a market where resources are mobile, the "prevailing" wage rate in a profession or trade is determined by the interplay of the supply of and demand for labor in a given location and at a given time. This is the wage rate that workers consider in making their marketwork/house-work/leisure decisions and that employers attempt to equate to their marginal revenue product in their quest for profit optimization subject to institutional and social constraints. Workers leave their jobs because they find other employers willing and able to reward their skills and effort with a better wage rate, and employers fire workers because they do not add enough value to production in relation to what they are paid [Sørensen, 2007]. The wage rate is a variable that lends itself better to measuring the intricacies of disparities and diversity than does wage-and-salary income. While wages and salaries include the distracting effects of volume of labor input (*i.e.*, other things equal, at a specific wage rate, a worker who puts in twice as many hours as another worker will earn twice the amount in wages), the wage rate captures the worth per unit of time of a given worker in a given position relative to all other workers in all other positions.

Tables 5-27 and 5-28 present the distribution of South Florida pharmacists in the survey by hourly wage-rate bracket. Like wages and salaries, this indicator provides information that many practitioners (12.0 percent) prefer not to reveal. Only 2.4 percent of respondents who report their wage rate earn under $40 per hour. About half (49.0 percent) respond that they earn $40 or more but less than $50, another 43.8 percent earn $50 or more but less than $60, and the remaining 4.8 percent earn an hourly wage rate of $60 or more. Pharmacists' wage rates generally are higher in Collier, Hendry, Lee, and Monroe taken together and lower in Palm Beach and for pharmacists living outside South Florida. Judging by the relative concentration of male and female pharmacists in the various brackets, men earn slightly higher wage rates than do women. Blacks and Asian Americans earn lower wage rates than Non-Hispanic Whites, with Hispanics ranking in between. Here, too gender-ethnicity interaction occurs. The female wage rates of Non-Hispanic Whites are somewhat higher than those of male Non-Hispanic Whites, but within each of the three minority groups, the male wage rates tend to be higher than the female wage rates.

As with wage-and-salary income, non-disclosure of the wage rate increases with age. The concentration in the various wage-rate brackets suggests an inverted-U shape curve as well. The wage rate increases with age, reaching a peak in the 40–59 age range, and then declines. The gender gap is present throughout the entire age spectrum—it subsides from younger (less than 40 years) to middle-aged (40–59 years) groups as women leave behind their childbearing and childrearing years, but becomes more noticeable with older (60 years plus) pharmacists.

The distribution of median hourly wage rates by gender, ethnic group, and age group (see Tables 5-29 and 5-30) supports these generalizations. The overall male wage rate ($49.50) exceeds the female wage rate ($49.00) by a small margin. The wage-rate gap also is detected for all three minority groups and for younger and older practitioners. Within Non-Hispanic Whites, however, the median women's wage rate surpasses the men's wage rate.

HOUSEHOLD INCOME

Household income is another situation variable discussed in this chapter. It is important because the value of a person's time out of the labor market depends partly on his/her access to other sources of income in the absence of his/her wage-and-salary earnings. Several studies have hypothesized that income from non-labor sources reduces the amount of labor supplied in the market, thus constraining workers' potential earnings from wage-and-salary income, and have found supporting empirical evidence [Cohany and Sok, 2007; Hotchkiss, 2005; Mitra and Singh, 2006; Mosisa and Hipple, 2006; Mott, 2001; Shauman and Noonan, 2007; Tebaldi and Elmslie, 2006]. While the overwhelming majority of these studies focus on women relying on their husband's income while they care for their offspring, the mechanism also is applicable to individuals relying on savings or returns to investments, younger workers relying on parents' wealth, older workers relying on retirement pensions, or anybody relying on government welfare support. The process is the same: Access to other sources of income exerts an income effect on labor supply that reduces the number of hours workers are willing and able to work in the labor market, along with a reduction in the corresponding level of potential wage-and-salary earnings. Of course, an alternative explanation, at least in the case of the two-income household, is that women with a strong preference for housework are more successful in finding spouses with high permanent income levels, in which case there would be a self-selection bias [Brusentsev, 2006].

A high fraction (13.5 percent) of South Florida practitioners choose not to disclose their annual household income levels (see Tables 5-31 and 5-32), and the reluctance is evenly spread across both genders and all ethnic groups. Of those who provide information, 15.0 percent report an annual household income below $100,000; 40.4 percent report $100,000–149,999; 26.4 percent report $150,000–199,999; and the remaining 18.2 percent report an annual household income of $200,000 or more. Compared to the other counties, Broward pharmacists' households are wealthier and households outside the South Florida region are less wealthy. The gender distribution of the various brackets reveals that the household income reported by female pharmacist households exceeds the income reported by male pharmacist households. This lends credence to the contention that women tend to rely more than men on sources of support other than their labor while partially or fully out of the labor marke—raising their children, performing housework, etc. Non-Hispanic White and Hispanic pharmacist households show greater levels of household income relative to Black and Asian American pharmacist households, and within every ethnic group except Blacks, the household income of women is substantially greater than the household income of men. Black pharmacists have approximately the same household income distribution for men and women.

Older respondents are more reluctant than younger respondents to share information about their household income levels, perhaps due to the reduced likelihood of a working spouse being in the older age brackets. Their gender differential is the opposite of the gender differential in the other age groups. For pharmacists younger than 60 years of age, household income is greater for women than for men, but the inequality is reversed for the 60 year plus groups.

Pharmacists' median annual household income (see Tables 5-33 and 5-34) is $137,500, or $37,500 higher than their median income earned as pharmacists. Curiously, household income is highest for Hispanics, lowest for Asian Americans, and in between for Non-Hispanic Whites and Blacks. It also shows an inverted-U shape curve for age, reaching a peak in the 30–39 year old group. If the median annual income earned working as a pharmacist is subtracted from the median annual household income within each gender-ethnic and gender-age classification, the following values (in dollars) are obtained for other-than-own-work household income:

Ethnic Group	Gender		
	Both Genders	Men	Women
All ethnic groups	37,500	27,000	50,000
Non-Hispanic Whites	31,000	30,000	50,000
Non-Hispanic Blacks	28,000	25,000	28,000
Asian Americans	18,500	7,560	35,000
Hispanics	48,040	30,156	50,000
Other	47,560	50,000	10,000

Age Group	Gender		
	Both Genders	Men	Women
All age groups	37,500	27,000	50,000
Less than 30 years	20,000	13,000	20,000
30–39 years	49,000	25,000	52,000
40–49 years	36,000	20,000	50,000
50–59 years	37,000	32,500	45,000
60–69 years	35,000	38,000	2,500
70 years and older	40,000	37,000	20,000
Not known	52,500	14,000	65,000

Not only is the category for female pharmacists' other-than-own-work level of income almost double the corresponding level of male pharmacists, but in every category, except other ethnic groups and 60 years plus, income from other sources is greater for women than for men. The levels for Hispanics and "others" at the upper end and Asian Americans at the lower end sandwich in the levels for Non-Hispanic Whites and Blacks, and the older age brackets exhibit levels homogeneous with the other age groups.

WORKING SPOUSE

The analysis of the previous section leads to the formulation of an interesting path of inquiry: What is the breakdown of pharmacists' household income other than pharmacy wages and salaries? Specifically, what portion comes from spouse's work and what portion may be attributed to other sources such as retirement pensions, returns from non-labor factors of production, and so on? While these questions cannot be answered directly because the South Florida survey does not include data to this effect, a partial view may be captured by examining the gender, ethnic, and age distributions of married practitioners by whether or not their spouse works (see Tables 5-35 and 5-36).

On average, more than seven out of ten (71.5 percent) pharmacists' spouses have a job. Relatively fewer spouses of pharmacists living in Palm Beach and outside South Florida work compared to spouses from the other counties. Gender differences are notable: 91.3 percent of female pharmacists' husbands work, compared to only 56.4 percent of male pharmacists' wives. Women are more likely than men to have spouses active in the labor market, which accords with empirical findings throughout the literature [Shauman and Noonan, 2007] and is consistent with the gender household income differentials found above, whereby the median income value of women pharmacists' households surpasses the median income value of men pharmacists' households by 15.4 percent.

Ethnic differences are evident as well. Minority pharmacists, especially Hispanics, have a much greater incidence of working spouses relative to non-minority pharmacists, and the gender differential is replicated within each ethnic group. The incidence of working husbands is about the same for all ethnic groups, but the incidence of working wives varies in a very similar manner to the ethnic variation detected for median household income, that is, highest for Hispanics, lowest for Asian Americans, and in between for Non-Hispanic Whites and Blacks. Thus, it seems safe to conclude that a substantial portion of pharmacists' household income other than pharmacy wages and salaries is attributable to spouse's work.

The incidence of working spouses also is affected by age. It declines steadily as age rises, from 92.5 percent in the younger-than-30 group to 23.6 percent in the 70 year plus group. The gender gap is present in all age groups, but it is not as wide as it is within ethnic groups.

Table 5–1. Number of pharmacists who completed the survey questionnaire by county of residence, number of years working at current primary practice site, ethnic group, and gender.

County of Residence	Years at Current Practice Site	Gender	Number of Pharmacists					
			All Ethnic Groups	Non-Hispanic			Hispanic	Other
				White	Black	Asian		
All counties	All groups	Both genders	1,539	958	119	86	319	57
		Men	805	603	41	35	105	21
		Women	734	355	78	51	214	36
	Less than 3	Both genders	428	254	35	25	97	17
		Men	199	144	13	8	28	6
		Women	229	110	22	17	69	11
	3 - 9	Both genders	641	387	53	43	130	28
		Men	330	238	19	17	47	9
		Women	311	149	34	26	83	19
	10 - 19	Both genders	268	169	20	13	57	9
		Men	149	111	8	7	19	4
		Women	119	58	12	6	38	5
	20 and more	Both genders	149	105	6	4	31	3
		Men	96	80	1	3	10	2
		Women	53	25	5	1	21	1
	No response	Both genders	53	43	5	1	4	-
		Men	31	30	-	-	1	-
		Women	22	13	5	1	3	-
Broward	All groups	Both genders	508	316	55	35	70	32
		Men	270	199	22	11	26	12
		Women	238	117	33	24	44	20
	Less than 3	Both genders	135	79	15	7	24	10
		Men	61	44	6	-	8	3
		Women	74	35	9	7	16	7
	3 - 9	Both genders	239	144	27	25	26	17
		Men	127	90	11	10	9	7
		Women	112	54	16	15	17	10
	10 - 19	Both genders	72	44	9	2	12	5
		Men	37	26	4	-	5	2
		Women	35	18	5	2	7	3
	20 and more	Both genders	48	38	2	1	7	-
		Men	38	32	1	1	4	-
		Women	10	6	1	-	3	-
	No response	Both genders	14	11	2	-	1	-
		Men	7	7	-	-	-	-
		Women	7	4	2	-	1	-

Table 5–1. Number of pharmacists who completed the survey questionnaire by county of residence, number of years working at current primary practice site, ethnic group, and gender (continued).

County of Residence	Years at Current Practice Site	Gender	Number of Pharmacists					
			All Ethnic Groups	Non-Hispanic			Hispanic	Other
				White	Black	Asian		
Collier, Hendry, Lee, and Monroe	All groups	Both genders	202	181	4	5	12	-
		Men	111	99	2	3	7	-
		Women	91	82	2	2	5	-
	Less than 3	Both genders	60	49	2	3	6	-
		Men	28	23	1	1	3	-
		Women	32	26	1	2	3	-
	3 - 9	Both genders	72	64	1	1	6	-
		Men	41	35	1	1	4	-
		Women	31	29	-	-	2	-
	10 - 19	Both genders	42	41	-	1	-	-
		Men	25	24	-	1	-	-
		Women	17	17	-	-	-	-
	20 and more	Both genders	17	17	-	-	-	-
		Men	9	9	-	-	-	-
		Women	8	8	-	-	-	-
	No response	Both genders	11	10	1	-	-	-
		Men	8	8	-	-	-	-
		Women	3	2	1	-	-	-
Martin and Pasco	All groups	Both genders	96	76	4	6	5	5
		Men	57	46	-	5	3	3
		Women	39	30	4	1	2	2
	Less than 3	Both genders	23	17	3	1	1	1
		Men	8	6	-	1	-	1
		Women	15	11	3	-	1	-
	3 - 9	Both genders	42	35	1	2	2	2
		Men	28	24	-	1	2	1
		Women	14	11	1	1	-	1
	10 - 19	Both genders	21	16	-	3	1	1
		Men	14	10	-	3	-	1
		Women	7	6	-	-	1	-
	20 and more	Both genders	9	7	-	-	1	1
		Men	7	6	-	-	1	-
		Women	2	1	-	-	-	1
	No response	Both genders	1	1	-	-	-	-
		Men	-	-	-	-	-	-
		Women	1	1	-	-	-	-

Table 5–1. Number of pharmacists who completed the survey questionnaire by county of residence, number of years working at current primary practice site, ethnic group, and gender (continued).

County of Residence	Years at Current Practice Site	Gender	Number of Pharmacists					
			All Ethnic Groups	Non-Hispanic			Hispanic	Other
				White	Black	Asian		
Miami-Dade	All groups	Both genders	342	98	31	14	189	10
		Men	140	69	9	7	54	1
		Women	202	29	22	7	135	9
	Less than 3	Both genders	93	26	8	2	54	3
		Men	38	18	3	2	15	-
		Women	55	8	5	-	39	3
	3 - 9	Both genders	129	33	10	4	78	4
		Men	50	21	3	1	25	-
		Women	79	12	7	3	53	4
	10 - 19	Both genders	69	19	8	5	34	3
		Men	29	14	3	2	9	1
		Women	40	5	5	3	25	2
	20 and more	Both genders	42	14	4	3	21	-
		Men	19	13	-	2	4	-
		Women	23	1	4	1	17	-
	No response	Both genders	9	6	1	-	2	-
		Men	4	3	-	-	1	-
		Women	5	3	1	-	1	-
Palm Beach	All groups	Both genders	348	270	21	20	28	9
		Men	206	179	6	6	10	5
		Women	142	91	15	14	18	4
	Less than 3	Both genders	101	75	5	9	9	3
		Men	57	49	2	3	1	2
		Women	44	26	3	6	8	1
	3 - 9	Both genders	142	106	13	8	11	4
		Men	76	65	3	2	5	1
		Women	66	41	10	6	6	3
	10 - 19	Both genders	57	47	2	2	6	-
		Men	40	35	1	1	3	-
		Women	17	12	1	1	3	-
	20 and more	Both genders	32	28	-	-	2	2
		Men	22	19	-	-	1	2
		Women	10	9	-	-	1	-
	No response	Both genders	16	14	1	1	-	-
		Men	11	11	-	-	-	-
		Women	5	3	1	1	-	-

Table 5–1. Number of pharmacists who completed the survey questionnaire by county of residence, number of years working at current primary practice site, ethnic group, and gender (continued).

County of Residence	Years at Current Practice Site	Gender	Number of Pharmacists: All Ethnic Groups	Non-Hispanic: White	Non-Hispanic: Black	Non-Hispanic: Asian	Hispanic	Other
Other	All groups	Both genders	43	17	4	6	15	1
		Men	21	11	2	3	5	-
		Women	22	6	2	3	10	1
	Less than 3	Both genders	16	8	2	3	3	-
		Men	7	4	1	1	1	-
		Women	9	4	1	2	2	-
	3 - 9	Both genders	17	5	1	3	7	1
		Men	8	3	1	2	2	-
		Women	9	2	-	1	5	1
	10 - 19	Both genders	7	2	1	-	4	-
		Men	4	2	-	-	2	-
		Women	3	-	1	-	2	-
	20 and more	Both genders	1	1	-	-	-	-
		Men	1	1	-	-	-	-
		Women	-	-	-	-	-	-
	No response	Both genders	2	1	-	-	1	-
		Men	1	1	-	-	-	-
		Women	1	-	-	-	1	-

Table 5–2. Number of pharmacists who completed the survey questionnaire by county of residence, number of years working at current primary practice site, age group, and gender.

County of Residence	Years at Current Practice Site	Gender	Number of Pharmacists							
			All Age Groups	Less than 30	30-39	40-49	50-59	60-69	70 and Older	Not Known
All counties	All groups	Both genders	1,539	97	367	364	329	192	154	36
		Men	805	23	108	157	204	166	128	19
		Women	734	74	259	207	125	26	26	17
	Less than 3	Both genders	428	70	125	90	78	40	21	4
		Men	199	13	43	33	49	37	21	3
		Women	229	57	82	57	29	3	-	1
	3 - 9	Both genders	641	27	207	152	111	71	56	17
		Men	330	10	56	73	72	62	51	6
		Women	311	17	151	79	39	9	5	11
	10 - 19	Both genders	268	-	30	89	70	34	39	6
		Men	149	-	9	38	40	27	31	4
		Women	119	-	21	51	30	7	8	2
	20 and more	Both genders	149	-	-	23	58	36	25	7
		Men	96	-	-	10	37	31	14	4
		Women	53	-	-	13	21	5	11	3
	No response	Both genders	53	-	5	10	12	11	13	2
		Men	31	-	-	3	6	9	11	2
		Women	22	-	5	7	6	2	2	-
Broward	All groups	Both genders	508	25	124	136	110	60	40	13
		Men	270	4	36	70	69	51	34	6
		Women	238	21	88	66	41	9	6	7
	Less than 3	Both genders	135	17	40	33	28	12	4	1
		Men	61	2	12	14	18	10	4	1
		Women	74	15	28	19	10	2	-	-
	3 - 9	Both genders	239	8	72	69	38	24	19	9
		Men	127	2	20	39	24	21	18	3
		Women	112	6	52	30	14	3	1	6
	10 - 19	Both genders	72	-	11	23	19	10	8	1
		Men	37	-	4	12	8	7	6	-
		Women	35	-	7	11	11	3	2	1
	20 and more	Both genders	48	-	-	9	21	12	5	1
		Men	38	-	-	4	18	12	3	1
		Women	10	-	-	5	3	-	2	-
	No response	Both genders	14	-	1	2	4	2	4	1
		Men	7	-	-	1	1	1	3	1
		Women	7	-	1	1	3	1	1	-

Table 5–2. **Number of pharmacists who completed the survey questionnaire by county of residence, number of years working at current primary practice site, age group, and gender (continued).**

County of Residence	Years at Current Practice Site	Gender	Number of Pharmacists							
			All Age Groups	Less than 30	30-39	40-49	50-59	60-69	70 and Older	Not Known
Collier, Hendry, Lee, and Monroe	All groups	Both genders	202	16	40	49	58	22	13	4
		Men	111	5	13	20	39	19	12	3
		Women	91	11	27	29	19	3	1	1
	Less than 3	Both genders	60	12	14	16	13	4	1	-
		Men	28	3	6	3	12	3	1	-
		Women	32	9	8	13	1	1	-	-
	3 - 9	Both genders	72	4	22	14	18	9	5	-
		Men	41	2	7	7	11	9	5	-
		Women	31	2	15	7	7	-	-	-
	10 - 19	Both genders	42	-	2	14	15	3	4	4
		Men	25	-	-	6	9	3	4	3
		Women	17	-	2	8	6	-	-	1
	20 and more	Both genders	17	-	-	3	8	5	1	-
		Men	9	-	-	3	3	3	-	-
		Women	8	-	-	-	5	2	1	-
	No response	Both genders	11	-	2	2	4	1	2	-
		Men	8	-	-	1	4	1	2	-
		Women	3	-	2	1	-	-	-	-
Martin and Pasco	All groups	Both genders	96	6	18	23	29	12	7	1
		Men	57	2	8	7	21	11	7	1
		Women	39	4	10	16	8	1	-	-
	Less than 3	Both genders	23	3	8	4	6	-	2	-
		Men	8	2	2	-	2	-	2	-
		Women	15	1	6	4	4	-	-	-
	3 - 9	Both genders	42	3	8	12	11	8	-	-
		Men	28	-	6	5	10	7	-	-
		Women	14	3	2	7	1	1	-	-
	10 - 19	Both genders	21	-	2	6	7	3	2	1
		Men	14	-	-	2	6	3	2	1
		Women	7	-	2	4	1	-	-	-
	20 and more	Both genders	9	-	-	1	4	1	3	-
		Men	7	-	-	-	3	1	3	-
		Women	2	-	-	1	1	-	-	-
	No response	Both genders	1	-	-	-	1	-	-	-
		Men	-	-	-	-	-	-	-	-
		Women	1	-	-	-	1	-	-	-

Table 5–2. Number of pharmacists who completed the survey questionnaire by county of residence, number of years working at current primary practice site, age group, and gender (continued).

County of Residence	Years at Current Practice Site	Gender	Number of Pharmacists							
			All Age Groups	Less than 30	30-39	40-49	50-59	60-69	70 and Older	Not Known
Miami-Dade	All groups	Both genders	342	21	94	86	63	35	34	9
		Men	140	7	25	32	28	26	19	3
		Women	202	14	69	54	35	9	15	6
	Less than 3	Both genders	93	15	32	23	14	5	3	1
		Men	38	2	10	11	7	5	3	-
		Women	55	13	22	12	7	-	-	1
	3 - 9	Both genders	129	6	52	29	18	10	10	4
		Men	50	5	11	11	8	6	8	1
		Women	79	1	41	18	10	4	2	3
	10 - 19	Both genders	69	-	9	30	12	7	11	-
		Men	29	-	4	10	6	4	5	-
		Women	40	-	5	20	6	3	6	-
	20 and more	Both genders	42	-	-	2	17	11	9	3
		Men	19	-	-	-	7	9	2	1
		Women	23	-	-	2	10	2	7	2
	No response	Both genders	9	-	1	2	2	2	1	1
		Men	4	-	-	-	-	2	1	1
		Women	5	-	1	2	2	-	-	-
Palm Beach	All groups	Both genders	348	24	74	65	63	60	55	7
		Men	206	4	18	26	45	57	52	4
		Women	142	20	56	39	18	3	3	3
	Less than 3	Both genders	101	19	24	13	15	18	10	2
		Men	57	3	10	5	9	18	10	2
		Women	44	16	14	8	6	-	-	-
	3 - 9	Both genders	142	5	44	25	24	19	22	3
		Men	76	1	7	9	19	19	20	1
		Women	66	4	37	16	5	-	2	2
	10 - 19	Both genders	57	-	5	15	15	10	12	-
		Men	40	-	1	8	10	9	12	-
		Women	17	-	4	7	5	1	-	-
	20 and more	Both genders	32	-	-	8	8	7	7	2
		Men	22	-	-	3	6	6	6	1
		Women	10	-	-	5	2	1	1	1
	No response	Both genders	16	-	1	4	1	6	4	-
		Men	11	-	-	1	1	5	4	-
		Women	5	-	1	3	-	1	-	-

Table 5–2. Number of pharmacists who completed the survey questionnaire by county of residence, number of years working at current primary practice site, age group, and gender (continued).

County of Residence	Years at Current Practice Site	Gender	Number of Pharmacists							
			All Age Groups	Less than 30	30-39	40-49	50-59	60-69	70 and Older	Not Known
Other	All groups	Both genders	43	5	17	5	6	3	5	2
		Men	21	1	8	2	2	2	4	2
		Women	22	4	9	3	4	1	1	-
	Less than 3	Both genders	16	4	7	1	2	1	1	-
		Men	7	1	3	-	1	1	1	-
		Women	9	3	4	1	1	-	-	-
	3 - 9	Both genders	17	1	9	3	2	1	-	1
		Men	8	-	5	2	-	-	-	1
		Women	9	1	4	1	2	1	-	-
	10 - 19	Both genders	7	-	1	1	2	1	2	-
		Men	4	-	-	-	1	1	2	-
		Women	3	-	1	1	1	-	-	-
	20 and more	Both genders	1	-	-	-	-	-	-	1
		Men	1	-	-	-	-	-	-	1
		Women	-	-	-	-	-	-	-	-
	No response	Both genders	2	-	-	-	-	-	2	-
		Men	1	-	-	-	-	-	1	-
		Women	1	-	-	-	-	-	1	-

Table 5–3. Number of pharmacists who completed the survey questionnaire by county of residence, type of primary practice site, ethnic group, and gender.

County of Residence	Type of Primary Practice Site	Gender	Number of Pharmacists					
			All Ethnic Groups	Non-Hispanic			Hispanic	Other
				White	Black	Asian		
All counties	All groups	Both genders	1,539	958	119	86	319	57
		Men	805	603	41	35	105	21
		Women	734	355	78	51	214	36
	Retail community/ independent	Both genders	231	155	16	6	49	5
		Men	154	120	6	2	24	2
		Women	77	35	10	4	25	3
	Retail chain	Both genders	600	374	49	43	115	19
		Men	319	236	23	18	34	8
		Women	281	138	26	25	81	11
	Hospital	Both genders	377	216	28	22	92	19
		Men	173	124	6	10	26	7
		Women	204	92	22	12	66	12
	Other	Both genders	316	203	24	15	61	13
		Men	152	117	6	5	20	4
		Women	164	86	18	10	41	9
	No response	Both genders	15	10	2	-	2	1
		Men	7	6	-	-	1	-
		Women	8	4	2	-	1	1
Broward	All groups	Both genders	508	316	55	35	70	32
		Men	270	199	22	11	26	12
		Women	238	117	33	24	44	20
	Retail community/ independent	Both genders	76	52	8	4	9	3
		Men	51	39	3	1	6	2
		Women	25	13	5	3	3	1
	Retail chain	Both genders	173	103	25	14	19	12
		Men	95	66	14	5	5	5
		Women	78	37	11	9	14	7
	Hospital	Both genders	116	72	11	7	16	10
		Men	53	39	1	2	7	4
		Women	63	33	10	5	9	6
	Other	Both genders	137	85	10	10	25	7
		Men	67	52	4	3	7	1
		Women	70	33	6	7	18	6
	No response	Both genders	6	4	1	-	1	-
		Men	4	3	-	-	1	-
		Women	2	1	1	-	-	-

Table 5–3. Number of pharmacists who completed the survey questionnaire by county of residence, type of primary practice site, ethnic group, and gender (continued).

County of Residence	Type of Primary Practice Site	Gender	Number of Pharmacists					
			All Ethnic Groups	Non-Hispanic			Hispanic	Other
				White	Black	Asian		
Collier, Hendry, Lee, and Monroe	All groups	Both genders	202	181	4	5	12	-
		Men	111	99	2	3	7	-
		Women	91	82	2	2	5	-
	Retail community/ independent	Both genders	24	24	-	-	-	-
		Men	15	15	-	-	-	-
		Women	9	9	-	-	-	-
	Retail chain	Both genders	97	81	1	5	10	-
		Men	55	46	-	3	6	-
		Women	42	35	1	2	4	-
	Hospital	Both genders	45	43	1	-	1	-
		Men	23	22	1	-	-	-
		Women	22	21	-	-	1	-
	Other	Both genders	33	30	2	-	1	-
		Men	15	13	1	-	1	-
		Women	18	17	1	-	-	-
	No response	Both genders	3	3	-	-	-	-
		Men	3	3	-	-	-	-
		Women	-	-	-	-	-	-
Martin and Pasco	All groups	Both genders	96	76	4	6	5	5
		Men	57	46	-	5	3	3
		Women	39	30	4	1	2	2
	Retail community/ independent	Both genders	8	4	2	-	2	-
		Men	5	4	-	-	1	-
		Women	3	-	2	-	1	-
	Retail chain	Both genders	37	33	-	1	2	1
		Men	23	20	-	1	1	1
		Women	14	13	-	-	1	-
	Hospital	Both genders	28	23	-	3	-	2
		Men	16	14	-	2	-	-
		Women	12	9	-	1	-	2
	Other	Both genders	22	15	2	2	1	2
		Men	13	8	-	2	1	2
		Women	9	7	2	-	-	-
	No response	Both genders	1	1	-	-	-	-
		Men	-	-	-	-	-	-
		Women	1	1	-	-	-	-

Table 5–3. **Number of pharmacists who completed the survey questionnaire by county of residence, type of primary practice site, ethnic group, and gender (continued).**

County of Residence	Type of Primary Practice Site	Gender	Number of Pharmacists					
			All Ethnic Groups	Non-Hispanic			Hispanic	Other
				White	Black	Asian		
Miami-Dade	All groups	Both genders	342	98	31	14	189	10
		Men	140	69	9	7	54	1
		Women	202	29	22	7	135	9
	Retail community/ independent	Both genders	64	28	2	1	32	1
		Men	37	23	1	1	12	-
		Women	27	5	1	-	20	1
	Retail chain	Both genders	111	21	13	5	69	3
		Men	44	15	6	2	20	1
		Women	67	6	7	3	49	2
	Hospital	Both genders	107	27	10	7	60	3
		Men	37	17	1	4	15	-
		Women	70	10	9	3	45	3
	Other	Both genders	59	21	6	1	28	3
		Men	22	14	1	-	7	-
		Women	37	7	5	1	21	3
	No response	Both genders	1	1	-	-	-	-
		Men	-	-	-	-	-	-
		Women	1	1	-	-	-	-
Palm Beach	All groups	Both genders	348	270	21	20	28	9
		Men	206	179	6	6	10	5
		Women	142	91	15	14	18	4
	Retail community/ independent	Both genders	50	44	3	-	2	1
		Men	38	36	1	-	1	-
		Women	12	8	2	-	1	1
	Retail chain	Both genders	166	129	9	14	11	3
		Men	94	84	3	4	2	1
		Women	72	45	6	10	9	2
	Hospital	Both genders	71	48	5	4	10	4
		Men	41	30	2	2	4	3
		Women	30	18	3	2	6	1
	Other	Both genders	60	48	4	2	5	1
		Men	33	29	-	-	3	1
		Women	27	19	4	2	2	-
	No response	Both genders	1	1	-	-	-	-
		Men	-	-	-	-	-	-
		Women	1	1	-	-	-	-

Table 5–3. Number of pharmacists who completed the survey questionnaire by county of residence, type of primary practice site, ethnic group, and gender (continued).

County of Residence	Type of Primary Practice Site	Gender	Number of Pharmacists					
			All Ethnic Groups	Non-Hispanic			Hispanic	Other
				White	Black	Asian		
Other	All groups	Both genders	43	17	4	6	15	1
		Men	21	11	2	3	5	-
		Women	22	6	2	3	10	1
	Retail community/ independent	Both genders	9	3	1	1	4	-
		Men	8	3	1	-	4	-
		Women	1	-	-	1	-	-
	Retail chain	Both genders	16	7	1	4	4	-
		Men	8	5	-	3	-	-
		Women	8	2	1	1	4	-
	Hospital	Both genders	10	3	1	1	5	-
		Men	3	2	1	-	-	-
		Women	7	1	-	1	5	-
	Other	Both genders	5	4	-	-	1	-
		Men	2	1	-	-	1	-
		Women	3	3	-	-	-	-
	No response	Both genders	3	-	1	-	1	1
		Men	-	-	-	-	-	-
		Women	3	-	1	-	1	1

Table 5–4. Number of pharmacists who completed the survey questionnaire by county of residence, type of primary practice site, age group, and gender.

County of Residence	Type of Primary Practice Site	Gender	Number of Pharmacists							
			All Age Groups	Less than 30	30-39	40-49	50-59	60-69	70 and Older	Not Known
All counties	All groups	Both genders	1,539	97	367	364	329	192	154	36
		Men	805	23	108	157	204	166	128	19
		Women	734	74	259	207	125	26	26	17
	Retail community/ independent	Both genders	231	10	34	43	47	43	47	7
		Men	154	4	9	21	35	37	43	5
		Women	77	6	25	22	12	6	4	2
	Retail chain	Both genders	600	48	159	138	100	89	53	13
		Men	319	11	51	58	61	82	48	8
		Women	281	37	108	80	39	7	5	5
	Hospital	Both genders	377	24	96	105	99	23	21	9
		Men	173	5	29	47	59	19	11	3
		Women	204	19	67	58	40	4	10	6
	Other	Both genders	316	14	75	75	78	35	32	7
		Men	152	3	17	30	47	27	25	3
		Women	164	11	58	45	31	8	7	4
	No response	Both genders	15	1	3	3	5	2	1	-
		Men	7	-	2	1	2	1	1	-
		Women	8	1	1	2	3	1	-	-
Broward	All groups	Both genders	508	25	124	136	110	60	40	13
		Men	270	4	36	70	69	51	34	6
		Women	238	21	88	66	41	9	6	7
	Retail community/ independent	Both genders	76	4	12	21	12	16	9	2
		Men	51	2	3	12	11	14	8	1
		Women	25	2	9	9	1	2	1	1
	Retail chain	Both genders	173	10	49	46	24	23	13	8
		Men	95	-	18	26	14	21	12	4
		Women	78	10	31	20	10	2	1	4
	Hospital	Both genders	116	6	26	33	37	5	7	2
		Men	53	1	7	15	22	4	4	-
		Women	63	5	19	18	15	1	3	2
	Other	Both genders	137	5	34	35	35	16	11	1
		Men	67	1	6	16	21	12	10	1
		Women	70	4	28	19	14	4	1	-
	No response	Both genders	6	-	3	1	2	-	-	-
		Men	4	-	2	1	1	-	-	-
		Women	2	-	1	-	1	-	-	-

Table 5–4. Number of pharmacists who completed the survey questionnaire by county of residence, type of primary practice site, age group, and gender (continued).

County of Residence	Type of Primary Practice Site	Gender	Number of Pharmacists							
			All Age Groups	Less than 30	30-39	40-49	50-59	60-69	70 and Older	Not Known
Collier, Hendry, Lee, and Monroe	All groups	Both genders	202	16	40	49	58	22	13	4
		Men	111	5	13	20	39	19	12	3
		Women	91	11	27	29	19	3	1	1
	Retail community/ independent	Both genders	24	1	5	2	8	3	5	-
		Men	15	-	2	1	5	2	5	-
		Women	9	1	3	1	3	1	-	-
	Retail chain	Both genders	97	13	15	21	31	13	3	1
		Men	55	4	6	11	19	11	3	1
		Women	42	9	9	10	12	2	-	-
	Hospital	Both genders	45	-	10	19	11	3	1	1
		Men	23	-	3	7	8	3	1	1
		Women	22	-	7	12	3	-	-	-
	Other	Both genders	33	2	10	7	7	2	3	2
		Men	15	1	2	1	6	2	2	1
		Women	18	1	8	6	1	-	1	1
	No response	Both genders	3	-	-	-	1	1	1	-
		Men	3	-	-	-	1	1	1	-
		Women	-	-	-	-	-	-	-	-
Martin and Pasco	All groups	Both genders	96	6	18	23	29	12	7	1
		Men	57	2	8	7	21	11	7	1
		Women	39	4	10	16	8	1	-	-
	Retail community/ independent	Both genders	8	-	1	3	1	1	2	-
		Men	5	-	-	1	1	1	2	-
		Women	3	-	1	2	-	-	-	-
	Retail chain	Both genders	37	1	9	8	7	6	5	1
		Men	23	1	5	2	4	5	5	1
		Women	14	-	4	6	3	1	-	-
	Hospital	Both genders	28	4	6	5	12	1	-	-
		Men	16	1	3	2	9	1	-	-
		Women	12	3	3	3	3	-	-	-
	Other	Both genders	22	1	2	7	8	4	-	-
		Men	13	-	-	2	7	4	-	-
		Women	9	1	2	5	1	-	-	-
	No response	Both genders	1	-	-	-	1	-	-	-
		Men	-	-	-	-	-	-	-	-
		Women	1	-	-	-	1	-	-	-

Table 5–4. Number of pharmacists who completed the survey questionnaire by county of residence, type of primary practice site, age group, and gender (continued).

County of Residence	Type of Primary Practice Site	Gender	Number of Pharmacists							
			All Age Groups	Less than 30	30-39	40-49	50-59	60-69	70 and Older	Not Known
Miami-Dade	All groups	Both genders	342	21	94	86	63	35	34	9
		Men	140	7	25	32	28	26	19	3
		Women	202	14	69	54	35	9	15	6
	Retail community/ independent	Both genders	64	2	13	9	15	12	11	2
		Men	37	1	3	4	9	10	9	1
		Women	27	1	10	5	6	2	2	1
	Retail chain	Both genders	111	8	35	33	11	13	10	1
		Men	44	3	11	8	4	11	6	1
		Women	67	5	24	25	7	2	4	-
	Hospital	Both genders	107	9	29	31	20	6	8	4
		Men	37	2	6	15	8	4	2	-
		Women	70	7	23	16	12	2	6	4
	Other	Both genders	59	2	17	13	16	4	5	2
		Men	22	1	5	5	7	1	2	1
		Women	37	1	12	8	9	3	3	1
	No response	Both genders	1	-	-	-	1	-	-	-
		Men	-	-	-	-	-	-	-	-
		Women	1	-	-	-	1	-	-	-
Palm Beach	All groups	Both genders	348	24	74	65	63	60	55	7
		Men	206	4	18	26	45	57	52	4
		Women	142	20	56	39	18	3	3	3
	Retail community/ independent	Both genders	50	3	2	7	9	10	17	2
		Men	38	1	-	2	8	9	16	2
		Women	12	2	2	5	1	1	1	-
	Retail chain	Both genders	166	13	42	29	25	33	22	2
		Men	94	2	6	11	19	33	22	1
		Women	72	11	36	18	6	-	-	1
	Hospital	Both genders	71	5	20	16	18	7	4	1
		Men	41	1	9	7	12	7	4	1
		Women	30	4	11	9	6	-	-	-
	Other	Both genders	60	3	10	13	11	9	12	2
		Men	33	-	3	6	6	8	10	-
		Women	27	3	7	7	5	1	2	2
	No response	Both genders	1	-	-	-	-	1	-	-
		Men	-	-	-	-	-	-	-	-
		Women	1	-	-	-	-	1	-	-

Table 5–4. Number of pharmacists who completed the survey questionnaire by county of residence, type of primary practice site, age group, and gender (continued).

County of Residence	Type of Primary Practice Site	Gender	Number of Pharmacists							
			All Age Groups	Less than 30	30-39	40-49	50-59	60-69	70 and Older	Not Known
Other	All groups	Both genders	43	5	17	5	6	3	5	2
		Men	21	1	8	2	2	2	4	2
		Women	22	4	9	3	4	1	1	-
	Retail community/ independent	Both genders	9	-	1	1	2	1	3	1
		Men	8	-	1	1	1	1	3	1
		Women	1	-	-	-	1	-	-	-
	Retail chain	Both genders	16	3	9	1	2	1	-	-
		Men	8	1	5	-	1	1	-	-
		Women	8	2	4	1	1	-	-	-
	Hospital	Both genders	10	-	5	1	1	1	1	1
		Men	3	-	1	1	-	-	-	1
		Women	7	-	4	-	1	1	1	-
	Other	Both genders	5	1	2	-	1	-	1	-
		Men	2	-	1	-	-	-	1	-
		Women	3	1	1	-	1	-	-	-
	No response	Both genders	3	1	-	2	-	-	-	-
		Men	-	-	-	-	-	-	-	-
		Women	3	1	-	2	-	-	-	-

Table 5–5. Number of pharmacists who completed the survey questionnaire by county of residence, whether or not they primarily serve a specific patient population, ethnic group, and gender.

County of Residence	Primarily Serve a Patient Population	Gender	Number of Pharmacists					
			All Ethnic Groups	Non-Hispanic			Hispanic	Other
				White	Black	Asian		
All counties	All groups	Both genders	1,539	958	119	86	319	57
		Men	805	603	41	35	105	21
		Women	734	355	78	51	214	36
	Yes	Both genders	696	428	47	37	152	32
		Men	354	260	16	17	54	7
		Women	342	168	31	20	98	25
	No	Both genders	843	530	72	49	167	25
		Men	451	343	25	18	51	14
		Women	392	187	47	31	116	11
Broward	All groups	Both genders	508	316	55	35	70	32
		Men	270	199	22	11	26	12
		Women	238	117	33	24	44	20
	Yes	Both genders	209	136	19	12	26	16
		Men	108	85	6	4	10	3
		Women	101	51	13	8	16	13
	No	Both genders	299	180	36	23	44	16
		Men	162	114	16	7	16	9
		Women	137	66	20	16	28	7
Collier, Hendry, Lee, and Monroe	All groups	Both genders	202	181	4	5	12	-
		Men	111	99	2	3	7	-
		Women	91	82	2	2	5	-
	Yes	Both genders	92	81	3	1	7	-
		Men	47	39	2	1	5	-
		Women	45	42	1	-	2	-
	No	Both genders	110	100	1	4	5	-
		Men	64	60	-	2	2	-
		Women	46	40	1	2	3	-
Martin and Pasco	All groups	Both genders	96	76	4	6	5	5
		Men	57	46	-	5	3	3
		Women	39	30	4	1	2	2
	Yes	Both genders	46	36	2	2	4	2
		Men	25	21	-	2	2	-
		Women	21	15	2	-	2	2
	No	Both genders	50	40	2	4	1	3
		Men	32	25	-	3	1	3
		Women	18	15	2	1	-	-

Table 5–5. Number of pharmacists who completed the survey questionnaire by county of residence, whether or not they primarily serve a specific patient population, ethnic group, and gender (continued).

County of Residence	Primarily Serve a Patient Population	Gender	Number of Pharmacists					
			All Ethnic Groups	Non-Hispanic			Hispanic	Other
				White	Black	Asian		
Miami-Dade	All groups	Both genders	342	98	31	14	189	10
		Men	140	69	9	7	54	1
		Women	202	29	22	7	135	9
	Yes	Both genders	167	47	11	6	96	7
		Men	67	31	3	4	29	-
		Women	100	16	8	2	67	7
	No	Both genders	175	51	20	8	93	3
		Men	73	38	6	3	25	1
		Women	102	13	14	5	68	2
Palm Beach	All groups	Both genders	348	270	21	20	28	9
		Men	206	179	6	6	10	5
		Women	142	91	15	14	18	4
	Yes	Both genders	170	123	10	14	16	7
		Men	98	81	3	5	5	4
		Women	72	42	7	9	11	3
	No	Both genders	178	147	11	6	12	2
		Men	108	98	3	1	5	1
		Women	70	49	8	5	7	1
Other	All groups	Both genders	43	17	4	6	15	1
		Men	21	11	2	3	5	-
		Women	22	6	2	3	10	1
	Yes	Both genders	12	5	2	2	3	-
		Men	9	3	2	1	3	-
		Women	3	2	-	1	-	-
	No	Both genders	31	12	2	4	12	1
		Men	12	8	-	2	2	-
		Women	19	4	2	2	10	1

Table 5–6. Number of pharmacists who completed the survey questionnaire by county of residence, whether or not they primarily serve a specific patient population, age group, and gender.

County of Residence	Primarily Serve a Patient Population	Gender	Number of Pharmacists							
			All Age Groups	Less than 30	30-39	40-49	50- 59	60-69	70 and Older	Not Known
All counties	All groups	Both genders	1,539	97	367	364	329	192	154	36
		Men	805	23	108	157	204	166	128	19
		Women	734	74	259	207	125	26	26	17
	Yes	Both genders	696	50	162	151	147	89	85	12
		Men	354	12	41	61	94	71	69	6
		Women	342	38	121	90	53	18	16	6
	No	Both genders	843	47	205	213	182	103	69	24
		Men	451	11	67	96	110	95	59	13
		Women	392	36	138	117	72	8	10	11
Broward	All groups	Both genders	508	25	124	136	110	60	40	13
		Men	270	4	36	70	69	51	34	6
		Women	238	21	88	66	41	9	6	7
	Yes	Both genders	209	15	39	52	48	30	23	2
		Men	108	3	7	21	31	24	21	1
		Women	101	12	32	31	17	6	2	1
	No	Both genders	299	10	85	84	62	30	17	11
		Men	162	1	29	49	38	27	13	5
		Women	137	9	56	35	24	3	4	6
Collier, Hendry, Lee, and Monroe	All groups	Both genders	202	16	40	49	58	22	13	4
		Men	111	5	13	20	39	19	12	3
		Women	91	11	27	29	19	3	1	1
	Yes	Both genders	92	11	16	22	24	10	6	3
		Men	47	4	6	7	15	8	5	2
		Women	45	7	10	15	9	2	1	1
	No	Both genders	110	5	24	27	34	12	7	1
		Men	64	1	7	13	24	11	7	1
		Women	46	4	17	14	10	1	-	-
Martin and Pasco	All groups	Both genders	96	6	18	23	29	12	7	1
		Men	57	2	8	7	21	11	7	1
		Women	39	4	10	16	8	1	-	-
	Yes	Both genders	46	4	10	12	13	4	3	-
		Men	25	1	4	4	9	4	3	-
		Women	21	3	6	8	4	-	-	-
	No	Both genders	50	2	8	11	16	8	4	1
		Men	32	1	4	3	12	7	4	1
		Women	18	1	4	8	4	1	-	-

Table 5–6. Number of pharmacists who completed the survey questionnaire by county of residence, whether or not they primarily serve a specific patient population, age group, and gender (continued).

County of Residence	Primarily Serve a Patient Population	Gender	Number of Pharmacists							
			All Age Groups	Less than 30	30-39	40-49	50-59	60-69	70 and Older	Not Known
Miami-Dade	All groups	Both genders	342	21	94	86	63	35	34	9
		Men	140	7	25	32	28	26	19	3
		Women	202	14	69	54	35	9	15	6
	Yes	Both genders	167	7	48	39	32	20	18	3
		Men	67	3	10	18	15	12	8	1
		Women	100	4	38	21	17	8	10	2
	No	Both genders	175	14	46	47	31	15	16	6
		Men	73	4	15	14	13	14	11	2
		Women	102	10	31	33	18	1	5	4
Palm Beach	All groups	Both genders	348	24	74	65	63	60	55	7
		Men	206	4	18	26	45	57	52	4
		Women	142	20	56	39	18	3	3	3
	Yes	Both genders	170	12	43	24	30	24	34	3
		Men	98	1	10	9	24	22	31	1
		Women	72	11	33	15	6	2	3	2
	No	Both genders	178	12	31	41	33	36	21	4
		Men	108	3	8	17	21	35	21	3
		Women	70	9	23	24	12	1	-	1
Other	All groups	Both genders	43	5	17	5	6	3	5	2
		Men	21	1	8	2	2	2	4	2
		Women	22	4	9	3	4	1	1	-
	Yes	Both genders	12	1	6	2	-	1	1	1
		Men	9	-	4	2	-	1	1	1
		Women	3	1	2	-	-	-	-	-
	No	Both genders	31	4	11	3	6	2	4	1
		Men	12	1	4	-	2	1	3	1
		Women	19	3	7	3	4	1	1	-

Table 5–7. Number of pharmacists who completed the survey questionnaire by county of residence, type of primary pharmacy activity, ethnic group, and gender.

<table>
<tr><th rowspan="3">County of Residence</th><th rowspan="3">Primary Role as a Pharmacist</th><th rowspan="3">Gender</th><th colspan="6">Number of Pharmacists</th></tr>
<tr><th rowspan="2">All Ethnic Groups</th><th colspan="3">Non-Hispanic</th><th rowspan="2">Hispanic</th><th rowspan="2">Other</th></tr>
<tr><th>White</th><th>Black</th><th>Asian</th></tr>
<tr><td rowspan="18">All counties</td><td rowspan="3">All groups</td><td>Both genders</td><td>1,539</td><td>958</td><td>119</td><td>86</td><td>319</td><td>57</td></tr>
<tr><td>Men</td><td>805</td><td>603</td><td>41</td><td>35</td><td>105</td><td>21</td></tr>
<tr><td>Women</td><td>734</td><td>355</td><td>78</td><td>51</td><td>214</td><td>36</td></tr>
<tr><td rowspan="3">Clinical</td><td>Both genders</td><td>285</td><td>158</td><td>22</td><td>19</td><td>64</td><td>22</td></tr>
<tr><td>Men</td><td>125</td><td>81</td><td>9</td><td>8</td><td>22</td><td>5</td></tr>
<tr><td>Women</td><td>160</td><td>77</td><td>13</td><td>11</td><td>42</td><td>17</td></tr>
<tr><td rowspan="3">Dispensing</td><td>Both genders</td><td>1,010</td><td>636</td><td>80</td><td>64</td><td>203</td><td>27</td></tr>
<tr><td>Men</td><td>543</td><td>412</td><td>29</td><td>29</td><td>63</td><td>10</td></tr>
<tr><td>Women</td><td>467</td><td>224</td><td>51</td><td>35</td><td>140</td><td>17</td></tr>
<tr><td rowspan="3">Administrative</td><td>Both genders</td><td>194</td><td>121</td><td>16</td><td>4</td><td>42</td><td>11</td></tr>
<tr><td>Men</td><td>111</td><td>83</td><td>3</td><td>2</td><td>18</td><td>5</td></tr>
<tr><td>Women</td><td>83</td><td>38</td><td>13</td><td>2</td><td>24</td><td>6</td></tr>
<tr><td rowspan="3">Other</td><td>Both genders</td><td>112</td><td>73</td><td>5</td><td>4</td><td>25</td><td>5</td></tr>
<tr><td>Men</td><td>61</td><td>48</td><td>2</td><td>-</td><td>7</td><td>4</td></tr>
<tr><td>Women</td><td>51</td><td>25</td><td>3</td><td>4</td><td>18</td><td>1</td></tr>
<tr><td rowspan="3">No response</td><td>Both genders</td><td>14</td><td>11</td><td>2</td><td>1</td><td>-</td><td>-</td></tr>
<tr><td>Men</td><td>7</td><td>6</td><td>1</td><td>-</td><td>-</td><td>-</td></tr>
<tr><td>Women</td><td>7</td><td>5</td><td>1</td><td>1</td><td>-</td><td>-</td></tr>
<tr><td rowspan="18">Broward</td><td rowspan="3">All groups</td><td>Both genders</td><td>508</td><td>316</td><td>55</td><td>35</td><td>70</td><td>32</td></tr>
<tr><td>Men</td><td>270</td><td>199</td><td>22</td><td>11</td><td>26</td><td>12</td></tr>
<tr><td>Women</td><td>238</td><td>117</td><td>33</td><td>24</td><td>44</td><td>20</td></tr>
<tr><td rowspan="3">Clinical</td><td>Both genders</td><td>101</td><td>56</td><td>8</td><td>7</td><td>17</td><td>13</td></tr>
<tr><td>Men</td><td>43</td><td>27</td><td>4</td><td>1</td><td>7</td><td>4</td></tr>
<tr><td>Women</td><td>58</td><td>29</td><td>4</td><td>6</td><td>10</td><td>9</td></tr>
<tr><td rowspan="3">Dispensing</td><td>Both genders</td><td>304</td><td>189</td><td>39</td><td>26</td><td>35</td><td>15</td></tr>
<tr><td>Men</td><td>167</td><td>123</td><td>16</td><td>9</td><td>12</td><td>7</td></tr>
<tr><td>Women</td><td>137</td><td>66</td><td>23</td><td>17</td><td>23</td><td>8</td></tr>
<tr><td rowspan="3">Administrative</td><td>Both genders</td><td>70</td><td>44</td><td>10</td><td>2</td><td>7</td><td>7</td></tr>
<tr><td>Men</td><td>42</td><td>31</td><td>2</td><td>1</td><td>5</td><td>3</td></tr>
<tr><td>Women</td><td>28</td><td>13</td><td>8</td><td>1</td><td>2</td><td>4</td></tr>
<tr><td rowspan="3">Other</td><td>Both genders</td><td>50</td><td>35</td><td>2</td><td>1</td><td>11</td><td>1</td></tr>
<tr><td>Men</td><td>26</td><td>22</td><td>2</td><td>-</td><td>2</td><td>-</td></tr>
<tr><td>Women</td><td>24</td><td>13</td><td>-</td><td>1</td><td>9</td><td>1</td></tr>
<tr><td rowspan="3">No response</td><td>Both genders</td><td>7</td><td>6</td><td>-</td><td>1</td><td>-</td><td>-</td></tr>
<tr><td>Men</td><td>3</td><td>3</td><td>-</td><td>-</td><td>-</td><td>-</td></tr>
<tr><td>Women</td><td>4</td><td>3</td><td>-</td><td>1</td><td>-</td><td>-</td></tr>
</table>

Table 5–7. Number of pharmacists who completed the survey questionnaire by county of residence, type of primary pharmacy activity, ethnic group, and gender (continued).

County of Residence	Primary Role as a Pharmacist	Gender	Number of Pharmacists					
			All Ethnic Groups	Non-Hispanic			Hispanic	Other
				White	Black	Asian		
Collier, Hendry, Lee, and Monroe	All groups	Both genders	202	181	4	5	12	-
		Men	111	99	2	3	7	-
		Women	91	82	2	2	5	-
	Clinical	Both genders	26	24	2	-	-	-
		Men	9	8	1	-	-	-
		Women	17	16	1	-	-	-
	Dispensing	Both genders	151	132	3	5	11	-
		Men	87	75	2	3	7	-
		Women	64	57	1	2	4	-
	Administrative	Both genders	24	23	-	-	1	-
		Men	14	14	-	-	-	-
		Women	10	9	-	-	1	-
	Other	Both genders	8	8	-	-	-	-
		Men	6	6	-	-	-	-
		Women	2	2	-	-	-	-
	No response	Both genders	2	2	-	-	-	-
		Men	2	2	-	-	-	-
		Women	-	-	-	-	-	-
Martin and Pasco	All groups	Both genders	96	76	4	6	5	5
		Men	57	46	-	5	3	3
		Women	39	30	4	1	2	2
	Clinical	Both genders	28	21	-	4	-	3
		Men	18	14	-	3	-	1
		Women	10	7	-	1	-	2
	Dispensing	Both genders	55	44	3	4	4	-
		Men	30	24	-	4	2	-
		Women	25	20	3	-	2	-
	Administrative	Both genders	10	10	-	-	-	-
		Men	8	8	-	-	-	-
		Women	2	2	-	-	-	-
	Other	Both genders	6	2	1	-	1	2
		Men	5	2	-	-	1	2
		Women	1	-	1	-	-	-
	No response	Both genders	1	1	-	-	-	-
		Men	-	-	-	-	-	-
		Women	1	1	-	-	-	-

Table 5–7. **Number of pharmacists who completed the survey questionnaire by county of residence, type of primary pharmacy activity, ethnic group, and gender (continued).**

County of Residence	Primary Role as a Pharmacist	Gender	Number of Pharmacists					
			All Ethnic Groups	Non-Hispanic			Hispanic	Other
				White	Black	Asian		
Miami-Dade	All groups	Both genders	342	98	31	14	189	10
		Men	140	69	9	7	54	1
		Women	202	29	22	7	135	9
	Clinical	Both genders	66	18	6	3	34	5
		Men	27	12	2	2	11	-
		Women	39	6	4	1	23	5
	Dispensing	Both genders	231	67	21	11	126	6
		Men	97	48	7	6	35	1
		Women	134	19	14	5	91	5
	Administrative	Both genders	48	12	3	1	31	1
		Men	20	10	-	-	10	-
		Women	28	2	3	1	21	1
	Other	Both genders	21	8	1	-	11	1
		Men	9	5	-	-	3	1
		Women	12	3	1	-	8	-
	No response	Both genders	-	-	-	-	-	-
		Men	-	-	-	-	-	-
		Women	-	-	-	-	-	-
Palm Beach	All groups	Both genders	348	270	21	20	28	9
		Men	206	179	6	6	10	5
		Women	142	91	15	14	18	4
	Clinical	Both genders	53	34	5	4	9	1
		Men	24	18	1	2	3	-
		Women	29	16	4	2	6	1
	Dispensing	Both genders	240	193	12	13	17	5
		Men	149	134	4	4	5	2
		Women	91	59	8	9	12	3
	Administrative	Both genders	39	30	3	1	2	3
		Men	25	19	1	1	2	2
		Women	14	11	2	-	-	1
	Other	Both genders	23	18	1	3	-	1
		Men	13	12	-	-	-	1
		Women	10	6	1	3	-	-
	No response	Both genders	3	2	1	-	-	-
		Men	1	1	-	-	-	-
		Women	2	1	1	-	-	-

Table 5–7. Number of pharmacists who completed the survey questionnaire by county of residence, type of primary pharmacy activity, ethnic group, and gender (continued).

County of Residence	Primary Role as a Pharmacist	Gender	Number of Pharmacists					
			All Ethnic Groups	Non-Hispanic			Hispanic	Other
				White	Black	Asian		
Other	All groups	Both genders	43	17	4	6	15	1
		Men	21	11	2	3	5	-
		Women	22	6	2	3	10	1
	Clinical	Both genders	11	5	1	1	4	-
		Men	4	2	1	-	1	-
		Women	7	3	-	1	3	-
	Dispensing	Both genders	29	11	2	5	10	1
		Men	13	8	-	3	2	-
		Women	16	3	2	2	8	1
	Administrative	Both genders	3	2	-	-	1	-
		Men	2	1	-	-	1	-
		Women	1	1	-	-	-	-
	Other	Both genders	4	2	-	-	2	-
		Men	2	1	-	-	1	-
		Women	2	1	-	-	1	-
	No response	Both genders	1	-	1	-	-	-
		Men	1	-	1	-	-	-
		Women	-	-	-	-	-	-

Some pharmacists report more than one primary role; consequently, in any specific category the total may exceed the sum of the parts.

Table 5–8. Number of pharmacists who completed the survey questionnaire by county of residence, type of primary pharmacy activity, age group, and gender.

County of Residence	Primary Role as a Pharmacist	Gender	Number of Pharmacists							
			All Age Groups	Less than 30	30-39	40-49	50-59	60-69	70 and Older	Not Known
All counties	All groups	Both genders	1,539	97	367	364	329	192	154	36
		Men	805	23	108	157	204	166	128	19
		Women	734	74	259	207	125	26	26	17
	Clinical	Both genders	285	23	93	72	67	13	9	8
		Men	125	7	28	27	39	11	9	4
		Women	160	16	65	45	28	2	-	4
	Dispensing	Both genders	1,010	65	229	225	200	148	122	21
		Men	543	14	67	96	123	128	103	12
		Women	467	51	162	129	77	20	19	9
	Administrative	Both genders	194	10	42	57	51	20	9	5
		Men	111	2	14	31	39	17	6	2
		Women	83	8	28	26	12	3	3	3
	Other	Both genders	112	4	22	27	23	16	17	3
		Men	61	-	6	12	14	15	12	2
		Women	51	4	16	15	9	1	5	1
	No response	Both genders	14	-	1	6	5	2	-	-
		Men	7	-	-	3	3	1	-	-
		Women	7	-	1	3	2	1	-	-
Broward	All groups	Both genders	508	25	124	136	110	60	40	13
		Men	270	4	36	70	69	51	34	6
		Women	238	21	88	66	41	9	6	7
	Clinical	Both genders	101	5	31	30	24	5	3	3
		Men	43	2	8	12	12	5	3	1
		Women	58	3	23	18	12	-	-	2
	Dispensing	Both genders	304	16	72	78	59	43	27	9
		Men	167	2	24	40	37	37	23	4
		Women	137	14	48	38	22	6	4	5
	Administrative	Both genders	70	3	18	19	17	8	4	1
		Men	42	-	4	14	13	6	4	1
		Women	28	3	14	5	4	2	-	-
	Other	Both genders	50	2	9	14	14	3	7	1
		Men	26	-	-	8	9	3	5	1
		Women	24	2	9	6	5	-	2	-
	No response	Both genders	7	-	1	2	2	2	-	-
		Men	3	-	-	1	1	1	-	-
		Women	4	-	1	1	1	1	-	-

Table 5–8. Number of pharmacists who completed the survey questionnaire by county of residence, type of primary pharmacy activity, age group, and gender (continued).

County of Residence	Primary Role as a Pharmacist	Gender	Number of Pharmacists							
			All Age Groups	Less than 30	30-39	40-49	50-59	60-69	70 and Older	Not Known
Collier, Hendry, Lee, and Monroe	All groups	Both genders	202	16	40	49	58	22	13	4
		Men	111	5	13	20	39	19	12	3
		Women	91	11	27	29	19	3	1	1
	Clinical	Both genders	26	-	6	13	6	-	-	1
		Men	9	-	-	3	5	-	-	1
		Women	17	-	6	10	1	-	-	-
	Dispensing	Both genders	151	15	28	29	45	20	12	2
		Men	87	4	11	14	28	17	11	2
		Women	64	11	17	15	17	3	1	-
	Administrative	Both genders	24	1	5	8	7	2	-	1
		Men	14	1	2	3	6	2	-	-
		Women	10	-	3	5	1	-	-	1
	Other	Both genders	8	-	3	-	1	3	1	-
		Men	6	-	1	-	1	3	1	-
		Women	2	-	2	-	-	-	-	-
	No response	Both genders	2	-	-	1	1	-	-	-
		Men	2	-	-	1	1	-	-	-
		Women	-	-	-	-	-	-	-	-
Martin and Pasco	All groups	Both genders	96	6	18	23	29	12	7	1
		Men	57	2	8	7	21	11	7	1
		Women	39	4	10	16	8	1	-	-
	Clinical	Both genders	28	4	6	5	9	3	1	-
		Men	18	1	3	2	8	3	1	-
		Women	10	3	3	3	1	-	-	-
	Dispensing	Both genders	55	2	11	15	13	7	6	1
		Men	30	1	4	5	7	6	6	1
		Women	25	1	7	10	6	1	-	-
	Administrative	Both genders	10	-	1	3	6	-	-	-
		Men	8	-	1	1	6	-	-	-
		Women	2	-	-	2	-	-	-	-
	Other	Both genders	6	-	1	1	1	3	-	-
		Men	5	-	1	-	1	3	-	-
		Women	1	-	-	1	-	-	-	-
	No response	Both genders	1	-	-	-	1	-	-	-
		Men	-	-	-	-	-	-	-	-
		Women	1	-	-	-	1	-	-	-

Table 5–8. Number of pharmacists who completed the survey questionnaire by county of residence, type of primary pharmacy activity, age group, and gender (continued).

County of Residence	Primary Role as a Pharmacist	Gender	Number of Pharmacists							
			All Age Groups	Less than 30	30-39	40-49	50-59	60-69	70 and Older	Not Known
Miami-Dade	All groups	Both genders	342	21	94	86	63	35	34	9
		Men	140	7	25	32	28	26	19	3
		Women	202	14	69	54	35	9	15	6
	Clinical	Both genders	66	7	24	15	14	3	2	1
		Men	27	2	8	7	7	1	2	-
		Women	39	5	16	8	7	2	-	1
	Dispensing	Both genders	231	13	60	58	39	27	28	6
		Men	97	5	15	21	17	20	16	3
		Women	134	8	45	37	22	7	12	3
	Administrative	Both genders	48	2	10	16	9	7	3	1
		Men	20	-	3	6	5	6	-	-
		Women	28	2	7	10	4	1	3	1
	Other	Both genders	21	-	6	8	4	-	2	1
		Men	9	-	3	3	2	-	1	-
		Women	12	-	3	5	2	-	1	1
	No response	Both genders	-	-	-	-	-	-	-	-
		Men	-	-	-	-	-	-	-	-
		Women	-	-	-	-	-	-	-	-
Palm Beach	All groups	Both genders	348	24	74	65	63	60	55	7
		Men	206	4	18	26	45	57	52	4
		Women	142	20	56	39	18	3	3	3
	Clinical	Both genders	53	5	20	8	13	2	3	2
		Men	24	1	7	3	7	2	3	1
		Women	29	4	13	5	6	-	-	1
	Dispensing	Both genders	240	15	47	41	40	49	46	2
		Men	149	2	8	15	32	47	44	1
		Women	91	13	39	26	8	2	2	1
	Administrative	Both genders	39	4	6	11	11	3	2	2
		Men	25	1	3	7	8	3	2	1
		Women	14	3	3	4	3	-	-	1
	Other	Both genders	23	2	3	4	2	6	5	1
		Men	13	-	1	1	1	5	4	1
		Women	10	2	2	3	1	1	1	-
	No response	Both genders	3	-	-	2	1	-	-	-
		Men	1	-	-	-	1	-	-	-
		Women	2	-	-	2	-	-	-	-

Table 5–8. **Number of pharmacists who completed the survey questionnaire by county of residence, type of primary pharmacy activity, age group, and gender (continued).**

County of Residence	Primary Role as a Pharmacist	Gender	Number of Pharmacists							
			All Age Groups	Less than 30	30-39	40-49	50-59	60-69	70 and Older	Not Known
Other	All groups	Both genders	43	5	17	5	6	3	5	2
		Men	21	1	8	2	2	2	4	2
		Women	22	4	9	3	4	1	1	-
	Clinical	Both genders	11	2	6	1	1	-	-	1
		Men	4	1	2	-	-	-	-	1
		Women	7	1	4	1	1	-	-	-
	Dispensing	Both genders	29	4	11	4	4	2	3	1
		Men	13	-	5	1	2	1	3	1
		Women	16	4	6	3	2	1	-	-
	Administrative	Both genders	3	-	2	-	1	-	-	-
		Men	2	-	1	-	1	-	-	-
		Women	1	-	1	-	-	-	-	-
	Other	Both genders	4	-	-	-	1	1	2	-
		Men	2	-	-	-	-	1	1	-
		Women	2	-	-	-	1	-	1	-
	No response	Both genders	1	-	-	1	-	-	-	-
		Men	1	-	-	1	-	-	-	-
		Women	-	-	-	-	-	-	-	-

Some pharmacists report more than one primary role; consequently, in any specific category the total may exceed the sum of the parts.

Table 5–9. Number of pharmacists who completed the survey questionnaire by county of residence, location of primary practice site, ethnic group, and gender.

County of Residence	Location of Primary Practice Site	Gender	Number of Pharmacists					
			All Ethnic Groups	Non-Hispanic			Hispanic	Other
				White	Black	Asian		
All counties	All groups	Both genders	1,539	958	119	86	319	57
		Men	805	603	41	35	105	21
		Women	734	355	78	51	214	36
	Large city	Both genders	847	424	93	46	244	40
		Men	423	278	36	18	75	16
		Women	424	146	57	28	169	24
	Suburb or small city	Both genders	596	465	20	37	60	14
		Men	339	288	5	17	25	4
		Women	257	177	15	20	35	10
	Town or rural area	Both genders	63	45	5	3	8	2
		Men	32	26	-	-	5	1
		Women	31	19	5	3	3	1
	No response	Both genders	33	24	1	-	7	1
		Men	11	11	-	-	-	-
		Women	22	13	1	-	7	1
Broward	All groups	Both genders	508	316	55	35	70	32
		Men	270	199	22	11	26	12
		Women	238	117	33	24	44	20
	Large city	Both genders	299	166	45	18	46	24
		Men	157	106	20	5	16	10
		Women	142	60	25	13	30	14
	Suburb or small city	Both genders	183	135	7	16	19	6
		Men	101	84	2	6	8	1
		Women	82	51	5	10	11	5
	Town or rural area	Both genders	9	2	3	1	2	1
		Men	5	2	-	-	2	1
		Women	4	-	3	1	-	-
	No response	Both genders	17	13	-	-	3	1
		Men	7	7	-	-	-	-
		Women	10	6	-	-	3	1
Collier, Hendry, Lee, and Monroe	All groups	Both genders	202	181	4	5	12	-
		Men	111	99	2	3	7	-
		Women	91	82	2	2	5	-
	Large city	Both genders	47	41	1	2	3	-
		Men	27	24	-	1	2	-
		Women	20	17	1	1	1	-
	Suburb or small city	Both genders	137	125	3	3	6	-
		Men	74	66	2	2	4	-
		Women	63	59	1	1	2	-
	Town or rural area	Both genders	16	13	-	-	3	-
		Men	8	7	-	-	1	-
		Women	8	6	-	-	2	-
	No response	Both genders	2	2	-	-	-	-
		Men	2	2	-	-	-	-
		Women	-	-	-	-	-	-

Table 5–9. Number of pharmacists who completed the survey questionnaire by county of residence, location of primary practice site, ethnic group, and gender (continued).

County of Residence	Location of Primary Practice Site	Gender	Number of Pharmacists					
			All Ethnic Groups	Non-Hispanic			Hispanic	Other
				White	Black	Asian		
Martin and Pasco	All groups	Both genders	96	76	4	6	5	5
		Men	57	46	-	5	3	3
		Women	39	30	4	1	2	2
	Large city	Both genders	30	18	2	4	1	5
		Men	18	11	-	3	1	3
		Women	12	7	2	1	-	2
	Suburb or small city	Both genders	45	38	1	2	4	-
		Men	30	26	-	2	2	-
		Women	15	12	1	-	2	-
	Town or rural area	Both genders	19	18	1	-	-	-
		Men	9	9	-	-	-	-
		Women	10	9	1	-	-	-
	No response	Both genders	2	2	-	-	-	-
		Men	-	-	-	-	-	-
		Women	2	2	-	-	-	-
Miami-Dade	All groups	Both genders	342	98	31	14	189	10
		Men	140	69	9	7	54	1
		Women	202	29	22	7	135	9
	Large city	Both genders	291	82	29	10	162	8
		Men	119	58	9	5	46	1
		Women	172	24	20	5	116	7
	Suburb or small city	Both genders	38	13	1	2	21	1
		Men	18	10	-	2	6	-
		Women	20	3	1	-	15	1
	Town or rural area	Both genders	7	1	1	2	2	1
		Men	3	1	-	-	2	-
		Women	4	-	1	2	-	1
	No response	Both genders	6	2	-	-	4	-
		Men	-	-	-	-	-	-
		Women	6	2	-	-	4	-
Palm Beach	All groups	Both genders	348	270	21	20	28	9
		Men	206	179	6	6	10	5
		Women	142	91	15	14	18	4
	Large city	Both genders	149	106	12	10	19	2
		Men	89	72	5	4	6	2
		Women	60	34	7	6	13	-
	Suburb or small city	Both genders	183	150	8	10	8	7
		Men	108	98	1	2	4	3
		Women	75	52	7	8	4	4
	Town or rural area	Both genders	11	10	-	-	1	-
		Men	7	7	-	-	-	-
		Women	4	3	-	-	1	-
	No response	Both genders	5	4	1	-	-	-
		Men	2	2	-	-	-	-
		Women	3	2	1	-	-	-

Table 5–9. Number of pharmacists who completed the survey questionnaire by county of residence, location of primary practice site, ethnic group, and gender (continued).

County of Residence	Location of Primary Practice Site	Gender	Number of Pharmacists					
			All Ethnic Groups	Non-Hispanic			Hispanic	Other
				White	Black	Asian		
Other	All groups	Both genders	43	17	4	6	15	1
		Men	21	11	2	3	5	-
		Women	22	6	2	3	10	1
	Large city	Both genders	31	11	4	2	13	1
		Men	13	7	2	-	4	-
		Women	18	4	2	2	9	1
	Suburb or small city	Both genders	10	4	-	4	2	-
		Men	8	4	-	3	1	-
		Women	2	-	-	1	1	-
	Town or rural area	Both genders	1	1	-	-	-	-
		Men	-	-	-	-	-	-
		Women	1	1	-	-	-	-
	No response	Both genders	1	1	-	-	-	-
		Men	-	-	-	-	-	-
		Women	1	1	-	-	-	-

Table 5–10. Number of pharmacists who completed the survey questionnaire by county of residence, location of primary practice site, age group, and gender.

County of Residence	Location of Primary Practice Site	Gender	Number of Pharmacists							
			All Age Groups	Less than 30	30-39	40-49	50-59	60-69	70 and Older	Not Known
All counties	All groups	Both genders	1,539	97	367	364	329	192	154	36
		Men	805	23	108	157	204	166	128	19
		Women	734	74	259	207	125	26	26	17
	Large city	Both genders	847	58	217	205	161	97	88	21
		Men	423	16	64	91	96	82	64	10
		Women	424	42	153	114	65	15	24	11
	Suburb or small city	Both genders	596	34	135	136	134	84	61	12
		Men	339	7	42	59	87	77	59	8
		Women	257	27	93	77	47	7	2	4
	Town or rural area	Both genders	63	4	11	13	23	7	4	1
		Men	32	-	2	6	15	5	4	-
		Women	31	4	9	7	8	2	-	1
	No response	Both genders	33	1	4	10	11	4	1	2
		Men	11	-	-	1	6	2	1	1
		Women	22	1	4	9	5	2	-	1
Broward	All groups	Both genders	508	25	124	136	110	60	40	13
		Men	270	4	36	70	69	51	34	6
		Women	238	21	88	66	41	9	6	7
	Large city	Both genders	299	19	73	81	65	31	25	5
		Men	157	4	20	41	42	26	21	3
		Women	142	15	53	40	23	5	4	2
	Suburb or small city	Both genders	183	3	48	49	35	28	14	6
		Men	101	-	16	25	21	25	12	2
		Women	82	3	32	24	14	3	2	4
	Town or rural area	Both genders	9	2	-	3	3	-	-	1
		Men	5	-	-	3	2	-	-	-
		Women	4	2	-	-	1	-	-	1
	No response	Both genders	17	1	3	3	7	1	1	1
		Men	7	-	-	1	4	-	1	1
		Women	10	1	3	2	3	1	-	-
Collier, Hendry, Lee, and Monroe	All groups	Both genders	202	16	40	49	58	22	13	4
		Men	111	5	13	20	39	19	12	3
		Women	91	11	27	29	19	3	1	1
	Large city	Both genders	47	4	12	10	9	7	3	2
		Men	27	1	6	5	5	7	2	1
		Women	20	3	6	5	4	-	1	1
	Suburb or small city	Both genders	137	11	25	35	42	12	10	2
		Men	74	4	7	14	28	9	10	2
		Women	63	7	18	21	14	3	-	-
	Town or rural area	Both genders	16	1	3	4	6	2	-	-
		Men	8	-	-	1	5	2	-	-
		Women	8	1	3	3	1	-	-	-
	No response	Both genders	2	-	-	-	1	1	-	-
		Men	2	-	-	-	1	1	-	-
		Women	-	-	-	-	-	-	-	-

Table 5–10. **Number of pharmacists who completed the survey questionnaire by county of residence, location of primary practice site, age group, and gender (continued).**

County of Residence	Location of Primary Practice Site	Gender	Number of Pharmacists							
			All Age Groups	Less than 30	30-39	40-49	50-59	60-69	70 and Older	Not Known
Martin and Pasco	All groups	Both genders	96	6	18	23	29	12	7	1
		Men	57	2	8	7	21	11	7	1
		Women	39	4	10	16	8	1	-	-
	Large city	Both genders	30	4	7	7	6	4	2	-
		Men	18	1	2	3	6	4	2	-
		Women	12	3	5	4	-	-	-	-
	Suburb or small city	Both genders	45	2	9	14	9	7	3	1
		Men	30	1	6	4	8	7	3	1
		Women	15	1	3	10	1	-	-	-
	Town or rural area	Both genders	19	-	2	1	13	1	2	-
		Men	9	-	-	-	7	-	2	-
		Women	10	-	2	1	6	1	-	-
	No response	Both genders	2	-	-	1	1	-	-	-
		Men	-	-	-	-	-	-	-	-
		Women	2	-	-	1	1	-	-	-
Miami-Dade	All groups	Both genders	342	21	94	86	63	35	34	9
		Men	140	7	25	32	28	26	19	3
		Women	202	14	69	54	35	9	15	6
	Large city	Both genders	291	16	81	68	55	32	32	7
		Men	119	6	21	26	23	24	17	2
		Women	172	10	60	42	32	8	15	5
	Suburb or small city	Both genders	38	5	11	10	8	2	1	1
		Men	18	1	4	4	5	2	1	1
		Women	20	4	7	6	3	-	-	-
	Town or rural area	Both genders	7	-	1	4	-	1	1	-
		Men	3	-	-	2	-	-	1	-
		Women	4	-	1	2	-	1	-	-
	No response	Both genders	6	-	1	4	-	-	-	1
		Men	-	-	-	-	-	-	-	-
		Women	6	-	1	4	-	-	-	1
Palm Beach	All groups	Both genders	348	24	74	65	63	60	55	7
		Men	206	4	18	26	45	57	52	4
		Women	142	20	56	39	18	3	3	3
	Large city	Both genders	149	12	30	34	24	21	23	5
		Men	89	3	10	14	20	20	20	2
		Women	60	9	20	20	4	1	3	3
	Suburb or small city	Both genders	183	12	39	28	37	34	31	2
		Men	108	1	6	12	23	33	31	2
		Women	75	11	33	16	14	1	-	-
	Town or rural area	Both genders	11	-	5	1	1	3	1	-
		Men	7	-	2	-	1	3	1	-
		Women	4	-	3	1	-	-	-	-
	No response	Both genders	5	-	-	2	1	2	-	-
		Men	2	-	-	-	1	1	-	-
		Women	3	-	-	2	-	1	-	-

Table 5–10. Number of pharmacists who completed the survey questionnaire by county of residence, location of primary practice site, age group, and gender (continued).

County of Residence	Location of Primary Practice Site	Gender	Number of Pharmacists							
			All Age Groups	Less than 30	30-39	40-49	50-59	60-69	70 and Older	Not Known
Other	All groups	Both genders	43	5	17	5	6	3	5	2
		Men	21	1	8	2	2	2	4	2
		Women	22	4	9	3	4	1	1	-
	Large city	Both genders	31	3	14	5	2	2	3	2
		Men	13	1	5	2	-	1	2	2
		Women	18	2	9	3	2	1	1	-
	Suburb or small city	Both genders	10	1	3	-	3	1	2	-
		Men	8	-	3	-	2	1	2	-
		Women	2	1	-	-	1	-	-	-
	Town or rural area	Both genders	1	1	-	-	-	-	-	-
		Men	-	-	-	-	-	-	-	-
		Women	1	1	-	-	-	-	-	-
	No response	Both genders	1	-	-	-	1	-	-	-
		Men	-	-	-	-	-	-	-	-
		Women	1	-	-	-	1	-	-	-

Table 5–11. Number of pharmacists who completed the survey questionnaire by county of residence, distance from home to work, ethnic group, and gender.

County of Residence	Distance from Home to Work (miles)	Gender	Number of Pharmacists					
			All Ethnic Groups	Non-Hispanic			Hispanic	Other
				White	Black	Asian		
All counties	All groups	Both genders	1,539	958	119	86	319	57
		Men	805	603	41	35	105	21
		Women	734	355	78	51	214	36
	Less than 5	Both genders	296	194	9	17	66	10
		Men	150	116	4	4	24	2
		Women	146	78	5	13	42	8
	5 - 9	Both genders	353	225	22	23	67	16
		Men	192	143	9	9	25	6
		Women	161	82	13	14	42	10
	10 - 14	Both genders	302	193	31	17	52	9
		Men	161	123	11	9	15	3
		Women	141	70	20	8	37	6
	15 - 19	Both genders	179	102	12	14	42	9
		Men	97	67	3	9	13	5
		Women	82	35	9	5	29	4
	20 or more	Both genders	323	195	38	13	64	13
		Men	163	120	11	4	23	5
		Women	160	75	27	9	41	8
	No response	Both genders	86	49	7	2	28	-
		Men	42	34	3	-	5	-
		Women	44	15	4	2	23	-
Broward	All groups	Both genders	508	316	55	35	70	32
		Men	270	199	22	11	26	12
		Women	238	117	33	24	44	20
	Less than 5	Both genders	96	68	5	8	12	3
		Men	46	37	2	1	5	1
		Women	50	31	3	7	7	2
	5 - 9	Both genders	100	59	8	10	13	10
		Men	53	37	3	4	6	3
		Women	47	22	5	6	7	7
	10 - 14	Both genders	109	73	15	6	9	6
		Men	64	51	7	2	1	3
		Women	45	22	8	4	8	3
	15 - 19	Both genders	61	36	5	3	12	5
		Men	32	23	2	1	4	2
		Women	29	13	3	2	8	3
	20 or more	Both genders	125	71	21	7	18	8
		Men	67	45	7	3	9	3
		Women	58	26	14	4	9	5
	No response	Both genders	17	9	1	1	6	-
		Men	8	6	1	-	1	-
		Women	9	3	-	1	5	-

Table 5–11. Number of pharmacists who completed the survey questionnaire by county of residence, distance from home to work, ethnic group, and gender (continued).

County of Residence	Distance from Home to Work (miles)	Gender	Number of Pharmacists					
			All Ethnic Groups	Non-Hispanic			Hispanic	Other
				White	Black	Asian		
Collier, Hendry, Lee, and Monroe	All groups	Both genders	202	181	4	5	12	-
		Men	111	99	2	3	7	-
		Women	91	82	2	2	5	-
	Less than 5	Both genders	45	42	-	1	2	-
		Men	25	23	-	1	1	-
		Women	20	19	-	-	1	-
	5 - 9	Both genders	59	54	-	-	5	-
		Men	32	30	-	-	2	-
		Women	27	24	-	-	3	-
	10 - 14	Both genders	40	36	-	3	1	-
		Men	23	21	-	2	-	-
		Women	17	15	-	1	1	-
	15 - 19	Both genders	19	17	1	-	1	-
		Men	12	11	-	-	1	-
		Women	7	6	1	-	-	-
	20 or more	Both genders	28	23	1	1	3	-
		Men	12	8	1	-	3	-
		Women	16	15	-	1	-	-
	No response	Both genders	11	9	2	-	-	-
		Men	7	6	1	-	-	-
		Women	4	3	1	-	-	-
Martin and Pasco	All groups	Both genders	96	76	4	6	5	5
		Men	57	46	-	5	3	3
		Women	39	30	4	1	2	2
	Less than 5	Both genders	10	9	1	-	-	-
		Men	6	6	-	-	-	-
		Women	4	3	1	-	-	-
	5 - 9	Both genders	23	18	1	1	3	-
		Men	14	12	-	1	1	-
		Women	9	6	1	-	2	-
	10 - 14	Both genders	19	16	1	1	-	1
		Men	9	8	-	1	-	-
		Women	10	8	1	-	-	1
	15 - 19	Both genders	9	5	-	3	-	1
		Men	8	4	-	3	-	1
		Women	1	1	-	-	-	-
	20 or more	Both genders	33	26	1	1	2	3
		Men	19	15	-	-	2	2
		Women	14	11	1	1	-	1
	No response	Both genders	2	2	-	-	-	-
		Men	1	1	-	-	-	-
		Women	1	1	-	-	-	-

Table 5–11. Number of pharmacists who completed the survey questionnaire by county of residence, distance from home to work, ethnic group, and gender (continued).

County of Residence	Distance from Home to Work (miles)	Gender	Number of Pharmacists					
			All Ethnic Groups	Non-Hispanic			Hispanic	Other
				White	Black	Asian		
Miami-Dade	All groups	Both genders	342	98	31	14	189	10
		Men	140	69	9	7	54	1
		Women	202	29	22	7	135	9
	Less than 5	Both genders	74	23	1	3	43	4
		Men	32	16	1	1	14	-
		Women	42	7	-	2	29	4
	5 - 9	Both genders	78	28	6	3	38	3
		Men	41	23	4	1	12	1
		Women	37	5	2	2	26	2
	10 - 14	Both genders	66	15	9	4	37	1
		Men	27	10	3	2	12	-
		Women	39	5	6	2	25	1
	15 - 19	Both genders	41	12	3	2	23	1
		Men	17	8	-	2	7	-
		Women	24	4	3	-	16	1
	20 or more	Both genders	53	12	10	2	28	1
		Men	16	8	1	1	6	-
		Women	37	4	9	1	22	1
	No response	Both genders	30	8	2	-	20	-
		Men	7	4	-	-	3	-
		Women	23	4	2	-	17	-
Palm Beach	All groups	Both genders	348	270	21	20	28	9
		Men	206	179	6	6	10	5
		Women	142	91	15	14	18	4
	Less than 5	Both genders	62	49	2	5	4	2
		Men	36	32	1	1	1	1
		Women	26	17	1	4	3	1
	5 - 9	Both genders	85	63	6	6	7	3
		Men	49	40	1	2	4	2
		Women	36	23	5	4	3	1
	10 - 14	Both genders	60	48	6	2	3	1
		Men	33	30	1	1	1	-
		Women	27	18	5	1	2	1
	15 - 19	Both genders	44	30	3	5	4	2
		Men	25	19	1	2	1	2
		Women	19	11	2	3	3	-
	20 or more	Both genders	71	59	2	1	8	1
		Men	44	41	1	-	2	-
		Women	27	18	1	1	6	1
	No response	Both genders	26	21	2	1	2	-
		Men	19	17	1	-	1	-
		Women	7	4	1	1	1	-

Table 5–11. **Number of pharmacists who completed the survey questionnaire by county of residence, distance from home to work, ethnic group, and gender (continued).**

County of Residence	Distance from Home to Work (miles)	Gender	Number of Pharmacists					
			All Ethnic Groups	Non-Hispanic			Hispanic	Other
				White	Black	Asian		
Other	All groups	Both genders	43	17	4	6	15	1
		Men	21	11	2	3	5	-
		Women	22	6	2	3	10	1
	Less than 5	Both genders	9	3	-	-	5	1
		Men	5	2	-	-	3	-
		Women	4	1	-	-	2	1
	5 - 9	Both genders	8	3	1	3	1	-
		Men	3	1	1	1	-	-
		Women	5	2	-	2	1	-
	10 - 14	Both genders	8	5	-	1	2	-
		Men	5	3	-	1	1	-
		Women	3	2	-	-	1	-
	15 - 19	Both genders	5	2	-	1	2	-
		Men	3	2	-	1	-	-
		Women	2	-	-	-	2	-
	20 or more	Both genders	13	4	3	1	5	-
		Men	5	3	1	-	1	-
		Women	8	1	2	1	4	-
	No response	Both genders	-	-	-	-	-	-
		Men	-	-	-	-	-	-
		Women	-	-	-	-	-	-

Table 5–12. Number of pharmacists who completed the survey questionnaire by county of residence, distance from home to work, age group, and gender.

County of Residence	Distance from Home to Work (miles)	Gender	Number of Pharmacists							
			All Age Groups	Less than 30	30-39	40-49	50-59	60-69	70 and Older	Not Known
All counties	All groups	Both genders	1,539	97	367	364	329	192	154	36
		Men	805	23	108	157	204	166	128	19
		Women	734	74	259	207	125	26	26	17
	Less than 5	Both genders	296	16	65	73	67	44	27	4
		Men	150	3	20	27	38	40	20	2
		Women	146	13	45	46	29	4	7	2
	5 - 9	Both genders	353	22	91	80	74	47	32	7
		Men	192	7	25	46	48	35	27	4
		Women	161	15	66	34	26	12	5	3
	10 - 14	Both genders	302	23	75	67	55	37	34	11
		Men	161	6	21	31	36	34	27	6
		Women	141	17	54	36	19	3	7	5
	15 - 19	Both genders	179	17	43	39	42	18	18	2
		Men	97	2	20	13	27	18	15	2
		Women	82	15	23	26	15	-	3	-
	20 or more	Both genders	323	18	77	86	65	35	31	11
		Men	163	4	21	33	43	29	28	5
		Women	160	14	56	53	22	6	3	6
	No response	Both genders	86	1	16	19	26	11	12	1
		Men	42	1	1	7	12	10	11	-
		Women	44	-	15	12	14	1	1	1
Broward	All groups	Both genders	508	25	124	136	110	60	40	13
		Men	270	4	36	70	69	51	34	6
		Women	238	21	88	66	41	9	6	7
	Less than 5	Both genders	96	3	28	30	16	13	6	-
		Men	46	-	7	13	8	13	5	-
		Women	50	3	21	17	8	-	1	-
	5 - 9	Both genders	100	3	28	27	19	13	9	1
		Men	53	-	8	15	14	8	8	-
		Women	47	3	20	12	5	5	1	1
	10 - 14	Both genders	109	5	24	26	18	19	10	7
		Men	64	1	7	15	12	18	8	3
		Women	45	4	17	11	6	1	2	4
	15 - 19	Both genders	61	4	13	15	19	4	6	-
		Men	32	1	5	5	11	4	6	-
		Women	29	3	8	10	8	-	-	-
	20 or more	Both genders	125	9	29	35	30	10	7	5
		Men	67	1	9	20	21	7	6	3
		Women	58	8	20	15	9	3	1	2
	No response	Both genders	17	1	2	3	8	1	2	-
		Men	8	1	-	2	3	1	1	-
		Women	9	-	2	1	5	-	1	-

Table 5–12. Number of pharmacists who completed the survey questionnaire by county of residence, distance from home to work, age group, and gender (continued).

County of Residence	Distance from Home to Work (miles)	Gender	Number of Pharmacists							
			All Age Groups	Less than 30	30-39	40-49	50-59	60-69	70 and Older	Not Known
Collier, Hendry, Lee, and Monroe	All groups	Both genders	202	16	40	49	58	22	13	4
		Men	111	5	13	20	39	19	12	3
		Women	91	11	27	29	19	3	1	1
	Less than 5	Both genders	45	2	6	10	16	6	5	-
		Men	25	-	3	2	10	5	5	-
		Women	20	2	3	8	6	1	-	-
	5 - 9	Both genders	59	5	12	17	18	4	3	-
		Men	32	3	2	8	12	4	3	-
		Women	27	2	10	9	6	-	-	-
	10 - 14	Both genders	40	4	9	10	8	3	4	2
		Men	23	1	3	6	5	3	3	2
		Women	17	3	6	4	3	-	1	-
	15 - 19	Both genders	19	4	7	1	3	3	-	1
		Men	12	1	4	-	3	3	-	1
		Women	7	3	3	1	-	-	-	-
	20 or more	Both genders	28	1	4	8	9	5	-	1
		Men	12	-	1	2	6	3	-	-
		Women	16	1	3	6	3	2	-	1
	No response	Both genders	11	-	2	3	4	1	1	-
		Men	7	-	-	2	3	1	1	-
		Women	4	-	2	1	1	-	-	-
Martin and Pasco	All groups	Both genders	96	6	18	23	29	12	7	1
		Men	57	2	8	7	21	11	7	1
		Women	39	4	10	16	8	1	-	-
	Less than 5	Both genders	10	-	1	4	4	1	-	-
		Men	6	-	1	1	3	1	-	-
		Women	4	-	-	3	1	-	-	-
	5 - 9	Both genders	23	1	5	5	7	5	-	-
		Men	14	1	3	2	3	5	-	-
		Women	9	-	2	3	4	-	-	-
	10 - 14	Both genders	19	3	3	4	6	-	2	1
		Men	9	-	-	1	5	-	2	1
		Women	10	3	3	3	1	-	-	-
	15 - 19	Both genders	9	-	3	3	2	-	1	-
		Men	8	-	3	2	2	-	1	-
		Women	1	-	-	1	-	-	-	-
	20 or more	Both genders	33	2	6	7	8	6	4	-
		Men	19	1	1	1	7	5	4	-
		Women	14	1	5	6	1	1	-	-
	No response	Both genders	2	-	-	-	2	-	-	-
		Men	1	-	-	-	1	-	-	-
		Women	1	-	-	-	1	-	-	-

Table 5–12. Number of pharmacists who completed the survey questionnaire by county of residence, distance from home to work, age group, and gender (continued).

County of Residence	Distance from Home to Work (miles)	Gender	Number of Pharmacists							
			All Age Groups	Less than 30	30-39	40-49	50-59	60-69	70 and Older	Not Known
Miami-Dade	All groups	Both genders	342	21	94	86	63	35	34	9
		Men	140	7	25	32	28	26	19	3
		Women	202	14	69	54	35	9	15	6
	Less than 5	Both genders	74	6	15	18	13	8	10	4
		Men	32	2	5	6	6	6	5	2
		Women	42	4	10	12	7	2	5	2
	5 - 9	Both genders	78	2	23	18	13	12	8	2
		Men	41	-	8	11	10	6	5	1
		Women	37	2	15	7	3	6	3	1
	10 - 14	Both genders	66	5	19	18	12	6	5	1
		Men	27	3	5	7	5	5	2	-
		Women	39	2	14	11	7	1	3	1
	15 - 19	Both genders	41	4	10	11	8	3	5	-
		Men	17	-	3	6	3	3	2	-
		Women	24	4	7	5	5	-	3	-
	20 or more	Both genders	53	4	17	14	11	3	3	1
		Men	16	2	4	1	4	3	2	-
		Women	37	2	13	13	7	-	1	1
	No response	Both genders	30	-	10	7	6	3	3	1
		Men	7	-	-	1	-	3	3	-
		Women	23	-	10	6	6	-	-	1
Palm Beach	All groups	Both genders	348	24	74	65	63	60	55	7
		Men	206	4	18	26	45	57	52	4
		Women	142	20	56	39	18	3	3	3
	Less than 5	Both genders	62	5	14	9	15	15	4	-
		Men	36	1	3	5	9	14	4	-
		Women	26	4	11	4	6	1	-	-
	5 - 9	Both genders	85	9	19	13	16	13	12	3
		Men	49	3	2	10	9	12	11	2
		Women	36	6	17	3	7	1	1	1
	10 - 14	Both genders	60	4	16	9	11	7	13	-
		Men	33	-	3	2	9	7	12	-
		Women	27	4	13	7	2	-	1	-
	15 - 19	Both genders	44	5	6	9	10	8	6	-
		Men	25	-	3	-	8	8	6	-
		Women	19	5	3	9	2	-	-	-
	20 or more	Both genders	71	1	17	19	5	11	14	4
		Men	44	-	6	7	5	11	13	2
		Women	27	1	11	12	-	-	1	2
	No response	Both genders	26	-	2	6	6	6	6	-
		Men	19	-	1	2	5	5	6	-
		Women	7	-	1	4	1	1	-	-

Table 5–12. Number of pharmacists who completed the survey questionnaire by county of residence, distance from home to work, age group, and gender (continued).

County of Residence	Distance from Home to Work (miles)	Gender	Number of Pharmacists							
			All Age Groups	Less than 30	30-39	40-49	50-59	60-69	70 and Older	Not Known
Other	All groups	Both genders	43	5	17	5	6	3	5	2
		Men	21	1	8	2	2	2	4	2
		Women	22	4	9	3	4	1	1	-
	Less than 5	Both genders	9	-	1	2	3	1	2	-
		Men	5	-	1	-	2	1	1	-
		Women	4	-	-	2	1	-	1	-
	5 - 9	Both genders	8	2	4	-	1	-	-	1
		Men	3	-	2	-	-	-	-	1
		Women	5	2	2	-	1	-	-	-
	10 - 14	Both genders	8	2	4	-	-	2	-	-
		Men	5	1	3	-	-	1	-	-
		Women	3	1	1	-	-	1	-	-
	15 - 19	Both genders	5	-	4	-	-	-	-	1
		Men	3	-	2	-	-	-	-	1
		Women	2	-	2	-	-	-	-	-
	20 or more	Both genders	13	1	4	3	2	-	3	-
		Men	5	-	-	2	-	-	3	-
		Women	8	1	4	1	2	-	-	-
	No response	Both genders	-	-	-	-	-	-	-	-
		Men	-	-	-	-	-	-	-	-
		Women	-	-	-	-	-	-	-	-

Table 5–13. Median distance from home to work of pharmacists who completed the survey questionnaire by county of residence, ethnic group, and gender.

County of Residence	Gender	Median Distance from Home to Work (miles)					
		All Ethnic Groups	Non-Hispanic			Hispanic	Other
			White	Black	Asian		
All counties	Both genders	10.0	10.0	12.0	10.0	10.0	10.0
	Men	10.0	10.0	10.0	10.0	10.0	10.0
	Women	10.0	10.0	12.0	8.0	10.0	9.5
Broward	Both genders	10.0	10.0	13.5	9.0	12.5	10.0
	Men	11.0	11.0	13.0	9.5	15.0	10.0
	Women	10.0	10.0	15.0	8.0	10.0	10.5
Collier, Hendry, Lee, and Monroe	Both genders	8.0	8.0	27.5	10.0	7.5	-
	Men	8.0	8.0	40.0	10.0	15.0	-
	Women	8.0	8.0	15.0	15.0	6.0	-
Martin and Pasco	Both genders	12.0	11.5	-	15.0	7.0	40.0
	Men	14.0	10.0	7.5	15.0	28.0	50.0
	Women	12.0	12.0	7.5	20.0	7.0	26.5
Miami-Dade	Both genders	10.0	7.5	12.0	10.0	10.0	6.5
	Men	8.0	7.0	8.5	12.0	8.0	5.0
	Women	10.0	10.0	16.5	5.0	10.0	8.0
Palm Beach	Both genders	10.0	10.0	10.0	7.0	10.0	8.0
	Men	10.0	10.0	10.0	9.0	6.0	8.0
	Women	10.0	10.0	10.0	6.0	15.0	8.5
Other	Both genders	10.0	10.0	25.0	7.5	10.0	4.0
	Men	10.0	12.0	15.0	10.0	3.0	-
	Women	10.0	8.0	112.5	5.0	15.0	4.0

Table 5–14. Median distance from home to work of pharmacists who completed the survey questionnaire by county of residence, age group, and gender.

County of Residence	Gender	Median Distance from Home to Work (miles)							
		All Age Groups	Less than 30	30-39	40-49	50-59	60-69	70 and Older	Not Known
All counties	Both genders	10.0	10.0	10.0	10.0	10.0	9.0	10.0	10.0
	Men	10.0	10.0	10.0	9.5	10.0	10.0	10.0	10.0
	Women	10.0	10.0	10.0	10.0	10.0	8.0	10.0	11.0
Broward	Both genders	10.0	15.0	10.0	10.0	14.0	10.0	11.5	12.0
	Men	11.0	15.0	10.5	10.0	14.0	10.0	12.0	27.5
	Women	10.0	15.0	10.0	10.0	12.5	8.0	10.0	12.0
Collier, Hendry, Lee, and Monroe	Both genders	8.0	10.0	10.0	7.5	7.0	12.0	6.0	12.5
	Men	8.0	8.0	10.0	8.0	8.0	10.0	8.0	10.0
	Women	8.0	10.0	8.0	7.5	5.5	20.0	10.0	20.0
Martin and Pasco	Both genders	12.0	12.5	13.5	10.0	10.0	16.5	20.0	12.0
	Men	14.0	22.5	11.5	10.0	14.0	9.0	20.0	12.0
	Women	12.0	12.5	16.0	11.0	7.0	24.0	-	-
Miami-Dade	Both genders	10.0	10.0	10.0	10.0	10.0	7.5	6.0	5.0
	Men	8.0	10.0	8.0	8.0	8.0	8.5	6.0	2.0
	Women	10.0	10.5	10.0	10.0	10.0	7.5	6.0	8.0
Palm Beach	Both genders	10.0	7.0	10.0	12.0	8.0	8.0	11.5	20.0
	Men	10.0	5.5	15.0	6.5	10.0	9.0	12.0	14.5
	Women	10.0	9.0	7.0	15.0	5.0	6.0	10.0	20.0
Other	Both genders	10.0	10.0	12.0	25.0	5.0	10.0	25.0	10.0
	Men	10.0	10.0	11.0	39.0	3.0	5.5	25.0	10.0
	Women	10.0	8.0	15.0	4.0	18.0	10.0	2.0	-

Table 5–15. Number of pharmacists who completed the survey questionnaire by county of residence, average one-way commute time to work, ethnic group, and gender.

County of Residence	One-Way Commute Time to Work (minutes)	Gender	Number of Pharmacists					
			All Ethnic Groups	Non-Hispanic			Hispanic	Other
				White	Black	Asian		
All counties	All groups	Both genders	1,539	958	119	86	319	57
		Men	805	603	41	35	105	21
		Women	734	355	78	51	214	36
	Less than 15	Both genders	359	228	17	24	78	12
		Men	175	136	3	6	27	3
		Women	184	92	14	18	51	9
	15 - 29	Both genders	542	356	30	37	98	21
		Men	284	218	14	19	25	8
		Women	258	138	16	18	73	13
	30 - 44	Both genders	376	231	33	16	81	15
		Men	203	149	14	6	29	5
		Women	173	82	19	10	52	10
	45 or more	Both genders	193	103	26	8	48	8
		Men	112	74	10	4	20	4
		Women	81	29	16	4	28	4
	No response	Both genders	69	40	13	1	14	1
		Men	31	26	-	-	4	1
		Women	38	14	13	1	10	-
Broward	All groups	Both genders	508	316	55	35	70	32
		Men	270	199	22	11	26	12
		Women	238	117	33	24	44	20
	Less than 15	Both genders	110	73	5	10	18	4
		Men	52	44	1	1	5	1
		Women	58	29	4	9	13	3
	15 - 29	Both genders	176	111	20	13	19	13
		Men	89	62	7	5	9	6
		Women	87	49	13	8	10	7
	30 - 44	Both genders	140	86	17	8	19	10
		Men	81	63	7	3	6	2
		Women	59	23	10	5	13	8
	45 or more	Both genders	67	37	13	4	9	4
		Men	41	25	7	2	5	2
		Women	26	12	6	2	4	2
	No response	Both genders	15	9	-	-	5	1
		Men	7	5	-	-	1	1
		Women	8	4	-	-	4	-

Table 5–15. Number of pharmacists who completed the survey questionnaire by county of residence, average one-way commute time to work, ethnic group, and gender (continued).

County of Residence	One-Way Commute Time to Work (minutes)	Gender	Number of Pharmacists					
			All Ethnic Groups	Non-Hispanic			Hispanic	Other
				White	Black	Asian		
Collier, Hendry, Lee, and Monroe	All groups	Both genders	202	181	4	5	12	-
		Men	111	99	2	3	7	-
		Women	91	82	2	2	5	-
	Less than 15	Both genders	52	46	-	2	4	-
		Men	26	23	-	1	2	-
		Women	26	23	-	1	2	-
	15 - 29	Both genders	83	76	1	2	4	-
		Men	51	47	1	2	1	-
		Women	32	29	-	-	3	-
	30 - 44	Both genders	43	40	1	1	1	-
		Men	20	19	-	-	1	-
		Women	23	21	1	1	-	-
	45 or more	Both genders	14	10	1	-	3	-
		Men	8	4	1	-	3	-
		Women	6	6	-	-	-	-
	No response	Both genders	10	9	1	-	-	-
		Men	6	6	-	-	-	-
		Women	4	3	1	-	-	-
Martin and Pasco	All groups	Both genders	96	76	4	6	5	5
		Men	57	46	-	5	3	3
		Women	39	30	4	1	2	2
	Less than 15	Both genders	22	17	2	2	1	-
		Men	14	11	-	2	1	-
		Women	8	6	2	-	-	-
	15 - 29	Both genders	31	26	1	1	2	1
		Men	18	17	-	1	-	-
		Women	13	9	1	-	2	1
	30 - 44	Both genders	26	20	1	3	1	1
		Men	14	10	-	2	1	1
		Women	12	10	1	1	-	-
	45 or more	Both genders	16	12	-	-	1	3
		Men	11	8	-	-	1	2
		Women	5	4	-	-	-	1
	No response	Both genders	1	1	-	-	-	-
		Men	-	-	-	-	-	-
		Women	1	1	-	-	-	-

Table 5–15. **Number of pharmacists who completed the survey questionnaire by county of residence, average one-way commute time to work, ethnic group, and gender (continued).**

County of Residence	One-Way Commute Time to Work (minutes)	Gender	Number of Pharmacists					
			All Ethnic Groups	Non-Hispanic			Hispanic	Other
				White	Black	Asian		
Miami-Dade	All groups	Both genders	342	98	31	14	189	10
		Men	140	69	9	7	54	1
		Women	202	29	22	7	135	9
	Less than 15	Both genders	79	22	3	3	46	5
		Men	34	16	2	-	15	1
		Women	45	6	1	3	31	4
	15 - 29	Both genders	107	35	7	5	57	3
		Men	42	25	2	4	11	-
		Women	65	10	5	1	46	3
	30 - 44	Both genders	88	26	8	3	49	2
		Men	39	18	3	1	17	-
		Women	49	8	5	2	32	2
	45 or more	Both genders	54	10	12	3	29	-
		Men	20	8	2	2	8	-
		Women	34	2	10	1	21	-
	No response	Both genders	14	5	1	-	8	-
		Men	5	2	-	-	3	-
		Women	9	3	1	-	5	-
Palm Beach	All groups	Both genders	348	270	21	20	28	9
		Men	206	179	6	6	10	5
		Women	142	91	15	14	18	4
	Less than 15	Both genders	88	66	7	5	7	3
		Men	44	40	-	1	2	1
		Women	44	26	7	4	5	2
	15 - 29	Both genders	141	104	9	13	12	3
		Men	79	64	4	5	4	2
		Women	62	40	5	8	8	1
	30 - 44	Both genders	64	51	4	1	6	2
		Men	41	34	2	-	3	2
		Women	23	17	2	1	3	-
	45 or more	Both genders	36	33	-	-	2	1
		Men	29	28	-	-	1	-
		Women	7	5	-	-	1	1
	No response	Both genders	19	16	1	1	1	-
		Men	13	13	-	-	-	-
		Women	6	3	1	1	1	-

Table 5–15. Number of pharmacists who completed the survey questionnaire by county of residence, average one-way commute time to work, ethnic group, and gender (continued).

County of Residence	One-Way Commute Time to Work (minutes)	Gender	Number of Pharmacists					
			All Ethnic Groups	Non-Hispanic			Hispanic	Other
				White	Black	Asian		
Other	All groups	Both genders	43	17	4	6	15	1
		Men	21	11	2	3	5	-
		Women	22	6	2	3	10	1
	Less than 15	Both genders	8	4	-	2	2	-
		Men	5	2	-	1	2	-
		Women	3	2	-	1	-	-
	15 - 29	Both genders	13	4	1	3	4	1
		Men	5	3	-	2	-	-
		Women	8	1	1	1	4	1
	30 - 44	Both genders	16	8	3	-	5	-
		Men	8	5	2	-	1	-
		Women	8	3	1	-	4	-
	45 or more	Both genders	6	1	-	1	4	-
		Men	3	1	-	-	2	-
		Women	3	-	-	1	2	-
	No response	Both genders	-	-	-	-	-	-
		Men	-	-	-	-	-	-
		Women	-	-	-	-	-	-

Table 5–16. Number of pharmacists who completed the survey questionnaire by county of residence, average one-way commute time to work, age group, and gender.

County of Residence	One-Way Commute Time to Work (minutes)	Gender	Number of Pharmacists							
			All Age Groups	Less than 30	30-39	40-49	50-59	60-69	70 and Older	Not Known
All counties	All groups	Both genders	1,539	97	367	364	329	192	154	36
		Men	805	23	108	157	204	166	128	19
		Women	734	74	259	207	125	26	26	17
	Less than 15	Both genders	359	23	95	85	76	47	29	4
		Men	175	4	26	31	43	44	25	2
		Women	184	19	69	54	33	3	4	2
	15 - 29	Both genders	551	43	135	123	113	67	53	17
		Men	284	11	36	58	73	56	41	9
		Women	267	32	99	65	40	11	12	8
	30 - 44	Both genders	377	21	90	98	76	42	40	10
		Men	203	3	34	44	48	35	33	6
		Women	174	18	56	54	28	7	7	4
	45 or more	Both genders	193	9	38	44	46	26	25	5
		Men	112	4	12	20	30	22	22	2
		Women	81	5	26	24	16	4	3	3
	No response	Both genders	59	1	9	14	18	10	7	-
		Men	31	1	-	4	10	9	7	-
		Women	28	-	9	10	8	1	-	-
Broward	All groups	Both genders	508	25	124	136	110	60	40	13
		Men	270	4	36	70	69	51	34	6
		Women	238	21	88	66	41	9	6	7
	Less than 15	Both genders	110	5	35	31	18	13	8	-
		Men	52	-	8	13	11	12	8	-
		Women	58	5	27	18	7	1	-	-
	15 - 29	Both genders	176	8	48	42	36	23	12	7
		Men	89	1	14	23	21	18	9	3
		Women	87	7	34	19	15	5	3	4
	30 - 44	Both genders	140	6	25	45	32	16	12	4
		Men	81	-	9	23	22	15	10	2
		Women	59	6	16	22	10	1	2	2
	45 or more	Both genders	67	5	13	15	18	7	7	2
		Men	41	2	5	10	12	5	6	1
		Women	26	3	8	5	6	2	1	1
	No response	Both genders	15	1	3	3	6	1	1	-
		Men	7	1	-	1	3	1	1	-
		Women	8	-	3	2	3	-	-	-

Table 5–16. Number of pharmacists who completed the survey questionnaire by county of residence, average one-way commute time to work, age group, and gender (continued).

County of Residence	One-Way Commute Time to Work (minutes)	Gender	Number of Pharmacists							
			All Age Groups	Less than 30	30-39	40-49	50-59	60-69	70 and Older	Not Known
Collier, Hendry, Lee, and Monroe	All groups	Both genders	202	16	40	49	58	22	13	4
		Men	111	5	13	20	39	19	12	3
		Women	91	11	27	29	19	3	1	1
	Less than 15	Both genders	52	2	10	15	16	3	6	-
		Men	26	-	4	5	8	3	6	-
		Women	26	2	6	10	8	-	-	-
	15 - 29	Both genders	83	11	13	19	25	9	5	1
		Men	51	5	3	10	19	8	5	1
		Women	32	6	10	9	6	1	-	-
	30 - 44	Both genders	43	3	13	8	8	7	1	3
		Men	20	-	6	2	5	5	-	2
		Women	23	3	7	6	3	2	1	1
	45 or more	Both genders	14	-	2	5	5	2	-	-
		Men	8	-	-	2	4	2	-	-
		Women	6	-	2	3	1	-	-	-
	No response	Both genders	10	-	2	2	4	1	1	-
		Men	6	-	-	1	3	1	1	-
		Women	4	-	2	1	1	-	-	-
Martin and Pasco	All groups	Both genders	96	6	18	23	29	12	7	1
		Men	57	2	8	7	21	11	7	1
		Women	39	4	10	16	8	1	-	-
	Less than 15	Both genders	22	1	4	5	8	4	-	-
		Men	14	1	3	1	5	4	-	-
		Women	8	-	1	4	3	-	-	-
	15 - 29	Both genders	31	2	6	9	9	2	2	1
		Men	18	-	3	4	6	2	2	1
		Women	13	2	3	5	3	-	-	-
	30 - 44	Both genders	26	2	8	5	4	3	4	-
		Men	14	-	2	2	4	2	4	-
		Women	12	2	6	3	-	1	-	-
	45 or more	Both genders	16	1	-	4	7	3	1	-
		Men	11	1	-	-	6	3	1	-
		Women	5	-	-	4	1	-	-	-
	No response	Both genders	1	-	-	-	1	-	-	-
		Men	-	-	-	-	-	-	-	-
		Women	1	-	-	-	1	-	-	-

Table 5–16. Number of pharmacists who completed the survey questionnaire by county of residence, average one-way commute time to work, age group, and gender (continued).

County of Residence	One-Way Commute Time to Work (minutes)	Gender	Number of Pharmacists							
			All Age Groups	Less than 30	30-39	40-49	50-59	60-69	70 and Older	Not Known
Miami-Dade	All groups	Both genders	342	21	94	86	63	35	34	9
		Men	140	7	25	32	28	26	19	3
		Women	202	14	69	54	35	9	15	6
	Less than 15	Both genders	79	6	21	21	12	9	7	3
		Men	34	2	6	7	7	8	3	1
		Women	45	4	15	14	5	1	4	2
	15 - 29	Both genders	107	6	31	26	18	11	11	4
		Men	42	1	9	10	9	6	5	2
		Women	65	5	22	16	9	5	6	2
	30 - 44	Both genders	88	6	24	23	19	6	10	-
		Men	39	3	7	10	8	5	6	-
		Women	49	3	17	13	11	1	4	-
	45 or more	Both genders	54	3	15	12	11	6	5	2
		Men	20	1	3	4	4	4	4	-
		Women	34	2	12	8	7	2	1	2
	No response	Both genders	14	-	3	4	3	3	1	-
		Men	5	-	-	1	-	3	1	-
		Women	9	-	3	3	3	-	-	-
Palm Beach	All groups	Both genders	348	24	74	65	63	60	55	7
		Men	206	4	18	26	45	57	52	4
		Women	142	20	56	39	18	3	3	3
	Less than 15	Both genders	88	8	22	12	21	17	8	-
		Men	44	1	3	5	11	16	8	-
		Women	44	7	19	7	10	1	-	-
	15 - 29	Both genders	141	13	33	25	23	21	22	4
		Men	79	3	5	11	17	21	20	2
		Women	62	10	28	14	6	-	2	2
	30 - 44	Both genders	64	3	12	16	11	9	11	2
		Men	41	-	6	6	9	8	11	1
		Women	23	3	6	10	2	1	-	1
	45 or more	Both genders	36	-	6	7	4	8	10	1
		Men	29	-	4	3	4	8	9	1
		Women	7	-	2	4	-	-	1	-
	No response	Both genders	19	-	1	5	4	5	4	-
		Men	13	-	-	1	4	4	4	-
		Women	6	-	1	4	-	1	-	-

Table 5–16. **Number of pharmacists who completed the survey questionnaire by county of residence, average one-way commute time to work, age group, and gender (continued).**

County of Residence	One-Way Commute Time to Work (minutes)	Gender	Number of Pharmacists							
			All Age Groups	Less than 30	30-39	40-49	50-59	60-69	70 and Older	Not Known
Other	All groups	Both genders	43	5	17	5	6	3	5	2
		Men	21	1	8	2	2	2	4	2
		Women	22	4	9	3	4	1	1	-
	Less than 15	Both genders	8	1	3	1	1	1	-	1
		Men	5	-	2	-	1	1	-	1
		Women	3	1	1	1	-	-	-	-
	15 - 29	Both genders	13	3	4	2	2	1	1	-
		Men	5	1	2	-	1	1	-	-
		Women	8	2	2	2	1	-	1	-
	30 - 44	Both genders	16	1	8	1	2	1	2	1
		Men	8	-	4	1	-	-	2	1
		Women	8	1	4	-	2	1	-	-
	45 or more	Both genders	6	-	2	1	1	-	2	-
		Men	3	-	-	1	-	-	2	-
		Women	3	-	2	-	1	-	-	-
	No response	Both genders	-	-	-	-	-	-	-	-
		Men	-	-	-	-	-	-	-	-
		Women	-	-	-	-	-	-	-	-

Table 5–17. Median one-way commute time to work of pharmacists who completed the survey questionnaire by county of residence, ethnic group, and gender.

County of Residence	Gender	Median One-Way Commute Time to Work (minutes)					
		All Ethnic Groups	Non-Hispanic			Hispanic	Other
			White	Black	Asian		
All counties	Both genders	20.0	20.0	30.0	20.0	20.0	20.0
	Men	20.0	20.0	30.0	20.0	25.0	25.0
	Women	20.0	20.0	25.0	15.0	20.0	20.0
Broward	Both genders	25.0	20.0	30.0	20.0	20.0	25.0
	Men	25.0	25.0	30.0	20.0	25.0	25.0
	Women	20.0	20.0	25.0	15.0	20.0	27.5
Collier, Hendry, Lee, and Monroe	Both genders	20.0	20.0	30.0	15.0	20.0	-
	Men	20.0	20.0	37.5	15.0	30.0	-
	Women	20.0	20.0	30.0	20.0	20.0	-
Martin and Pasco	Both genders	22.0	20.0	10.0	29.0	15.0	50.0
	Men	25.0	20.0	-	28.0	40.0	60.0
	Women	20.0	22.0	10.0	30.0	15.0	32.5
Miami-Dade	Both genders	23.0	20.0	30.0	22.5	20.0	12.5
	Men	20.0	20.0	30.0	25.0	25.0	10.0
	Women	25.0	25.0	30.0	20.0	20.0	15.0
Palm Beach	Both genders	20.0	20.0	15.0	15.0	20.0	20.0
	Men	20.0	20.0	22.5	19.0	20.0	20.0
	Women	18.0	20.0	14.5	15.0	20.0	16.5
Other	Both genders	30.0	30.0	30.0	15.0	30.0	20.0
	Men	30.0	30.0	30.0	15.0	30.0	-
	Women	25.0	22.5	25.0	15.0	30.0	20.0

Table 5–18. Median one-way commute time to work of pharmacists who completed the survey questionnaire by county of residence, age group, and gender.

County of Residence	Gender	Median One-Way Commute Time to Work (minutes)							
		All Age Groups	Less than 30	30-39	40-49	50-59	60-69	70 and Older	Not Known
All counties	Both genders	20.0	20.0	20.0	25.0	20.0	20.0	25.0	25.0
	Men	20.0	20.0	25.0	25.0	20.0	20.0	25.0	25.0
	Women	20.0	20.0	20.0	20.0	20.0	21.0	24.0	25.0
Broward	Both genders	25.0	25.0	20.0	25.0	25.0	20.0	25.0	25.0
	Men	25.0	45.0	22.5	25.0	30.0	20.0	25.0	27.5
	Women	20.0	25.0	20.0	20.0	20.0	20.0	27.5	25.0
Collier, Hendry, Lee, and Monroe	Both genders	20.0	20.0	20.0	20.0	16.5	20.0	12.5	30.0
	Men	20.0	20.0	28.0	20.0	16.5	20.0	10.0	30.0
	Women	20.0	23.0	20.0	17.5	17.5	30.0	40.0	30.0
Martin and Pasco	Both genders	22.0	25.0	22.5	20.0	20.0	27.5	30.0	25.0
	Men	25.0	27.5	17.5	20.0	28.0	20.0	30.0	25.0
	Women	20.0	25.0	30.0	20.0	15.0	40.0	-	-
Miami-Dade	Both genders	23.0	25.0	20.0	25.0	27.5	20.0	25.0	15.0
	Men	20.0	30.0	20.0	25.0	20.0	20.0	30.0	15.0
	Women	25.0	20.0	24.0	25.0	30.0	20.0	23.0	15.0
Palm Beach	Both genders	20.0	15.0	15.0	25.0	20.0	20.0	25.0	25.0
	Men	20.0	17.5	30.0	20.0	20.0	20.0	25.0	25.0
	Women	18.0	15.0	15.0	25.0	11.0	20.0	20.0	25.0
Other	Both genders	30.0	15.0	30.0	20.0	25.0	20.0	40.0	20.0
	Men	30.0	20.0	27.5	52.5	13.5	14.5	42.5	20.0
	Women	25.0	15.0	30.0	20.0	35.0	40.0	15.0	-

Table 5–19. Number of pharmacists who completed the survey questionnaire by county of residence, average number of hours worked per week, ethnic group, and gender.

County of Residence	Average Work Week (hours)	Gender	Number of Pharmacists					
			All Ethnic Groups	Non-Hispanic			Hispanic	Other
				White	Black	Asian		
All counties	All groups	Both genders	1,539	958	119	86	319	57
		Men	805	603	41	35	105	21
		Women	734	355	78	51	214	36
	Less than 20	Both genders	96	79	-	3	13	1
		Men	60	58	-	-	2	-
		Women	36	21	-	3	11	1
	20 - 29	Both genders	119	83	4	4	26	2
		Men	56	51	1	-	4	-
		Women	63	32	3	4	22	2
	30 - 39	Both genders	190	135	6	13	30	6
		Men	83	70	1	3	8	1
		Women	107	65	5	10	22	5
	40 - 44	Both genders	821	458	86	54	190	33
		Men	422	290	28	24	67	13
		Women	399	168	58	30	123	20
	45 or more	Both genders	282	179	21	12	55	15
		Men	172	123	10	8	24	7
		Women	110	56	11	4	31	8
	No response	Both genders	31	24	2	-	5	-
		Men	12	11	1	-	-	-
		Women	19	13	1	-	5	-
Broward	All groups	Both genders	508	316	55	35	70	32
		Men	270	199	22	11	26	12
		Women	238	117	33	24	44	20
	Less than 20	Both genders	21	17	-	-	3	1
		Men	11	11	-	-	-	-
		Women	10	6	-	-	3	1
	20 - 29	Both genders	34	25	2	2	4	1
		Men	17	17	-	-	-	-
		Women	17	8	2	2	4	1
	30 - 39	Both genders	62	41	3	5	8	5
		Men	25	17	1	2	4	1
		Women	37	24	2	3	4	4
	40 - 44	Both genders	270	152	39	24	39	16
		Men	136	95	14	6	13	8
		Women	134	57	25	18	26	8
	45 or more	Both genders	112	74	11	4	14	9
		Men	78	56	7	3	9	3
		Women	34	18	4	1	5	6
	No response	Both genders	9	7	-	-	2	-
		Men	3	3	-	-	-	-
		Women	6	4	-	-	2	-

Table 5–19. Number of pharmacists who completed the survey questionnaire by county of residence, average number of hours worked per week, ethnic group, and gender (continued).

County of Residence	Average Work Week (hours)	Gender	Number of Pharmacists					
			All Ethnic Groups	Non-Hispanic			Hispanic	Other
				White	Black	Asian		
Collier, Hendry, Lee, and Monroe	All groups	Both genders	202	181	4	5	12	-
		Men	111	99	2	3	7	-
		Women	91	82	2	2	5	-
	Less than 20	Both genders	20	19	-	-	1	-
		Men	11	11	-	-	-	-
		Women	9	8	-	-	1	-
	20 - 29	Both genders	11	11	-	-	-	-
		Men	6	6	-	-	-	-
		Women	5	5	-	-	-	-
	30 - 39	Both genders	35	29	-	3	3	-
		Men	17	14	-	1	2	-
		Women	18	15	-	2	1	-
	40 - 44	Both genders	99	88	3	2	6	-
		Men	57	49	1	2	5	-
		Women	42	39	2	-	1	-
	45 or more	Both genders	31	28	1	-	2	-
		Men	17	16	1	-	-	-
		Women	14	12	-	-	2	-
	No response	Both genders	6	6	-	-	-	-
		Men	3	3	-	-	-	-
		Women	3	3	-	-	-	-
Martin and Pasco	All groups	Both genders	96	76	4	6	5	5
		Men	57	46	-	5	3	3
		Women	39	30	4	1	2	2
	Less than 20	Both genders	4	4	-	-	-	-
		Men	3	3	-	-	-	-
		Women	1	1	-	-	-	-
	20 - 29	Both genders	5	4	-	-	1	-
		Men	2	2	-	-	-	-
		Women	3	2	-	-	1	-
	30 - 39	Both genders	13	11	1	-	1	-
		Men	5	4	-	-	1	-
		Women	8	7	1	-	-	-
	40 - 44	Both genders	62	49	2	5	2	4
		Men	40	32	-	4	2	2
		Women	22	17	2	1	-	2
	45 or more	Both genders	11	7	1	1	1	1
		Men	7	5	-	1	-	1
		Women	4	2	1	-	1	-
	No response	Both genders	1	1	-	-	-	-
		Men	-	-	-	-	-	-
		Women	1	1	-	-	-	-

Table 5–19. Number of pharmacists who completed the survey questionnaire by county of residence, average number of hours worked per week, ethnic group, and gender (continued).

County of Residence	Average Work Week (hours)	Gender	Number of Pharmacists					
			All Ethnic Groups	Non-Hispanic			Hispanic	Other
				White	Black	Asian		
Miami-Dade	All groups	Both genders	342	98	31	14	189	10
		Men	140	69	9	7	54	1
		Women	202	29	22	7	135	9
	Less than 20	Both genders	13	5	-	1	7	-
		Men	6	5	-	-	1	-
		Women	7	-	-	1	6	-
	20 - 29	Both genders	28	10	2	-	15	1
		Men	10	6	1	-	3	-
		Women	18	4	1	-	12	1
	30 - 39	Both genders	30	11	2	4	12	1
		Men	10	9	-	-	1	-
		Women	20	2	2	4	11	1
	40 - 44	Both genders	195	40	25	7	117	6
		Men	76	30	7	5	34	-
		Women	119	10	18	2	83	6
	45 or more	Both genders	69	28	2	2	35	2
		Men	35	16	1	2	15	1
		Women	34	12	1	-	20	1
	No response	Both genders	7	4	-	-	3	-
		Men	3	3	-	-	-	-
		Women	4	1	-	-	3	-
Palm Beach	All groups	Both genders	348	270	21	20	28	9
		Men	206	179	6	6	10	5
		Women	142	91	15	14	18	4
	Less than 20	Both genders	35	33	-	2	-	-
		Men	27	27	-	-	-	-
		Women	8	6	-	2	-	-
	20 - 29	Both genders	38	32	-	1	5	-
		Men	19	19	-	-	-	-
		Women	19	13	-	1	5	-
	30 - 39	Both genders	47	42	-	1	4	-
		Men	26	26	-	-	-	-
		Women	21	16	-	1	4	-
	40 - 44	Both genders	171	119	15	14	17	6
		Men	102	78	5	6	10	3
		Women	69	41	10	8	7	3
	45 or more	Both genders	51	39	5	2	2	3
		Men	30	27	1	-	-	2
		Women	21	12	4	2	2	1
	No response	Both genders	6	5	1	-	-	-
		Men	2	2	-	-	-	-
		Women	4	3	1	-	-	-

Table 5–19. Number of pharmacists who completed the survey questionnaire by county of residence, average number of hours worked per week, ethnic group, and gender (continued).

County of Residence	Average Work Week (hours)	Gender	Number of Pharmacists					
			All Ethnic Groups	Non-Hispanic			Hispanic	Other
				White	Black	Asian		
Other	All groups	Both genders	43	17	4	6	15	1
		Men	21	11	2	3	5	-
		Women	22	6	2	3	10	1
	Less than 20	Both genders	3	1	-	-	2	-
		Men	2	1	-	-	1	-
		Women	1	-	-	-	1	-
	20 - 29	Both genders	3	1	-	1	1	-
		Men	2	1	-	-	1	-
		Women	1	-	-	1	-	-
	30 - 39	Both genders	3	1	-	-	2	-
		Men	-	-	-	-	-	-
		Women	3	1	-	-	2	-
	40 - 44	Both genders	24	10	2	2	9	1
		Men	11	6	1	1	3	-
		Women	13	4	1	1	6	1
	45 or more	Both genders	8	3	1	3	1	-
		Men	5	3	-	2	-	-
		Women	3	-	1	1	1	-
	No response	Both genders	2	1	1	-	-	-
		Men	1	-	1	-	-	-
		Women	1	1	-	-	-	-

Table 5–20. Number of pharmacists who completed the survey questionnaire by county of residence, average number of hours worked per week, age group, and gender.

County of Residence	Average Work Week (hours)	Gender	Number of Pharmacists							
			All Age Groups	Less than 30	30-39	40-49	50-59	60-69	70 and Older	Not Known
All counties	All groups	Both genders	1,539	97	367	364	329	192	154	36
		Men	805	23	108	157	204	166	128	19
		Women	734	74	259	207	125	26	26	17
	Less than 20	Both genders	96	2	10	12	6	16	46	4
		Men	60	-	-	-	1	16	41	2
		Women	36	2	10	12	5	-	5	2
	20 - 29	Both genders	119	3	19	21	16	17	37	6
		Men	56	-	-	2	7	14	29	4
		Women	63	3	19	19	9	3	8	2
	30 - 39	Both genders	190	3	47	44	36	28	25	7
		Men	83	1	8	9	14	23	24	4
		Women	107	2	39	35	22	5	1	3
	40 - 44	Both genders	821	65	226	205	178	94	36	17
		Men	422	15	78	96	115	84	26	8
		Women	399	50	148	109	63	10	10	9
	45 or more	Both genders	282	24	60	74	83	33	7	1
		Men	172	7	22	47	62	27	7	-
		Women	110	17	38	27	21	6	-	1
	No response	Both genders	31	-	5	8	10	4	3	1
		Men	12	-	-	3	5	2	1	1
		Women	19	-	5	5	5	2	2	-
Broward	All groups	Both genders	508	25	124	136	110	60	40	13
		Men	270	4	36	70	69	51	34	6
		Women	238	21	88	66	41	9	6	7
	Less than 20	Both genders	21	1	2	4	2	2	9	1
		Men	11	-	-	-	1	2	8	-
		Women	10	1	2	4	1	-	1	1
	20 - 29	Both genders	34	-	2	10	7	4	10	1
		Men	17	-	-	1	4	3	8	1
		Women	17	-	2	9	3	1	2	-
	30 - 39	Both genders	62	1	17	16	11	7	6	4
		Men	25	1	3	4	4	5	6	2
		Women	37	-	14	12	7	2	-	2
	40 - 44	Both genders	270	16	81	71	51	31	13	7
		Men	136	1	26	38	29	29	10	3
		Women	134	15	55	33	22	2	3	4
	45 or more	Both genders	112	7	21	33	34	15	2	-
		Men	78	2	7	26	29	12	2	-
		Women	34	5	14	7	5	3	-	-
	No response	Both genders	9	-	1	2	5	1	-	-
		Men	3	-	-	1	2	-	-	-
		Women	6	-	1	1	3	1	-	-

Table 5–20. Number of pharmacists who completed the survey questionnaire by county of residence, average number of hours worked per week, age group, and gender (continued).

County of Residence	Average Work Week (hours)	Gender	Number of Pharmacists							
			All Age Groups	Less than 30	30-39	40-49	50-59	60-69	70 and Older	Not Known
Collier, Hendry, Lee, and Monroe	All groups	Both genders	202	16	40	49	58	22	13	4
		Men	111	5	13	20	39	19	12	3
		Women	91	11	27	29	19	3	1	1
	Less than 20	Both genders	20	-	4	3	2	3	8	-
		Men	11	-	-	-	-	3	8	-
		Women	9	-	4	3	2	-	-	-
	20 - 29	Both genders	11	1	1	-	3	1	4	1
		Men	6	-	-	-	1	1	3	1
		Women	5	1	1	-	2	-	1	-
	30 - 39	Both genders	35	1	6	12	12	4	-	-
		Men	17	-	3	4	6	4	-	-
		Women	18	1	3	8	6	-	-	-
	40 - 44	Both genders	99	13	20	26	28	10	-	2
		Men	57	5	8	12	22	8	-	2
		Women	42	8	12	14	6	2	-	-
	45 or more	Both genders	31	1	6	8	11	4	-	1
		Men	17	-	2	4	8	3	-	-
		Women	14	1	4	4	3	1	-	1
	No response	Both genders	6	-	3	-	2	-	1	-
		Men	3	-	-	-	2	-	1	-
		Women	3	-	3	-	-	-	-	-
Martin and Pasco	All groups	Both genders	96	6	18	23	29	12	7	1
		Men	57	2	8	7	21	11	7	1
		Women	39	4	10	16	8	1	-	-
	Less than 20	Both genders	4	-	-	1	-	1	2	-
		Men	3	-	-	-	-	1	2	-
		Women	1	-	-	1	-	-	-	-
	20 - 29	Both genders	5	-	-	2	2	-	1	-
		Men	2	-	-	-	1	-	1	-
		Women	3	-	-	2	1	-	-	-
	30 - 39	Both genders	13	1	2	4	2	1	2	1
		Men	5	-	-	-	1	1	2	1
		Women	8	1	2	4	1	-	-	-
	40 - 44	Both genders	62	5	13	13	20	9	2	-
		Men	40	2	7	5	16	8	2	-
		Women	22	3	6	8	4	1	-	-
	45 or more	Both genders	11	-	3	3	4	1	-	-
		Men	7	-	1	2	3	1	-	-
		Women	4	-	2	1	1	-	-	-
	No response	Both genders	1	-	-	-	1	-	-	-
		Men	-	-	-	-	-	-	-	-
		Women	1	-	-	-	1	-	-	-

Table 5–20. Number of pharmacists who completed the survey questionnaire by county of residence, average number of hours worked per week, age group, and gender (continued).

County of Residence	Average Work Week (hours)	Gender	Number of Pharmacists							
			All Age Groups	Less than 30	30-39	40-49	50-59	60-69	70 and Older	Not Known
Miami-Dade	All groups	Both genders	342	21	94	86	63	35	34	9
		Men	140	7	25	32	28	26	19	3
		Women	202	14	69	54	35	9	15	6
	Less than 20	Both genders	13	-	-	3	1	3	4	2
		Men	6	-	-	-	-	3	2	1
		Women	7	-	-	3	1	-	2	1
	20 - 29	Both genders	28	-	4	5	3	4	8	4
		Men	10	-	-	1	1	2	4	2
		Women	18	-	4	4	2	2	4	2
	30 - 39	Both genders	30	-	12	4	3	5	6	-
		Men	10	-	1	-	1	3	5	-
		Women	20	-	11	4	2	2	1	-
	40 - 44	Both genders	195	12	56	58	38	16	12	3
		Men	76	3	18	23	14	12	6	-
		Women	119	9	38	35	24	4	6	3
	45 or more	Both genders	69	9	21	14	17	6	2	-
		Men	35	4	6	7	11	5	2	-
		Women	34	5	15	7	6	1	-	-
	No response	Both genders	7	-	1	2	1	1	2	-
		Men	3	-	-	1	1	1	-	-
		Women	4	-	1	1	-	-	2	-
Palm Beach	All groups	Both genders	348	24	74	65	63	60	55	7
		Men	206	4	18	26	45	57	52	4
		Women	142	20	56	39	18	3	3	3
	Less than 20	Both genders	35	1	4	1	1	7	20	1
		Men	27	-	-	-	-	7	19	1
		Women	8	1	4	1	1	-	1	-
	20 - 29	Both genders	38	2	11	4	1	6	14	-
		Men	19	-	-	-	-	6	13	-
		Women	19	2	11	4	1	-	1	-
	30 - 39	Both genders	47	-	9	7	8	10	11	2
		Men	26	-	1	1	2	10	11	1
		Women	21	-	8	6	6	-	-	1
	40 - 44	Both genders	171	15	44	35	38	28	8	3
		Men	102	3	14	17	33	27	7	1
		Women	69	12	30	18	5	1	1	2
	45 or more	Both genders	51	6	6	15	15	7	2	-
		Men	30	1	3	8	10	6	2	-
		Women	21	5	3	7	5	1	-	-
	No response	Both genders	6	-	-	3	-	2	-	1
		Men	2	-	-	-	-	1	-	1
		Women	4	-	-	3	-	1	-	-

Table 5–20. Number of pharmacists who completed the survey questionnaire by county of residence, average number of hours worked per week, age group, and gender (continued).

County of Residence	Average Work Week (hours)	Gender	Number of Pharmacists							
			All Age Groups	Less than 30	30-39	40-49	50-59	60-69	70 and Older	Not Known
Other	All groups	Both genders	43	5	17	5	6	3	5	2
		Men	21	1	8	2	2	2	4	2
		Women	22	4	9	3	4	1	1	-
	Less than 20	Both genders	3	-	-	-	-	-	3	-
		Men	2	-	-	-	-	-	2	-
		Women	1	-	-	-	-	-	1	-
	20 - 29	Both genders	3	-	1	-	-	2	-	-
		Men	2	-	-	-	-	2	-	-
		Women	1	-	1	-	-	-	-	-
	30 - 39	Both genders	3	-	1	1	-	1	-	-
		Men	-	-	-	-	-	-	-	-
		Women	3	-	1	1	-	1	-	-
	40 - 44	Both genders	24	4	12	2	3	-	1	2
		Men	11	1	5	1	1	-	1	2
		Women	13	3	7	1	2	-	-	-
	45 or more	Both genders	8	1	3	1	2	-	1	-
		Men	5	-	3	-	1	-	1	-
		Women	3	1	-	1	1	-	-	-
	No response	Both genders	2	-	-	1	1	-	-	-
		Men	1	-	-	1	-	-	-	-
		Women	1	-	-	-	1	-	-	-

Table 5–21. Median number of hours worked per week by pharmacists who completed the survey questionnaire by county of residence, ethnic group, and gender.

County of Residence	Gender	Median Number of Hours Worked per Week					
		All Ethnic Groups	Non-Hispanic			Hispanic	Other
			White	Black	Asian		
All counties	Both genders	40.0	40.0	40.0	40.0	40.0	40.0
	Men	40.0	40.0	41.0	40.0	40.0	40.0
	Women	40.0	40.0	40.0	40.0	40.0	40.0
Broward	Both genders	40.0	40.0	40.0	40.0	40.0	40.0
	Men	40.0	40.0	42.0	40.0	40.5	40.0
	Women	40.0	40.0	40.0	40.0	40.0	40.0
Collier, Hendry, Lee, and Monroe	Both genders	40.0	40.0	42.0	36.0	40.0	-
	Men	40.0	40.0	42.5	40.0	40.0	-
	Women	40.0	40.0	40.0	33.0	40.0	-
Martin and Pasco	Both genders	40.0	40.0	40.0	40.0	40.0	40.0
	Men	40.0	40.0	-	40.0	40.0	40.0
	Women	40.0	40.0	40.0	40.0	43.5	40.0
Miami-Dade	Both genders	40.0	40.0	40.0	40.0	40.0	40.0
	Men	40.0	40.0	40.0	40.0	40.0	88.0
	Women	40.0	40.0	40.0	32.0	40.0	40.0
Palm Beach	Both genders	40.0	40.0	40.0	40.0	40.0	44.0
	Men	40.0	40.0	42.0	40.0	40.0	42.0
	Women	40.0	40.0	40.0	40.0	40.0	44.0
Other	Both genders	40.0	40.0	40.0	42.5	40.0	40.0
	Men	40.0	40.0	40.0	45.0	40.0	-
	Women	40.0	40.0	50.0	40.0	40.0	40.0

Table 5–22. **Median number of hours worked per week by pharmacists who completed the survey questionnaire by county of residence, age group, and gender.**

County of Residence	Gender	Median Number of Hours Worked per Week							
		All Age Groups	Less than 30	30-39	40-49	50-59	60-69	70 and Older	Not Known
All counties	Both genders	40.0	40.0	40.0	40.0	40.0	40.0	25.0	40.0
	Men	40.0	44.0	40.0	40.0	40.0	40.0	25.0	34.5
	Women	40.0	40.0	40.0	40.0	40.0	40.0	25.0	40.0
Broward	Both genders	40.0	40.0	40.0	40.0	40.0	40.0	32.5	40.0
	Men	40.0	50.0	40.0	41.0	42.0	40.0	32.5	37.5
	Women	40.0	40.0	40.0	40.0	40.0	40.0	32.0	40.0
Collier, Hendry, Lee, and Monroe	Both genders	40.0	40.0	40.0	40.0	40.0	40.0	17.0	40.0
	Men	40.0	44.0	40.0	40.0	40.0	40.0	16.0	40.0
	Women	40.0	40.0	40.0	40.0	38.0	40.0	20.0	50.0
Martin and Pasco	Both genders	40.0	40.0	40.0	40.0	40.0	40.0	35.0	33.0
	Men	40.0	42.0	40.0	42.0	40.0	40.0	35.0	33.0
	Women	40.0	40.0	40.0	40.0	40.0	40.0	-	-
Miami-Dade	Both genders	40.0	42.0	40.0	40.0	40.0	40.0	33.5	20.0
	Men	40.0	50.0	40.0	40.0	40.0	40.0	35.0	20.0
	Women	40.0	40.0	40.0	40.0	40.0	40.0	32.0	32.0
Palm Beach	Both genders	40.0	40.0	40.0	40.0	40.0	40.0	24.0	37.0
	Men	40.0	42.0	40.0	41.0	40.0	40.0	22.5	34.0
	Women	40.0	40.0	40.0	40.0	40.0	45.0	24.0	40.0
Other	Both genders	40.0	42.0	40.0	40.0	40.0	20.0	16.0	40.0
	Men	40.0	42.0	42.0	40.0	44.0	20.0	28.0	40.0
	Women	40.0	41.0	40.0	40.0	40.0	30.0	8.0	-

Table 5–23. Number of pharmacists who completed the survey questionnaire by county of residence, annual income earned working as a pharmacist, ethnic group, and gender.

County of Residence	Annual Income Earned (dollars)	Gender	Number of Pharmacists					
			All Ethnic Groups	Non-Hispanic			Hispanic	Other
				White	Black	Asian		
All counties	All groups	Both genders	1,539	958	119	86	319	57
		Men	805	603	41	35	105	21
		Women	734	355	78	51	214	36
	Less than 70,000	Both genders	198	143	6	5	40	4
		Men	99	91	1	1	5	1
		Women	99	52	5	4	35	3
	70,000 - 99,999	Both genders	341	203	31	24	70	13
		Men	150	119	6	6	17	2
		Women	191	84	25	18	53	11
	100,000 - 119,999	Both genders	593	344	58	46	119	26
		Men	300	204	21	24	41	10
		Women	293	140	37	22	78	16
	120,000 or more	Both genders	246	159	15	5	57	10
		Men	173	120	11	3	32	7
		Women	73	39	4	2	25	3
	No response	Both genders	161	109	9	6	33	4
		Men	83	69	2	1	10	1
		Women	78	40	7	5	23	3
Broward	All groups	Both genders	508	316	55	35	70	32
		Men	270	199	22	11	26	12
		Women	238	117	33	24	44	20
	Less than 70,000	Both genders	53	41	-	2	7	3
		Men	28	25	-	1	1	1
		Women	25	16	-	1	6	2
	70,000 - 99,999	Both genders	111	69	14	12	12	4
		Men	54	44	5	3	1	1
		Women	57	25	9	9	11	3
	100,000 - 119,999	Both genders	198	115	26	16	25	16
		Men	94	65	8	5	10	6
		Women	104	50	18	11	15	10
	120,000 or more	Both genders	89	58	11	2	13	5
		Men	64	43	8	1	9	3
		Women	25	15	3	1	4	2
	No response	Both genders	57	33	4	3	13	4
		Men	30	22	1	1	5	1
		Women	27	11	3	2	8	3

Table 5–23. Number of pharmacists who completed the survey questionnaire by county of residence, annual income earned working as a pharmacist, ethnic group, and gender (continued).

County of Residence	Annual Income Earned (dollars)	Gender	Number of Pharmacists					
			All Ethnic Groups	Non-Hispanic			Hispanic	Other
				White	Black	Asian		
Collier, Hendry, Lee, and Monroe	All groups	Both genders	202	181	4	5	12	-
		Men	111	99	2	3	7	-
		Women	91	82	2	2	5	-
	Less than 70,000	Both genders	26	25	-	-	1	-
		Men	13	13	-	-	-	-
		Women	13	12	-	-	1	-
	70,000 - 99,999	Both genders	35	32	-	2	1	-
		Men	17	16	-	-	1	-
		Women	18	16	-	2	-	-
	100,000 - 119,999	Both genders	80	65	4	3	8	-
		Men	44	34	2	3	5	-
		Women	36	31	2	-	3	-
	120,000 or more	Both genders	36	35	-	-	1	-
		Men	22	21	-	-	1	-
		Women	14	14	-	-	-	-
	No response	Both genders	25	24	-	-	1	-
		Men	15	15	-	-	-	-
		Women	10	9	-	-	1	-
Martin and Pasco	All groups	Both genders	96	76	4	6	5	5
		Men	57	46	-	5	3	3
		Women	39	30	4	1	2	2
	Less than 70,000	Both genders	10	9	-	-	1	-
		Men	6	6	-	-	-	-
		Women	4	3	-	-	1	-
	70,000 - 99,999	Both genders	28	20	2	3	1	2
		Men	12	8	-	2	1	1
		Women	16	12	2	1	-	1
	100,000 - 119,999	Both genders	38	32	1	3	-	2
		Men	24	20	-	3	-	1
		Women	14	12	1	-	-	1
	120,000 or more	Both genders	18	14	-	-	3	1
		Men	15	12	-	-	2	1
		Women	3	2	-	-	1	-
	No response	Both genders	2	1	1	-	-	-
		Men	-	-	-	-	-	-
		Women	2	1	1	-	-	-

Table 5–23. Number of pharmacists who completed the survey questionnaire by county of residence, annual income earned working as a pharmacist, ethnic group, and gender (continued).

County of Residence	Annual Income Earned (dollars)	Gender	Number of Pharmacists					
			All Ethnic Groups	Non-Hispanic			Hispanic	Other
				White	Black	Asian		
Miami-Dade	All groups	Both genders	342	98	31	14	189	10
		Men	140	69	9	7	54	1
		Women	202	29	22	7	135	9
	Less than 70,000	Both genders	42	11	3	-	27	1
		Men	12	8	1	-	3	-
		Women	30	3	2	-	24	1
	70,000 - 99,999	Both genders	79	17	7	3	46	6
		Men	24	11	1	1	11	-
		Women	55	6	6	2	35	6
	100,000 - 119,999	Both genders	27	33	14	8	70	2
		Men	51	22	4	5	19	1
		Women	76	11	10	3	51	1
	120,000 or more	Both genders	63	21	4	1	36	1
		Men	39	17	3	1	18	-
		Women	24	4	1	-	18	1
	No response	Both genders	31	16	3	2	10	-
		Men	14	11	-	-	3	-
		Women	17	5	3	2	7	-
Palm Beach	All groups	Both genders	348	270	21	20	28	9
		Men	206	179	6	6	10	5
		Women	142	91	15	14	18	4
	Less than 70,000	Both genders	60	55	1	2	2	-
		Men	37	37	-	-	-	-
		Women	23	18	1	2	2	-
	70,000 - 99,999	Both genders	79	61	8	3	7	-
		Men	40	38	-	-	2	-
		Women	39	23	8	3	5	-
	100,000 - 119,999	Both genders	131	90	11	14	10	6
		Men	76	57	5	6	6	2
		Women	55	33	6	8	4	4
	120,000 or more	Both genders	38	31	-	-	4	3
		Men	32	27	-	-	2	3
		Women	6	4	-	-	2	-
	No response	Both genders	40	33	1	1	5	-
		Men	21	20	1	-	-	-
		Women	19	13	-	1	5	-

Table 5–23. Number of pharmacists who completed the survey questionnaire by county of residence, annual income earned working as a pharmacist, ethnic group, and gender (continued).

County of Residence	Annual Income Earned (dollars)	Gender	Number of Pharmacists					
			All Ethnic Groups	Non-Hispanic			Hispanic	Other
				White	Black	Asian		
Other	All groups	Both genders	43	17	4	6	15	1
		Men	21	11	2	3	5	-
		Women	22	6	2	3	10	1
	Less than 70,000	Both genders	7	2	2	1	2	-
		Men	3	2	-	-	1	-
		Women	4	-	2	1	1	-
	70,000 - 99,999	Both genders	9	4	-	1	3	1
		Men	3	2	-	-	1	-
		Women	6	2	-	1	2	1
	100,000 - 119,999	Both genders	19	9	2	2	6	-
		Men	11	6	2	2	1	-
		Women	8	3	-	-	5	-
	120,000 or more	Both genders	2	-	-	2	-	-
		Men	1	-	-	1	-	-
		Women	1	-	-	1	-	-
	No response	Both genders	6	2	-	-	4	-
		Men	3	1	-	-	2	-
		Women	3	1	-	-	2	-

Table 5–24. Number of pharmacists who completed the survey questionnaire by county of residence, annual income earned working as a pharmacist, age group, and gender.

County of Residence	Gender	Annual Income Earned (dollars)	Number of Pharmacists							
			All Age Groups	Less than 30	30-39	40-49	50-59	60-69	70 and Older	Not Known
All counties	All groups	Both genders	1,539	97	367	364	329	192	154	36
		Men	805	23	108	157	204	166	128	19
		Women	734	74	259	207	125	26	26	17
	Less than 70,000	Both genders	198	5	26	33	24	32	71	7
		Men	99	-	-	4	9	26	56	4
		Women	99	5	26	29	15	6	15	3
	70,000 - 99,999	Both genders	341	34	98	63	66	43	31	6
		Men	150	5	23	19	32	36	29	6
		Women	191	29	75	44	34	7	2	-
	100,000 - 119,999	Both genders	593	40	169	166	130	56	21	11
		Men	300	9	57	74	88	50	19	3
		Women	293	31	112	92	42	6	2	8
	120,000 or more	Both genders	246	14	46	70	78	35	1	2
		Men	173	9	24	49	57	32	1	1
		Women	73	5	22	21	21	3	-	1
	No response	Both genders	161	4	28	32	31	26	30	10
		Men	83	-	4	11	18	22	23	5
		Women	78	4	24	21	13	4	7	5
Broward	All groups	Both genders	508	25	124	136	110	60	40	13
		Men	270	4	36	70	69	51	34	6
		Women	238	21	88	66	41	9	6	7
	Less than 70,000	Both genders	53	1	5	13	9	6	15	4
		Men	28	-	-	4	4	4	14	2
		Women	25	1	5	9	5	2	1	2
	70,000 - 99,999	Both genders	111	9	31	23	23	15	8	2
		Men	54	2	7	10	13	12	8	2
		Women	57	7	24	13	10	3	-	-
	100,000 - 119,999	Both genders	198	13	61	58	31	22	9	4
		Men	94	1	20	26	20	19	7	1
		Women	104	12	41	32	11	3	2	3
	120,000 or more	Both genders	89	1	20	28	28	12	-	-
		Men	64	1	9	21	22	11	-	-
		Women	25	-	11	7	6	1	-	-
	No response	Both genders	57	1	7	14	19	5	8	3
		Men	30	-	-	9	10	5	5	1
		Women	27	1	7	5	9	-	3	2

Table 5–24. Number of pharmacists who completed the survey questionnaire by county of residence, annual income earned working as a pharmacist, age group, and gender (continued).

County of Residence	Gender	Annual Income Earned (dollars)	Number of Pharmacists							
			All Age Groups	Less than 30	30-39	40-49	50-59	60-69	70 and Older	Not Known
Collier, Hendry, Lee, and Monroe	All groups	Both genders	202	16	40	49	58	22	13	4
		Men	111	5	13	20	39	19	12	3
		Women	91	11	27	29	19	3	1	1
	Less than 70,000	Both genders	26	1	4	4	5	4	8	-
		Men	13	-	-	-	2	4	7	-
		Women	13	1	4	4	3	-	1	-
	70,000 - 99,999	Both genders	35	3	6	6	11	8	1	-
		Men	17	-	3	2	5	6	1	-
		Women	18	3	3	4	6	2	-	-
	100,000 - 119,999	Both genders	80	6	14	25	28	4	-	3
		Men	44	2	4	12	21	3	-	2
		Women	36	4	10	13	7	1	-	1
	120,000 or more	Both genders	36	5	7	10	11	3	-	-
		Men	22	3	4	4	8	3	-	-
		Women	14	2	3	6	3	-	-	-
	No response	Both genders	25	1	9	4	3	3	4	1
		Men	15	-	2	2	3	3	4	1
		Women	10	1	7	2	-	-	-	-
Martin and Pasco	All groups	Both genders	96	6	18	23	29	12	7	1
		Men	57	2	8	7	21	11	7	1
		Women	39	4	10	16	8	1	-	-
	Less than 70,000	Both genders	10	-	-	3	2	2	3	-
		Men	6	-	-	-	1	2	3	-
		Women	4	-	-	3	1	-	-	-
	70,000 - 99,999	Both genders	28	2	8	5	6	4	2	1
		Men	12	-	2	-	3	4	2	1
		Women	16	2	6	5	3	-	-	-
	100,000 - 119,999	Both genders	38	2	7	10	13	4	2	-
		Men	24	1	4	3	11	3	2	-
		Women	14	1	3	7	2	1	-	-
	120,000 or more	Both genders	18	2	3	4	7	2	-	-
		Men	15	1	2	4	6	2	-	-
		Women	3	1	1	-	1	-	-	-
	No response	Both genders	2	-	-	1	1	-	-	-
		Men	-	-	-	-	-	-	-	-
		Women	2	-	-	1	1	-	-	-

Table 5–24. Number of pharmacists who completed the survey questionnaire by county of residence, annual income earned working as a pharmacist, age group, and gender (continued).

County of Residence	Gender	Annual Income Earned (dollars)	Number of Pharmacists							
			All Age Groups	Less than 30	30-39	40-49	50-59	60-69	70 and Older	Not Known
Miami-Dade	All groups	Both genders	342	21	94	86	63	35	34	9
		Men	140	7	25	32	28	26	19	3
		Women	202	14	69	54	35	9	15	6
	Less than 70,000	Both genders	42	-	5	8	3	8	16	2
		Men	12	-	-	-	1	5	5	1
		Women	30	-	5	8	2	3	11	1
	70,000 - 99,999	Both genders	79	10	30	17	11	4	7	-
		Men	24	2	4	6	4	3	5	-
		Women	55	8	26	11	7	1	2	-
	100,000 - 119,999	Both genders	127	6	45	37	27	6	5	1
		Men	51	2	15	13	11	5	5	-
		Women	76	4	30	24	16	1	-	1
	120,000 or more	Both genders	63	4	12	19	16	11	-	1
		Men	39	3	6	13	8	9	-	-
		Women	24	1	6	6	8	2	-	1
	No response	Both genders	31	1	2	5	6	6	6	5
		Men	14	-	-	-	4	4	4	2
		Women	17	1	2	5	2	2	2	3
Palm Beach	All groups	Both genders	348	24	74	65	63	60	55	7
		Men	206	4	18	26	45	57	52	4
		Women	142	20	56	39	18	3	3	3
	Less than 70,000	Both genders	60	2	11	4	5	10	27	1
		Men	37	-	-	-	1	10	25	1
		Women	23	2	11	4	4	-	2	-
	70,000 - 99,999	Both genders	79	10	20	10	13	12	12	2
		Men	40	1	6	1	7	11	12	2
		Women	39	9	14	9	6	1	-	-
	100,000 - 119,999	Both genders	131	9	31	34	29	20	5	3
		Men	76	2	8	18	23	20	5	-
		Women	55	7	23	16	6	-	-	3
	120,000 or more	Both genders	38	2	3	9	15	7	1	1
		Men	32	1	2	7	13	7	1	1
		Women	6	1	1	2	2	-	-	-
	No response	Both genders	40	1	9	8	1	11	10	-
		Men	21	-	2	-	1	9	9	-
		Women	19	1	7	8	-	2	1	-

Table 5–24. **Number of pharmacists who completed the survey questionnaire by county of residence, annual income earned working as a pharmacist, age group, and gender (continued).**

County of Residence	Annual Income Earned (dollars)	Gender	Number of Pharmacists							
			All Age Groups	Less than 30	30-39	40-49	50-59	60-69	70 and Older	Not Known
Other	All groups	Both genders	43	5	17	5	6	3	5	2
		Men	21	1	8	2	2	2	4	2
		Women	22	4	9	3	4	1	1	-
	Less than 70,000	Both genders	7	1	1	1	-	2	2	-
		Men	3	-	-	-	-	1	2	-
		Women	4	1	1	1	-	1	-	-
	70,000 - 99,999	Both genders	9	-	3	2	2	-	1	1
		Men	3	-	1	-	-	-	1	1
		Women	6	-	2	2	2	-	-	-
	100,000 - 119,999	Both genders	19	4	11	2	2	-	-	-
		Men	11	1	6	2	2	-	-	-
		Women	8	3	5	-	-	-	-	-
	120,000 or more	Both genders	2	-	1	-	1	-	-	-
		Men	1	-	1	-	-	-	-	-
		Women	1	-	-	-	1	-	-	-
	No response	Both genders	6	-	1	-	1	1	2	1
		Men	3	-	-	-	-	1	1	1
		Women	3	-	1	-	1	-	1	-

Table 5–25. Median annual income earned working as a pharmacist of pharmacists who completed the survey questionnaire by county of residence, ethnic group, and gender.

County of Residence	Gender	Median Annual Income Earned Working as a Pharmacist (dollars)					
		All Ethnic Groups	Non-Hispanic			Hispanic	Other
			White	Black	Asian		
All counties	Both genders	100,000	100,000	102,000	100,000	101,960	102,440
	Men	103,000	100,000	105,000	102,440	109,844	110,000
	Women	100,000	100,000	100,000	100,000	100,000	100,000
Broward	Both genders	101,920	101,000	105,000	100,000	105,000	104,000
	Men	103,000	101,000	110,000	100,000	114,000	110,000
	Women	100,000	100,500	102,220	100,000	100,000	100,000
Collier, Hendry, Lee, and Monroe	Both genders	103,140	104,000	104,000	100,000	102,440	-
	Men	104,000	105,000	102,000	100,000	104,000	-
	Women	100,000	100,000	107,000	88,000	100,000	-
Martin and Pasco	Both genders	100,000	101,000	97,500	97,500	120,000	100,000
	Men	105,000	105,000	-	100,000	120,000	100,000
	Women	98,000	99,000	97,500	95,000	107,000	94,750
Miami-Dade	Both genders	100,400	100,000	102,000	100,000	101,000	95,800
	Men	105,000	100,000	105,000	102,960	110,000	110,000
	Women	100,000	101,500	101,000	100,000	100,000	95,800
Palm Beach	Both genders	100,000	100,000	100,000	105,000	101,000	110,000
	Men	100,000	100,000	100,000	110,000	105,000	120,000
	Women	99,840	97,500	97,000	102,000	93,000	106,000
Other	Both genders	100,000	104,000	84,500	107,500	100,000	90,000
	Men	104,750	106,000	105,000	115,000	95,000	-
	Women	95,000	102,000	64,500	85,000	100,000	90,000

Table 5–26. Median annual income earned working as a pharmacist of pharmacists who completed the survey questionnaire by county of residence, age group, and gender.

County of Residence	Gender	Median Annual Income Earned Working as a Pharmacist (dollars)							
		All Age Groups	Less than 30	30-39	40-49	50-59	60-69	70 and Older	Not Known
All counties	Both genders	100,000	100,000	101,000	104,000	104,000	100,000	59,000	97,500
	Men	103,000	112,000	105,000	110,000	108,500	100,000	63,000	86,000
	Women	100,000	100,000	100,000	100,000	100,000	96,000	40,000	100,000
Broward	Both genders	101,920	100,000	105,000	103,000	105,000	98,725	70,000	78,500
	Men	103,000	99,000	105,000	110,000	110,000	101,500	70,000	70,000
	Women	100,000	100,000	102,440	100,000	100,000	99,450	101,920	100,000
Collier, Hendry, Lee, and Monroe	Both genders	103,140	110,000	104,000	106,000	102,440	96,000	25,000	106,000
	Men	104,000	120,000	110,000	108,000	103,500	93,000	27,500	108,000
	Women	100,000	107,000	101,480	105,000	100,000	97,000	25,000	100,000
Martin and Pasco	Both genders	100,000	108,344	100,000	104,000	109,000	102,000	80,000	90,000
	Men	105,000	128,344	100,000	120,000	110,000	99,000	80,000	90,000
	Women	98,000	99,000	96,250	98,000	99,000	105,040	-	-
Miami-Dade	Both genders	100,450	99,500	101,500	104,000	104,000	100,000	59,000	81,000
	Men	105,000	110,000	109,844	108,500	102,000	101,500	79,000	15,000
	Women	100,000	98,000	100,000	101,000	104,000	93,600	37,000	100,000
Palm Beach	Both genders	100,000	99,840	100,000	105,000	102,000	100,000	50,000	100,000
	Men	100,000	107,500	100,000	110,000	105,500	100,000	60,000	90,000
	Women	99,840	98,000	98,000	100,000	97,000	89,000	40,000	100,000
Other	Both genders	100,000	102,000	102,000	90,000	110,000	58,000	24,000	85,000
	Men	104,750	112,000	104,750	112,500	112,500	60,000	24,000	85,000
	Women	95,000	101,000	100,000	90,000	93,600	56,000	-	-

Table 5–27. Number of pharmacists who completed the survey questionnaire by county of residence, hourly wage rate, ethnic group, and gender.

County of Residence	Wage Rate (dollars per hour)	Gender	Number of Pharmacists					
			All Ethnic Groups	Non-Hispanic			Hispanic	Other
				White	Black	Asian		
All counties	All groups	Both genders	1,539	958	119	86	319	57
		Men	805	603	41	35	105	21
		Women	734	355	78	51	214	36
	Less than 40	Both genders	33	19	2	1	9	2
		Men	21	17	1	1	2	-
		Women	12	2	1	-	7	2
	40 - 49	Both genders	664	396	58	42	142	26
		Men	328	254	19	14	35	6
		Women	336	142	39	28	107	20
	50 - 59	Both genders	593	377	39	34	120	23
		Men	319	225	18	18	47	11
		Women	274	152	21	16	73	12
	60 or more	Both genders	65	43	3	2	14	3
		Men	44	32	1	1	8	2
		Women	21	11	2	1	6	1
	No response	Both genders	184	123	17	7	34	3
		Men	93	75	2	1	13	2
		Women	91	48	15	6	21	1
Broward	All groups	Both genders	508	316	55	35	70	32
		Men	270	199	22	11	26	12
		Women	238	117	33	24	44	20
	Less than 40	Both genders	9	6	-	1	-	2
		Men	6	5	-	1	-	-
		Women	3	1	-	-	-	2
	40 - 49	Both genders	231	141	27	22	29	12
		Men	117	91	9	6	7	4
		Women	114	50	18	16	22	8
	50 - 59	Both genders	174	107	21	7	24	15
		Men	93	62	11	3	12	5
		Women	81	45	10	4	12	10
	60 or more	Both genders	19	11	2	1	4	1
		Men	12	8	1	-	2	1
		Women	7	3	1	1	2	-
	No response	Both genders	75	51	5	4	13	2
		Men	42	33	1	1	5	2
		Women	33	18	4	3	8	-

Table 5–27. Number of pharmacists who completed the survey questionnaire by county of residence, hourly wage rate, ethnic group, and gender (continued).

County of Residence	Wage Rate (dollars per hour)	Gender	Number of Pharmacists					
			All Ethnic Groups	Non-Hispanic			Hispanic	Other
				White	Black	Asian		
Collier, Hendry, Lee, and Monroe	All groups	Both genders	202	181	4	5	12	-
		Men	111	99	2	3	7	-
		Women	91	82	2	2	5	-
	Less than 40	Both genders	2	2	-	-	-	-
		Men	2	2	-	-	-	-
		Women	-	-	-	-	-	-
	40 - 49	Both genders	45	40	1	1	3	-
		Men	27	23	1	-	3	-
		Women	18	17	-	1	-	-
	50 - 59	Both genders	125	110	2	4	9	-
		Men	66	58	1	3	4	-
		Women	59	52	1	1	5	-
	60 or more	Both genders	10	10	-	-	-	-
		Men	6	6	-	-	-	-
		Women	4	4	-	-	-	-
	No response	Both genders	20	19	1	-	-	-
		Men	10	10	-	-	-	-
		Women	10	9	1	-	-	-
Martin and Pasco	All groups	Both genders	96	76	4	6	5	5
		Men	57	46	-	5	3	3
		Women	39	30	4	1	2	2
	Less than 40	Both genders	3	2	1	-	-	-
		Men	2	2	-	-	-	-
		Women	1	-	1	-	-	-
	40 - 49	Both genders	37	26	1	4	2	4
		Men	19	12	-	3	2	2
		Women	18	14	1	1	-	2
	50 - 59	Both genders	44	39	1	2	2	-
		Men	26	24	-	2	-	-
		Women	18	15	1	-	2	-
	60 or more	Both genders	7	5	-	-	1	1
		Men	7	5	-	-	1	1
		Women	-	-	-	-	-	-
	No response	Both genders	5	4	1	-	-	-
		Men	3	3	-	-	-	-
		Women	2	1	1	-	-	-

Table 5–27. Number of pharmacists who completed the survey questionnaire by county of residence, hourly wage rate, ethnic group, and gender (continued).

County of Residence	Wage Rate (dollars per hour)	Gender	Number of Pharmacists					
			All Ethnic Groups	Non-Hispanic			Hispanic	Other
				White	Black	Asian		
Miami-Dade	All groups	Both genders	342	98	31	14	189	10
		Men	140	69	9	7	54	1
		Women	202	29	22	7	135	9
	Less than 40	Both genders	8	2	-	-	6	-
		Men	3	2	-	-	1	-
		Women	5	-	-	-	5	-
	40 - 49	Both genders	144	41	11	2	82	8
		Men	50	29	3	-	18	-
		Women	94	12	8	2	64	8
	50 - 59	Both genders	135	32	15	11	76	1
		Men	62	24	6	6	25	1
		Women	73	8	9	5	51	-
	60 or more	Both genders	19	8	1	1	8	1
		Men	9	4	-	1	4	-
		Women	10	4	1	-	4	1
	No response	Both genders	36	15	4	-	17	-
		Men	16	10	-	-	6	-
		Women	20	5	4	-	11	-
Palm Beach	All groups	Both genders	348	270	21	20	28	9
		Men	206	179	6	6	10	5
		Women	142	91	15	14	18	4
	Less than 40	Both genders	10	7	1	-	2	-
		Men	7	6	1	-	-	-
		Women	3	1	-	-	2	-
	40 - 49	Both genders	183	141	14	10	17	1
		Men	106	94	4	4	4	-
		Women	77	47	10	6	13	1
	50 - 59	Both genders	104	83	-	7	7	7
		Men	66	54	-	2	5	5
		Women	38	29	-	5	2	2
	60 or more	Both genders	10	9	-	-	1	-
		Men	10	9	-	-	1	-
		Women	-	-	-	-	-	-
	No response	Both genders	41	30	6	3	1	1
		Men	17	16	1	-	-	-
		Women	24	14	5	3	1	1

Table 5–27. Number of pharmacists who completed the survey questionnaire by county of residence, hourly wage rate, ethnic group, and gender (continued).

County of Residence	Wage Rate (dollars per hour)	Gender	Number of Pharmacists					
			All Ethnic Groups	Non-Hispanic			Hispanic	Other
				White	Black	Asian		
Other	All groups	Both genders	43	17	4	6	15	1
		Men	21	11	2	3	5	-
		Women	22	6	2	3	10	1
	Less than 40	Both genders	1	-	-	-	1	-
		Men	1	-	-	-	1	-
		Women	-	-	-	-	-	-
	40 - 49	Both genders	24	7	4	3	9	1
		Men	9	5	2	1	1	-
		Women	15	2	2	2	8	1
	50 - 59	Both genders	11	6	-	3	2	-
		Men	6	3	-	2	1	-
		Women	5	3	-	1	1	-
	60 or more	Both genders	-	-	-	-	-	-
		Men	-	-	-	-	-	-
		Women	-	-	-	-	-	-
	No response	Both genders	7	4	-	-	3	-
		Men	5	3	-	-	2	-
		Women	2	1	-	-	1	-

Table 5–28. Number of pharmacists who completed the survey questionnaire by county of residence, hourly wage rate, age group, and gender.

County of Residence	Wage Rate (dollars per hour)	Gender	Number of Pharmacists							
			All Age Groups	Less than 30	30-39	40-49	50-59	60-69	70 and Older	Not Known
All counties	All groups	Both genders	1,539	97	367	364	329	192	154	36
		Men	805	23	108	157	204	166	128	19
		Women	734	74	259	207	125	26	26	17
	Less than 40	Both genders	33	3	4	5	3	4	13	1
		Men	21	1	2	3	3	3	8	1
		Women	12	2	2	2	-	1	5	-
	40 - 49	Both genders	664	46	185	130	122	79	86	16
		Men	328	8	47	48	72	71	72	10
		Women	336	38	138	82	50	8	14	6
	50 - 59	Both genders	593	38	136	162	147	66	33	11
		Men	319	13	48	74	91	58	31	4
		Women	274	25	88	88	56	8	2	7
	60 or more	Both genders	65	1	9	22	18	12	3	-
		Men	44	1	3	12	14	11	3	-
		Women	21	-	6	10	4	1	-	-
	No response	Both genders	184	9	33	45	39	31	19	8
		Men	93	-	8	20	24	23	14	4
		Women	91	9	25	25	15	8	5	4
Broward	All groups	Both genders	508	25	124	136	110	60	40	13
		Men	270	4	36	70	69	51	34	6
		Women	238	21	88	66	41	9	6	7
	Less than 40	Both genders	9	1	3	1	1	1	2	-
		Men	6	-	2	1	1	1	1	-
		Women	3	1	1	-	-	-	1	-
	40 - 49	Both genders	231	12	61	58	52	20	21	7
		Men	117	2	16	27	32	18	19	3
		Women	114	10	45	31	20	2	2	4
	50 - 59	Both genders	174	9	44	50	34	23	10	4
		Men	93	2	15	27	20	19	9	1
		Women	81	7	29	23	14	4	1	3
	60 or more	Both genders	19	-	3	8	3	4	1	-
		Men	12	-	-	4	3	4	1	-
		Women	7	-	3	4	-	-	-	-
	No response	Both genders	75	3	13	19	20	12	6	2
		Men	42	-	3	11	13	9	4	2
		Women	33	3	10	8	7	3	2	-

Table 5–28. Number of pharmacists who completed the survey questionnaire by county of residence, hourly wage rate, age group, and gender (continued).

County of Residence	Wage Rate (dollars per hour)	Gender	Number of Pharmacists: All Age Groups	Less than 30	30-39	40-49	50-59	60-69	70 and Older	Not Known
Collier, Hendry, Lee, and Monroe	All groups	Both genders	202	16	40	49	58	22	13	4
		Men	111	5	13	20	39	19	12	3
		Women	91	11	27	29	19	3	1	1
	Less than 40	Both genders	2	-	-	-	-	1	1	-
		Men	2	-	-	-	-	1	1	-
		Women	-	-	-	-	-	-	-	-
	40 - 49	Both genders	45	3	10	7	14	5	5	1
		Men	27	-	2	3	12	4	5	1
		Women	18	3	8	4	2	1	-	-
	50 - 59	Both genders	125	12	24	35	34	11	7	2
		Men	66	5	8	15	20	10	6	2
		Women	59	7	16	20	14	1	1	-
	60 or more	Both genders	10	-	1	3	4	2	-	-
		Men	6	-	1	-	3	2	-	-
		Women	4	-	-	3	1	-	-	-
	No response	Both genders	20	1	5	4	6	3	-	1
		Men	10	-	2	2	4	2	-	-
		Women	10	1	3	2	2	1	-	1
Martin and Pasco	All groups	Both genders	96	6	18	23	29	12	7	1
		Men	57	2	8	7	21	11	7	1
		Women	39	4	10	16	8	1	-	-
	Less than 40	Both genders	3	-	1	-	-	1	1	-
		Men	2	-	-	-	-	1	1	-
		Women	1	-	1	-	-	-	-	-
	40 - 49	Both genders	37	2	10	8	8	6	3	-
		Men	19	-	4	1	5	6	3	-
		Women	18	2	6	7	3	-	-	-
	50 - 59	Both genders	44	4	6	12	16	2	3	1
		Men	26	2	3	4	12	1	3	1
		Women	18	2	3	8	4	1	-	-
	60 or more	Both genders	7	-	1	1	4	1	-	-
		Men	7	-	1	1	4	1	-	-
		Women	-	-	-	-	-	-	-	-
	No response	Both genders	5	-	-	2	1	2	-	-
		Men	3	-	-	1	-	2	-	-
		Women	2	-	-	1	1	-	-	-

Table 5–28. Number of pharmacists who completed the survey questionnaire by county of residence, hourly wage rate, age group, and gender (continued).

County of Residence	Wage Rate (dollars per hour)	Gender	Number of Pharmacists							
			All Age Groups	Less than 30	30-39	40-49	50-59	60-69	70 and Older	Not Known
Miami-Dade	All groups	Both genders	342	21	94	86	63	35	34	9
		Men	140	7	25	32	28	26	19	3
		Women	202	14	69	54	35	9	15	6
	Less than 40	Both genders	8	-	-	2	-	1	4	1
		Men	3	-	-	1	-	-	1	1
		Women	5	-	-	1	-	1	3	-
	40 - 49	Both genders	144	12	45	26	22	14	22	3
		Men	50	4	8	6	9	10	11	2
		Women	94	8	37	20	13	4	11	1
	50 - 59	Both genders	135	8	38	41	29	12	4	3
		Men	62	3	15	17	13	10	4	-
		Women	73	5	23	24	16	2	-	3
	60 or more	Both genders	19	-	4	7	5	3	-	-
		Men	9	-	1	4	2	2	-	-
		Women	10	-	3	3	3	1	-	-
	No response	Both genders	36	1	7	10	7	5	4	2
		Men	16	-	1	4	4	4	3	-
		Women	20	1	6	6	3	1	1	2
Palm Beach	All groups	Both genders	348	24	74	65	63	60	55	7
		Men	206	4	18	26	45	57	52	4
		Women	142	20	56	39	18	3	3	3
	Less than 40	Both genders	10	2	-	2	2	-	4	-
		Men	7	1	-	1	2	-	3	-
		Women	3	1	-	1	-	-	1	-
	40 - 49	Both genders	183	14	47	28	24	32	34	4
		Men	106	2	12	10	14	32	33	3
		Women	77	12	35	18	10	-	1	1
	50 - 59	Both genders	104	3	19	22	32	18	9	1
		Men	66	-	4	10	25	18	9	-
		Women	38	3	15	12	7	-	-	1
	60 or more	Both genders	10	1	-	3	2	2	2	-
		Men	10	1	-	3	2	2	2	-
		Women	-	-	-	-	-	-	-	-
	No response	Both genders	41	4	8	10	3	8	6	2
		Men	17	-	2	2	2	5	5	1
		Women	24	4	6	8	1	3	1	1

Table 5–28. Number of pharmacists who completed the survey questionnaire by county of residence, hourly wage rate, age group, and gender (continued).

County of Residence	Wage Rate (dollars per hour)	Gender	Number of Pharmacists							
			All Age Groups	Less than 30	30-39	40-49	50-59	60-69	70 and Older	Not Known
Other	All groups	Both genders	43	5	17	5	6	3	5	2
		Men	21	1	8	2	2	2	4	2
		Women	22	4	9	3	4	1	1	-
	Less than 40	Both genders	1	-	-	-	-	-	1	-
		Men	1	-	-	-	-	-	1	-
		Women	-	-	-	-	-	-	-	-
	40 - 49	Both genders	24	3	12	3	2	2	1	1
		Men	9	-	5	1	-	1	1	1
		Women	15	3	7	2	2	1	-	-
	50 - 59	Both genders	11	2	5	2	2	-	-	-
		Men	6	1	3	1	1	-	-	-
		Women	5	1	2	1	1	-	-	-
	60 or more	Both genders	-	-	-	-	-	-	-	-
		Men	-	-	-	-	-	-	-	-
		Women	-	-	-	-	-	-	-	-
	No response	Both genders	7	-	-	-	2	1	3	1
		Men	5	-	-	-	1	1	2	1
		Women	2	-	-	-	1	-	1	-

Table 5–29. Median hourly wage rate of pharmacists who completed the survey questionnaire by county of residence, ethnic group, and gender.

County of Residence	Gender	Median Hourly Wage Rate (dollars)					
		All Ethnic Groups	Non-Hispanic			Hispanic	Other
			White	Black	Asian		
All counties	Both genders	49.5	49.5	49.0	49.0	49.0	49.5
	Men	49.5	49.5	49.5	50.0	50.0	50.0
	Women	49.0	50.0	49.0	49.0	48.5	48.5
Broward	Both genders	49.0	49.0	49.0	49.0	49.5	50.0
	Men	49.0	49.0	50.0	49.0	50.5	50.0
	Women	49.0	49.0	49.0	49.0	49.0	49.5
Collier, Hendry, Lee, and Monroe	Both genders	50.0	50.0	50.0	50.0	51.5	-
	Men	50.0	50.0	48.5	50.0	49.5	-
	Women	50.5	50.0	50.0	49.0	52.0	-
Martin and Pasco	Both genders	50.0	50.0	47.0	49.0	50.0	48.0
	Men	50.0	50.5	-	49.0	45.0	49.0
	Women	49.5	49.5	47.0	49.0	51.5	45.5
Miami-Dade	Both genders	49.5	49.0	50.0	50.0	49.0	47.5
	Men	50.0	49.0	50.0	52.0	50.0	53.0
	Women	49.0	49.5	50.0	50.0	49.0	47.0
Palm Beach	Both genders	48.5	49.0	47.0	49.5	48.0	52.0
	Men	49.0	48.0	47.5	49.0	50.0	52.0
	Women	48.5	49.0	47.0	49.5	47.0	51.0
Other	Both genders	48.0	49.0	48.5	49.5	45.0	49.0
	Men	49.0	48.5	49.0	53.0	45.0	-
	Women	47.5	50.0	46.5	49.0	45.0	49.0

Table 5–30. Median hourly wage rate of pharmacists who completed the survey questionnaire by county of residence, age group, and gender.

County of Residence	Gender	Median Hourly Wage Rate (dollars)							
		All Age Groups	Less than 30	30-39	40-49	50-59	60-69	70 and Older	Not Known
All counties	Both genders	49.5	49.0	49.0	50.0	50.0	49.5	47.0	48.0
	Men	49.5	51.0	49.5	50.0	50.0	49.5	47.0	48.0
	Women	49.0	48.0	49.0	50.0	50.0	49.0	43.0	49.5
Broward	Both genders	49.0	49.0	49.0	49.0	49.0	50.0	48.0	48.0
	Men	49.0	49.0	49.0	50.0	49.0	50.0	48.0	48.0
	Women	49.0	49.0	49.0	49.0	48.5	50.0	47.0	49.0
Collier, Hendry, Lee, and Monroe	Both genders	50.0	52.0	50.0	51.0	50.5	50.0	50.0	51.0
	Men	50.0	54.0	50.5	51.5	50.0	50.0	49.0	51.0
	Women	50.5	50.0	50.0	51.0	52.0	45.0	50.0	-
Martin and Pasco	Both genders	50.0	51.0	49.0	50.0	53.0	49.0	48.5	50.5
	Men	50.0	51.5	49.5	51.0	55.0	49.0	48.5	50.5
	Women	49.5	49.5	48.5	49.5	50.0	50.5	-	-
Miami-Dade	Both genders	49.5	46.5	49.0	50.0	50.0	49.5	45.0	48.0
	Men	50.0	46.0	50.5	50.0	50.0	50.0	47.0	40.0
	Women	49.0	49.0	48.5	50.0	50.0	47.5	42.0	50.0
Palm Beach	Both genders	48.5	48.0	48.0	49.0	50.0	49.0	47.0	48.0
	Men	49.0	48.5	48.0	50.0	50.0	49.0	47.0	48.0
	Women	48.5	48.0	49.0	48.0	49.5	-	40.0	53.5
Other	Both genders	48.0	48.0	48.5	49.0	47.5	41.0	32.0	41.0
	Men	49.0	52.0	49.0	52.0	50.0	40.0	32.0	41.0
	Women	47.5	48.0	45.0	49.0	45.0	42.0	-	-

Table 5–31. Number of pharmacists who completed the survey questionnaire by county of residence, annual household income, ethnic group, and gender.

County of Residence	Annual Household Income (dollars)	Gender	Number of Pharmacists					
			All Ethnic Groups	Non-Hispanic			Hispanic	Other
				White	Black	Asian		
All counties	All groups	Both genders	1,539	958	119	86	319	57
		Men	805	603	41	35	105	21
		Women	734	355	78	51	214	36
	Less than 100,000	Both genders	200	125	11	13	41	10
		Men	109	88	2	5	12	2
		Women	91	37	9	8	29	8
	100,000 - 149,999	Both genders	538	344	52	38	89	15
		Men	319	231	24	20	39	5
		Women	219	113	28	18	50	10
	150,000 - 199,999	Both genders	352	214	26	16	81	15
		Men	175	130	10	5	24	6
		Women	177	84	16	11	57	9
	200,000 or more	Both genders	242	139	14	11	65	13
		Men	96	63	3	3	21	6
		Women	146	76	11	8	44	7
	No response	Both genders	207	136	16	8	43	4
		Men	106	91	2	2	9	2
		Women	101	45	14	6	34	2
Broward	All groups	Both genders	508	316	55	35	70	32
		Men	270	199	22	11	26	12
		Women	238	117	33	24	44	20
	Less than 100,000	Both genders	56	38	4	8	4	2
		Men	36	29	2	3	1	1
		Women	20	9	2	5	3	1
	100,000 - 149,999	Both genders	164	109	26	8	13	8
		Men	96	70	13	3	8	2
		Women	68	39	13	5	5	6
	150,000 - 199,999	Both genders	119	67	12	9	20	11
		Men	59	42	5	2	6	4
		Women	60	25	7	7	14	7
	200,000 or more	Both genders	96	58	4	8	19	7
		Men	42	28	2	2	7	3
		Women	54	30	2	6	12	4
	No response	Both genders	73	44	9	2	14	4
		Men	37	30	-	1	4	2
		Women	36	14	9	1	10	2

Table 5–31. Number of pharmacists who completed the survey questionnaire by county of residence, annual household income, ethnic group, and gender (continued).

County of Residence	Annual Household Income (dollars)	Gender	Number of Pharmacists					
			All Ethnic Groups	Non-Hispanic			Hispanic	Other
				White	Black	Asian		
Collier, Hendry, Lee, and Monroe	All groups	Both genders	202	181	4	5	12	-
		Men	111	99	2	3	7	-
		Women	91	82	2	2	5	-
	Less than 100,000	Both genders	24	22	-	1	1	-
		Men	14	13	-	-	1	-
		Women	10	9	-	1	-	-
	100,000 - 149,999	Both genders	78	66	2	2	8	-
		Men	49	40	1	2	6	-
		Women	29	26	1	-	2	-
	150,000 - 199,999	Both genders	45	42	-	1	2	-
		Men	22	22	-	-	-	-
		Women	23	20	-	1	2	-
	200,000 or more	Both genders	28	27	1	-	-	-
		Men	9	9	-	-	-	-
		Women	19	18	1	-	-	-
	No response	Both genders	27	24	1	1	1	-
		Men	17	15	1	1	-	-
		Women	10	9	-	-	1	-
Martin and Pasco	All groups	Both genders	96	76	4	6	5	5
		Men	57	46	-	5	3	3
		Women	39	30	4	1	2	2
	Less than 100,000	Both genders	13	9	1	1	-	2
		Men	7	5	-	1	-	1
		Women	6	4	1	-	-	1
	100,000 - 149,999	Both genders	45	37	1	3	3	1
		Men	29	24	-	3	2	-
		Women	16	13	1	-	1	1
	150,000 - 199,999	Both genders	22	20	-	2	-	-
		Men	13	12	-	1	-	-
		Women	9	8	-	1	-	-
	200,000 or more	Both genders	11	7	1	-	1	2
		Men	6	3	-	-	1	2
		Women	5	4	1	-	-	-
	No response	Both genders	5	3	1	-	1	-
		Men	2	2	-	-	-	-
		Women	3	1	1	-	1	-

Table 5–31. Number of pharmacists who completed the survey questionnaire by county of residence, annual household income, ethnic group, and gender (continued).

County of Residence	Annual Household Income (dollars)	Gender	Number of Pharmacists					
			All Ethnic Groups	Non-Hispanic			Hispanic	Other
				White	Black	Asian		
Miami-Dade	All groups	Both genders	342	98	31	14	189	10
		Men	140	69	9	7	54	1
		Women	202	29	22	7	135	9
	Less than 100,000	Both genders	51	13	3	1	29	5
		Men	16	9	-	1	6	-
		Women	35	4	3	-	23	5
	100,000 - 149,999	Both genders	107	34	13	8	50	2
		Men	56	28	6	4	17	1
		Women	51	6	7	4	33	1
	150,000 - 199,999	Both genders	78	17	7	1	52	1
		Men	28	10	2	1	15	-
		Women	50	7	5	-	37	1
	200,000 or more	Both genders	63	14	5	2	40	2
		Men	22	7	1	1	13	-
		Women	41	7	4	1	27	2
	No response	Both genders	43	20	3	2	18	-
		Men	18	15	-	-	3	-
		Women	25	5	3	2	15	-
Palm Beach	All groups	Both genders	348	270	21	20	28	9
		Men	206	179	6	6	10	5
		Women	142	91	15	14	18	4
	Less than 100,000	Both genders	46	39	2	2	3	-
		Men	31	29	-	-	2	-
		Women	15	10	2	2	1	-
	100,000 - 149,999	Both genders	126	93	7	13	9	4
		Men	81	66	2	6	5	2
		Women	45	27	5	7	4	2
	150,000 - 199,999	Both genders	84	66	7	2	6	3
		Men	51	43	3	-	3	2
		Women	33	23	4	2	3	1
	200,000 or more	Both genders	40	30	3	1	4	2
		Men	16	15	-	-	-	1
		Women	24	15	3	1	4	1
	No response	Both genders	52	42	2	2	6	-
		Men	27	26	1	-	-	-
		Women	25	16	1	2	6	-

Table 5–31. Number of pharmacists who completed the survey questionnaire by county of residence, annual household income, ethnic group, and gender (continued).

County of Residence	Annual Household Income (dollars)	Gender	Number of Pharmacists					
			All Ethnic Groups	Non-Hispanic			Hispanic	Other
				White	Black	Asian		
Other	All groups	Both genders	43	17	4	6	15	1
		Men	21	11	2	3	5	-
		Women	22	6	2	3	10	1
	Less than 100,000	Both genders	10	4	1	-	4	1
		Men	5	3	-	-	2	-
		Women	5	1	1	-	2	1
	100,000 - 149,999	Both genders	18	5	3	4	6	-
		Men	8	3	2	2	1	-
		Women	10	2	1	2	5	-
	150,000 - 199,999	Both genders	4	2	-	1	1	-
		Men	2	1	-	1	-	-
		Women	2	1	-	-	1	-
	200,000 or more	Both genders	4	3	-	-	1	-
		Men	1	1	-	-	-	-
		Women	3	2	-	-	1	-
	No response	Both genders	7	3	-	1	3	-
		Men	5	3	-	-	2	-
		Women	2	-	-	1	1	-

Table 5–32. Number of pharmacists who completed the survey questionnaire by county of residence, annual household income, age group, and gender.

County of Residence	Annual Household Income (dollars)	Gender	Number of Pharmacists: All Age Groups	Less than 30	30-39	40-49	50-59	60-69	70 and Older	Not Known
All counties	All groups	Both genders	1,539	97	367	364	329	192	154	36
		Men	805	23	108	157	204	166	128	19
		Women	734	74	259	207	125	26	26	17
	Less than 100,000	Both genders	200	15	34	30	28	31	57	5
		Men	109	2	12	11	14	22	43	5
		Women	91	13	22	19	14	9	14	-
	100,000 - 149,999	Both genders	538	40	125	138	122	67	39	7
		Men	319	11	52	70	83	61	37	5
		Women	219	29	73	68	39	6	2	2
	150,000 - 199,999	Both genders	352	15	100	83	89	43	14	8
		Men	175	4	20	32	62	40	14	3
		Women	177	11	80	51	27	3	-	5
	200,000 or more	Both genders	242	21	72	71	54	18	1	5
		Men	96	6	17	26	28	18	1	-
		Women	146	15	55	45	26	-	-	5
	No response	Both genders	207	6	36	42	36	33	43	11
		Men	106	-	7	18	17	25	33	6
		Women	101	6	29	24	19	8	10	5
Broward	All groups	Both genders	508	25	124	136	110	60	40	13
		Men	270	4	36	70	69	51	34	6
		Women	238	21	88	66	41	9	6	7
	Less than 100,000	Both genders	56	1	12	12	8	10	11	2
		Men	36	-	4	7	6	7	10	2
		Women	20	1	8	5	2	3	1	-
	100,000 - 149,999	Both genders	164	8	38	46	37	20	14	1
		Men	96	1	16	25	22	18	13	1
		Women	68	7	22	21	15	2	1	-
	150,000 - 199,999	Both genders	119	6	32	30	27	17	4	3
		Men	59	1	6	13	19	15	4	1
		Women	60	5	26	17	8	2	-	2
	200,000 or more	Both genders	96	8	31	29	19	6	-	3
		Men	42	2	8	12	14	6	-	-
		Women	54	6	23	17	5	-	-	3
	No response	Both genders	73	2	11	19	19	7	11	4
		Men	37	-	2	13	8	5	7	2
		Women	36	2	9	6	11	2	4	2

Table 5–32. Number of pharmacists who completed the survey questionnaire by county of residence, annual household income, age group, and gender (continued).

County of Residence	Annual Household Income (dollars)	Gender	Number of Pharmacists							
			All Age Groups	Less than 30	30-39	40-49	50-59	60-69	70 and Older	Not Known
Collier, Hendry, Lee, and Monroe	All groups	Both genders	202	16	40	49	58	22	13	4
		Men	111	5	13	20	39	19	12	3
		Women	91	11	27	29	19	3	1	1
	Less than 100,000	Both genders	24	-	5	3	6	4	6	-
		Men	14	-	2	2	2	3	5	-
		Women	10	-	3	1	4	1	1	-
	100,000 - 149,999	Both genders	78	6	16	19	27	6	4	-
		Men	49	3	6	9	23	4	4	-
		Women	29	3	10	10	4	2	-	-
	150,000 - 199,999	Both genders	45	3	7	12	15	5	-	3
		Men	22	1	2	4	8	5	-	2
		Women	23	2	5	8	7	-	-	1
	200,000 or more	Both genders	28	5	6	10	5	2	-	-
		Men	9	1	2	2	2	2	-	-
		Women	19	4	4	8	3	-	-	-
	No response	Both genders	27	2	6	5	5	5	3	1
		Men	17	-	1	3	4	5	3	1
		Women	10	2	5	2	1	-	-	-
Martin and Pasco	All groups	Both genders	96	6	18	23	29	12	7	1
		Men	57	2	8	7	21	11	7	1
		Women	39	4	10	16	8	1	-	-
	Less than 100,000	Both genders	13	1	1	3	3	2	3	-
		Men	7	-	-	-	2	2	3	-
		Women	6	1	1	3	1	-	-	-
	100,000 - 149,999	Both genders	45	2	9	13	11	8	1	1
		Men	29	1	5	5	9	7	1	1
		Women	16	1	4	8	2	1	-	-
	150,000 - 199,999	Both genders	22	2	6	5	8	1	-	-
		Men	13	1	2	2	7	1	-	-
		Women	9	1	4	3	1	-	-	-
	200,000 or more	Both genders	11	1	1	1	6	1	1	-
		Men	6	-	1	-	3	1	1	-
		Women	5	1	-	1	3	-	-	-
	No response	Both genders	5	-	1	1	1	-	2	-
		Men	2	-	-	-	-	-	2	-
		Women	3	-	1	1	1	-	-	-

Table 5–32. Number of pharmacists who completed the survey questionnaire by county of residence, annual household income, age group, and gender (continued).

County of Residence	Annual Household Income (dollars)	Gender	Number of Pharmacists							
			All Age Groups	Less than 30	30-39	40-49	50-59	60-69	70 and Older	Not Known
Miami-Dade	All groups	Both genders	342	21	94	86	63	35	34	9
		Men	140	7	25	32	28	26	19	3
		Women	202	14	69	54	35	9	15	6
	Less than 100,000	Both genders	51	8	6	6	8	6	16	1
		Men	16	2	2	2	2	2	5	1
		Women	35	6	4	4	6	4	11	-
	100,000 - 149,999	Both genders	107	7	34	29	18	9	8	2
		Men	56	3	12	16	8	8	8	1
		Women	51	4	22	13	10	1	-	1
	150,000 - 199,999	Both genders	78	1	28	26	15	6	2	-
		Men	28	-	5	8	8	5	2	-
		Women	50	1	23	18	7	1	-	-
	200,000 or more	Both genders	63	4	21	17	15	4	-	
		Men	22	2	5	5	6	4	-	-
		Women	41	2	16	12	9	-	-	2
	No response	Both genders	43	1	5	8	7	10	8	4
		Men	18	-	1	1	4	7	4	1
		Women	25	1	4	7	3	3	4	3
Palm Beach	All groups	Both genders	348	24	74	65	63	60	55	7
		Men	206	4	18	26	45	57	52	4
		Women	142	20	56	39	18	3	3	3
	Less than 100,000	Both genders	46	5	8	4	2	7	19	1
		Men	31	-	3	-	2	7	18	1
		Women	15	5	5	4	-	-	1	-
	100,000 - 149,999	Both genders	126	12	20	30	26	24	11	3
		Men	81	2	8	14	20	24	11	2
		Women	45	10	12	16	6	-	-	1
	150,000 - 199,999	Both genders	84	3	25	9	23	14	8	2
		Men	51	1	4	5	19	14	8	-
		Women	33	2	21	4	4	-	-	2
	200,000 or more	Both genders	40	3	11	13	8	5	-	-
		Men	16	1	1	6	3	5	-	-
		Women	24	2	10	7	5	-	-	-
	No response	Both genders	52	1	10	9	4	10	17	1
		Men	27	-	2	1	1	7	15	1
		Women	25	1	8	8	3	3	2	-

Table 5–32. Number of pharmacists who completed the survey questionnaire by county of residence, annual household income, age group, and gender (continued).

County of Residence	Annual Household Income (dollars)	Gender	Number of Pharmacists							
			All Age Groups	Less than 30	30-39	40-49	50-59	60-69	70 and Older	Not Known
Other	All groups	Both genders	43	5	17	5	6	3	5	2
		Men	21	1	8	2	2	2	4	2
		Women	22	4	9	3	4	1	1	-
	Less than 100,000	Both genders	10	-	2	2	1	2	2	1
		Men	5	-	1	-	-	1	2	1
		Women	5	-	1	2	1	1	-	-
	100,000 - 149,999	Both genders	18	5	8	1	3	-	1	-
		Men	8	1	5	1	1	-	-	-
		Women	10	4	3	-	2	-	1	-
	150,000 - 199,999	Both genders	4	-	2	1	1	-	-	-
		Men	2	-	1	-	1	-	-	-
		Women	2	-	1	1	-	-	-	-
	200,000 or more	Both genders	4	-	2	1	1	-	-	-
		Men	1	-	-	1	-	-	-	-
		Women	3	-	2	-	1	-	-	-
	No response	Both genders	7	-	3	-	-	1	2	1
		Men	5	-	1	-	-	1	2	1
		Women	2	-	2	-	-	-	-	-

Table 5–33. Median annual household income of pharmacists who completed the survey questionnaire by county of residence, ethnic group, and gender.

County of Residence	Gender	Median Annual Household Income (dollars)					
		All Ethnic Groups	Non-Hispanic			Hispanic	Other
			White	Black	Asian		
All counties	Both genders	137,500	131,000	130,000	118,500	150,000	150,000
	Men	130,000	130,000	130,000	110,000	140,000	160,000
	Women	150,000	150,000	128,000	135,000	150,000	110,000
Broward	Both genders	145,000	140,000	123,000	150,000	160,000	165,000
	Men	131,500	130,000	120,000	115,000	160,000	175,000
	Women	151,000	150,000	128,000	160,000	171,800	155,000
Collier, Hendry, Lee, and Monroe	Both genders	140,000	140,000	120,000	112,500	120,000	-
	Men	132,500	137,500	120,000	112,500	110,000	-
	Women	150,000	150,000	165,000	123,000	145,000	-
Martin and Pasco	Both genders	135,000	138,000	120,000	103,960	140,000	100,000
	Men	130,000	132,500	-	101,920	140,000	200,000
	Women	139,000	140,000	120,000	180,000	140,000	94,750
Miami-Dade	Both genders	140,000	122,000	140,000	127,500	150,000	101,500
	Men	125,000	120,000	140,000	127,500	150,000	110,000
	Women	150,000	155,000	140,000	140,000	150,000	98,000
Palm Beach	Both genders	129,500	129,500	150,000	112,000	125,000	150,000
	Men	125,000	125,000	150,000	112,500	107,500	150,000
	Women	140,000	150,000	145,000	112,000	150,000	135,000
Other	Both genders	107,500	111,000	105,000	115,000	102,000	90,000
	Men	107,500	108,500	105,000	115,000	95,000	-
	Women	107,000	130,000	90,000	120,000	104,000	90,000

Table 5–34. Median annual household income of pharmacists who completed the survey questionnaire by county of residence, age group, and gender.

County of Residence	Gender	Median Annual Household Income (dollars)							
		All Age Groups	Less than 30	30-39	40-49	50-59	60-69	70 and Older	Not Known
All counties	Both genders	137,500	120,000	150,000	140,000	141,000	135,000	99,000	150,000
	Men	130,000	125,000	130,000	130,000	141,000	138,000	100,000	100,000
	Women	150,000	120,000	152,000	150,000	145,000	98,500	60,000	165,000
Broward	Both genders	145,000	152,000	160,000	150,000	150,000	140,000	100,000	160,000
	Men	131,500	196,500	132,500	130,000	150,000	141,500	100,000	93,500
	Women	151,000	150,000	170,000	150,000	120,000	100,000	82,000	200,000
Collier, Hendry, Lee, and Monroe	Both genders	140,000	160,000	140,000	149,000	131,000	140,000	85,000	150,000
	Men	132,500	142,500	135,000	140,000	130,000	145,000	90,000	150,000
	Women	150,000	160,000	140,000	150,000	150,000	100,000	60,000	160,000
Martin and Pasco	Both genders	135,000	145,844	140,000	117,500	147,500	132,500	98,000	125,000
	Men	130,000	145,844	140,000	125,000	145,000	135,000	98,000	125,000
	Women	139,000	147,500	140,000	110,000	150,000	130,000	-	125,000
Miami-Dade	Both genders	140,000	107,500	150,000	150,000	150,000	138,000	92,500	110,000
	Men	125,000	110,000	135,000	130,000	150,000	140,000	110,000	75,000
	Women	150,000	105,000	150,000	160,000	145,000	86,800	57,000	200,000
Palm Beach	Both genders	129,500	114,000	150,000	130,000	150,000	130,000	99,500	105,000
	Men	125,000	137,500	127,500	130,000	145,000	130,000	100,000	100,000
	Women	140,000	112,000	155,569	120,000	150,000	-	65,000	150,000
Other	Both genders	107,500	110,000	107,500	110,000	135,000	75,000	40,000	90,000
	Men	107,500	112,000	105,000	165,500	137,500	60,000	34,500	90,000
	Women	107,000	106,000	110,000	90,000	135,000	90,000	100,000	-

Table 5–35. Number of pharmacists who completed the survey questionnaire and reported being married by county of residence, whether or not spouse works, ethnic group, and gender.

County of Residence	Does Spouse Work?	Gender	Number of Pharmacists					
			All Ethnic Groups	Non-Hispanic			Hispanic	Other
				White	Black	Asian		
All counties	All groups	Both genders	1,120	728	79	55	218	40
		Men	635	483	32	23	79	18
		Women	485	245	47	32	139	22
	Yes	Both genders	801	483	61	41	182	34
		Men	358	260	18	11	54	15
		Women	443	223	43	30	128	19
	No	Both genders	319	245	18	14	36	6
		Men	277	223	14	12	25	3
		Women	42	22	4	2	11	3
Broward	All groups	Both genders	369	240	33	23	49	24
		Men	207	157	17	6	18	9
		Women	162	83	16	17	31	15
	Yes	Both genders	277	169	23	20	42	23
		Men	127	91	9	4	14	9
		Women	150	78	14	16	28	14
	No	Both genders	92	71	10	3	7	1
		Men	80	66	8	2	4	-
		Women	12	5	2	1	3	1
Collier, Hendry, Lee, and Monroe	All groups	Both genders	151	134	4	3	10	-
		Men	89	80	2	2	5	-
		Women	62	54	2	1	5	-
	Yes	Both genders	113	99	4	3	7	-
		Men	56	50	2	2	2	-
		Women	57	49	2	1	5	-
	No	Both genders	38	35	-	-	3	-
		Men	33	30	-	-	3	-
		Women	5	5	-	-	-	-
Martin and Pasco	All groups	Both genders	77	62	3	4	5	3
		Men	48	39	-	3	3	3
		Women	29	23	3	1	2	-
	Yes	Both genders	52	42	3	2	3	2
		Men	27	23	-	1	1	2
		Women	25	19	3	1	2	-
	No	Both genders	25	20	-	2	2	1
		Men	21	16	-	2	2	1
		Women	4	4	-	-	-	-

Table 5–35. Number of pharmacists who completed the survey questionnaire and reported being married by county of residence, whether or not spouse works, ethnic group, and gender (continued).

County of Residence	Does Spouse Work?	Gender	Number of Pharmacists					
			All Ethnic Groups	Non-Hispanic			Hispanic	Other
				White	Black	Asian		
Miami-Dade	All groups	Both genders	221	65	18	9	124	5
		Men	100	47	6	5	41	1
		Women	121	18	12	4	83	4
	Yes	Both genders	170	39	13	6	109	3
		Men	61	25	2	2	32	-
		Women	109	14	11	4	77	3
	No	Both genders	51	26	5	3	15	2
		Men	39	22	4	3	9	1
		Women	12	4	1	-	6	1
Palm Beach	All groups	Both genders	273	216	18	11	21	7
		Men	178	155	6	4	8	5
		Women	95	61	12	7	13	2
	Yes	Both genders	175	129	16	9	16	5
		Men	85	70	5	2	4	4
		Women	90	59	11	7	12	1
	No	Both genders	98	87	2	2	5	2
		Men	93	85	1	2	4	1
		Women	5	2	1	-	1	1
Other	All groups	Both genders	29	11	3	5	9	1
		Men	13	5	1	3	4	-
		Women	16	6	2	2	5	1
	Yes	Both genders	14	5	2	1	5	1
		Men	2	1	-	-	1	-
		Women	12	4	2	1	4	1
	No	Both genders	15	6	1	4	4	-
		Men	11	4	1	3	3	-
		Women	4	2	-	1	1	-

Two unrelated, Non-Hispanic White men living in Broward County, who indicated they have a domestic partner, have been classified as married.

A Non-Hispanic man living in Broward County, an Hispanic woman living in Broward County, and a Non-Hispanic White man living outside the nine counties did not respond; they have been classified as "spouse not working."

Table 5–36. Number of pharmacists who completed the survey questionnaire and reported being married by county of residence, whether or not spouse works, age group, and gender.

County of Residence	Does Spouse Work?	Gender	Number of Married Pharmacists							
			All Age Groups	Less than 30	30-39	40-49	50-59	60-69	70 and Older	Not Known
All counties	All groups	Both genders	1,120	53	265	261	234	157	123	27
		Men	635	13	75	115	154	146	115	17
		Women	485	40	190	146	80	11	8	10
	Yes	Both genders	801	49	229	215	188	74	29	17
		Men	358	13	50	79	116	66	27	7
		Women	443	36	179	136	72	8	2	10
	No	Both genders	319	4	36	46	46	83	94	10
		Men	277	-	25	36	38	80	88	10
		Women	42	4	11	10	8	3	6	-
Broward	All groups	Both genders	369	16	90	97	74	49	33	10
		Men	207	3	23	50	48	46	32	5
		Women	162	13	67	47	26	3	1	5
	Yes	Both genders	277	15	80	79	61	26	8	8
		Men	127	3	17	34	38	24	8	3
		Women	150	12	63	45	23	2	-	5
	No	Both genders	92	1	10	18	13	23	25	2
		Men	80	-	6	16	10	22	24	2
		Women	12	1	4	2	3	1	1	-
Collier, Hendry, Lee, and Monroe	All groups	Both genders	151	9	30	38	40	18	12	4
		Men	89	3	10	16	28	17	12	3
		Women	62	6	20	22	12	1	-	1
	Yes	Both genders	113	9	26	32	31	6	5	4
		Men	56	3	7	13	20	5	5	3
		Women	57	6	19	19	11	1	-	1
	No	Both genders	38	-	4	6	9	12	7	-
		Men	33	-	3	3	8	12	7	-
		Women	5	-	1	3	1	-	-	-
Martin and Pasco	All groups	Both genders	77	2	14	18	24	12	6	1
		Men	48	1	5	6	18	11	6	1
		Women	29	1	9	12	6	1	-	-
	Yes	Both genders	52	2	13	13	16	7	1	-
		Men	27	1	4	4	11	6	1	-
		Women	25	1	9	9	5	1	-	-
	No	Both genders	25	-	1	5	8	5	5	1
		Men	21	-	1	2	7	5	5	1
		Women	4	-	-	3	1	-	-	-

Table 5–36. Number of pharmacists who completed the survey questionnaire and reported being married by county of residence, whether or not spouse works, age group, and gender (continued).

County of Residence	Does Spouse Work?	Gender	Number of Married Pharmacists							
			All Age Groups	Less than 30	30-39	40-49	50-59	60-69	70 and Older	Not Known
Miami-Dade	All groups	Both genders	221	7	61	58	46	22	22	5
		Men	100	2	16	20	23	20	16	3
		Women	121	5	45	38	23	2	6	2
	Yes	Both genders	170	7	55	48	38	11	9	2
		Men	61	2	13	11	17	11	7	-
		Women	109	5	42	37	21	-	2	2
	No	Both genders	51	-	6	10	8	11	13	3
		Men	39	-	3	9	6	9	9	3
		Women	12	-	3	1	2	2	4	-
Palm Beach	All groups	Both genders	273	16	58	46	48	53	46	6
		Men	178	4	15	22	37	50	46	4
		Women	95	12	43	24	11	3	-	2
	Yes	Both genders	175	14	50	39	40	23	6	3
		Men	85	4	8	16	30	20	6	1
		Women	90	10	42	23	10	3	-	2
	No	Both genders	98	2	8	7	8	30	40	3
		Men	93	-	7	6	7	30	40	3
		Women	5	2	1	1	1	-	-	-
Other	All groups	Both genders	29	3	12	4	2	3	4	1
		Men	13	-	6	1	-	2	3	1
		Women	16	3	6	3	2	1	1	-
	Yes	Both genders	14	2	5	4	2	1	-	-
		Men	2	-	1	1	-	-	-	-
		Women	12	2	4	3	2	1	-	-
	No	Both genders	15	1	7	-	-	2	4	1
		Men	11	-	5	-	-	2	3	1
		Women	4	1	2	-	-	-	1	-

Two unrelated, 40-49 year old men living in Broward County, who indicated they have a domestic partner, have been classified as married.

A 40-49 year old man living in Broward County, a 50-59 year old woman living in Broward County, and a man who did not report his age, living outside the nine counties, did not respond; they have been classified as "spouse not working."

OPINION VARIABLES 6

Chapter 6 addresses variations in pharmacists' job-related perceptions, attitudes, and opinions that lead to, and are derived from, disparities in labor market outcomes. These perceptions, attitudes, and opinions are conditioned by the intrinsic and extrinsic rewards that different individuals, and different groups of individuals, experience in their work environment [Malka and Chatman, 2003]. Persons with a heavy intrinsic orientation value highly the satisfaction derived from performing the work itself, feelings of self-determination and competence, personal development, and interaction with coworkers, in contrast with persons oriented toward extrinsic rewards such as financial compensation, promotion, and prestige. Intrinsically satisfying jobs are characterized by the absence of excessive supervision and offer workers discretion on how to perform their tasks and evaluate their own performance. In addition, employers can offer their employees what Miller [2006] calls "psychic income" to improve their performance and retain them in the organization. This is done by connecting employees with a higher purpose and integrating them into a cohesive group.

The opinion variables discussed here focus on how much pharmacists like their jobs and specific aspects of their professional activities. They are designed to ascertain pharmacists' perceptions of their role in the healthcare delivery system as well as their individual working conditions, and relate to various aspects of job satisfaction. They develop in response to values, social cues, and work experiences that may affect groups (*i.e.*, gender groups, ethnic groups, age groups, etc.) differently, or simply be interpreted differently by the various groups.

Work values are beliefs held by individuals as standards guiding their behavior at work. They shape job-related perceptions, attitudes, and opinions. Brown [2002] identifies financial prosperity, altruism, achievement, and responsibility as examples of work values, and argues that they are crystalized when workers become aware of them and the influence of these values on their work behavior. Obviously, interpretation of who one is and what one can be exerts a powerful influence on occupational attainment and quality of work. Persons who aim high and believe in their ability to succeed in life, regardless of their definition of success, are likely to be more successful than their counterparts with less ambition and lower expectations. Perhaps people carry within themselves genetic and/or learned behavioral predispositions to specific situations in which environments present them with sets of normally distributed opportunities, risks, and potential rewards, in such a way that they end up accomplishing what they expect to accomplish, but no more. That might explain why workers of different genders, ethnic groups, and age groups tend to set and attain different dimensions and standards of professional fulfillment [Carvajal *et al.*, 1996; Deaux and Major, 1987].

Men and women differ in their emotional perceptions of the advantages and disadvantages offered by available jobs. Men usually seek jobs in which pecuniary factors such as pay, overtime hours, and advancement opportunities are emphasized, while women tend to prefer jobs with flexible schedules, good interaction with coworkers, and other non-pecuniary aspects, that is, a substantially different set of characteristics [Carvajal and Hardigan, 2008; Theodossiou and Vasileiou, 2007]. Some empirical evidence suggests that women are more risk adverse than men, and this preference leads them to choose jobs with less risk of physical injury or death, an amenity that may warrant lower pay as a compensation differential [DeLeire and Levy, 2004; Hersch, 2006]. Others argue that the extent to which people believe in gender role differences reflects their level of social conservatism and anti-egalitarianism; according to this view, the intensity of belief in gender-role differences correlates with endorsement of traditional marital roles and the intensity to which people consider men's and women's positions in the family and in the labor market to be fair and satisfactory [Poeschl, 2003; Poeschl *et al.*, 2001/2002]. Married women who hold relatively egalitarian attitudes toward gendered family roles and whose husbands participate in a relatively wider share of household work activities tend to work more hours and exhibit greater labor force attachment than their less egalitarian counterparts [Cunningham, 2008]. And still others report that men are more anti-egalitarian than women, as they generally do not believe that domestic work is within men's purview; they consider an unequal division of family chores to be fairer and more satisfactory, and they exhibit a higher level of both hostile and benevolent sexism [Poeschl *et al.*, 2006].

Expectations of male and female behavior often result from gender-role stereotypes that affect interpretation of performance. Young women are more likely than young men to attribute (and have others attribute) their success to luck or absence of difficulty from a specific task, and their failures to lack of ability, while young men exhibit the opposite pattern [Gitelson *et al.*, 1982; Stipek, 1984]. Within this context of early-life socialization, it is only "natural" that men rather than women get the more prestigious jobs, the higher salaries, and the more frequent promotions since they are "more likely" or expected to succeed more often than are women. Consequently, men end up defining their success more in terms of professional accomplishments in their roles as providers and women, along their primary responsibility to nurture their families, tend to measure their success more in terms of the quality of their relationships with other people and the stability of their homes [Cook, 1993; Kinnier *et al.*, 1991]. Implicit in this dichotomy of pursuits is the assumption that whatever the average woman sacrifices in the labor market by choosing a discontinuous workforce attachment and flexible work conditions is gained by an increase in the utility of time spent with her family.

In addition to the numerous internal barriers to success arising from the frequently adverse early gender-role socialization process experienced by women, including lack of self-confidence, limited career expectations, and fear of competition [Nolen-Hoeksema *et al.*, 1999], women also are at a disadvantage in the pursuit of occupational status because of role stereotyping. As seen in the previous chapter, occupational success demands commitment to the job and the profession, but women frequently are unable to make that commitment because they face choices between family and career that men normally do not have to face. As a result, many women choose a discontinuous career pattern, either working part time or dropping out of the labor force for extended periods to bear and raise children, or opting for less important, less prestigious positions, which demand less commitment and are closer to home or childcare centers, are characterized by more flexibility, and offer lots of support by coworkers and supervisors, for the sake of accommodating their families' needs.

The incidence of otherwise normally distributed opportunities, risks, potential rewards, and preferences also may be altered by patterns of ethnic stereotyping as Blacks, Hispanics, Asian Americans, and non-minorities perceive and interpret themselves differently [Carvajal and Hardigan, 1999]. In the eyes of ethnic minorities, desirable jobs may appear to be—even when they are not—dominated so effectively by non-minorities that a whole range of stereotypical ethnic characteristics may become identified with them, thus affecting minorities' aspirations to attain such jobs. Or the palatable jobs may be perceived as requiring attitudes, actions, or lifestyles inconsistent with "proper" ethnically established norms and mores. Whatever the case, the underrepresentation of ethnic minorities in a profession or field of work sends the wrong message to potential students and the rest of the world, namely, that minorities do not or cannot belong in that area of the workforce.

Maume and Sebastian [2007] make reference to two abstractions relevant to ethnic stereotyping—the similarity-attraction paradigm and the social categorization paradigm. Proponents of the similarity-attraction paradigm contend that, in the absence of detailed information about others, individuals have a tendency to like persons who are similar to them on visible characteristics such as race and ethnicity. According to this view, people believe that similar others have similar life experiences and values that make communication easier. Interacting and socializing with similar others enhance individual self-esteem and foster group identification. Proponents of the social categorization paradigm claim that human beings tend to define others as either belonging to their social circle or not, and non-group persons are less likely than group persons to be viewed as honest and trustworthy. As a minority group grows in size, political influence, and economic strength, the non-minority group tends to view it as an increasing threat in the competition for scarce resources.

Apart from the obvious ethnic dissimilarities of Blacks, Hispanics, and, to a lesser extent, Asian Americans vis-à-vis the non-minority population, other patterns of ethnic stereotyping can be disguised by variations in income and wealth. Relatively more minority than non-minority young men and women come from lower-income households and experience the burden of financial constraints in pursuing their education and making early career and family-life decisions not confronted by many of their non-minority peers whose parents' greater income and wealth can afford them a wider variety of choices.

Although the barriers and distortion of expectations faced by women and minorities, which condition their perceptions, attitudes, and opinions, work through different channels, the outcomes are very similar, namely, what McClelland [1990] calls a process of cumulative disadvantage in the internalization of objective chances of success. A specific accomplishment such as completing a report on time or a year free of dispensing errors may be perceived differently by a woman, Black, or Hispanic than by a non-minority male. The non-minority male tends to see it as a logical consequence of his actions (i.e., working hard, paying attention, etc.), but the woman or member of a minority ethnic group may be constantly haunted by the feeling that he/she is succeeding in spite of adverse odds that eventually may catch up with him/her. Furthermore, while non-minority males are likely to relate on a regular basis to family and friends who have succeeded in the performance of professional tasks, the paucity of successful female and/or minority peers, relatives, and role models usually constitutes a formidable handicap for the affected groups.

Cumulative disadvantage is an ongoing, systematic selection process by virtue of which men and women, non-minorities and minorities, tend to develop different patterns of response in their perceptions, attitudes, and opinions. It transcends specific individuals as it becomes institutionalized with the actions and omissions of social selectors or gatekeepers. Cumulative disadvantage is reinforced when women and minorities receive, either directly or indirectly, fewer or less intense messages of encouragement compared to non-minority males; when their family-related or cultural needs and preferences are not properly understood; or, worst of all, when they are the object of prejudice, bias, discrimination, or harassment [Carvajal *et al.*, 1996]. Thus, identical job incentives for men and women; non-minorities and minorities; and, to a lesser extent, all age groups, disregard crucial environmental stimuli and tend to preserve stereotypical gender, ethnic, and age disparities in expectations, aspirations, and, ultimately, achievement.

While age considerations may not be as severe as the gender and ethnic concerns identified above, employers need to increase their awareness of issues affecting mature workers in order to cope with workforce shortages more effectively. In some instances, not only should older workers be retained, but retired workers should be encouraged to return to work, although some evidence suggests that it is difficult to entice people to return after they have retired from the labor force [Hirsch, 2003]. Whether to convince older workers to stay or come back, employers must show them that working is a more attractive option than leisure, and that requires offering non-pecuniary incentives.

Armstrong-Stassen [2006] points out six crucial strategies to this effect. These strategies are offering flexible working options, including adaptable work days and schedules, part-time alternatives, job sharing, and unpaid leaves of absence for purposes of elderly care; providing training and development practices designed for mature employees to upgrade their skills and for managers to utilize their mature employees more effectively; designing practices which provide older workers with challenging and meaningful tasks and assignments, including new roles such as mentoring; recognizing the contributions of mature workers and treating them with respect; implementing performance evaluation appraisals free of age bias and providing older employees with useful feedback on their performance; and offering more financial compensation and improved benefits.

Regardless of whether or not perceptions conform to reality, they ultimately configure beliefs, shape attitudes, and induce behavior. Thus, systematic patterns by gender, ethnic group, and age are important. To illustrate, Hunt [2004] recently has explored people's views on wealth and poverty along three perspectives—individualistic beliefs identify the causes of poverty in characteristics of poor people themselves as well as their actions, structural beliefs search for the causes of poverty in the socioeconomic system in which poor people live, and fatalistic beliefs explain the causes of poverty in terms of forces that can be controlled neither by individuals nor by the socioeconomic system (*i.e.*, bad luck, illness, etc.). He finds that women are more likely than men to blame the system for poverty. Ethnic minorities are more likely than Non-Hispanic Whites to identify systematic biases at work in explaining the existence of wealthy people, although they are simultaneously more individualistic and more structuralist than are non-minorities on the subject of poverty. Being foreign born increases individualistic beliefs about poverty. African Americans and Hispanics also tend to attribute economic outcomes to God's will more frequently compared to Non-Hispanic Whites. Finally, older persons hold more individualistic beliefs on poverty than do younger respondents. The same reality is viewed differently by persons of different gender, ethnic identification, and age group, along with the behavioral consequences that such differences imply.

The job-related opinions of South Florida pharmacists analyzed in this chapter include satisfaction with current job and with the profession, amount of work in relation to other workers as an indicator of workload, amount of stress in relation to other workers, availability of advancement opportunities, job security, job autonomy, overall fairness in the workplace, rating of supervisor's performance in helping and supporting the pharmacist, job atmosphere in the workplace, scheduling flexibility, coworkers' overall professional quality, and coworkers' willingness to render help and support. The opinion variables are measured along zero-to-ten intensity scales, ten showing the greatest intensity. This procedure has the advantage of response homogeneity insofar as pharmacists are able to express their perception of various facets of their professional life following a common measurement rod. Since there is no room for outliers, the mean provides an adequate measure of central tendency.

JOB AND CAREER SATISFACTION

When workers assess available opportunities in the labor market, they review jobs with multiple combinations of characteristics, which include earnings, fringe benefits, location, working conditions, effort requirements, advancement opportunities, etc. These characteristics appear in fixed bundles, in such a way that workers seldom are able to choose all the characteristics that are precious to them and/or eschew all the characteristics that they perceive as problematic. Jobs that pay well may offer unpalatable benefit packages, a promotion may require moving to an undesirable location, and so on. How can workers compare the entire spectrum of characteristics and weigh the advantages and disadvantages of alternative jobs? A central metric is needed to relate to one another different aspects with different measurement rods. This central metric is provided by job satisfaction [Bender *et al.*, 2005; Benz, 2005; Bond and Raehl, 2001; Carvajal and Hardigan, 2000; Clark, 2001; Cox and Fitzpatrick, 1999; Donohue and Heywood, 2004; Hamermesh, 2001; Hardigan and Carvajal, 2007; Shields and Ward, 2001] and has received increasing recognition in the sociobehavioral sciences as a reliable proxy for utility [Frey and Stutzer, 2002b]. It is a positive emotional state resulting from workers' self-appraisal of their jobs that takes place when certain unspecified conditions are met [Andresen *et al.*, 2007]. When the appraisal is negative, a gap arises between what is desired and what is expected; when the appraisal is positive, outcome-desire fulfillment occurs [Testa, 2001].

Personality has been linked repeatedly to job satisfaction. For example, O'Connell [1991] asserts that if an individual's personality is incongruent with the personalities of others in the same field of work, friction induced in the individual tends to cause alterations in behavior. If the mismatch is considerable, the individual may not be able to respond appropriately and may not be able to work in that field successfully or find much enjoyment in it. Mathews [1992] and Stewart and Felicetti [1992] support this view of personality congruence when they confirm that people with specific personality styles tend to choose particular professions. Mathews [1992] maintains that mathematics majors have different personality styles from the styles of education majors, while Stewart and Felicetti [1992] find differences within majors—students pursuing marketing management degrees have personality styles different from students seeking advertising degrees. Additional evidence of personality congruence is provided by Rowe *et al.* [1992], who use the Myers Briggs Type Indicator to conclude that vocational teacher education students prefer sensing-judging, whereas marketing education majors exhibit a higher intuitive-thinking temperament.

The Myers Briggs Type Indicator has been used in pharmacy education to establish a database of pharmacy students' personality styles as they relate to vocational choice. Hardigan and Cohen [1998] report that pharmacy students' personality styles differ from the styles of students enrolled in osteopathic medicine, physical therapy, physician assistant, and occupational therapy programs. They report that while pharmacy attracts all personality types, it is especially attractive to students with introverted, sensing, thinking, and judging personalities. A review of the pharmacy literature reveals that most research involving vocational choice and personality style revolves around students and little has been done with practicing pharmacists. One exception is the work conducted by Hardigan *et al.* [2001a]. They report that, in contrast to the findings of Rezler *et al.* [1976], definite personality types choose to work in specific pharmacy practice sites, and marginally significant relationships appear only when gender is included in the analysis.

Cohrs *et al.* [2006] and Kim [2005] identify three groups of theories that have been proposed in the literature regarding the determinants of job satisfaction: situational theories, dispositional approaches, and interactive theories. Situational theories view job satisfaction as the product of the nature of one's job or other aspects of the environment, dispositional approaches maintain that job satisfaction is ingrained in the individual's personological make-up, and interactive theories consider job satisfaction as resulting from the interplay of both the environment and personality. The distinction between job satisfaction as an evaluative judgment or as an attitude is not a trivial one. Brief and Weiss [2002] maintain that job satisfaction is influenced by what Watson [2000] calls temperaments. These temperaments may be neuroticism or negative affectivity and extraversion or positive affectivity. Individuals with negative affectivity tend to experience anxiety, depression, hostility, and guilt, whereas individuals with positive affectivity are cheerful, enthusiastic, confident, active, and energetic, all of which provide a context for perceiving and interpreting job characteristics, thus shaping the extent to which people derive pleasure from their work experience.

In a study conducted by Hardigan *et al.* [2001b] to ascertain the relevance of affectivity in measuring practicing pharmacists' job satisfaction levels, both positive and negative affectivity prove to be statistically significant in the prediction of job satisfaction. Positive affectivity is directly correlated with job satisfaction while negative affectivity shows a negative relationship. In other words, pharmacists predisposed to be happy generally experience greater job satisfaction levels than do pharmacists predisposed to be unhappy.

Regardless of the approach, job satisfaction reflects workers' comprehensive evaluation of their jobs, focusing on the mixture, good and bad, of their experiences in a given position, within a specific setting, or both. It is a global abstraction that allows social and behavioral scientists to approximate the fundamental concept of aggregate well-being generated from a job. Individuals are asked to assess their objective conditions subjectively, often by means of comparison groups. Their responses are influenced by intrinsic and extrinsic forces, and it is up to the worker to decide the relative importance of each aspect of his/her employment. Intrinsic forces, sometimes called motivators, include considerations such as whether the job is interesting, the mechanics are challenging, and the objectives are worthwhile, whereas extrinsic forces, sometimes called hygiene factors, include financial remuneration in the form of pay and benefits, job security, opportunities for advancement, adequacy of resources, and similar concerns. According to Goris *et al.* [2000] and Robbins [2002], job and career satisfaction occur when workers experience three psychological states related to intrinsic forces—meaningfulness (*i.e.*, what they do is perceived as important and valuable), responsibility, and knowledge of results (*i.e.*, when they receive feedback about how effectively the work is performed). Campbell [2007] points out that 28 percent of workers in a recent survey identify the feeling of accomplishment as the most important contributor to job satisfaction, followed by 22 percent who identify technical challenge. However, the empirical results from other studies suggest that today's workers place greater emphasis on extrinsic than intrinsic factors [Andrews *et al.*, 2002; Jennings, 2000; Karl and Sutton, 1998], and this trend has been attributed to recent massive layoffs and increasing healthcare costs [Cameron, 1994; Schroder, 2008b]. Some of the aspects that pharmacists identify systematically as sources of job satisfaction include salary and fringe benefits, job security and flexibility, patient care and interaction, contact with medical staff, job opportunities, the nature of the work and work environment, and professional trust and respect [Cardinale, 2005].

Job satisfaction plays a crucial role in shaping labor market outcomes. It has been linked positively to motivation, job performance, productivity, organizational commitment and good citizenship behavior, and customer satisfaction, and negatively to absenteeism, tardiness, complaints and grievances against management, theft, job turnover and turnover intent, stress, and burnout [Bolin and Heatherly, 2001; Brief and Weiss, 2002; Byrd *et al.*, 2000; Clugston, 2000; Fisher, 2000; Frey and Stutzer, 2002a; Gordon and Denisi, 1995; Heslop *et al.*, 2002; Hulin and Judge, 2003; Johns, 2002; Judge and Bono, 2001; Judge *et al.*, 2002; Kim, 2005; Kirkman and Shapiro, 2001; Kulas *et al.*, 2007; Lambert *et al.*, 2005; Lin *et al.*, 2007; Mitchell and Lee, 2001; Rosser, 2004; Schappe, 1998; Smerek and Peterson, 2007; Sochalski, 2004; Sousa-Poza and Sousa-Poza, 2000a; Thomas and Au, 2002; Woods and Weasmer, 2002; Wright *et al.*, 2002]. Excessive turnover is costly to employers. Its direct costs include workers' loss of performance, interviewing potential employees, advertising and other recruitment expenses, selection/hiring/training of the newly hired, overtime wages to cover vacated positions, and administrative time to rearrange schedules, while indirect costs include loss of social networks, increased use of inexperienced or tired employees, insufficient staffing, and low morale, ultimately resulting in a drop in the quality of services provided and an increase in the risk to safety [Abbasi and Hollman, 2000; Lambert and Hogan, 2009; Watrous *et al.*, 2006].

More satisfied workers generally see their organization in a positive manner and are appreciative toward the organization for providing them with a job that makes them happy; thus, they are less likely to leave their job voluntarily than are less satisfied workers. Instead, they tend to invest in firm-specific human capital, which increases their commitment to their employer [Hamermesh, 2001]. According to Necowitz and Roznowski [1994], unfulfilled workers often manifest their dissatisfaction through unproductive and dysfunctional behaviors such as wandering around pretending to be busy, using the phone or computer for non-work purposes, and drinking alcohol or using drugs. And Clark and Oswald [1996] argue that workers' level of satisfaction constitutes a measure of the utility derived from their jobs, and consequently represents a relevant indicator of their attitudes and behavior. Hence, the determinants of workers' satisfaction with their jobs have important implications for organizational management and performance.

In spite of their widespread use, however, career- and job-satisfaction indices are viewed by some with scepticism [Long, 2005]. One concern is that well-being measures are too subjective and may not be comparable among individuals. Critics argue that job satisfaction indices are ordinal measures of very intangible concepts; as such, they may be an improper representation of what is intended to be measured. A fundamental issue here is whether job satisfaction is comparable across individuals and if it translates into meaningful and understandable behavior. Then there is discrepancy about whether job satisfaction should be measured by a global indicator or be derived, as a composite measure, from various indices of satisfaction with key aspects of a job such as pay and fringe benefits, the nature of work, supervision, coworkers, operating conditions, promotions, and recognition [Fields, 2002]. Lambert *et al.* [2001] argue that using a global measure avoids problems concerning weighting the various facets of one's job, accounting for different frames of reference, and ensuring that all relevant areas comprising job satisfaction are identified; yet, after concluding that a single-item variable overestimates satisfaction and underestimates dissatisfaction, Oshagbemi [1999] suggests that, whenever possible, both single- and multiple-item measures of job satisfaction be used.

Part of the controversy surrounding the use of job satisfaction has to do with its measurement. Not only do different studies conceptualize job satisfaction differently, sample different populations, and focus on different time periods, but they also use different measurements. Differences in measurement techniques are especially problematic since a multitude of indicators have been developed and it is questionable whether they measure the same thing [Jiang, 2004]. This methodological quagmire may be illustrated with the use of Likert scales.

In studies of job satisfaction among practicing pharmacists, it often is assumed that a well-constructed set of Likert questions provides interval-level scores [Maio *et al.*, 2004; Olson and Lawson, 1996; Riggins and Plowman, 2000]. Specifically, Olson and Lawson [1996] examine the relationship between hospital pharmacists' job satisfaction and clinical activities. They measure job satisfaction using a five-point scale that reads as follows: 1 for "strongly agree," 2 for "tend to agree," 3 for "neither agree nor disagree," 4 for "tend to disagree," and 5 for "strongly disagree." From the original data gathered, a mean satisfaction score is calculated. However, the Likert response categories represent an ordinal level of measurement. With ordinal levels the categories represent an inherent order, but the numbers assigned to the categories do not indicate the magnitude of the difference between categories. Interval properties imply equally spaced points on a scale, whereby a > b > c > . . . and also (a - b) = (b - c) = (c - d) = ... But Cohen *et al.* [2000] argue that it is incorrect to assume that the intensity of feeling between "strongly disagree" and "disagree" is equivalent to the intensity of feeling between other consecutive categories on the Likert scale. The authenticity in assuming an interval scale for Likert type categories is an important issue because the appropriate inferential statistics differ for ordinal and interval variables, and if the wrong statistical technique is used, the researcher increases the chance of reaching the wrong conclusion about the significance of his/her empirical results [Godfrey, 2005; Jamieson, 2004].

In principle, Likert scale data can be used as a basis for obtaining interval-level estimates on a continuum by applying the Rasch model [Sivakumar *et al.*, 2005; Wright and Stone, 1979]. The Rasch model, however, poses the advantage of allowing tests of hypotheses that reflect varying levels of an attitude or trait. For example, past research indicates that the neutral category does not represent a level of attitude or trait between the "disagree" and "agree" categories [Wright and Stone, 1979]. Rasch analysis amplifies this assumption. It recognizes that results from a survey can be compared meaningfully only if the survey functions in the same way for everyone who completes the questionnaire. If a questionnaire functions differently for different groups, then comparisons across groups may not be valid.

Rasch analysis, a form of item response theory, is used in the examination of categorical data [Anderson, 1997; Bond and Fox, 2001]. It converts raw scores into standardized units. These units are then aligned on a ruler that measures each component of the model. With survey research, Likert items typically are analyzed using the rating scale model. The rating scale model produces measures of a person's latent trait (*i.e.*, job satisfaction) on the same scale with measures of item difficulty using a logit scale [Bond and Fox, 2001]. A logit scale uses the log-odds of obtaining a particular rating to estimate the level of the latent trait and item difficulty. In contrast, traditional statistical analysis treats all items as having equal value and describes data in terms of averages, percentages, and probabilities [Linacre, 2002; McHorney *et al.*, 1992]. A study conducted by Hardigan and Carvajal [2008] shows that the use of Rasch analysis in the evaluation of job satisfaction among practicing pharmacists is superior to other approaches. Their conclusions reveal that Rasch estimates provide more precise scores than the traditional estimates and also provide more precise estimates when mean scores are more diverse (*i.e.*, larger). The study results demonstrate the usefulness of Rasch analysis in assessing the psychometric properties of a scale and suggest that further use of this technique to assess job satisfaction in other clinical groups is warranted.

An interesting phenomenon that emerges in the measurement of job satisfaction is the so-called gender paradox or paradox of the contented female worker, namely, that women's reported job satisfaction levels are consistently greater than the levels reported by their male counterparts [Bender and Heywood, 2006; Bilimoria *et al.*, 2006; Brown and McIntosh, 2003; Gazioğlu and Tansel, 2002; Kaiser, 2007; Kim, 2005; Kramen-Kahn and Hansen, 1998; Lambert *et al.*, 2001; Lin *et al.*, 2007; Long, 2005; McDuff, 2001; McMurray *et al.*, 2000; Sousa-Poza and Sousa-Poza, 2000a; Tanner *et al.*, 1999] in spite of women holding less glamorous jobs, earning lower levels of income, and receiving fewer promotions relative to men, all situations which would be expected to limit satisfaction. One reason for this phenomenon may be that insofar as women are primarily responsible for childcare and housework, they feel less social pressure to be successful at work compared to men, who are bestowed, in the eyes of society, with the financial responsibility for the household. Thus, women who are dissatisfied with their jobs may opt more freely to leave the labor market, and consequently their dissatisfaction would not count in surveys. Another reason for the paradox is that since satisfaction is a function of expectations, if women have lower expectations than do men about labor market outcomes, their expectations would be fulfilled more readily [Clark, 1997]. In other words, women's satisfaction gap between what is expected and what is attained is comparatively small. Women may be comparing their outcomes to the outcomes of other women, so their target may be less demanding than men's target. Phelan [1994] also argues that women may be more satisfied in their jobs than are men because subjective rewards, which are distributed more equitably, are relatively more appealing to women than are objective rewards, which are distributed less equitably between genders. In any event, Sousa-Poza and Sousa-Poza [2003] predict that this paradox is a transitory occurrence; according to them, as employment conditions and opportunities converge for men and women, job satisfaction differences by gender are expected to disappear.

A third explanation for the paradox of the contented female worker is that the job characteristics valued by men and women are different [Bilimoria *et al.*, 2006]. Women do not place as much emphasis on financial remuneration as do men, but instead identify social relations at work as the most important contributor to job satisfaction [Clark, 1997]. In fact, some empirical evidence suggests that greater earnings add more to the job satisfaction of men than to women's job satisfaction, and the job satisfaction of women increases with female share of the workplace [Donohue and Heywood, 2004; Sloane and Williams, 2000]. Furthermore, women in male-dominated jobs frequently are less satisfied than women in jobs not dominated by men [Bender *et al.*, 2005; Loscocco and Spitze, 1991]. These studies point out that men and women make workplace choices based on heterogeneous preferences over job characteristics, so the higher satisfaction of women reported in female-dominated jobs exists because those jobs have special characteristics, probably difficult to measure, which women value. Therefore, Bender *et al.* [2005] conclude that policies that enforce equality or changes in the gender composition of job characteristics are likely to be dysfunctional and could end up reducing the job satisfaction of both men and women.

A fourth explanation for the paradox of the contented female worker is provided by Hagan and Kay [2007]. They argue that gender job satisfaction comparisons obscure a more notable difference in men's and women's feelings of depression and despondency. According to this view, women tend to respond to their professional disillusionment by experiencing internalized feelings of despondency rather than conveying externalized statements of job dissatisfaction. In other words, while men publicize their job-related problems through complaints, protests, and grievances, women are more likely to translate them into signs of distress, especially those arising from work-family conflict. Thus, the greater incidence of female than male professional work-induced depression is a more relevant indicator of how women and men respond to differences in occupational status, earnings, and promotions. This is consistent with the findings by Hull [1999], namely, that women are less satisfied than are their men peers with specific features of the context in which they work.

In contrast with gender composition, the effect on job satisfaction of the ethnic composition of workgroups has not received much attention in the literature. Maume and Sebastian [2007] explore a basic proposition of the ethnic segregation hypothesis whereby organizations tend to devalue the pay and promotion policies of jobs increasingly held by minorities. The authors find that Non-Hispanic Whites exhibit high levels of job dissatisfaction while working with minorities, not because they are biased against minority coworkers, but rather they become dissatisfied with the less favored jobs they share with minorities. McHugh [1999] detects no differences in job satisfaction among ethnic groups, but Bender and Heywood [2006], Byrd *et al.* [2000], Rosser [2005], and Smerek and Peterson [2007] find that minorities report lower levels of job satisfaction than do Non-Hispanic Whites. Obviously it is important to know how non-minorities react to minority coworkers not only because of the impact on ethnic relations, but also because of the specific implications for managing a widely diverse workforce, especially in places like South Florida.

Several studies indicate that age has a U-shape effect on job satisfaction [Brown and McIntosh, 2003; Brown and Sargeant, 2007; Hochwarter *et al.*, 2001; Kaiser, 2007; Long, 2005; Theodossiou and Vasileiou, 2007]. Both younger and older workers seem happier with their work relative to middle-aged workers. According to Gazioğlu and Tansel [2002], younger workers experience relatively high levels of satisfaction with their jobs because they possess little labor market experience and are not able to judge accurately their own working conditions. As they acquire experience throughout the years, they are better able to judge their own work and their satisfaction drops in the middle ages. When they get older, their aspirations are reduced as they realize that they face limited choices in the workplace [Schroder, 2008b; Smerek and Peterson, 2007; Spector, 1997]. With a broader perspective of life and approaching retirement, aging workers are likely to attach less importance to professional ambitions, or perhaps they acquire a growing awareness of areas within the profession from which they derive a greater level of job satisfaction [Cimete *et al.*, 2003]. Or they may have adapted to the working conditions, policies, and interpersonal relationships of a specific employer, or type of organization, for which they have worked over several years [Schroder, 2008a]. An alternative explanation may be that older workers' satisfaction is subject to a self-selection process; since dissatisfied mature workers may decide to leave the labor market and retire, perform volunteer work, etc., individuals who remain in the market and report their opinions are the more satisfied workers.

Some of the general findings pertaining to job satisfaction and other variables are as follows: Job satisfaction varies positively with income [Gazioğlu and Tansel, 2002; Kaiser, 2007], autonomy [Carvajal and Hardigan, 2000], job security [Gazioğlu and Tansel, 2002; Theodossiou and Vasileiou, 2007], availability of training opportunities [Gazioğlu and Tansel, 2002], perceived importance of the job [Carvajal and Hardigan, 2000], and self-efficacy [Bradley and Roberts, 2004]. It varies negatively with formal schooling [Bender *et al.*, 2005; Clark and Oswald, 1996; Johnson and Johnson, 2000], size of firm [Bender *et al.*, 2005; Gazioğlu and Tansel, 2002; Theodossiou and Vasileiou, 2007], number of hours worked [Burchell and Fagan, 2004; Gazioğlu and Tansel, 2002], and income disparities in the workplace [Donohue and Heywood, 2004]. Married workers report less satisfaction than single workers [Brown and McIntosh, 2003; Gazioğlu and Tansel, 2002; Thomas and Talpade, 1999], rural workers are less satisfied than are their urban colleagues with the infrastructure of the areas where they work [Arnold *et al.*, 1997], and practice site seems to play a significant role in the literature. Yet other studies find no relationship between job satisfaction and demographic variables [Brewer and McMahan-Landers, 2003; Petty *et al.*, 2005]. Specifically for pharmacy practitioners, separate findings indicate that pharmacists practicing in independent settings are more satisfied with their work than those in other ambulatory settings [McHugh, 1999], community pharmacists report higher levels of job satisfaction than do hospital and clinical pharmacists [Lin *et al.*, 2007], and practitioners working in chain pharmacies exhibit the lowest level of job satisfaction of all settings [Ukens, 2004].

The results of the South Florida pharmacists survey reveal that practitioners' overall level of satisfaction with their jobs is moderately high (see Tables 6-1 and 6-2). This is consistent with the findings of similar surveys nationwide [Cardinale, 2005; Lapane and Hughes, 2006; Levy, 2008; LoBuono, 2003; Ukens, 2007]. The levels of job satisfaction are about the same throughout all county categories. Men and women show virtually identical levels, so there does not seem to be a paradox of the contented female worker in South Florida, but ethnic disparities are apparent. Hispanic pharmacists' job satisfaction levels are greater than the satisfaction of nonminority pharmacists, which in turn exceeds the job satisfaction levels of Black and Asian American pharmacists. Gender differences do appear within ethnic groups. Male pharmacists' job satisfaction indices exceed the female indices for Blacks and Asian Americans, but Hispanic female pharmacists are more satisfied with their jobs than are Hispanic male pharmacists. Nonminority men and women report approximately the same job satisfaction levels. In terms of age, the only evident pattern is that practitioners 70 years or older exhibit a much greater level of satisfaction with their jobs compared to the other age groups.

Career satisfaction is a similar concept to job satisfaction, with two obvious variations. One is that it entails a longer-term perspective; the other is that the spectrum of characteristics being compared transcends a specific job setting and refers to broader activities within the profession. In contrast with earlier findings by Carvajal and Hardigan [2008], whereby both male and female pharmacists' job satisfaction indices exceed career satisfaction indices, South Florida pharmacists report approximately the same overall levels of satisfaction with their careers as with their current jobs, although the composition by group is quite different (see Tables 6-3 and 6-4). Pharmacists living in the four-county area of Collier, Hendry, Lee, and Monroe express lower levels of satisfaction with their careers compared to the rest of the sample. With the exception of Black and Asian American practitioners, female pharmacists are more satisfied with their profession relative to male pharmacists. Non-Hispanic Whites report the lowest levels of career satisfaction, Hispanics report the highest, and Blacks and Asian Americans score in between. And age exhibits the classic U-shape function found elsewhere, with pharmacists younger than 40 years of age and 70 years or older reporting higher levels of career satisfaction than their 40–69 year old peers.

WORKLOAD

An excessive workload is one of the main causes of pharmacists' dissatisfaction with their jobs [Lapane and Hughes, 2006; Tanner, 1999]. It generates stress among practitioners, leads to medication dispensing errors, and reduces the opportunities for pharmacists to interact with patients and perform care activities [Mahrous and Maziarz, 2008]. Workers who perceive themselves as victims of an excessive overload tend to feel angry at their employers, resent their coworkers, consider searching for another job, experience work-family conflict, and suffer deteriorating health [Galinsky *et al.*, 2001]. Several nationwide surveys reveal a consensus that pharmacists' workload, already perceived as onerous, continues to increase, with more time spent on dispensing and administrative functions instead of counseling and clinical activities [Cardinale, 2005; Knapp and Cultice, 2007; Levy, 2008; Schommer *et al.*, 2002; Ukens, 2007]. Lo Buono [2003] reports that chain pharmacists dispense an average of 177 prescriptions daily, HMO pharmacists dispense 157 prescriptions, hospital pharmacists dispense 149 prescriptions, independent pharmacists dispense 142 prescriptions, discount/mass merchandisers dispense 138 prescriptions, and supermarket pharmacists dispense an average of 118 prescriptions per day. An obvious question raised by this situation is whether the increasing workload will allow pharmacists to keep in place appropriate quality control mechanisms and meet adequate standards of patient care.

Manassee and Speedie [2007] argue that the increase in workload, frequently measured as the number of prescriptions dispensed per period of time, can be attributed to an influx of new drugs for previously untreated diseases as well as other drugs for previously treated disorders. In addition, the incidence of chronic illnesses is on the rise because of the increase in the population of patients, primarily baby boomers, reaching age brackets when chronic illnesses usually emerge. Moreover, Medicare now pays automatically for prescription medications. Obviously the rise in workload is closely related to the shortage of pharmacists.

In pharmacy and other professions men often carry a heavier workload than do women, but women consider their job more exhausting than do men [Green *et al.*, 2007; McMurray *et al.*, 2000; Weeks and Wallace, 2006a]. This perception may arise out of the commonly accepted gender division of labor, namely, that in addition to working in the labor market, women are responsible for the brunt of childcare and household activities.

In the South Florida survey workload is measured by the respondent's perceived amount of work in relation to other workers (see Tables 6-5 and 6-6). The rating for this variable is fairly high, indicating that excessive workload is an important issue for South Florida pharmacists. There seems to be no variation among counties regarding workload, but women complain more than men about the amount of work assigned to them. This is consistent with the findings of other studies cited above, and the gender disparity is replicated within every ethnic group except Asian Americans. On average, pharmacists from all three minority groups report a heavier workload than Non-Hispanic White pharmacists, and pharmacists 60 years of age and older seem to be less concerned with their workload relative to their younger colleagues.

STRESS

Job-related stress, a non-specific, negative response of the body to job demands, conditions, and expected performance standards, is related in the literature to low levels of job satisfaction and organizational commitment, disillusionment, and excessive turnover [Acker, 2004; Baggerly and Osborn, 2006; DeMato and Curcio, 2004; Gaither, 1998, 1999; Lambert and Paoline, 2008; Mor-Barak *et al.*, 2001; Rayle, 2006]. It involves feelings of work-related tension, anxiety, frustration, worry, emotional exhaustion, and distress [Grossi *et al.*, 1996; Van Voorhis *et al.*, 1991]. In several studies pharmacists have expressed very high levels of job-related stress, and many perceive that their jobs are becoming increasingly stressful [Levy, 2008; Ukens, 2007]; yet their relatively high levels of job satisfaction seem to suggest that pharmacists have come to accept stress as a characteristic of their profession normally rewarded with higher income levels. Nevertheless Mott *et al.* [2004] issue a stern warning that unless pharmacists' job-related stress declines in the near future, their physical and mental health, as well as the safety of their patients, may be in jeopardy.

Stress normally emerges with negative working conditions and/or poor workplace relationships over which workers have little or no control [Burchell and Fagan, 2004; Spector *et al.*, 2000]. Common causes of job-related stress include increased regulation, downsizing, irregular work schedules, role ambiguity (coping with the absence of clear guidelines for performing tasks in the workplace), role conflict (managing multiple roles), lack of power, and perceptions of organizational politics [Day and Chamberlain, 2006; Lewandowski, 2003; Miller *et al.*, 2008; Nelson and Burke, 2000]. Mott *et al.* [2004] and Ukens [2004] have found substantially greater stress levels in chain, mass merchandiser/supermarket, and hospital pharmacies relative to independent pharmacies. The perception of less stress reported by independent pharmacists compared to pharmacists who practice in other settings is not surprising since many independent pharmacists own and/or manage their establishment. Owning or managing their business allows these pharmacists the opportunity to set the rules and determine the policies for their pharmacy as well as practice their profession in the manner they choose. The ability to have more control over responsibilities may in part influence the higher levels of satisfaction and lower perceived stress levels observed in this group. As a general rule, the worst stressors are a heavy work volume, inadequate staff support, too much paperwork, and perceptions of unfriendliness or hostility in the workplace [Ukens, 2007]. Other stressors include being interrupted by phone calls, not being able to practice pharmacy the way practitioners would like to practice it, working unusual hours, not receiving constructive feedback from supervisors, experiencing job policies enforced inconsistently, and keeping up with new developments to maintain professional competence [Andresen *et al.*, 2007; Lapane and Hughes, 2006; Mott *et al.*, 2004].

While some stress may be necessary for workers to experience drive and motivation, extremely stressful conditions often are the cause of short tempers and poor relationships among employees. Stack [2003] identifies five progressive stages of job-related stress, as follows: the physical stage, characterized by illness and fatigue; the social stage, when negativity, blaming things on others, missing deadlines, and working through lunch take place; the cerebral stage, during which clock watching, errors in assignments, minor accidents, absentmindedness, and indecisiveness occur; the emotional stage, when feelings of anger, sadness, crying, yelling, being overwhelmed, and depression arise; and the spiritual stage, characterized by brooding, wanting to make drastic changes in life, not relating well with people, and cooling off personal relationships. Stress, in association with intensity of work, appears to be responsible for a wide variety of health-related symptoms such as headaches, backaches, stomachaches, anxiety, irritability, sleeping problems, and skin disorders [Winchert, 2002]. It also has been linked to divorce, substance abuse, and suicide [Cheek, 1984]. Workers who experience relatively high levels of stress tend to blame their employers for creating or allowing the stress, which leads to less organizational commitment on their part [Lambert, 2004; Lambert and Paoline, 2008].

Burnout may be defined as a phase beyond stress. It develops in response to prolonged exposure to stressful situations [Cartwright, 1987] and consists of a psychological syndrome of emotional exhaustion, depersonalization, and reduced personal accomplishment that pervades nonwork aspects of one's existence, brought about by excessive and chronic job-related interpersonal stressors [Lewandowski, 2003; Maslach *et al.*, 2001]. Symptoms include a sense of helplessness, cynical attitudes toward symbols of authority, progressive apathy, and becoming angry with patients and coworkers. Healthcare professionals are particularly susceptible to burnout because the nature of their work engages them with patients in emotionally demanding situations and exposes them to their problems over the long run [Kirk-Brown and Wallace, 2004; Kumar *et al.*, 2007; Patton and Goddard, 2003].

Not all stressors affect all individuals or groups of individuals in a similar manner. Compared to their Non-Hispanic White male counterparts, women and minorities are reported to experience more stress in their jobs [McMurray *et al.*, 2000; Trower and Chait, 2002]. According to Cartwright [1987], women respond to stress by diluting or diminishing their careers (*i.e.*, working fewer hours) and reducing or limiting the demands of intimacy (*i.e.*, less likely to get married, getting married at an older age, more likely to get divorced, and likely to have fewer children) to a greater extent than do men. Auster [2001] identifies time pressures, life balance, office politics, and work-family support as the four main factors that influence professional women's midcareer stress and satisfaction. Of particular interest are women with strong ethnic minority identities, who frequently struggle to cope with two different worlds—the dominant Non-Hispanic White male culture in the workplace and a personal world full of different and often conflicting mores and expectations ingrained in the ethnic community to which they belong [Bell, 1990]. This biculturalism leads to additional stress-inducing situations of isolation and rejection [Zweigenhaft, 1994].

Tables 6-7 and 6-8 show the average rating of perceived stress, in relation to other workers, of South Florida pharmacists who participated in the survey. The overall level of perceived stress is moderate to high, with minor inter-county differences other than for pharmacists living outside the South Florida area, who exhibit higher levels of job-related stress compared to the rest of the sample. Women report more job-related stress than men. The gender disparity, however, applies only to Non-Hispanic Whites and, with less intensity, Hispanics; male and female Black pharmacists exhibit virtually identical levels, and male Asian American pharmacists complain about stress substantially more than do female Asian American pharmacists. On average, non-minorities experience the lowest levels of stress, while Blacks and Hispanics report the highest levels, and this variable seems to fit a dome-shape function for age. Stress levels increase with age, reaching a peak in the 40–59 year-old group, then decline to their lowest levels for pharmacists 70 years and older.

ADVANCEMENT OPPORTUNITIES

Several studies suggest that pharmacy as a profession experiences shortcomings in satisfying the work ambitions of its practitioners, as a generalized perception of limited opportunities for career advancement seems to be prevalent [Carvajal and Hardigan, 2008; Levy, 2008; Tanner *et al.*, 1999]. This is a universal problem that affects men and women alike in many professions, although throughout the world men seem to have access to more and better advancement opportunities than do women [Blau and DeVaro, 2007; Long, 2005; Sousa-Poza and Sousa-Poza, 2000a]. A term used in the literature, which may apply to this situation and tends to perpetuate gender and ethnic inequalities in the workplace, is the glass ceiling [Kee, 2006]. It refers to a metaphorical barrier preventing women and minorities from advancing further along the organizational structure once they have attained a certain level. They watch their Non-Hispanic White male peers being promoted while they are not. Yet it is not uncommon for women to show greater satisfaction than do men with the promotions they receive [Kim, 2005]. A plausible explanation for this apparent inconsistency may be that women pharmacists are not as interested as are their men counterparts in getting promotions that often are accompanied by increased stress and work commitments inconsistent with their household responsibilities. Furthermore, since female pharmacists' husbands earn greater income levels compared to male pharmacists' wives, as was established in Chapter 5, women indeed may experience less pressure than men to be promoted. Thus, the fact that women are promoted less frequently than are men might be attributed, at least partially, to a matter of choice rather than a lack of opportunities. Obviously this argument may not be used as readily to explain the existence of ethnic glass ceilings, so the statistics reflect a complex situation that probably responds to the interplay of several factors. Smerek and Peterson [2007], for example, find that non-minorities are more satisfied with their advancement opportunities than are minorities.

According to Kahaleh and Gaither [2007], pharmacists who work in independent settings report greater levels of perceived advancement opportunities than those who work in chain or hospital pharmacies. Apparently having access to training and advancement opportunities reduces the likelihood of job turnover. In other studies training and advancement opportunities are viewed as exerting a stronger impact on job satisfaction compared to workload or pay [Bender and Heywood, 2006; Gazioğlu and Tansel, 2002].

South Florida pharmacists assign to their perceived availability of advancement opportunities the lowest overall ratings of any variable in the survey (see Tables 6-9 and 6-10), although pharmacists residing outside South Florida are less pessimistic about their advancement prospects relative to the rest of the sample. Women practitioners report substantially more and better professional opportunities than do men, and the differential is replicated within each ethnic group, thus lending credence to the contented female worker hypothesis. Black, Asian American, and Hispanic pharmacists also are more optimistic in their perception of advancement opportunities than are Non-Hispanic White pharmacists, which accords with the findings of Maume and Sebastian [2007] regarding the ethnic segregation hypothesis and might serve as the empirical basis for formulating and examining a contented minority worker hypothesis. Pharmacists younger than 30 years of age exhibit the greatest levels of optimism regarding the range of advancement opportunities available to them, and the average rating declines steadily and uninterruptedly with each older group. Perhaps the greater levels of optimism observed in younger practitioners is due in part to the attainment of the Pharm.D. degree. Possessing a Pharm.D. degree is likely to open more opportunities for long-term advancement.

JOB SECURITY

Subjective perceptions of risk of job loss exert important effects on the workforce, which have an impact on labor productivity, employment, and other outcomes. The relevance of these perceptions has become evident in the various downsizing, privatization, and contracting out practices undertaken in recent years by private and public organizations in response to economic pressures. For some time downsizing and contracting out were widely accepted as effective means to reorganize and promote the operating efficiency of firms through reducing unnecessary employees, improving the quality of human-capital stock of remaining employees, and increasing competitiveness. Surprisingly, downsizing, privatization, and contracting out have had adverse consequences on firms in terms of quality and customer service, and have failed to add to their value or enhance their productivity [Cascio, 2002; Chadwick *et al.*, 2004; Fisher and White, 2000; Howard, 2002; Landry, 2004; Rigby, 2002; Tsai *et al.*, 2007].

Workers in firms undergoing downsizing tend to suffer from decreased motivation, low morale, lack of competence, and increased stress, all symptoms of what Brockner [1992] labels the "survivor syndrome." They become suspicious of management, experience a decline in productivity, feel anxiety about the future, and report substantially lower levels of job satisfaction. They engage in extreme risk avoidance, develop physical illnesses, and many end up resigning [McKinley *et al.*, 1995; Mishra and Spreitzer, 1998; Perry and Mankin, 2007; Shah, 2000]. Along these lines, Green *et al.* [2000] show that a high risk of job loss is harmful to well-being, having all sorts of negative consequences on both the physical and mental health of employees and their families, and Prizzia [2005] reports that market reforms driven by privatization aggravate the disadvantaged status of women relative to men with regard to workplace conditions. Theodossiou and Vasileiou [2007] suggest that a visible reduction in the risk of job loss for the incumbent workforce can go a long way toward enhancing a well functioning labor market.

The significant effect of job security on job satisfaction is clearly established in the literature [Gazioğlu and Tansel, 2002; Kaiser, 2002; Moguerou, 2002; Sousa-Poza and Sousa-Poza, 2000b; Tocher *et al.*, 2006]. Specifically for pharmacists, job security is one of the top motivating influences to enter the profession [Cardinale, 2005; Tanner *et al.*, 1999]. There is evidence indicating that women display a greater level of satisfaction with job security than do men [Kaiser, 2007; Kim, 2005], and older workers tend to perceive a greater risk of job loss compared to younger workers [Theodossiou and Vasileiou, 2007]. This latter trend may reflect younger workers' relatively greater mobility early in their career in search for the most suitable job for them as well as apprehension by older workers about their options in the event of a negative outcome in their job.

Tables 6-11 and 6-12 summarize South Florida pharmacists' job-security ratings. The overall level of perceived job security is fairly high, as this is the opinion variable with the highest rating. Evidently practitioners believe that their jobs are endowed with a great deal of stability, which accords with earlier findings by Carvajal and Hardigan [2008]. The ongoing pharmacist shortage, as well as pharmacists' expanded role in the healthcare system and the increasing use of medications to treat chronic diseases in aging populations, are factors that probably contribute to pharmacists' general perception of job security. Also consistently with other studies identified above, female pharmacists perceive a lower risk of job loss relative to male pharmacists, and the differential is replicated within every ethnic group except Blacks. Average ratings are very similar for all ethnic groups, but variation by age is detected. The perception of job security declines steadily with age, in support of the findings by Theodossiou and Vasileiou [2007]. Only marginal regional differences are apparent, as pharmacists in the four-county area experience slightly more job security, and pharmacists in Martin and Pasco report feeling less secure, than the other practitioners in the sample.

AUTONOMY

Attractive jobs usually are free from overbearing supervision. These jobs allow workers to exercise their judgment in conducting professional activities and control how they allocate their time. Having more discretion provides pharmacists and other healthcare professionals, as well as workers in other fields, with a sense of autonomy and responsibility that is conducive to caring more about what they do, building confidence in their abilities, generating feelings of pride, rendering better care to patients and clients, and attaining higher levels of job satisfaction [Bolin and Shulman, 2005; Collins *et al.*, 2000; Gary, 2002; Hundley, 2001a; Kahaleh and Gaither, 2005; Linzer *et al.*, 2000; Spence Laschinger *et al.*, 2003; Weaver *et al.*, 2001; Zurmehly, 2008]. Workers who perceive that they have insufficient autonomy in their job tend to feel less valued [Tansey *et al.*, 2004] and are more likely to experience higher levels of job-related stress [Lazarus, 1999].

Some gender differences in autonomy are reported in the literature. Carvajal and Hardigan [2000] find that while both genders score very similar indices of perceived job autonomy, the influence of this variable on job satisfaction is stronger for female pharmacists than it is for their male peers. In a subsequent and broader study, however, Carvajal and Hardigan [2008] claim that perceived job autonomy is mediated by the number of hours worked. Within practitioners who work part time, men experience more job autonomy than do women, but for those who work at least 40 hours per week, no significant difference by gender is detected. Furthermore, men's perception of the importance of job autonomy tends to decline as the level of work effort rises, but no such trend is detected for women. In other studies, relatively fewer female than male physicians are satisfied with autonomy in their jobs [McMurray *et al.*, 2000; Seifert and Umbach, 2008] and community pharmacists report perceiving more autonomy in their jobs compared to pharmacists working in hospitals and clinics [Lin *et al.*, 2007].

Carlson and Mellor [2004] advance an interesting explanation of why these gender differences in the perception of autonomy exist. According to them, men and women differ in how they interpret their actualized self. Men tend to define their selves through separation from others as part of their own identity, so they search for jobs that provide independence in performing their tasks and allow them to experience satisfaction through self-actualization opportunities. In contrast, women tend to be happier in jobs that allow them to pursue care and connectedness with others within their relational self-definition because they are more likely than men to develop connected selves. Generally women place greater importance on interpersonal relationships, including working with others, than on individual self-actualization [Konrad *et al.*, 2000b].

According to the South Florida pharmacists survey results (see Tables 6-13 and 6-14), practitioners who responded perceive that they enjoy moderate to high levels of autonomy in their jobs. Pharmacists in Martin and Pasco, the periphery counties, report the lowest indices of job autonomy. Men and women report very similar indices, and differences among ethnic groups and among age groups are small.

FAIRNESS IN THE WORKPLACE

The issue of fairness in the workplace, also known as organizational justice, points to a fundamental consideration in the analysis of labor market determinants and outcomes, namely, whether interpersonal comparisons of perceptions possess methodological validity [Long, 2005]. Harsanyi [1987] argues that economists tend to exaggerate the shortcomings of making interpersonal comparisons. Van Praag [1991] claims that, in most instances, survey respondents place approximately the same number value on different subjective responses, but Clark and Oswald [1996], Ng [1997], and Sloane and Williams [2000] validate the procedure of analyzing comparisons of subjective perceptions among individuals, concluding that perceived disparities in how workers are treated account for a great deal of job dissatisfaction.

While inequality and unfairness may be related to each other, they are by no means synonymous. Unfairness is subject to perception and interpretation, which involve feelings; inequality is a *de facto* situation reflecting, in part, an objective match (or lack thereof) between heterogeneous workers and heterogeneous employers. Other things equal, the better the quality of the match between the supply of and demand for labor, the less inequality one would expect to find [Sørensen, 2007]. Thus, the level of inequality in a given profession, say pharmacy, may be approximated by measuring the nature and intensity of organizational as well as workforce heterogeneity in that labor market [Carroll and Hannan, 2004].

Hegtvedt and Markovsky [1994] and Vandenberghe and Tremblay [2008], among others, identify two mechanisms in the perception of fairness—distributive justice, which refers to the perceived fairness of the distribution of workplace rewards, that is, the decision outcomes, and procedural justice, which addresses perceived fairness in the methods by which rewards are distributed. Workers perceive distributive justice when the outcomes received (*i.e.*, salaries, bonuses, benefits, promotions, etc.) are congruent with their expectations, whereas procedural justice has to do with the means used to attain the outcomes. Means are perceived to be fair when they are free of bias and are applied consistently across individuals and time, when they allow for accurate representation of the opinions of affected individuals, and when corrective mechanisms are in place should a bad decision be made [Clay-Warner *et al.*, 2005]. In most organizations workers seem to be very concerned with the procedures in place, even though these procedures may not affect outcomes significantly [Huo *et al.*, 1997].

Inequality and unfairness may be manifested in multiple ways [Bilimoria *et al.*, 2006; Preston, 2004; Valian, 2004]. Perhaps the most salient is inequalities in pay, even when controlling for age, work experience, and job level, obviously a matter of distributive justice. Although some progress has been attained in the last few decades, women and minorities continue to earn, on average, a fraction of what their Non-Hispanic White male counterparts earn [Allen *et al.*, 2006; Blau and Khan, 2006; Ezeala-Harrison, no date; Fry and Lowell, 2006; Graham and Smith, 2005; Hersch, 2006; Meyer and Mukerjee, 2007; Reimers, 2000]. While a substantial portion of this disparity may be attributed to differences in human-capital stock and individual preferences, as discussed in other parts of this book, major unexplained gender and ethnic wage gaps remain, which point to unequal treatment of presumably equal workers, notwithstanding their gender and/or ethnicity. Luce and Brenner [2006] point out that while 39 percent of Non-Hispanic White women and 44 percent of Asian American women worked in management, professional, and related occupations in 2004, only 31 percent of African American women and 22 percent of Hispanic women did so. Women are slowly increasing their participation in management, professional, and related occupations, including pharmacy, but there are still broad differences across races. Thus, it is not surprising to find studies reporting that women and minorities perceive more inequalities in the workplace compared to non-minority men [Griffin *et al.*, 2005; Hagedorn and Laden, 2002; Townsend and LaPaglia, 2000]. By the same token, minority employees generally see benefits stemming from diversity management and fairness in the workplace above and beyond those experienced by Non-Hispanic White workers [Pitts, 2009]. Diversity management is a component of human resources management that embraces training programs, family-friendly policies, mentoring opportunities, and advocacy groups, all sensitive to the special needs of women and minorities [Kellough and Naff, 2004; Mathews, 1998].

Other disparities also are identified in the literature. For example, it is not uncommon for women and minority workers to get less office and work space allocated to them, or receive fewer services from support staff, relative to their non-minority male peers [Park, 1996]. Women and minorities also are reported to work, against their preference, proportionately more non-standard hours and shifts [Presser, 2003]. In many instances they are not given equal opportunity to advance within their organization [Igbaria and Baroudi, 1995; Igbaria and Chidambaram, 1997; Smucker *et al.*, 2003]; they are ignored, disregarded, or neglected when they make suggestions or attempt to contribute to collective outcomes in group situations [Yoder and McDonald, 1998]; or they are treated as tokens and are deprived of the full benefits of being part of the inner circles of power, even when they succeed in being included [Whelan-Berry and Gordon, 2000; Yoder, 1991]. Disparities in treatment lead frequently to feelings of pessimism, overall dissatisfaction, and turnover in women and minorities, all associated with increased work conflict, lower prestige and power on the job, and multiple career uncertainties [Ackah *et al.*, 1999; Gutek *et al.*, 1996; Sicherman, 1996]. Thus, the lower levels of job satisfaction experienced by minority workers relative to Non-Hispanic Whites, reported by Bender and Heywood [2006], may be influenced by perceptions of unequal and/or unfair treatment in the workplace [Clay-Warner *et al.*, 2005; Seifert and Umbach, 2008], and the healthcare sector provides an interesting setting for examining changes in the gender and ethnic composition of its various professions. Healthcare is an unequal workplace [Queneau, 2006]. Women, Blacks, and Hispanics are overrepresented in lower-paying occupations (*e.g.*, health and nursing aids), underrepresented in higher-paying occupations (*e.g.*, physicians and dentists), and in transition in other occupations such as pharmacy, more rapidly so in places of great ethnic diversity like South Florida. They also are less likely to hold positions of authority relative to Non-Hispanic White men [Smith and Elliott, 2002].

Age also may be a factor in the perception of fairness in the workplace, although disparities may not be as noticeable as they are with gender and ethnic identification. Rix [2006] points out that age discrimination, mandatory retirement rules in many establishments, job dislocation, and skills obsolescence plague older workers systematically, which may have a negative effect on the way they are treated. At the other end of the age scale, younger workers' lack of experience and seniority may be responsible for the assignment of less desirable tasks, shifts, etc., a practice perceived by some as unfair.

The perception of fairness in the workplace has been linked to positive labor outcomes, which promote organizational goals such as organizational commitment, good citizenship behavior, and trust in management [Colquitt *et al.*, 2001; Cropanzano *et al.*, 2001a; Masterson *et al.*, 2000; O'Neill and Mone, 1998]. From an ethnic perspective, minority workers tend to report higher levels of job satisfaction than those reported by non-minority workers when diversity management is implemented, which lends support to the contention that poor diversity management is responsible for the relatively low levels of job satisfaction frequently reported by ethnic minorities [Pitts, 2009]. The research consensus seems to be that if more workers perceive their workplace as fair, they are more likely to be satisfied with their jobs [Kidwell and Bennett, 1994; Masterson *et al.*, 2000; Randall and Mueller, 1995]. Moreover, Diekmann *et al.* [2007] find that self-perceived status moderates the relationship between procedural fairness and job satisfaction; the higher the self-perceived status, the stronger the positive relationship between both variables. Yet Irving *et al.* [2005] argue that while employers may influence the satisfaction of their workers by implementing fair procedures when allocating rewards and resources, fair procedures do not uniformly result in positive outcomes, including job satisfaction, because negative affectivity makes some individuals perceive the environment in adverse terms regardless of what is happening. Therefore, they suggest that employers consider individual differences when developing organizational interventions. Widespread opinions of inequality and unfairness on the part of women and minorities may lead to a reduction in the motivation by these groups to gain the education, skills, and experience needed to advance in the workforce because the desired outcomes are not perceived as happening [Anderson and Shinew, 2001].

When asked to rate the overall fairness which they perceive in the workplace, South Florida pharmacists respond with moderately high levels (see Tables 6-15 and 6-16). No major differences among counties are detected. On average, male pharmacists perceive more fairness in the workplace than do female pharmacists, and this gender differential is replicated within every ethnic group other than Asian Americans. Relatively more Non-Hispanic White and Hispanic practitioners than Black and Asian American practitioners consider their institution to be a fair place to hold a job. Little variation is detected among groups younger than 70 years of age, but pharmacists 70 years or older report substantially higher scores than the rest of the pharmacist workforce in the sample regarding perceived fairness in the workplace.

SUPPORT FROM SUPERVISOR

Support from one's supervisor is another opinion variable frequently associated with job and career satisfaction. The support may be transmitted in the form of information, appraisal, assistance with tasks, or merely conveying feelings of empathy or emotional concern [Baggerly and Osborn, 2006; Deelstra *et al.*, 2003; Harris *et al.*, 2007a; Logan and Ganster, 2005]. Support is viewed as adding to work contentment by increasing confidence and relieving anxiety [Kong, 1995; North and Kirk, 1990] as well as providing adequate facilities and equipment [Baker, 2007]. According to Kahaleh and Gaither [2007], this occurs by virtue of pharmacists acquiring empowerment, which in turn engenders greater organizational commitment among employees. They claim that pharmacists who work in independent settings enjoy more support from their supervisors than practitioners who work in hospitals or chain pharmacies, and consequently are more empowered. Supervisors can play a crucial role in fostering a non-controlling environment that empowers employees' self-development. Supportive supervisors encourage workers to voice their opinions and concerns, provide positive feedback, and implement participative strategic planning processes contributing to organizational effectiveness [Kim, 2002; London *et al.*, 1999]. They also provide recognition and praise deserving employees. According to a study by Rath and Clifton [2004], workers who receive recognition and praise respond by increasing their productivity and job satisfaction.

Newstrom *et al.* [1999] claim that job-related self-esteem (*i.e.*, the extent to which workers believe they are capable and successful in performing their work) is a powerful determinant of workers' attitudes, motivation, and job-related behavior. They argue that supervisors have the responsibility to enhance employees' individual self-esteem and raise it to organization-based self-esteem, defined as individuals' self-perceived value working with the organization. This may be attained by soliciting employees' suggestions about how to improve things at work, providing emotional support needed to make employees feel good about what they do, basing promotions and other rewards on people's contributions to the organization, and eliminating restrictive rules and procedures perceived by workers as unnecessary or of little significance. They contend that not only do workers with higher organization-based self-esteem levels typically perceive themselves as important and worthwhile, but these workers also tend to be more productive and effective than employees with lower levels of organization-based self-esteem.

Kim [2005] finds that women are more likely than men to consider matters pertaining to job supervision important, and Taylor *et al.* [1990] conclude that women value workplace social support more than do men. Supervisors' actions directed toward mentoring junior professionals also are perceived to be more valuable by women than by men [Bilimoria *et al.*, 2006]. Specifically in the field of pharmacy, Carvajal and Hardigan [2000] report that supervisor's reliability, in terms of providing help and support, contributes to increase female pharmacists' job satisfaction but is not relevant for male pharmacists. Another interesting finding is that women supervisors who perceive greater responsibility and trust bestowed upon them by their organization respond by improving their job performance and increasing the closeness of supervision of employees under their management [Valentine, 2001].

Smith and Elliott [2002] point out that Black men have uniquely limited access to positions of high authority. They conclude that Blacks specifically, not necessarily ethnic minorities in general, have a disadvantage relative to Non-Hispanic Whites in the process of attaining authority, and the disadvantage is more noticeable in Black women than in Black men. They also report that Hispanics working under Hispanic supervisors are less prone to be in positions of authority than are Hispanics working under non-Hispanic supervisors. All in all, however, the key mechanism linking ethnic concentration with enhanced minority authority opportunity seems to be ethnic matching from below. In other words, the ethnicity of subordinate work groups influences the ethnicity of appointed supervisors. Three possible reasons are suggested for this phenomenon: to minimize ethnic tension and maximize organizational harmony and commitment of workers being supervised, because the operation of internal labor markets dictates that employers draw supervisors from subordinate workers who show leadership qualities, and because subordinate workers tend to contribute to bottom-up ethnic matching by a process of self-selection.

South Florida pharmacists perceive their supervisors as only moderately helpful and supportive in their jobs (see Tables 6-17 and 6-18). This is the opinion variable in the survey with the second lowest overall score. Pharmacists in Martin and Pasco complain of receiving less help and support from their supervisors than do pharmacists in other counties, while pharmacists living outside South Florida report experiencing much higher levels of help and support. There seems to be no major overall gender differential, but within counties gender differences are observed. In the periphery counties men report receiving more help and support from their supervisors compared to women, while the opposite is the case for Palm Beach and the four smaller counties. Ethnic disparities are apparent. Hispanic pharmacists exhibit the highest average score in terms of their supervisors' helpfulness and support, and Asian Americans show the lowest, with Non-Hispanic White and Black pharmacists scoring in between. Although average scores vary among age groups, there is no consistent trend.

JOB ATMOSPHERE

Job atmosphere, also known as workplace or organizational climate, is a proxy for the extent to which harmony pervades operations and interpersonal relations at work. It reflects whether the job environment is perceived by workers as personally beneficial or detrimental to their sense of well-being [James *et al.*, 1990]. More specifically, it refers to an organization's typical practices and behaviors that prevail in the perception of its members, especially practices and behaviors which accord with expectations and consequently are rewarded. In a healthy job atmosphere workers look forward to going to work, are excited about their employer's vision, agree with their organization's operating values, go beyond the call of duty gladly when required, trust their coworkers and consider them friends, feel pride in being part of a team effort, are personally satisfied when the team performs well, and believe that their work contributes directly to the team's success [Gegax, 2006]. In a positive climate good, new ideas are accepted readily and unnecessary rules are eliminated. The focus of management is on getting the best people to attain organizational goals rather than establishing long lines of authority. Workers are allowed to introduce innovations without constantly seeking approval from their supervisors, are given ample opportunity to participate in the goal setting and planning processes, are recognized and rewarded for good performance, and know exactly what is expected from them [Watkin, 2001]. In this type of environment workers develop attitudinal commitments, which lead to emotional, mental, and cognitive bonds with their employers, and these bonds are reflected frequently in higher levels of job performance as well as less absenteeism and turnover [Lambert and Paoline, 2008; Lambert *et al.*, 2005; Neal and Griffin, 1999; Neal *et al.*, 2005; Perry and Mankin, 2007].

The term "organizational commitment" summarizes these psychological real bonds that reduce the likelihood of an employee leaving his/her job voluntarily [Allen and Meyer, 1996]. Amos and Weathington [2008] identify three types of commitment: continuance commitment occurs when employees stay with an organization because it would cost them more to leave than to stay, affective commitment is emotional and responds to employees' desire to stay, and normative commitment occurs when employees remain with an organization because they feel that it is the right thing to do. In all three types certain commonalities can be found, namely, a strong belief in, and acceptance of, the organization's goals and values; a willingness to exert considerable effort on behalf of the organization; and a strong desire to continue being a member of the organization [Schroder, 2008b].

Conversely, the perception of organizational politics is detrimental to both job satisfaction and organizational efficiency. Organizational politics commonly refers to subjective evaluations of others' self-serving work behaviors not sanctioned by authority, and its perception may be fueled by uncertainty regarding organizational decisions, ambiguity of expectations, conflicting roles and procedures, and competition within the organization for scarce resources [Kacmar and Baron, 1999; Miller *et al.*, 2008]. It is characterized by its parochial and divisive nature, and aggravates absenteeism and turnover problems [Ferris *et al.*, 2002].

The ethical climate of an organization is a subset of the overall organizational climate. It refers to the shared perceptions by employer and employees of what is or is not ethically correct behavior and how ethical issues should be handled within the institution [Peterson, 2002]. It has been shown to exert a major influence on workers' ethical behavior, as organizations whose attitude toward employee deviance is perceived as permissive tend to experience a greater prevalence of unethical behaviors compared to organizations in which deviance is not tolerated [Deshpande *et al.*, 2000; Fritzsche, 2000]. Kulas *et al.* [2007] identify two major categories of employee deviance in terms of potential harm to their employers—property deviance and production deviance. Examples of property deviance include misuse of employee discounts; taking supplies, merchandise, or information for personal use or sale; filching money or products; and falsifying records. Production deviance, also known as work withdrawal behavior, leads to reductions in productivity and encompasses reduced job involvement, low levels of organizational commitment, and occasions in which there is a reduction of time working such as tardiness, absenteeism, abuse of sick time, and unauthorized breaks or leaves of absence [Hanisch *et al.*, 1998]. All these instances involve various kinds of theft—money, physical property, information, or time theft, and their magnitude is ten times more costly than street crime [Greenberg, 1997].

Barnett and Schubert [2002] contend that employees' perception of a solid ethical work climate fosters the development of a covenantal relationship with the organization. A covenantal relationship is a special form of contract between workers and the institution where they work. Unlike transactional contracts, which rely on economic exchange, or relational contracts based on social exchange and fairness, a covenantal relationship rests on employer-employee commitment and their allegiance to shared values [Graham and Organ, 1993]. Both parties must be willing to subordinate their own private interests to promote higher, more important goals. A covenantal relationship demands mutual loyalty and support, and in the long run workers who develop this relationship feel appreciated by their organization and are likely to engage in behavior patterns beneficial to the organization.

Key to addressing the workplace environment and practitioners' organizational commitment are understanding and responding to the ways pharmacists are treated by management, other pharmacists, technicians, members of other healthcare professions, and patients. The quality of job atmosphere improves when workers are allowed more participation in the decision-making process, perceive that the organization values their contributions, and believe that supervisors and coworkers care about their personal and professional well-being [Buerhaus *et al.*, 2006; Kahaleh and Gaither, 2005; Rhoades and Eisenberger, 2002]. Perceived organizational support fulfills workers' socioemotional needs and is used by employees to infer their employer's willingness and ability to reward increased efforts made on its behalf [Chen *et al.*, 2009; Harris *et al.*, 2007b]. Along these lines Benz [2005] reports that employees of non-profit institutions usually are more satisfied with their work than are employees of for-profit organizations because non-profit firms tend to hire self-motivated workers who internalize institutional values. In general, women seem to be affected more than men by this opinion variable [Kim, 2005], and Cline and Mott [2000] suggest that since female pharmacists are more likely than their male peers to be married to a relatively highly paid spouse, they tend to downplay the importance of wages and instead focus their attention on working conditions, choosing places characterized by an absence of crises and conflicts, as well as other amenities such as scheduling flexibility.

One line of inquiry that has yet to be developed is the extent to which characteristics of physical settings such as temperature, noise, and lighting influence the way workers feel and act [Brief and Weiss, 2002]. Oldham *et al.* [1995] report that music improves the mood states of workers, while White [1996] successfully links physical cues or symbols in organizations to the emotions reported by potential participants. The way organizations are perceived by their workers may depend largely on the physical environment to which they are exposed.

The average ratings of job atmosphere, as perceived by South Florida pharmacists in the survey, are shown in Tables 6-19 and 6-20. The overall scores are moderately high and some variation is detected among counties. Practitioners residing outside South Florida report the highest levels of satisfaction with the job atmosphere in their workplace, while practitioners in the periphery counties show substantially lower levels. Virtually identical levels are reported by male and female pharmacists; however, gender differences exist within ethnic groups: A friendlier job atmosphere is perceived by Black men compared to Black women, but Hispanic men have a less optimistic perception of this variable relative to Hispanic women. Hispanic pharmacists show the highest level of satisfaction with job atmosphere of all ethnic groups. The scores remain approximately constant for all groups under 70 years of age, then increase to the highest levels of all age groups for both men and women 70 years and older.

FLEXIBILITY

Flexible work arrangements are a crucial element in the bundle of job characteristics appealing to various groups of workers. They may take different forms, such as working fewer hours per day, fewer days per week, or working the same number of hours but with greater discretion over when the hours are worked. Regardless of the specific format, their purpose is to allow workers to accommodate other activities that are important to them [Almer and Kaplan, 2002]. Job flexibility is attractive to women because it enables them to pursue household-related activities and take care of children or elderly family members [Bender and Heywood, 2006; Cline and Mott, 2000; Donohue and Heywood, 2004; Hersch, 2006; Mott, 2001; O'Halloran, 2003]; to ethnic minorities when it encompasses both the informal culture of the institution and its formal policies, as manifested by attitudes towards, and individual accommodations for, specific worker needs [Bender *et al.*, 2005]; to Generation X'ers because of their lifestyle preferences [Report of the ASHP Task Force on Pharmacy's Changing Demographics, 2007]; and to older workers insofar as it allows them to reduce gradually the intensity of their work effort [Armstrong-Stassen, 2006]. It is conducive to less burnout, fewer stressors, and greater levels of satisfaction [Almer and Kaplan, 2002]. Consequently, several recent studies recommend developing and implementing programs that offer more flexibility in dealing with workers, not only on work hours and scheduling matters, but also on rewards, family issues, and matching individual competencies with job requirements [Gardner and Stowe, 2007; Nguyen, 2008; Teeter, 2004].

Traditionally, pharmacists have been fairly satisfied with the scheduling flexibility of their jobs [Cardinale, 2005; LoBuono, 2003]. South Florida pharmacists seem to be no exception (see Tables 6-21 and 6-22). Overall scores are similar for all county classifications and for male and female practitioners, but within minority ethnic groups women perceive more flexibility in the workplace than do men. Ethnic disparities also are detected: On average, Hispanic pharmacists perceive the greatest level of flexibility and Black pharmacists perceive the lowest; Non-Hispanic Whites and Asian Americans score in between. Practitioners' perception of flexibility declines steadily with age for pharmacists under 70 years, then jumps up to the highest level for pharmacists 70 years and older.

COWORKERS

Coworkers are members of an organization who hold approximately the same power or level of authority and with whom an employee interacts in performing his/her job. They are an influential and powerful component of most working environments [Miller *et al.*, 2005], providing a dynamic and interactive background for self-expression. They are important because they constitute organizations' emergent informal networks, characterized by a horizontal flow of information, as opposed to formal networks, which configure the usual channels of authority through which orders and information are transmitted downward and upward. Coworkers' support is conducive to greater levels of job satisfaction [Ducharme and Martin, 2000]. Stevenson and Gilly [1991] show that employees prefer to communicate and discuss work-related problems, ideas, and opinions with their peers rather than with supervisors, and Tan and Lim [2009] conclude that trust in coworkers is important because it contributes to the attainment of desired organizational outcomes. Coworkers generally are the most common source of job-related support identified by employees [Allen and Finkelstein, 2003]. Ferres *et al.* [2004] also find that coworker trust is conducive to greater levels of perceived organizational support and lower turnover intention, and Adkins *et al.* [1996] argue that normally employees experience higher levels of job satisfaction when their values match the values of their coworkers.

Coworkers' values tend to match when there is person-environment congruence. Muchinsky and Monahan [1987] identify two types of congruence. Supplementary congruence occurs when somebody possesses characteristics similar to others in the environment, while complementary congruence refers to a situation in which somebody's characteristics round out the characteristics of others. They view supplementary in terms of similarity and complementary as a reflection of mutual needs. Within this context, personalities are compatible when one person's trait expression offers opportunities for other persons to express their traits [Tett and Murphy, 2002]. In other words, workers prefer to interact with other workers who let them be themselves—autonomous workers avoid dominant coworkers because they fear that their independence may be in jeopardy and workers afraid of making decisions welcome the company of dominant coworkers because the latter provide a setting for dependence.

It is reasonable to expect that employees' trust in their coworkers exerts a positive influence on their trust in their employer insofar as they are likely to regard their peers' perceptions as relevant and socially acceptable. The importance of these perceptions tends to increase during periods of uncertainty; when workers are unsure about what is happening at work, they look toward similar others for information about how to cope with unexpected or unfamiliar conditions, which fosters a greater awareness of mutual support and assistance [Griskevicius *et al.*, 2008]. This gives rise to the so-called reciprocity norm. If workers do not get along with one another, and do not support one another when the workflow experiences bottlenecks, teamwork becomes dysfunctional and the organization suffers [Newstrom *et al.*, 1999].

When an employee feels supported and helped by his/her peers, the norm of reciprocity suggests that he/she reciprocate by supporting and helping others at work. Employees who provide favorable treatment do so with the expectation that the debt will be repaid, although the nature and timing of the reciprocity may not be clear. An unspecified obligation toward the community of workers is delineated, whereby every individual who endorses the reciprocity norm contributes to the stability and long-term benefits of the workgroup as well as the smooth functioning of the organization [Cropanzano *et al.*, 2001b;

Deckop *et al.*, 2003; Eder and Eisenberger, 2008; Eisenberger *et al.*, 2001].

Some empirical evidence suggests that a worker's ability, defined by his/her job competence, knowledge, and skills, determines his/her quality rating in the eyes of his/her coworkers, and this perception is related to trust [Mayer and Davis, 1999; Mayer and Gavin, 2005]. Perceiving coworkers as trustworthy increases the likelihood that the trustor will engage in excellent relations, which ultimately will enable him/her to perform better [Colquitt *et al.*, 2007; Dirks and Ferrin, 2002], and being perceived as trustworthy by coworkers relates positively to the trustee's performance [Dirks and Skarlicki, 2009]. Obviously the link between being perceived as trustworthy and performance becomes more complex upon the realization that trustworthiness seldom is based on a single factor but rather has multiple facets such as benevolence, congeniality, integrity, and so on, each possessing its own implications for reciprocity and performance. All in all, Semerek and Peterson [2007] find that, compared to minorities, non-minorities enjoy better relations with their coworkers.

The South Florida pharmacists survey includes two coworker-related variables: one measures practitioners' perception of the collective professional quality of coworkers (see Tables 6-23 and 6-24) and the other deals with how practitioners rate their coworkers in terms of their willingness to provide help and support (see Tables 6-25 and 6-26). Pharmacists respond with an overall favorable perception on both counts. An exception to this generalization is detected with practitioners living outside the South Florida area, who are more critical about the professional quality of their coworkers than the other pharmacists combined. Men and women show very similar scores, with the exception of Black and Asian American pharmacists. Black women are more critical of their coworkers, especially in matters pertaining to providing help and support, thus suggesting that they abide less by the reciprocity norm, compared to Black male practitioners. Asian American women seem to appreciate their coworkers' quality more frequently than their male counterparts.

Ethnic differences appear in terms of quality of coworkers and, to a lesser extent, in terms of their willingness to provide help and support. Hispanic pharmacists exhibit the highest ratings in both indicators, and Asian American pharmacists exhibit the lowest, of all ethnic groups. Age-group variations also are detected. The rating scores of coworkers' professional quality go up with age, and the score for pharmacists 70 years or older is substantially higher than for any other age group. In other words, younger practitioners tend to be more critical of their coworker's quality of work than are older practitioners. Perhaps this differential is influenced by the fact that younger practitioners are more likely to possess a Pharm.D. degree, that is, more formal education, which may lead them to be more critical of coworkers who may not have the same level of training. When it comes to assessing coworkers' willingness to provide help and support, the scores of all age groups are similar, except for pharmacists 70 years or older, who are very appreciative of their coworkers' efforts.

Table 6–1. **Average rating of satisfaction with current job (0–10 scale) of pharmacists who completed the survey questionnaire by county of residence, ethnic group, and gender.**

County of Residence	Gender	Average Rating of Satisfaction with Current Job (0–10 scale)					
		All Ethnic Groups	Non-Hispanic			Hispanic	Other
			White	Black	Asian		
All counties	Both genders	7.23	7.22	6.79	6.94	7.52	7.29
	Men	7.25	7.24	7.10	7.12	7.35	7.50
	Women	7.22	7.18	6.63	6.82	7.61	7.17
Broward	Both genders	7.23	7.37	6.51	6.91	7.26	7.52
	Men	7.32	7.38	6.95	7.27	6.77	8.36
	Women	7.13	7.34	6.21	6.75	7.56	7.05
Collier, Hendry, Lee, and Monroe	Both genders	7.11	7.13	7.25	8.50	6.36	-
	Men	7.09	7.14	7.00	8.00	6.29	-
	Women	7.14	7.11	7.50	9.00	6.50	-
Martin and Pasco	Both genders	7.27	7.30	6.75	7.33	8.60	5.80
	Men	7.39	7.56	-	7.40	8.00	4.33
	Women	7.08	6.90	6.75	7.00	9.50	8.00
Miami-Dade	Both genders	7.31	7.02	7.00	6.07	7.60	7.60
	Men	7.20	7.03	7.67	6.43	7.40	10.00
	Women	7.39	7.00	6.73	5.71	7.68	7.33
Palm Beach	Both genders	7.21	7.14	7.20	6.90	8.14	7.11
	Men	7.20	7.16	7.20	6.83	8.20	7.00
	Women	7.24	7.11	7.20	6.93	8.11	7.25
Other	Both genders	7.26	7.41	6.50	7.83	7.31	6.00
	Men	7.52	7.00	6.00	7.67	9.20	-
	Women	7.00	8.17	7.00	8.00	6.10	6.00

Table 6–2. **Average rating of satisfaction with current job (0–10 scale) of pharmacists who completed the survey questionnaire by county of residence, age group, and gender.**

County of Residence	Gender	Average Rating of Satisfaction with Current Job (0–10 scale)							
		All Age Groups	Less than 30	30-39	40-49	50-59	60-69	70 and Older	Not Known
All counties	Both genders	7.23	7.03	7.24	7.03	7.32	7.15	7.75	7.35
	Men	7.25	7.05	7.15	6.90	7.28	7.24	7.70	7.72
	Women	7.22	7.03	7.28	7.12	7.40	6.50	8.00	6.94
Broward	Both genders	7.23	7.16	7.18	6.89	7.43	7.30	7.98	7.31
	Men	7.32	6.50	7.17	6.87	7.43	7.49	7.85	8.33
	Women	7.13	7.29	7.18	6.91	7.43	6.13	8.67	6.43
Collier, Hendry, Lee, and Monroe	Both genders	7.11	5.87	7.10	7.32	6.91	7.52	7.69	8.25
	Men	7.09	5.60	6.92	6.95	7.00	7.56	7.50	8.00
	Women	7.14	6.00	7.19	7.59	6.74	7.33	10.00	9.00
Martin and Pasco	Both genders	7.27	7.83	6.89	7.35	7.39	6.50	8.33	8.00
	Men	7.39	6.00	7.25	7.57	7.48	6.91	8.33	8.00
	Women	7.08	8.75	6.60	7.25	7.14	2.00	-	-
Miami-Dade	Both genders	7.31	7.76	7.50	6.73	7.63	6.85	8.00	6.88
	Men	7.20	7.57	7.40	6.77	7.32	6.80	7.68	8.33
	Women	7.39	7.86	7.54	6.70	7.89	7.00	8.50	6.00
Palm Beach	Both genders	7.21	6.70	7.24	7.38	7.10	7.12	7.42	7.50
	Men	7.20	8.67	7.06	6.92	7.14	7.18	7.46	6.00
	Women	7.24	6.40	7.30	7.68	7.00	5.50	6.67	9.00
Other	Both genders	7.26	7.40	6.88	7.00	8.00	8.00	7.40	7.00
	Men	7.52	10.00	6.75	6.50	7.50	7.50	9.25	7.00
	Women	7.00	6.75	7.00	7.33	8.25	9.00	0.00	-

Table 6–3. Average rating of satisfaction with the profession of pharmacy (0–10 scale) of pharmacists who completed the survey questionnaire by county of residence, ethnic group, and gender.

County of Residence	Gender	Average Rating of Satisfaction with the Profession of Pharmacy (0–10 scale)					
		All Ethnic Groups	Non-Hispanic			Hispanic	Other
			White	Black	Asian		
All counties	Both genders	7.32	7.08	7.58	7.41	7.90	7.41
	Men	7.17	7.00	8.08	7.44	7.57	7.65
	Women	7.49	7.22	7.33	7.39	8.06	7.28
Broward	Both genders	7.40	7.34	7.40	7.26	7.59	7.71
	Men	7.41	7.23	8.09	7.91	7.50	8.45
	Women	7.39	7.54	6.94	6.96	7.64	7.30
Collier, Hendry, Lee, and Monroe	Both genders	6.77	6.71	9.00	7.75	6.45	-
	Men	6.56	6.49	8.50	7.50	6.57	-
	Women	7.02	6.98	9.50	8.00	6.25	-
Martin and Pasco	Both genders	7.31	7.25	8.00	8.00	7.80	6.20
	Men	7.41	7.56	-	8.00	7.00	4.67
	Women	7.15	6.80	8.00	8.00	9.00	8.50
Miami-Dade	Both genders	7.59	6.75	7.55	7.00	8.12	6.80
	Men	7.17	6.62	8.11	6.86	7.74	8.00
	Women	7.89	7.07	7.32	7.14	8.28	6.67
Palm Beach	Both genders	7.24	7.08	8.00	7.70	7.71	7.78
	Men	7.07	7.03	8.40	7.00	6.90	7.60
	Women	7.48	7.18	7.87	8.00	8.17	8.00
Other	Both genders	7.53	7.41	6.50	7.50	8.00	7.00
	Men	7.57	7.18	6.50	7.00	9.20	-
	Women	7.50	7.83	6.50	8.00	7.40	7.00

Table 6–4. Average rating of satisfaction with the profession of pharmacy (0–10 scale) of pharmacists who completed the survey questionnaire by county of residence, age group, and gender.

County of Residence	Gender	Average Rating of Satisfaction with the Profession of Pharmacy (0–10 scale)							
		All Age Groups	Less than 30	30-39	40-49	50-59	60-69	70 and Older	Not Known
All counties	Both genders	7.32	7.43	7.53	7.30	7.17	6.97	7.51	7.49
	Men	7.17	6.91	7.29	7.18	7.21	6.92	7.27	7.63
	Women	7.49	7.59	7.63	7.39	7.11	7.32	8.72	7.31
Broward	Both genders	7.40	7.88	7.56	7.23	7.26	7.12	7.76	7.54
	Men	7.41	6.50	7.64	7.25	7.41	7.12	7.90	8.67
	Women	7.39	8.14	7.52	7.22	7.00	7.13	8.67	6.57
Collier, Hendry, Lee, and Monroe	Both genders	6.77	6.80	6.73	7.00	6.35	6.86	7.00	8.75
	Men	6.56	5.80	6.62	6.65	6.22	6.79	6.75	8.67
	Women	7.02	7.30	6.78	7.26	6.58	7.33	10.00	9.00
Martin and Pasco	Both genders	7.31	7.50	7.61	7.57	7.31	6.25	7.17	8.00
	Men	7.41	6.00	7.88	8.43	7.76	6.09	7.17	8.00
	Women	7.15	8.25	7.40	7.19	6.13	8.00	-	-
Miami-Dade	Both genders	7.59	7.67	7.83	7.46	7.68	7.06	7.55	7.75
	Men	7.17	7.43	7.16	7.26	7.54	6.96	6.47	8.33
	Women	7.89	7.79	8.07	7.57	7.80	7.33	9.00	7.40
Palm Beach	Both genders	7.24	7.04	7.55	7.32	7.17	6.91	7.26	6.86
	Men	7.07	7.67	6.83	7.00	7.22	6.90	7.29	5.75
	Women	7.48	6.95	7.79	7.54	7.06	7.00	6.67	8.33
Other	Both genders	7.53	7.80	7.41	7.80	7.00	8.00	8.60	5.50
	Men	7.57	10.00	7.63	7.00	7.50	7.50	8.25	5.50
	Women	7.50	7.25	7.22	8.33	6.75	9.00	10.00	-

Table 6–5. **Average rating of perceived amount of work in relation to other workers (0–10 scale) of pharmacists who completed the survey questionnaire by county of residence, ethnic group, and gender.**

County of Residence	Gender	Average Rating of Perceived Amount of Work in Relation to Other Workers (0–10 scale)					
		All Ethnic Groups	Non-Hispanic			Hispanic	Other
			White	Black	Asian		
All counties	Both genders	7.67	7.53	7.82	7.91	7.93	7.95
	Men	7.49	7.41	7.72	8.41	7.59	7.55
	Women	7.86	7.73	7.87	7.58	8.09	8.17
Broward	Both genders	7.76	7.66	7.80	7.94	7.88	8.16
	Men	7.67	7.57	7.91	8.55	7.56	8.27
	Women	7.86	7.81	7.73	7.67	8.07	8.10
Collier, Hendry, Lee, and Monroe	Both genders	7.38	7.28	7.25	8.50	8.55	-
	Men	7.20	7.07	7.00	9.50	8.43	-
	Women	7.60	7.54	7.50	7.50	8.75	-
Martin and Pasco	Both genders	7.56	7.49	8.25	8.67	8.20	6.20
	Men	7.66	7.58	-	9.00	8.67	5.67
	Women	7.42	7.34	8.25	7.00	7.50	7.00
Miami-Dade	Both genders	7.77	7.69	7.58	7.57	7.88	7.44
	Men	7.47	7.60	6.56	8.29	7.41	4.00
	Women	7.98	7.90	8.00	6.86	8.06	7.88
Palm Beach	Both genders	7.64	7.55	8.10	7.68	7.96	8.44
	Men	7.47	7.41	9.00	7.83	7.40	7.80
	Women	7.90	7.82	7.80	7.61	8.28	9.25
Other	Both genders	7.67	6.76	9.00	8.17	8.12	10.00
	Men	6.80	5.73	8.50	7.67	8.25	-
	Women	8.50	8.67	8.75	8.67	8.06	10.00

Table 6–6. **Average rating of perceived amount of work in relation to other workers (0–10 scale) of pharmacists who completed the survey questionnaire by county of residence, age group, and gender.**

County of Residence	Gender	Average Rating of Perceived Amount of Work in Relation to Other Workers (0–10 scale)							
		All Age Groups	Less than 30	30-39	40-49	50-59	60-69	70 and Older	Not Known
All counties	Both genders	7.67	7.81	7.67	7.79	7.85	7.42	7.26	7.50
	Men	7.49	7.32	7.49	7.65	7.76	7.42	7.10	6.83
	Women	7.86	7.96	7.75	7.89	8.00	7.46	8.08	8.25
Broward	Both genders	7.76	7.92	7.62	7.71	8.12	7.44	7.64	7.92
	Men	7.67	7.75	7.33	7.63	8.07	7.43	7.61	7.67
	Women	7.86	7.95	7.74	7.80	8.22	7.50	7.83	8.14
Collier, Hendry, Lee, and Monroe	Both genders	7.38	8.67	7.46	7.34	7.49	7.32	5.46	7.25
	Men	7.20	9.20	7.38	7.15	7.44	7.21	5.67	6.67
	Women	7.60	8.40	7.50	7.48	7.58	8.00	3.00	9.00
Martin and Pasco	Both genders	7.56	8.00	8.06	7.26	7.43	7.67	7.67	5.00
	Men	7.66	9.00	8.25	7.86	7.43	7.55	7.67	5.00
	Women	7.42	7.50	7.90	7.00	7.43	9.00	-	-
Miami-Dade	Both genders	7.77	7.48	7.55	8.07	7.89	7.41	7.85	8.38
	Men	7.47	5.43	7.60	7.87	7.68	7.48	7.00	8.00
	Women	7.98	8.50	7.54	8.18	8.06	7.22	9.00	8.60
Palm Beach	Both genders	7.64	7.39	7.94	8.00	7.76	7.46	7.08	6.83
	Men	7.47	6.67	7.67	7.81	7.70	7.47	7.14	6.00
	Women	7.90	7.50	8.03	8.13	7.89	7.00	6.00	7.67
Other	Both genders	7.67	7.80	7.65	9.00	8.92	6.00	6.25	5.00
	Men	6.80	8.00	6.88	7.50	9.00	5.00	6.25	5.00
	Women	8.50	7.75	8.33	10.00	8.88	7.00	-	5.00

Table 6–7. Average rating of perceived amount of stress in relation to other workers (0–10 scale) of pharmacists who completed the survey questionnaire by county of residence, ethnic group, and gender.

County of Residence	Gender	Average Rating of Perceived Amount of Stress in Relation to Other Workers (0–10 scale)					
		All Ethnic Groups	Non-Hispanic			Hispanic	Other
			White	Black	Asian		
All counties	Both genders	6.94	6.70	7.34	7.02	7.37	7.45
	Men	6.76	6.55	7.35	7.56	7.30	7.75
	Women	7.14	6.98	7.33	6.66	7.41	7.28
Broward	Both genders	6.91	6.69	7.53	6.60	7.23	7.61
	Men	6.75	6.48	7.77	6.82	7.35	8.00
	Women	7.09	7.05	7.36	6.50	7.16	7.40
Collier, Hendry, Lee, and Monroe	Both genders	6.92	6.86	7.75	7.25	7.55	-
	Men	6.93	6.78	8.50	8.50	8.00	-
	Women	6.92	6.95	7.00	6.00	6.75	-
Martin and Pasco	Both genders	6.67	6.62	4.75	8.00	7.00	7.00
	Men	6.82	6.69	-	7.80	7.00	7.00
	Women	6.45	6.52	4.75	9.00	7.00	7.00
Miami-Dade	Both genders	7.16	6.86	7.00	7.14	7.37	6.60
	Men	6.73	6.54	5.56	6.86	7.15	7.00
	Women	7.45	7.11	7.59	7.43	7.45	6.56
Palm Beach	Both genders	6.76	6.55	7.35	7.12	7.71	7.78
	Men	6.62	6.41	7.40	8.67	8.00	7.80
	Women	6.96	6.82	7.33	6.46	7.56	7.75
Other	Both genders	7.65	7.24	9.50	7.67	7.47	10.00
	Men	7.38	7.09	9.50	8.67	6.40	-
	Women	7.91	7.50	9.50	6.67	8.00	10.00

Table 6–8. Average rating of perceived amount of stress in relation to other workers (0–10 scale) of pharmacists who completed the survey questionnaire by county of residence, age group, and gender.

County of Residence	Gender	Average Rating of Perceived Amount of Stress in Relation to Other Workers (0–10 scale)							
		All Age Groups	Less than 30	30-39	40-49	50-59	60-69	70 and Older	Not Known
All counties	Both genders	6.94	6.96	6.97	7.26	7.23	6.65	5.89	6.71
	Men	6.76	6.73	7.00	7.18	7.26	6.52	5.70	5.89
	Women	7.14	7.03	6.96	7.33	7.16	7.58	6.84	7.63
Broward	Both genders	6.91	7.20	6.98	7.00	7.26	6.67	5.80	6.38
	Men	6.75	7.75	6.92	7.13	7.13	6.59	5.47	5.00
	Women	7.09	7.10	7.01	6.86	7.49	7.13	6.00	7.57
Collier, Hendry, Lee, and Monroe	Both genders	6.92	8.40	6.36	6.81	7.24	6.68	6.15	7.75
	Men	6.93	8.60	6.62	6.60	7.42	6.63	6.08	7.00
	Women	6.92	8.30	6.23	6.96	6.89	7.00	7.00	10.00
Martin and Pasco	Both genders	6.67	6.17	6.78	6.65	6.75	6.58	7.50	2.00
	Men	6.82	7.50	7.13	6.71	7.00	6.27	7.50	2.00
	Women	6.45	5.50	6.50	6.63	6.00	10.00	-	-
Miami-Dade	Both genders	7.16	6.05	7.01	7.76	7.52	7.09	5.79	8.38
	Men	6.73	4.71	6.72	7.71	7.43	6.72	4.68	8.00
	Women	7.45	6.71	7.12	7.79	7.60	8.11	7.29	8.60
Palm Beach	Both genders	6.76	6.70	7.03	7.56	7.05	6.37	5.79	4.33
	Men	6.62	6.67	7.44	7.19	7.29	6.37	5.90	3.33
	Women	6.96	6.70	6.90	7.82	6.44	6.50	4.00	5.33
Other	Both genders	7.65	7.40	8.00	9.00	7.17	7.00	5.60	9.50
	Men	7.38	6.00	7.75	7.50	8.00	6.50	6.00	9.50
	Women	7.91	7.55	8.22	10.00	6.75	8.00	4.00	-

Table 6–9. **Average rating of perceived availability of advancement opportunities (0–10 scale) of pharmacists who completed the survey questionnaire by county of residence, ethnic group, and gender.**

County of Residence	Gender	Average Rating of Perceived Availability of Advancement Opportunities (0–10 scale)					
		All Ethnic Groups	Non-Hispanic			Hispanic	Other
			White	Black	Asian		
All counties	Both genders	4.63	4.31	5.16	5.60	5.12	4.58
	Men	4.10	3.86	4.92	4.59	4.75	5.47
	Women	5.20	5.08	5.28	6.27	5.30	4.11
Broward	Both genders	4.53	4.30	4.80	5.49	4.57	5.13
	Men	4.13	4.00	4.82	3.64	3.77	6.60
	Women	4.98	4.82	4.79	6.33	5.05	4.40
Collier, Hendry, Lee, and Monroe	Both genders	4.47	4.38	7.50	5.25	4.64	-
	Men	3.68	3.58	7.50	1.50	4.57	-
	Women	5.45	5.34	7.50	9.00	4.75	-
Martin and Pasco	Both genders	4.69	4.93	5.50	4.67	2.80	2.40
	Men	5.15	5.55	-	5.00	2.33	2.33
	Women	4.03	4.00	5.50	3.00	3.50	2.50
Miami-Dade	Both genders	4.87	4.41	4.97	5.71	5.12	3.00
	Men	4.51	4.07	4.00	5.86	5.08	0.00
	Women	5.10	5.17	5.36	5.57	5.14	3.33
Palm Beach	Both genders	4.53	4.10	5.40	6.15	6.39	5.67
	Men	3.64	3.38	5.40	5.33	4.80	6.20
	Women	5.80	5.49	5.40	6.50	7.28	5.00
Other	Both genders	5.30	3.76	7.75	5.33	6.40	5.00
	Men	4.86	3.09	6.50	5.00	8.00	-
	Women	5.73	5.00	9.00	5.67	5.60	5.00

Table 6–10. Average rating of perceived availability of advancement opportunities (0–10 scale) of pharmacists who completed the survey questionnaire by county of residence, age group, and gender.

County of Residence	Gender	Average Rating of Perceived Availability of Advancement Opportunities (0–10 scale)							
		All Age Groups	Less than 30	30-39	40-49	50-59	60-69	70 and Older	Not Known
All counties	Both genders	4.63	6.15	5.32	5.07	4.54	3.32	2.86	3.94
	Men	4.10	5.77	4.81	5.19	4.17	3.38	2.63	4.11
	Women	5.20	6.26	5.54	4.98	5.13	2.88	4.00	3.75
Broward	Both genders	4.53	6.04	5.46	4.63	4.14	3.46	2.71	5.08
	Men	4.13	5.75	4.69	4.94	3.93	3.55	2.31	7.50
	Women	4.98	6.10	5.77	4.31	4.51	2.88	4.83	3.00
Collier, Hendry, Lee, and Monroe	Both genders	4.47	6.40	4.64	5.15	4.46	3.05	1.62	5.00
	Men	3.68	7.00	5.08	4.30	3.71	3.38	1.00	3.67
	Women	5.45	6.10	4.42	5.78	5.84	4.33	9.00	9.00
Martin and Pasco	Both genders	4.69	4.50	4.67	4.87	4.96	3.27	6.60	2.00
	Men	5.15	3.50	5.00	7.00	5.38	3.55	6.60	2.00
	Women	4.03	5.00	4.40	3.94	3.71	0.00	-	-
Miami-Dade	Both genders	4.87	6.62	5.19	5.60	5.03	2.97	2.91	3.13
	Men	4.51	6.29	4.68	6.33	4.54	3.00	2.84	2.67
	Women	5.10	6.79	5.38	5.19	5.43	2.89	3.00	3.40
Palm Beach	Both genders	4.53	5.83	5.82	5.22	4.52	3.37	2.75	2.67
	Men	3.64	4.00	4.72	4.69	4.02	3.47	2.63	1.00
	Women	5.80	6.10	6.18	5.58	6.06	0.50	4.67	4.33
Other	Both genders	5.30	7.40	5.18	6.00	4.83	5.67	4.40	2.50
	Men	4.86	6.00	5.38	5.00	5.50	5.50	4.00	2.50
	Women	5.73	7.75	5.00	6.67	4.50	6.00	6.00	-

Table 6–11. Average rating of perceived job security (0–10 scale) of pharmacists who completed the survey questionnaire by county of residence, ethnic group, and gender.

County of Residence	Gender	Average Rating of Perceived Job Security (0–10 scale)					
		All Ethnic Groups	Non-Hispanic			Hispanic	Other
			White	Black	Asian		
All counties	Both genders	7.84	7.80	7.84	7.88	8.02	7.39
	Men	7.67	7.63	8.20	7.15	7.94	7.30
	Women	8.02	8.09	7.65	8.37	8.06	7.44
Broward	Both genders	7.71	7.83	7.62	7.89	7.59	6.65
	Men	7.69	7.75	7.91	7.00	7.62	7.09
	Women	7.72	7.98	7.42	8.29	7.58	6.40
Collier, Hendry, Lee, and Monroe	Both genders	8.14	8.16	8.25	7.75	7.91	-
	Men	7.81	7.88	8.00	6.00	7.43	-
	Women	8.54	8.51	8.50	9.50	8.75	-
Martin and Pasco	Both genders	7.44	7.53	7.00	6.33	8.20	7.00
	Men	7.64	7.98	-	5.60	8.00	5.67
	Women	7.15	6.87	7.00	10.00	8.50	9.00
Miami-Dade	Both genders	7.99	7.44	7.84	8.64	8.20	8.90
	Men	7.82	7.34	8.44	8.71	8.17	10.00
	Women	8.11	7.69	7.59	8.57	8.21	8.78
Palm Beach	Both genders	7.82	7.76	8.55	7.90	7.57	8.44
	Men	7.48	7.46	9.20	6.67	7.10	8.20
	Women	8.31	8.36	8.33	8.43	7.83	8.75
Other	Both genders	7.81	7.12	7.75	7.75	8.67	8.00
	Men	7.52	6.27	8.00	8.00	9.60	-
	Women	8.09	8.67	7.50	7.50	8.20	8.00

Table 6–12. Average rating of perceived job security (0–10 scale) of pharmacists who completed the survey questionnaire by county of residence, age group, and gender.

County of Residence	Gender	Average Rating of Perceived Job Security (0–10 scale)							
		All Age Groups	Less than 30	30-39	40-49	50-59	60-69	70 and Older	Not Known
All counties	Both genders	7.84	8.41	8.12	7.81	7.86	7.71	7.10	7.50
	Men	7.67	8.68	7.80	7.95	7.66	7.76	6.91	7.83
	Women	8.02	8.33	8.25	7.71	8.11	7.42	8.04	7.13
Broward	Both genders	7.71	8.36	7.93	7.69	7.37	7.79	7.44	7.62
	Men	7.69	8.50	7.67	8.09	7.18	8.02	7.24	8.17
	Women	7.72	8.33	8.03	7.28	7.70	6.38	8.50	7.14
Collier, Hendry, Lee, and Monroe	Both genders	8.14	8.80	8.41	7.77	8.33	8.45	6.23	9.25
	Men	7.81	9.60	7.46	7.26	8.11	8.53	6.00	9.23
	Women	8.54	8.40	8.88	8.15	8.74	8.00	9.00	9.00
Martin and Pasco	Both genders	7.44	8.17	7.56	7.70	7.10	7.08	7.33	10.00
	Men	7.64	10.00	7.88	8.71	7.24	7.09	7.33	10.00
	Women	7.15	7.25	7.30	7.25	6.75	7.00	-	-
Miami-Dade	Both genders	7.99	8.29	8.28	8.06	8.21	7.15	7.67	6.25
	Men	7.82	7.86	8.32	8.06	8.21	6.92	7.47	7.00
	Women	8.11	8.50	8.26	8.06	8.20	7.78	7.93	5.80
Palm Beach	Both genders	7.82	8.26	8.41	7.80	7.96	7.88	6.53	8.50
	Men	7.48	8.00	7.61	7.77	7.79	7.84	6.52	8.33
	Women	8.31	8.30	8.66	7.82	8.39	9.00	6.67	8.67
Other	Both genders	7.81	9.00	7.24	8.20	9.33	6.33	8.80	4.00
	Men	7.52	10.00	7.63	8.00	9.00	5.50	8.50	4.00
	Women	8.09	8.75	6.89	8.33	9.50	8.00	10.00	-

Table 6–13. Average rating of perceived job autonomy (0–10 scale) of pharmacists who completed the survey questionnaire by county of residence, ethnic group, and gender.

County of Residence	Gender	Average Rating of Perceived Job Autonomy (0–10 scale)					
		All Ethnic Groups	Non-Hispanic			Hispanic	Other
			White	Black	Asian		
All counties	Both genders	6.99	6.95	7.06	6.87	7.10	7.04
	Men	6.96	6.94	7.25	6.91	7.01	6.89
	Women	7.02	6.97	6.96	6.84	7.14	7.12
Broward	Both genders	6.96	7.04	6.90	6.65	6.89	6.71
	Men	7.15	7.28	6.86	6.55	6.54	7.60
	Women	6.72	6.61	6.93	6.70	7.12	6.22
Collier, Hendry, Lee, and Monroe	Both genders	6.80	6.82	7.75	7.50	5.91	-
	Men	6.52	6.48	7.00	8.00	6.43	-
	Women	7.14	7.22	8.50	7.00	5.00	-
Martin and Pasco	Both genders	6.56	6.49	7.00	6.33	8.20	6.00
	Men	6.84	7.04	-	6.00	8.00	4.00
	Women	6.16	5.62	7.00	8.00	8.50	9.00
Miami-Dade	Both genders	7.12	7.30	7.00	7.21	7.11	8.20
	Men	6.95	6.73	7.56	7.57	6.98	10.00
	Women	7.23	7.72	6.75	6.86	7.16	8.00
Palm Beach	Both genders	7.15	7.09	7.42	7.10	7.50	7.56
	Men	6.99	6.92	8.60	7.17	7.50	6.60
	Women	7.39	7.41	7.00	7.07	7.50	8.75
Other	Both genders	6.78	6.06	7.25	6.60	7.60	5.00
	Men	6.85	5.70	7.00	7.00	9.00	
	Women	6.71	6.67	7.50	6.00	6.90	5.00

Table 6–14. Average rating of perceived job autonomy (0–10 scale) of pharmacists who completed the survey questionnaire by county of residence, age group, and gender.

County of Residence	Gender	Average Rating of Perceived Job Autonomy (0–10 scale)							
		All Age Groups	Less than 30	30-39	40-49	50-59	60-69	70 and Older	Not Known
All counties	Both genders	6.99	7.07	7.08	6.93	7.05	6.67	7.09	7.06
	Men	6.96	6.36	7.18	7.05	6.98	6.81	6.92	7.06
	Women	7.02	7.29	7.04	6.84	7.18	5.71	7.96	7.07
Broward	Both genders	6.96	6.78	7.16	6.87	6.85	6.95	7.11	6.69
	Men	7.15	6.50	7.34	7.31	6.85	7.37	6.91	7.67
	Women	6.72	6.84	7.09	6.42	6.86	4.38	8.40	5.86
Collier, Hendry, Lee, and Monroe	Both genders	6.80	6.71	6.95	6.64	6.87	6.82	6.33	8.33
	Men	6.52	5.60	6.62	5.40	7.00	6.74	6.73	8.00
	Women	7.14	7.33	7.12	7.56	6.61	7.33	2.00	9.00
Martin and Pasco	Both genders	6.56	7.17	5.44	7.70	6.64	5.67	7.17	2.00
	Men	6.84	7.00	6.38	8.43	7.00	6.09	7.17	2.00
	Women	6.16	7.25	4.70	7.38	5.57	1.00	-	-
Miami-Dade	Both genders	7.12	7.48	7.19	6.77	7.52	6.12	7.59	8.14
	Men	6.95	6.71	7.52	7.00	7.15	6.13	6.72	8.33
	Women	7.23	7.86	7.07	6.64	7.82	6.11	8.71	8.00
Palm Beach	Both genders	7.15	7.74	7.31	7.09	7.25	6.86	6.90	7.67
	Men	6.99	6.00	7.28	7.15	7.07	6.84	6.96	7.33
	Women	7.39	8.00	7.32	7.05	7.72	7.50	6.00	8.00
Other	Both genders	6.78	4.40	7.00	8.20	7.40	6.67	7.50	4.50
	Men	6.85	7.00	6.88	9.00	7.00	5.50	7.67	4.50
	Women	6.71	3.75	7.11	7.67	7.67	9.00	7.00	-

Table 6–15. Average rating of perceived overall fairness in the workplace (0–10 scale) of pharmacists who completed the survey questionnaire by county of residence, ethnic group, and gender.

County of Residence	Gender	Average Rating of Perceived Overall Fairness in the Workplace (0–10 scale)					
		All Ethnic Groups	Non-Hispanic			Hispanic	Other
			White	Black	Asian		
All counties	Both genders	7.08	7.18	6.77	6.59	7.13	6.55
	Men	7.19	7.23	7.20	6.35	7.21	7.16
	Women	6.96	7.09	6.55	6.75	7.09	6.22
Broward	Both genders	6.99	7.25	6.62	6.37	6.62	6.53
	Men	7.41	7.54	7.23	6.27	6.92	7.60
	Women	6.52	6.75	6.21	6.42	6.44	6.00
Collier, Hendry, Lee, and Monroe	Both genders	7.35	7.39	7.25	7.75	6.73	-
	Men	7.11	7.17	7.00	7.00	6.43	-
	Women	7.65	7.65	7.50	8.50	7.25	-
Martin and Pasco	Both genders	6.72	6.69	7.50	6.33	8.80	5.00
	Men	7.04	7.09	-	6.80	9.00	4.67
	Women	6.26	6.07	7.50	4.00	8.50	5.50
Miami-Dade	Both genders	7.04	7.04	6.55	6.07	7.20	6.90
	Men	7.12	7.24	6.78	5.43	7.21	10.00
	Women	6.97	6.59	6.45	6.71	7.19	6.56
Palm Beach	Both genders	7.21	7.20	7.40	6.85	7.46	7.11
	Men	7.06	7.02	8.80	6.67	6.90	7.20
	Women	7.44	7.55	6.93	6.93	7.78	7.00
Other	Both genders	7.00	6.35	6.25	8.33	7.73	6.00
	Men	6.95	6.18	5.00	7.00	9.40	-
	Women	7.05	6.67	7.50	7.67	6.90	6.00

Table 6–16. Average rating of perceived overall fairness in the workplace (0–10 scale) of pharmacists who completed the survey questionnaire by county of residence, age group, and gender.

County of Residence	Gender	Average Rating of Perceived Overall Fairness in the Workplace (0–10 scale)							
		All Age Groups	Less than 30	30-39	40-49	50-59	60-69	70 and Older	Not Known
All counties	Both genders	7.08	6.97	7.01	6.95	7.07	6.99	7.82	7.00
	Men	7.19	6.91	6.97	7.01	7.11	7.14	7.77	7.71
	Women	6.96	6.99	7.02	6.90	7.01	5.96	8.09	6.25
Broward	Both genders	6.99	6.60	6.89	6.79	6.93	7.16	8.15	6.92
	Men	7.41	6.00	7.19	7.37	7.18	7.42	8.06	9.00
	Women	6.52	6.71	6.76	6.18	6.49	5.50	8.67	5.43
Collier, Hendry, Lee, and Monroe	Both genders	7.35	7.60	7.42	7.13	7.17	7.36	8.00	8.75
	Men	7.11	7.40	6.62	6.25	7.14	7.47	8.00	8.33
	Women	7.65	7.70	7.84	7.78	7.21	6.67	8.00	10.00
Martin and Pasco	Both genders	6.72	6.50	5.89	7.30	6.79	6.08	8.00	8.00
	Men	7.04	6.50	6.88	7.57	7.05	6.27	8.00	8.00
	Women	6.26	6.50	5.10	7.19	6.00	4.00	-	-
Miami-Dade	Both genders	7.04	6.86	7.06	6.65	7.24	6.53	8.26	7.00
	Men	7.12	6.57	7.28	6.45	7.21	6.76	8.26	9.00
	Women	6.97	7.00	6.99	6.77	7.26	5.89	8.25	5.80
Palm Beach	Both genders	7.21	7.30	7.23	7.45	7.06	7.07	7.19	7.17
	Men	7.06	7.33	6.50	7.19	6.95	7.11	7.22	6.67
	Women	7.44	7.30	7.46	7.63	7.33	6.00	6.67	7.67
Other	Both genders	7.00	6.40	6.82	6.20	8.17	8.33	8.40	3.00
	Men	6.95	10.00	6.75	6.50	6.50	7.50	8.75	3.00
	Women	7.05	5.50	6.89	6.00	9.00	10.00	7.00	-

Table 6–17. Average rating of performance of supervisor in helping and supporting the pharmacist in his/her job (0–10 scale) of pharmacists who completed the survey questionnaire by county of residence, ethnic group, and gender.

County of Residence	Gender	Average Rating of Supervisor's Performance in Helping/Supporting the Pharmacist (0–10 scale)					
		All Ethnic Groups	Non-Hispanic			Hispanic	Other
			White	Black	Asian		
All counties	Both genders	6.63	6.55	6.63	6.13	7.02	6.58
	Men	6.54	6.49	6.69	5.91	6.97	6.89
	Women	6.73	6.66	6.60	6.28	7.05	6.42
Broward	Both genders	6.51	6.58	6.22	5.56	6.81	6.87
	Men	6.64	6.61	6.41	5.36	7.23	7.60
	Women	6.38	6.52	6.09	5.65	6.56	6.50
Collier, Hendry, Lee, and Monroe	Both genders	6.79	6.82	7.25	6.25	6.27	-
	Men	6.48	6.57	8.00	6.50	4.86	-
	Women	7.16	7.13	6.50	6.00	8.75	-
Martin and Pasco	Both genders	6.02	6.10	7.25	5.67	7.00	3.60
	Men	6.36	6.53	-	6.40	8.50	2.33
	Women	5.50	5.43	7.25	2.00	4.00	5.50
Miami-Dade	Both genders	6.74	6.60	6.42	5.36	6.99	6.60
	Men	6.64	6.70	6.22	5.14	6.79	10.00
	Women	6.81	6.38	6.50	5.57	7.06	6.22
Palm Beach	Both genders	6.71	6.50	7.72	6.95	7.67	7.22
	Men	6.36	6.26	8.25	5.83	7.11	7.60
	Women	7.19	6.97	7.57	7.43	7.94	6.75
Other	Both genders	7.17	5.81	7.75	8.83	7.86	7.00
	Men	7.25	5.70	7.50	8.67	9.40	-
	Women	7.10	6.00	8.00	9.00	7.00	7.00

Table 6–18. Average rating of performance of supervisor in helping and supporting the pharmacist in his/her job (0–10 scale) of pharmacists who completed the survey questionnaire by county of residence, age group, and gender.

County of Residence	Gender	Average Rating of Supervisor's Performance in Helping/Supporting the Pharmacist (0–10 scale)							
		All Age Groups	Less than 30	30-39	40-49	50-59	60-69	70 and Older	Not Known
All counties	Both genders	6.63	6.37	6.80	6.68	6.61	5.91	7.21	6.52
	Men	6.54	6.71	6.52	6.80	6.46	5.97	7.04	6.65
	Women	6.73	6.27	6.91	6.60	6.85	5.48	8.04	6.38
Broward	Both genders	6.51	6.24	6.46	6.60	6.53	6.20	6.95	6.58
	Men	6.64	6.50	6.50	6.94	6.46	6.51	6.63	7.80
	Women	6.38	6.19	6.45	6.28	6.67	4.14	8.67	5.71
Collier, Hendry, Lee, and Monroe	Both genders	6.79	5.87	7.13	7.15	6.73	6.18	6.67	7.25
	Men	6.48	5.60	5.92	6.75	6.94	6.11	6.36	6.33
	Women	7.16	6.00	7.76	7.46	6.37	6.67	10.00	10.00
Martin and Pasco	Both genders	6.02	5.83	5.17	6.68	6.09	5.09	7.33	8.00
	Men	6.36	4.50	5.88	7.71	6.29	5.60	7.33	8.00
	Women	5.50	6.50	4.60	6.20	5.50	0.00	-	-
Miami-Dade	Both genders	6.74	6.62	6.92	6.27	7.18	5.50	7.85	6.75
	Men	6.64	7.29	6.63	6.52	7.04	5.10	7.68	7.33
	Women	6.81	6.29	7.03	6.13	7.29	6.44	8.07	6.40
Palm Beach	Both genders	6.71	6.64	7.27	7.06	6.28	5.85	7.02	5.83
	Men	6.36	8.50	6.28	6.56	6.02	5.89	7.08	5.00
	Women	7.19	6.45	7.59	7.41	6.89	5.00	6.00	6.67
Other	Both genders	7.17	7.00	7.47	6.80	7.00	6.67	8.67	5.00
	Men	7.25	10.00	8.50	7.50	2.50	5.50	8.67	5.00
	Women	7.10	6.25	6.56	6.33	9.25	9.00	-	-

Table 6–19. Average rating of perceived job atmosphere in the workplace (0–10 scale) of pharmacists who completed the survey questionnaire by county of residence, ethnic group, and gender.

County of Residence	Gender	Average Rating of Perceived Job Atmosphere in the Workplace (0–10 scale)					
		All Ethnic Groups	Non-Hispanic			Hispanic	Other
			White	Black	Asian		
All counties	Both genders	7.15	7.10	6.97	6.86	7.46	7.00
	Men	7.16	7.14	7.15	6.91	7.33	7.40
	Women	7.13	7.03	6.88	6.82	7.53	6.78
Broward	Both genders	7.07	7.23	6.69	6.57	6.99	6.97
	Men	7.24	7.33	7.00	6.55	6.62	8.27
	Women	6.88	7.05	6.48	6.58	7.21	6.25
Collier, Hendry, Lee, and Monroe	Both genders	7.06	7.07	6.25	7.75	7.00	-
	Men	6.81	6.85	6.50	6.50	6.43	-
	Women	7.38	7.34	6.00	9.00	8.00	-
Martin and Pasco	Both genders	6.64	6.61	7.25	7.50	7.60	4.60
	Men	6.73	6.69	-	7.80	8.67	3.67
	Women	6.50	6.48	7.25	6.00	6.00	6.00
Miami-Dade	Both genders	7.33	6.96	7.03	6.29	7.63	7.50
	Men	7.23	7.12	7.56	6.14	7.42	10.00
	Women	7.39	6.59	6.82	6.43	7.72	7.22
Palm Beach	Both genders	7.22	7.14	7.75	6.95	7.61	7.89
	Men	7.25	7.19	7.60	7.50	8.00	7.20
	Women	7.18	7.03	7.80	6.71	7.39	8.75
Other	Both genders	7.50	7.35	7.00	8.33	7.50	7.00
	Men	7.67	7.18	6.50	7.67	9.20	-
	Women	7.33	7.67	7.50	9.00	6.56	7.00

Table 6–20. Average rating of perceived job atmosphere in the workplace (0–10 scale) of pharmacists who completed the survey questionnaire by county of residence, age group, and gender.

County of Residence	Gender	Average Rating of Perceived Job Atmosphere in the Workplace (0–10 scale)							
		All Age Groups	Less than 30	30-39	40-49	50-59	60-69	70 and Older	Not Known
All counties	Both genders	7.15	7.01	7.15	7.04	7.16	6.82	7.78	7.59
	Men	7.16	6.90	6.82	7.11	7.13	6.92	7.73	8.44
	Women	7.13	7.04	7.28	6.99	7.20	6.13	8.04	6.63
Broward	Both genders	7.07	6.64	7.12	6.96	7.07	6.78	7.79	7.77
	Men	7.24	5.25	7.11	7.22	7.22	6.94	7.74	9.50
	Women	6.88	6.90	7.13	6.69	6.78	5.75	8.20	6.29
Collier, Hendry, Lee, and Monroe	Both genders	7.06	6.53	7.23	7.00	6.92	7.14	7.54	8.25
	Men	6.81	7.20	6.08	6.45	6.69	7.26	7.50	7.67
	Women	7.38	6.20	7.81	7.41	7.34	6.33	8.00	10.00
Martin and Pasco	Both genders	6.64	7.00	5.56	7.30	6.75	6.08	7.33	8.00
	Men	6.73	5.50	5.63	7.57	7.05	6.18	7.33	8.00
	Women	6.50	7.75	5.50	7.19	5.86	5.00	-	-
Miami-Dade	Both genders	7.33	7.40	7.49	6.92	7.49	6.76	8.18	7.13
	Men	7.23	7.33	7.28	6.97	7.32	6.80	7.97	7.67
	Women	7.39	7.43	7.57	6.89	7.63	6.67	8.50	6.80
Palm Beach	Both genders	7.22	7.39	7.08	7.28	7.30	6.84	7.57	7.33
	Men	7.25	7.67	6.44	7.38	7.27	6.95	7.68	8.67
	Women	7.18	7.35	7.29	7.21	7.39	4.00	5.67	6.00
Other	Both genders	7.50	7.00	7.24	7.40	7.67	8.33	8.50	7.50
	Men	7.67	10.00	7.38	7.00	6.50	8.00	8.50	7.50
	Women	7.33	6.25	7.11	7.67	8.25	9.00	-	-

Table 6–21. Average rating of perceived scheduling flexibility in the workplace (0–10 scale) of pharmacists who completed the survey questionnaire by county of residence, ethnic group, and gender.

County of Residence	Gender	Average Rating of Perceived Scheduling Flexibility in the Workplace (0–10 scale)					
		All Ethnic Groups	Non-Hispanic			Hispanic	Other
			White	Black	Asian		
All counties	Both genders	7.01	7.00	6.50	6.84	7.37	6.43
	Men	6.94	7.02	6.30	6.59	6.95	6.65
	Women	7.08	6.98	6.60	7.00	7.57	6.31
Broward	Both genders	7.01	7.18	6.22	6.86	7.33	6.23
	Men	7.15	7.32	6.32	7.18	6.65	6.82
	Women	6.86	6.94	6.15	6.71	7.74	5.90
Collier, Hendry, Lee, and Monroe	Both genders	6.86	6.90	7.50	6.75	6.09	-
	Men	6.50	6.64	5.00	5.00	5.43	-
	Women	7.31	7.22	10.00	8.50	7.25	-
Martin and Pasco	Both genders	6.85	6.97	5.75	7.17	7.60	4.80
	Men	7.00	7.31	-	6.60	7.00	3.00
	Women	6.63	6.45	5.75	10.00	8.50	7.50
Miami-Dade	Both genders	7.13	7.09	6.55	6.36	7.30	7.20
	Men	6.82	7.01	5.89	4.86	6.94	10.00
	Women	7.34	7.28	6.82	7.86	7.44	6.89
Palm Beach	Both genders	7.03	6.89	6.85	7.05	8.43	7.00
	Men	6.97	6.89	6.60	7.50	7.70	7.80
	Women	7.12	6.90	6.93	6.86	8.83	6.00
Other	Both genders	6.83	6.24	8.00	6.83	7.14	8.00
	Men	7.10	5.73	8.50	7.67	9.20	-
	Women	6.57	7.17	7.50	6.00	6.00	8.00

Table 6–22. **Average rating of perceived scheduling flexibility in the workplace (0–10 scale) of pharmacists who completed the survey questionnaire by county of residence, age group, and gender.**

County of Residence	Gender	Average Rating of Perceived Scheduling Flexibility in the Workplace (0–10 scale)							
		All Age Groups	Less than 30	30-39	40-49	50-59	60-69	70 and Older	Not Known
All counties	Both genders	7.01	7.22	7.17	6.89	6.85	6.43	7.76	7.35
	Men	6.94	6.86	6.76	6.81	6.91	6.53	7.70	8.11
	Women	7.08	7.33	7.34	6.95	6.74	5.75	8.04	6.50
Broward	Both genders	7.01	7.16	7.11	7.00	6.80	6.53	7.78	9.50
	Men	7.15	7.00	7.11	7.31	6.85	6.73	7.65	7.54
	Women	6.86	7.19	7.10	6.68	6.70	5.25	8.50	5.86
Collier, Hendry, Lee, and Monroe	Both genders	6.86	6.93	7.82	6.40	6.94	5.27	8.08	6.25
	Men	6.50	5.80	7.00	5.50	7.06	5.53	8.00	5.67
	Women	7.31	7.50	8.23	7.07	6.74	3.67	9.00	8.00
Martin and Pasco	Both genders	6.85	7.67	6.11	7.52	6.86	4.92	9.00	10.00
	Men	7.00	5.00	4.75	8.29	7.76	5.36	9.00	10.00
	Women	6.63	9.00	7.20	7.19	4.14	0.00	-	-
Miami-Dade	Both genders	7.13	6.90	7.15	6.80	7.22	6.70	8.03	8.38
	Men	6.82	7.29	6.08	6.77	6.68	6.46	8.00	9.33
	Women	7.34	6.71	7.54	6.81	7.66	7.33	8.07	7.80
Palm Beach	Both genders	7.03	7.48	7.39	6.77	6.56	6.91	7.40	6.50
	Men	6.97	8.00	7.06	6.04	6.78	7.00	7.44	7.67
	Women	7.12	7.40	7.50	7.26	6.00	4.50	6.67	5.33
Other	Both genders	6.83	8.00	6.35	8.60	5.83	7.00	7.25	5.50
	Men	7.10	9.00	8.25	8.00	3.50	5.50	7.25	5.50
	Women	6.57	7.75	4.67	9.00	7.00	10.00	-	-

Table 6–23. Average rating of coworkers' overall professional quality (0–10 scale) of pharmacists who completed the survey questionnaire by county of residence, ethnic group, and gender.

County of Residence	Gender	Average Rating of Coworkers' Overall Professional Quality (0–10 scale)					
		All Ethnic Groups	Non-Hispanic			Hispanic	Other
			White	Black	Asian		
All counties	Both genders	7.45	7.44	7.34	6.84	7.75	7.18
	Men	7.47	7.48	7.68	6.65	7.61	7.45
	Women	7.43	7.37	7.17	6.96	7.82	7.03
Broward	Both genders	7.46	7.57	7.42	6.74	7.43	7.35
	Men	7.58	7.65	7.73	6.64	7.00	8.27
	Women	7.33	7.42	7.21	6.79	7.70	6.85
Collier, Hendry, Lee, and Monroe	Both genders	7.36	7.47	6.00	7.00	6.27	-
	Men	7.31	7.40	7.00	7.00	6.29	-
	Women	7.42	7.55	5.00	7.00	6.25	-
Martin and Pasco	Both genders	7.22	7.31	7.25	7.33	7.80	5.20
	Men	7.25	7.42	-	7.00	8.67	3.67
	Women	7.18	7.14	7.25	9.00	6.50	7.50
Miami-Dade	Both genders	7.63	7.44	7.19	6.07	7.95	7.10
	Men	7.54	7.47	8.00	5.71	7.79	8.00
	Women	7.70	7.38	6.86	6.43	8.02	7.00
Palm Beach	Both genders	7.43	7.38	7.40	7.10	8.07	7.67
	Men	7.46	7.46	6.80	6.83	8.10	7.80
	Women	7.39	7.24	7.60	7.21	8.06	7.50
Other	Both genders	6.98	6.12	8.50	7.67	7.00	8.00
	Men	7.10	5.82	8.50	7.67	9.00	-
	Women	6.85	6.80	8.50	7.67	6.11	8.00

Table 6–24. Average rating of coworkers' overall professional quality (0–10 scale) of pharmacists who completed the survey questionnaire by county of residence, age group, and gender.

County of Residence	Gender	Average Rating of Coworkers' Overall Professional Quality (0–10 scale)							
		All Age Groups	Less than 30	30-39	40-49	50-59	60-69	70 and Older	Not Known
All counties	Both genders	7.45	7.14	7.38	7.39	7.51	7.36	8.04	7.12
	Men	7.47	6.86	7.14	7.40	7.48	7.39	8.00	7.72
	Women	7.43	7.22	7.47	7.39	7.56	7.17	8.25	6.44
Broward	Both genders	7.46	7.00	7.51	7.38	7.39	7.46	8.00	7.54
	Men	7.58	6.75	7.67	7.44	7.46	7.57	7.88	8.67
	Women	7.33	7.05	7.45	7.31	7.27	6.71	8.67	6.57
Collier, Hendry, Lee, and Monroe	Both genders	7.36	6.47	6.36	7.04	7.51	7.73	8.08	8.00
	Men	7.31	6.20	6.77	6.85	7.37	7.74	8.00	8.33
	Women	7.42	6.60	7.65	7.19	7.76	7.67	9.00	7.00
Martin and Pasco	Both genders	7.22	7.33	6.22	7.57	7.50	6.83	8.33	7.00
	Men	7.25	5.50	6.13	8.00	7.62	6.64	8.33	7.00
	Women	7.18	8.25	6.30	7.38	7.14	9.00	-	-
Miami-Dade	Both genders	7.63	7.10	7.71	7.39	7.84	7.24	8.42	7.50
	Men	7.54	6.71	7.28	7.48	7.64	7.20	8.42	8.67
	Women	7.70	7.29	7.87	7.33	8.00	7.33	8.43	6.80
Palm Beach	Both genders	7.43	7.52	7.19	7.56	7.48	7.27	7.81	6.33
	Men	7.46	8.33	6.61	7.35	7.50	7.33	7.90	7.33
	Women	7.39	7.40	7.38	7.71	7.44	5.50	6.33	5.33
Other	Both genders	6.98	8.00	6.59	8.20	6.20	8.00	7.75	3.50
	Men	7.10	10.00	7.13	8.50	6.00	7.50	7.75	3.50
	Women	6.85	7.50	6.11	8.00	6.33	9.00	-	-

Table 6–25. Average rating of coworkers' willingness to help and support (0–10 scale) of pharmacists who completed the survey questionnaire by county of residence, ethnic group, and gender.

County of Residence	Gender	Average Rating of Coworkers' Willingness to Help and Support (0–10 scale)					
		All Ethnic Groups	Non-Hispanic			Hispanic	Other
			White	Black	Asian		
All counties	Both genders	7.76	7.76	7.46	7.45	7.99	7.52
	Men	7.80	7.80	8.12	7.32	7.88	7.70
	Women	7.71	7.70	7.12	7.53	8.04	7.42
Broward	Both genders	7.74	7.90	7.40	7.26	7.64	7.58
	Men	8.00	8.00	8.32	7.64	7.62	8.73
	Women	7.45	7.73	6.79	7.08	7.65	6.95
Collier, Hendry, Lee, and Monroe	Both genders	7.66	7.72	7.00	7.25	7.18	-
	Men	7.61	7.66	8.00	7.50	6.86	-
	Women	7.73	7.79	6.00	7.00	7.75	-
Martin and Pasco	Both genders	7.56	7.72	7.25	7.00	9.00	4.80
	Men	7.57	7.84	-	7.40	8.67	2.67
	Women	7.55	7.52	7.25	5.00	9.50	8.00
Miami-Dade	Both genders	7.75	7.53	7.19	6.50	8.06	7.60
	Men	7.56	7.51	7.89	6.00	7.75	9.00
	Women	7.88	7.55	6.91	7.00	8.18	7.44
Palm Beach	Both genders	7.88	7.76	7.95	8.25	8.50	8.56
	Men	7.87	7.83	7.60	7.33	8.90	8.20
	Women	7.90	7.62	8.07	8.64	8.28	9.00
Other	Both genders	7.83	7.12	8.50	8.67	8.00	9.00
	Men	7.75	6.30	8.50	9.00	9.60	-
	Women	7.90	8.50	8.50	8.33	7.11	9.00

Table 6–26. Average rating of coworkers' willingness to help and support (0–10 scale) of pharmacists who completed the survey questionnaire by county of residence, age group, and gender.

County of Residence	Gender	Average Rating of Coworkers' Willingness to Help and Support (0–10 scale)							
		All Age Groups	Less than 30	30-39	40-49	50-59	60-69	70 and Older	Not Known
All counties	Both genders	7.76	7.62	7.65	7.72	7.70	7.72	8.38	7.71
	Men	7.80	7.32	7.44	7.77	7.69	7.77	8.36	8.50
	Women	7.71	7.71	7.74	7.68	7.71	7.35	8.50	6.81
Broward	Both genders	7.74	7.52	7.64	7.79	7.58	7.82	8.28	8.08
	Men	8.00	7.75	8.06	7.94	7.79	8.10	8.15	9.33
	Women	7.45	7.48	7.47	7.63	7.19	5.86	9.00	7.00
Collier, Hendry, Lee, and Monroe	Both genders	7.66	6.73	7.67	7.17	7.84	8.27	8.69	7.75
	Men	7.61	7.00	6.08	7.05	7.80	8.32	8.67	8.00
	Women	7.73	6.60	8.46	7.26	7.92	8.00	9.00	7.00
Martin and Pasco	Both genders	7.56	7.83	6.28	8.13	7.82	6.75	9.00	10.00
	Men	7.57	6.50	5.88	8.43	7.95	6.73	9.00	10.00
	Women	7.55	8.50	6.60	8.00	7.43	7.00	-	-
Miami-Dade	Both genders	7.75	7.24	7.84	7.61	7.73	7.50	8.50	7.63
	Men	7.56	6.71	7.48	7.61	7.36	7.20	8.56	8.67
	Women	7.88	7.50	7.97	7.61	8.03	8.33	8.43	7.00
Palm Beach	Both genders	7.88	8.43	7.70	7.90	7.73	7.75	8.26	7.33
	Men	7.87	8.33	7.33	7.81	7.64	7.81	8.30	8.67
	Women	7.90	8.45	7.82	7.97	7.94	6.00	7.67	6.00
Other	Both genders	7.83	8.40	7.94	8.60	7.33	7.33	8.00	5.50
	Men	7.75	10.00	8.63	9.00	5.50	6.00	8.00	5.50
	Women	7.90	8.00	7.33	8.33	8.25	10.00	-	-

AFTERWORD

One of the advantages of studies of this nature is that they usually provide the basis to explore and identify empirical relationships, beyond the original intent, for subsequent research endeavors. We anticipate that this will be the case with the data set gathered here. Meaningful and intellectually satisfying approaches to the study of pharmacist workforce undertaken in the future must inevitably recognize and deal with the interplay of numerous and often misunderstood economic, sociological, demographic, and behavioral indicators. Methodological advance should be deliberate and reflective, with constant reference to the full reality of a particular cultural context and its specific constraints, as well as to the quest for theoretical elegance and rigor.

While the empirical relationships established here may not be fully generalizable nationwide because they are largely configured by the unique conditions that characterize South Florida, the area's rich gender, ethnic, and age mix of both the population and practitioners provides a glimpse of the U.S. pharmacist workforce of the future—older, with an increasing participation of minorities, and with a clear majority of women. We hope that the comparisons and behavior of variables observed throughout this book shed some light into what to expect elsewhere in the years ahead.

REFERENCES

A note on the sequencing of items in the reference list. First, items are arranged alphabetically by the primary author's surname. In instances where the primary author has written more than one item in the reference list, the items are ordered by year of publication, earliest first. Single-author entries precede two-author entries beginning with the same surname, and two-author entries precede multiple-author entries beginning with the same surname. Items with three or more authors are ordered alphabetically by the primary author's surname, then chronologically by year of publication, earliest first.

Aanerud, Rebecca, Emory Morrison, Lori Homer, *et al.* (2007), "Widening the lens on gender and tenure: Looking beyond the academic labor market," *NWSA Journal* (Vol. 19, No. 3, Fall), pp. 105–123.

Abbasi, Sami M. and Kenneth W. Hollman (2000), "Turnover: The real bottom line," *Public Personnel Management* (Vol. 29, No. 3, Fall), pp. 333–342.

Accreditation Council for Pharmacy Education (2009), "Frequently asked questions," http://www.acpe-accredit.org/deans/faq.asp. Accessed August 31, 2009.

Ackah, Carol, Norma Heaton, and Gavin McWhinney (1999), "Women in management: The case of MBA graduates," *Women in Management Review* (Vol. 14, No. 4, April), pp. 136–145.

Acker, Gila M. (2004), "The effect of organizational conditions (role conflict, role ambiguity, opportunities for professional development, and social support) on job satisfaction and intention to leave among social workers in mental health care," *Community Mental Health Journal* (Vol. 40, No. 1, February), pp. 65–73.

Adams, Gary A., Lynda A. King, and Daniel W. King (1996), "Relationships of job and family involvement, family social support, and work-family conflict with job and life satisfaction," *Journal of Applied Psychology* (Vol. 81, No. 4, July), pp. 411–420.

Adkins, Cheryl L., Elizabeth C. Ravlin, and Bruce M. Meglino (1996), "Value congruence between co-workers and its relationship to work outcomes," *Group & Organization Management* (Vol. 21, No. 4, December), pp. 439–460.

Ahituv, Avner and Robert I. Lerman (2007), "How do marital status, work effort, and wage rates interact?," *Demography* (Vol. 44, No. 3, August), pp. 623–647.

Ahituv, Avner and Marta Tienda (2004), "Employment, motherhood, and school continuation decisions of young White, Black, and Hispanic women," *Journal of Labor Economics* (Vol. 22, No. 1, January), pp. 115–158.

Akresh, Ilana R. (2006), "Occupational mobility among legal immigrants to the United States," *International Migration Review* (Vol. 40, No. 4, Winter), pp. 854–884.

Akresh, Ilana R. (2007), "U.S. immigrants' labor market adjustment: Additional human capital investment and earnings growth," *Demography* (Vol. 44, No. 4, November), pp. 865–881.

Alba, Richard and Victor Nee (2003), *Remaking the American Mainstream: Assimilation and Contemporary Immigration* (Cambridge: Harvard University Press).

Albanesi, Stefania and Claudia Olivetti (2007), "Gender roles and technological progress," Columbia University, Department of Economics Discussion Paper No. 0607-1.

Alexander, Akash J. and Sharon B. Gatewood (2008), "Revealing undetected problems with medication therapy management services," *Consultant Pharmacist* (Vol. 23, No. 6, June), pp. 473–476.

Allen, Myria W., Deborah J. Armstrong, Cynthia K. Riemenschneider, *et al.* (2006), "Making sense of the barriers women face in the information technology work force: Standpoint theory, self-disclosure, and causal maps," *Sex Roles* (Vol. 54, No. 11/12, June), pp. 831–844.

Allen, Natalie J. and John P. Meyer (1996), "Affective continuance and normative commitment to the organization: An examination of construct validity," *Journal of Vocational Behavior* (Vol. 49, No. 3, December), pp. 252–276.

Allen, Tammy D. and Lisa M. Finkelstein (2003), "Beyond mentoring: Alternative sources and functions of developmental support," *The Career Development Quarterly* (Vol. 51, No. 4, June), pp. 346–355.

Allen, Tammy D., David E. Herst, Carly S. Bruck, *et al.* (2000), "Consequences associated with work-to-family conflict: A review and agenda for future research," *Journal of Occupational Health Psychology* (Vol. 5, No. 2, April), pp. 278–308.

Almer, Elizabeth D. and Steven E. Kaplan (2002), "The effects of flexible work arrangements on stressors, burnout, and behavioral job outcomes in public accounting," *Behavioral Research in Accounting* (Vol. 14), pp. 1–34.

Alon, Sigal, Debra Donahoe, and Marta Tienda (2001), "The effects of early work experience on young women's labor force attachment," *Social Forces* (Vol. 79, No. 3, March), pp. 1005–1034.

Altonji, Joseph G., Ulrich Doraszelski, and Lewis Segal (2000), "Black/White differences in wealth," *Economic Perspectives* (Vol. 24, No. 1, Spring), pp. 38–50.

American Association of Colleges of Pharmacy (2009), "Profile of pharmacy students: 2008–09," http://www.aacp.org/resources/research/institutionalresearch/Documents/2008_PPS_DegConf.pdf. Accessed September 6, 2009.

American College of Clinical Pharmacy (2009), "Frequently asked questions about board certification," http://www.accp.com/careers/boardFAQ.aspx. Accessed September 30, 2009.

American Human Development Project of the Social Science Research Council (2009), "The measure of America: American Human Development Report 2008–2009, American human development by state," http://www.measureofamerica.org/data-charts-from-the-measure-of-america/. Accessed November 25, 2009.

American Pharmacists Association (2010), "Code of ethics for pharmacists," http://www.pharmacist.com/AM/Template.cfm?Section=Search&template=/CM/HTMLDisplay.cfm&ContentID=2809. Accessed January 25, 2010.

American Society of Health-System Pharmacists (2010), "Mission and vision," http://www.ashp.org/mission-vision. Accessed January 25, 2010.

American Society of Hospital Pharmacists (1993), "ASHP statement on pharmaceutical care," *American Journal of Hospital Pharmacy* (Vol. 50, No. 8, August), pp. 1720–1723.

Amos, Elizabeth A. and Bart L. Weathington (2008), "An analysis of the relation between employee-organization value congruence and employee attitudes," *The Journal of Psychology* (Vol. 142, No. 6, November), pp. 615–631.

Anderson, Denise M. and Kimberly J. Shinew (2001), "A national examination of gender equity in public parks and recreation," *Journal of Leisure Research* (Vol. 33, No. 4, Fourth Quarter), pp. 470–491.

Anderson, Erling B. (1997), "The rating scale model." In *Handbook of Modern Item Response Theory*, edited by Wim J. van der Linden and Ronald K. Hambleton (New York: Springer-Verlag), pp. 67–84.

Andrén, Thomas (2003), "The choice of paid childcare, welfare, and labor supply of single mothers," *Labour Economics* (Vol. 10, No. 2, April), pp. 133–147.

Andresen, Maike, Michel E. Domsch, and Annett H. Cascorbi (2007), "Working unusual hours and its relationship to job satisfaction: A study of European maritime pilots," *Journal of Labor Research* (Vol. 28, No. 4, September), pp. 714–734.

Andrews, Jason D., Clayton W. Faubion, and Charles D. Palmer (2002), "The relationship between counselor satisfaction and extrinsic job factors in state rehabilitation agencies," *Rehabilitation Counseling Bulletin* (Vol. 45, No. 4, Summer), pp. 223–232.

Antecol, Heather and Kelly Bedard (2002), "The racial wage gap: The importance of labor force attachment differences," University of California at Santa Barbara, Department of Economics, Working Paper 7-02.

Apps, Patricia and Ray Rees (2005), "Gender, time use, and public policy over the life cycle," *Oxford Review of Economic Policy* (Vol. 21, No. 3, Autumn), pp. 439–461.

Armstrong-Stassen, Marjorie (2006), "Encouraging retirees to return to the workforce," *Human Resource Planning* (Vol. 29, No. 4, December), pp. 38–44.

Arnold, Nancy L., Tom Seekins, and Raymond E. Nelson (1997), "A comparison of vocational rehabilitation counselors: Rural and urban differences," *Rehabilitation Counseling Bulletin* (Vol. 41, No. 1, September), pp. 2–14.

Ash, Steven R. (2008), "Hispanics and Anglos: The role of group composition on satisfaction," *Public Personnel Management* (Vol. 37, No. 1, Spring), pp. 15–26.

Association of Academic Health Centers (2006), "The policy agenda to expand the health workforce," http://www.aahcdc.org/policy/meetinghighlights/110806workforce.php. Accessed January 25, 2010.

Auster, Ellen R. (2001), "Professional women's midcareer satisfaction: Toward an explanatory framework," *Sex Roles* (Vol. 44, No. 11/12, June), pp. 719–750.

Badgett, Mary V. (2001), *Money, Myths, and Change: The Economic Lives of Lesbians and Gay Men* (Chicago: The University of Chicago Press).

Baggerly, Jennifer and Debra Osborn (2006), "School counselors' career satisfaction and commitment: Correlates and predictors," *Professional School Counseling* (Vol. 9, No. 3, February), pp. 197–205.

Baker, Vicki D. (2007), "Relationship between job satisfaction and the perception of administrative support among early career secondary choral music educators," *Journal of Music Teacher Education* (Vol. 17, No. 1, Fall), pp. 77–90.

Bardwick, Judith M. (1986), *The Plateauing Trap: How to Avoid It in Your Career and Your Life* (New York: Amacom).

Barkan, Elazar (1992), *The Retreat of Scientific Racism: Changing Concepts of Race in Britain and the United States between the World Wars* (Cambridge: Cambridge University Press).

Barnett, Tim and Elizabeth Schubert (2002), "Perceptions of the ethical work climate and covenantal relationships," *Journal of Business Ethics* (Vol. 36, No. 3, March), pp. 279–290.

Barrow, Lisa and Cecilia E. Rouse (2006), "The economic value of education by race and ethnicity," *Economic Perspectives* (Vol. 30, No. 2, Second Quarter), pp. 14–27.

Baum II, Charles L. (2003), "Does early maternal employment harm child development? An analysis of the potential benefits of leave taking," *Journal of Labor Economics* (Vol. 21, No. 2, April), pp. 409–448.

Bayard, Kimberly, Judith Hellerstein, David Neumark, *et al.* (1999), "Why are racial and ethnic wage gaps larger for men than for women? Exploring the role of segregation using the new worker-establishment characteristics database," National Bureau of Economic Research, Working Paper 6,997.

Bedard, Kelly and Olivier Deschênes (2003), "Sex preferences, marital dissolution and the economic status of women," University of California at Santa Barbara, Department of Economics, Working Paper 6-03.

Belknap, Joanne (2001), *The Invisible Woman: Gender, Crime, and Justice* (Belmont, CA: Wadsworth Publishing).

Bell, Ella L. (1990), "The bicultural life experience of career-oriented Black women," *Journal of Organizational Behavior* (Vol. 11, No. 6, November), pp. 459–477.

Bender, Keith A. and John S. Heywood (2006), "Job satisfaction of the highly educated: The role of gender, academic tenure, and earnings," *Scottish Journal of Political Economy* (Vol. 53, No. 2, May), pp. 253–279.

Bender, Keith A., Susan M. Donohue, and John S. Heywood (2005), "Job satisfaction and gender segregation," *Oxford Economic Papers* (Vol. 57, No. 3, July), pp. 479–496.

Benz, Matthias (2005), "Not for the profit, but for the satisfaction? Evidence on worker well-being in non-profit firms," *KYKLOS* (Vol. 58, No. 2, May), pp. 155–176.

Berger, Lawrence M., Jennifer Hill, and Jane Waldfogel (2005), "Maternity leave, early maternal employment and child health and development in the US," *The Economic Journal* (Vol. 115, No. 501, February), pp. F29–F47.

Bergman, Bengt, Farooq Ahmad, and Donna E. Stewart (2003), "Physician health, stress and gender at a university hospital," *Journal of Psychosomatic Research* (Vol. 54, No. 2, February), pp. 171–178.

Bernstein, Robert and Tom Edwards (2009), "An older and more diverse nation by midcentury," *U.S. Census Bureau News* (Thursday, August 14, 2008), http://www.census.gov/Press-Release/www/releases/archives/population/012496.html. Accessed September 24, 2009.

Bierman, Arlene S., Nicole Lurie, Karen S. Collins, *et al.* (2002), "Addressing racial and ethnic barriers to effective health care: The need for better data," *Health Affairs* (Vol. 21, No. 3, May/June), pp. 91–102.

Bilimoria, Diana, Susan R. Perry, Xiangfen Liang, *et al.* (2006), "How do female and male faculty members construct job satisfaction? The roles of perceived institutional leadership and mentoring and their mediating processes," *Journal of Technology Transfer* (Vol. 31, No. 3, May), pp. 355–365.

Bissell, Paul, Janine M. Traulsen, and Lotte S. Haugbølle (2003), "Researching 'race,' ethnicity, and health: A critical review," *International Journal of Pharmacy Practice* (Vol. 11, No. 3, September 1), pp. 183–197.

Black, Dan, Natalia Kolesnikova, and Lowell J. Taylor (2007), "The labor supply of married women: Why does it differ across U.S. cities?," Federal Reserve Bank of St. Louis, Working Paper 2007-043B.

Blank, Rebecca M. and Heidi Shierholz (2006), "Exploring gender differences in employment and wage trends among less-skilled workers," National Bureau of Economic Research, Working Paper 12,494.

Blasius, Jeffrey J. and Eung-Kwon Pae (2005), "Work-pattern differences between male and female orthodontists," *American Journal of Orthodontics and Dentofacial Orthopedics* (Vol. 128, No. 3, September), pp. 283–290.

Blau, Francine D. and Jed DeVaro (2007), "New evidence on gender differences in promotion rates: An empirical analysis of a sample of new hires," *Industrial Relations* (Vol. 46, No. 3, July), pp. 511–550.

Blau, Francine D. and Lawrence M. Kahn (2005), "Gender and assimilation among Mexican Americans," National Bureau of Economic Research, Working Paper 11,512.

Blau, Francine D. and Lawrence M. Kahn (2006), "The U.S. gender gap in the 1990s: Slowing convergence," *Industrial and Labor Relations Review* (Vol. 60, No. 1, October), pp. 45–66.

Blau, Francine D., Marianne A. Ferber, and Anne E. Winkler (2002), *The Economics of Women, Men, and Work* (Upper Saddle River, NJ: Prentice Hall).

Bloom, David E., David Canning, Günther Fink, *et al.* (2007), "Fertility, female labor force participation, and the demographic dividend," National Bureau of Economic Research, Working Paper 13,583.

Bodenhorn, Howard and Christopher S. Ruebeck (2003), "The economics of identity and the endogeneity of race," National Bureau of Economic Research, Working Paper 9,962.

Bolin, Aaron and Linette Heatherly (2001), "Predictors of employee deviance: The relationship between bad attitudes and bad behavior," *Journal of Business and Psychology* (Vol. 15, No. 3, Spring), pp. 405–418.

Bolin, Kenneth A. and Jay D. Shulman (2005), "Nationwide survey of work environment perceptions and dentists' salaries in community health centers," *Journal of the American Dental Association* (Vol. 136, No. 2, February), pp. 214–220.

Bond, C. A. and Cynthia L. Raehl (2001), "Pharmacists' assessment of dispensing errors: Risk factors, practice sites, professional functions, and satisfaction," *Pharmacotherapy* (Vol. 21, No. 5, May), pp. 614–626.

Bond, Trevor G. and Christine M. Fox (2001), *Applying the Rasch Model: Fundamental Measurement in the Human Sciences* (Mahwah, NJ: LEA Publishers).

Booth, Alison L. and Jan C. van Ours (2007), "Job satisfaction and family happiness: The part-time work puzzle," Tilburg University, Discussion Paper 2007-69.

Bradbury, Katherine L. (2002), "Education and wages in the 1980s and 1990s: Are all groups moving up together?," *New England Economic Review* (First Quarter), pp. 19–46.

Bradford, Lisa, Jessica L. Buck, and Renee A. Meyers (2001), "Cultural and parental communicative influences on the career success of White and Black women," *Women's Studies in Communication* (Vol. 24, No. 2, Fall), pp. 194–217.

Bradley, Cathy J., David Neumark, Zhehui Luo, *et al.* (2005), "Employment-contingent health insurance, illness, and labor supply of women: Evidence from married women with breast cancer," National Bureau of Economic Research, Working Paper 11,304.

Bradley, Don E. and James A. Roberts (2004), "Self-employment and job satisfaction: Investigating the role of self-efficacy, depression, and seniority," *Journal of Small Business Management* (Vol. 42, No. 1, January), pp. 37–58.

Brandon, Peter D. and Jeromey B. Temple (2007), "Family provisions at the workplace and their relationship to absenteeism, retention, and productivity of workers: Timely evidence from prior data," *Australian Journal of Social Issues* (Vol. 42, No. 4, Summer), pp. 447–460.

Brewer, Ernest W. and Jama McMahan-Landers (2003), "Job satisfaction among industrial and technical teacher educators," *Journal of Industrial Teacher Education* (Vol. 40, No. 2, Winter), pp. 65–85.

Brief, Arthur P. and Howard M. Weiss (2002), "Organizational behavior: Affect in the workplace," *Annual Review of Psychology* (Vol. 53), pp. 279–307.

Brockner, Joel (1992), "Managing the effects of layoffs on survivors," *California Management Review* (Vol. 34, No. 2, Winter), pp. 9–28.

Brooks-Gunn, Jeanne, Wen-Jui Han, and Jane Waldfogel (2002), "Maternal employment and child cognitive outcomes in the first three years of life: The NICHD Study of Early Child Care," *Child Development* (Vol. 73, No. 4, July–August), pp. 1052–1072.

Brown, Donna and Steven McIntosh (2003), "Job satisfaction in the low wage service sector," *Applied Economics* (Vol. 35, No. 10, July 10), pp. 1241–1254.

Brown, Donna and Marcel A. Sargeant (2007), "Job satisfaction, organizational commitment, and religious commitment of full-time university employees," *Journal of Research on Christian Education* (Vol. 16, No. 2, July/December), pp. 211–241.

Brown, Duane (2002), "The role of work and cultural values in occupational choice, satisfaction, and success: A theoretical statement," *Journal of Counseling & Development* (Vol. 80, No. 1, Winter), pp. 48–56.

Brown, Lawrence M., John C. Schommer, Dave Mott, *et al.* (2006), "Examining gender salary disparities: An analysis of the 2003 multistate salary survey," *Research in Social and Administrative Pharmacy* (Vol. 2, No. 3, September), pp. 370–387.

Bruck, Carly S., Tammy D. Allen, and Paul E. Spector (2002), "The relation between work-family conflict and job satisfaction: A finer-grained analysis," *Journal of Vocational Behavior* (Vol. 60, No. 3, June), pp. 336–353.

Brusentsev, Vera (2006), "Evolution of female labor force participation in the United States: 1967 to 2003," *International Advances in Economic Research* (Vol. 12, No. 3, August), pp. 358–373.

Bryan, Mark L. and Almudena Sevilla Sanz (2007), "Does housework lower wages and why? Evidence for Britain," University of Oxford, Department of Economics Discussion Paper Series, No. 331.

Buerhaus, Peter I., Karen Donelan, Beth T. Ulrich, *et al.* (2006), "State of the registered nurse workforce in the United States," *Nursing Economics* (Vol. 24, No. 1, January/February), pp. 6–12.

Burchell, Brendan and Colette Fagan (2004), "Gender and the intensification of work: Evidence from the European working conditions surveys," *Eastern Economic Journal* (Vol. 30, No. 4, Fall), pp. 627–642.

Burda, Michael, Daniel S. Hamermesh, and Philippe Weil (2007), "Total work, gender, and social norms," National Bureau of Economic Research, Working Paper 13,000.

Byrd, Terry G., John K. Cochran, Ira J. Silverman, *et al.* (2000), "Behind bars: An assessment of the effects of job satisfaction, job-related stress, and anxiety on jail employees' inclinations to quit," *Journal of Crime and Justice* (Vol. 23, No. 2), pp. 69–93.

Cameron, Kim S. (1994), "Investigating organizational downsizing fundamental issues," *Human Resource Management* (Vol. 33, No. 2, Summer), pp. 183–188.

Campbell, Gillian (2007), "More than money," *Quality* (Vol. 46, No. 7, July), pp. 56–61.

Cantor, Joel C., Erika L. Miles, Laurence C. Baker, *et al.* (1996), "Physician service to the underserved: Implications for affirmative action in medical education," *Inquiry* (Vol. 33, No. 2, Summer), pp. 167–180.

Cardinale, Val (2005), "Flying high: Are rising wages and generous benefits enough to attract pharmacists and keep them from roaming?," *Drug Topics* (Vol. 149, No. 6, March 21), pp. 38–53.

Carlson, Jessica H. and Steven Mellor (2004), "Gender-related effects in the job-design-job-satisfaction relationship: An interactional approach," *Sex Roles* (Vol. 51, No. 3/4, August), pp. 237–247.

Carmichael, Fiona and Susan Charles (2003a), "Benefit payments, informal care and female labour supply," *Applied Economics Letters* (Vol. 10, No. 7, May), pp. 411–415.

Carmichael, Fiona and Susan Charles (2003b), "The opportunity costs of informal care: Does gender matter?," *Journal of Health Economics* (Vol. 22, No. 5, September), pp. 781–803.

Carroll, Glenn R. and Michael T. Hannan (2004), *The Demography of Corporations and Industries* (Princeton, NJ: Princeton University Press).

Cartwright, Lillian K. (1987), "Role montage: Life patterns of professional women," *Journal of American Medical Women's Association* (Vol. 42, No. 5, September–October), pp. 142–143 and 147-148.

Carvajal, Manuel J. (1997), "Hispanicity as a dimension of ethnic inequality: A review of Hispanics in the United States," *REDEN Revista Española de Estudios Norteamericanos* (Año VIII, No. 13), pp. 81–94.

Carvajal, Manuel J. (2004), "Measuring economic discrimination of Hispanic-owned architecture and engineering firms in South Florida," *Hispanic Journal of Behavioral Sciences* (Vol. 26, No. 1, February), pp. 79–101.

Carvajal, Manuel J. (2006), "Economic grounds for affirmative action: The evidence on architects and engineers in South Florida," *Review of Social Economy* (Vol. LXIV, No. 4, December), pp. 515–538.

Carvajal, Manuel J. and Irma T. De Alonso (2002), "Hispanics in the United States at the dawn of the twenty-first century: A growing, yet underdeveloped force," *REDEN Revista Española de Estudios Norteamericanos* (Año XIII, No. 23–24), pp. 97–114.

Carvajal, Manuel J. and Patrick C. Hardigan (1999), "First-job preferences and expectations of pharmacy students: Intergender and interethnic comparisons," *Journal of the American Pharmaceutical Association* (Vol. 39, No. 1, January/February), pp. 32–40.

Carvajal, Manuel J. and Patrick C. Hardigan (2000), "Pharmacists' sources of job satisfaction: Inter-gender differences in response," *American Journal of Pharmaceutical Education* (Vol. 64, No. 4, Winter), pp. 420–425.

Carvajal, Manuel J. and Patrick C. Hardigan (2004), "Gender and wage earnings differences among pharmacists," *Journal of Pharmaceutical Finance, Economics & Policy* (Vol. 13, No. 2), pp. 5–32.

Carvajal, Manuel J. and Patrick C. Hardigan (2007), "Gender differences in the labor supply function of U.S. pharmacists," *Journal of Pharmaceutical Finance, Economics & Policy* (Vol. 16, No. 2), pp. 87–110.

Carvajal, Manuel J. and Patrick C. Hardigan (2008), "Pharmacists' inter-gender differences in behavior and opinions: Is work input an important mediator?," *The Internet Journal of Allied Health Sciences and Practice* (Vol. 6, No. 2, April).

Carvajal, Manuel J., Julissa M. Barrios-Balbin, Beatriz M. Benitez, *et al.* (1996), "Career- and family-related preferences and expectations of college students: Some inter-gender and inter-ethnic comparisons," *International Journal of Sociology of the Family* (Vol. 26, No. 2, Autumn), pp. 79–100.

Cascio, Wayne F. (2002), "Strategies for responsible restructuring," *Academy of Management Executive* (Vol. 16, No. 3, August), pp. 80–91.

Casper, Lynne M. and Suzanne M. Bianchi (2002), *Continuity and Change in the American Family* (Thousand Oaks, CA: Sage Publications, Inc.).

Catanzarite, Lisa (2003), "Race-gender composition and occupational pay degradation," *Social Problems* (Vol. 50, No. 1, February), pp. 14–37.

Cattan, Peter (1993), "The diversity of Hispanics in the U.S. work force," *Monthly Labor Review* (Vol. 116, No. 8, August), pp. 3–15.

Chadwick, Clint, Larry W. Hunter, and Stephen L. Walston (2004), "Effects of downsizing practices on the performance of hospitals," *Strategic Management Journal* (Vol. 25, No. 5, May), pp. 405–427.

Chatterji, Pinka and Sara Markowitz (2005), "Does the length of maternity leave affect maternal health?," *Southern Economic Journal* (Vol. 72, No. 1, July), pp. 16–41.

Chatterji, Pinka and Sara Markowitz (2008), "Family leave after childbirth and the health of new mothers," National Bureau of Economic Research, Working Paper 14,156.

Cheek, Frances E. (1984), *Stress Management for Correctional Officers and Their Families* (College Park, MD: American Correctional Association).

Chen, Zhixia, Robert Eisenberger, Kelly M. Johnson, *et al.* (2009), "Perceived organizational support and extra-role performance: Which leads to which?," *The Journal of Social Psychology* (Vol. 149, No. 1, February), pp. 119–124.

Cherlin, Andrew J. (1992), *Marriage, Divorce, Remarriage* (Cambridge, MA: Harvard University Press).

Chiswick, Barry R., Yew L. Lee, and Paul W. Miller (2003), "Patterns of immigrant occupational attainment in a longitudinal survey," *International Migration* (Vol. 41, No. 4, December), pp. 47–69.

Chiu, Randy K. (1998), "Relationships among role conflicts, role satisfactions and life satisfaction: Evidence from Hong Kong," *Social Behavior and Personality* (Vol. 26, No. 4, October), pp. 409–414.

Chong, Dennis and Dukhong Kim (2006), "The experiences and effects of economic status among racial and ethnic minorities," *The American Political Science Review* (Vol. 100, No. 3, August), pp. 335–351.

Chowdhury, Mussaddeq and Roberto Pedace (2007), "Ethnic enclaves and labor markets: An analysis of immigrant outcomes in California," *Contemporary Economic Policy* (Vol. 25, No. 2, April), pp. 238–249.

Cimete, Güler, Nimet S. Gencalp, and Gülbahar Keskin (2003), "Quality of life and job satisfaction of nurses," *Journal of Nursing Care Quality* (Vol. 18, No. 2, April–June), pp. 151–158.

Clark, Andrew E. (1997), "Job satisfaction and gender: Why are women so happy at work?," *Labour Economics* (Vol. 4, No. 4, December), pp. 341–372.

Clark, Andrew E. (2001), "What really matters in a job? Hedonic measurement using quit data," *Labour Economics* (Vol. 8, No. 2, May), pp. 223–242.

Clark, Andrew E. and Andrew J. Oswald (1996), "Satisfaction and comparison income," *Journal of Public Economics* (Vol. 61, No. 3, September), pp. 359–381.

Clay-Warner, Jody, Jeremy Reynolds, and Paul Roman (2005), "Organizational justice and job satisfaction: A test of three competing models," *Social Justice Research* (Vol. 18, No. 4, December), pp. 391–409.

Cleveland, Jeanette N., Margaret Stockdale, and Kevin R. Murphy (2000), *Women and Men in Organizations: Sex and Gender Issues at Work* (Mahwah, NJ: Lawrence Erlbaum Associates).

Cline, Richard R. (2003), "Disequilibrium and human capital in pharmacy labor markets: Evidence from four states," *Journal of the American Pharmacists Association* (Vol. 43, No. 6, November/December), pp. 702–709.

Cline, Richard R. and David A. Mott (2000), "Job matching in pharmacy labor markets: A study in four states," *Pharmaceutical Research* (Vol. 17, No. 12, December), pp. 1537–1545.

Clugston, Michael (2000), "The mediating effects of multidimensional commitment on job satisfaction and intent to leave," *Journal of Organizational Behavior* (Vol. 21, No. 4, June), pp. 477–486.

Cohany, Sharon R. and Emy Sok (2007), "Trends in labor force participation of married mothers of infants," *Monthly Labor Review* (Vol. 130, Issue 2, February), pp. 9-16.

Cohen, Jordan J., Barbara A. Gabriel, and Charles Terrell (2002), "The case for diversity in the health care workforce," *Health Affairs* (Vol. 21, No. 5, September-October), pp. 90-102.

Cohen, Louis, Lawrence Manion, and Keith Morrison (2000), *Research Methods in Education* (London: Routledge Falmer).

Cohrs, J. Christopher, Andrea E. Abele, and Dorothea E. Dette (2006), "Integrating situational and dispositional determinants of job satisfaction: Findings from three samples of professionals," *The Journal of Psychology* (Vol. 140, No. 4, July), pp. 363-395.

Collins, K., M. L. Jones, A. Mcdonnell, *et al.* (2000), "Do new roles contribute to job satisfaction and retention of staff in nursing and professions allied to medicine?," *Journal of Nursing Management* (Vol. 8, No. 1, January), pp. 3-12.

Colquitt, Jason A., Donald E. Conlon, Michael J. Wesson, *et al.* (2001), "Justice at the millennium: A meta-analytic review of 25 years of organizational justice research," *Journal of Applied Psychology* (Vol. 86, No. 3, May), pp. 425-445.

Colquitt, Jason A., Brent A. Scott, and Jeffrey A. LePine (2007), "Trust, trustworthiness, and trust propensity: A meta-analytic test of their unique relationships with risk taking and job performance," *Journal of Applied Psychology* (Vol. 92, No. 4, July), pp. 909-927.

Coltrane, Scott (2000), "Research on household labor: Modeling and measuring the social embeddedness of routine family work," *Journal of Marriage and the Family* (Vol. 62, No. 4, November), pp. 1208-1233.

Coltrane, Scott and Michelle Adams (2001), "Men's family work: Child-centered fathering and the sharing of domestic labor." In *Working Families: The Transformation of the American Home*, edited by Rosanna Hertz and Nancy L. Marshall (Berkeley: University of California Press), pp. 72-102.

Cook, Ellen P. (1993), "The gendered context of life: Implications for women's and men's career-life plans," *Career Development Quarterly* (Vol. 41, No. 3, March), pp. 227-237.

Cooksey, Judith A., Katherine K. Knapp, Surrey M. Walton, *et al.* (2002), "Challenges to the pharmacist profession from escalating pharmaceutical demand," *Health Affairs* (Vol. 21, No. 5, September/October), pp. 182-188.

Cooper, Cary L. and Suzan Lewis (1999), "Gender and the changing nature of work." In *Handbook of Gender and Work*, edited by Gary N. Powell (Thousand Oaks, CA: Sage Publications, Inc.), pp. 37-46.

Correll, Shelley J. (2001), "Gender and the career choice process: The role of biased self-assessments," *American Journal of Sociology* (Vol. 106, No. 6, May), pp. 1691–1730.

Corrigall, Elizabeth A. and Alison M. Konrad (2007), "Gender role attitudes and careers: A longitudinal study," *Sex Roles* (Vol. 56, No. 11/12, June), pp. 847–855.

Costa, Jr., Paul T., Antonio Terracciano, and Robert R. McCrae (2001), "Gender differences in personality traits across cultures: Robust and surprising findings," *Journal of Personality and Social Psychology* (Vol. 81, No. 2, August), pp. 322–331.

Cox, Emily R. and Valerie Fitzpatrick (1999), "Pharmacists' job satisfaction and perceived utilization of skills," *American Journal of Health System Pharmacy* (Vol. 56, No. 17, September), pp. 1733–1737.

Cox, Jr., Taylor H. and Stacy Blake (1991), "Managing cultural diversity: Implications for organizational competitiveness," *The Academy of Management Executive* (Vol. 5, No. 3, August), pp. 45–56.

Crittenden, Ann (2001), *The Price of Motherhood: Why the Most Important Job in the World Is Still the Least Valued* (New York: Henry Holt and Company, LLC).

Cropanzano, Russell, Zinta S. Byrne, D. Ramona Bobocel, *et al.* (2001a), "Moral virtues, fairness heuristics, social entities, and other denizens of organizational justice," *Journal of Vocational Behavior* (Vol. 58, No. 2, April), pp. 164–209.

Cropanzano, Russell, Deborah E. Rupp, Carolyn J. Mohler, *et al.* (2001b), "Three roads to organizational justice." In *Research in Personnel and Human Resources Management*, Vol. 19, edited by Gerald R. Ferris (Greenwich, CT: JAI Press), pp. 1–113.

Cull, William L., Holly J. Mulvey, Karen G. O'Connor, *et al.* (2002), "Pediatricians working part-time: Past, present, and future," *Pediatrics* (Vol. 109, No. 6, June), pp. 1015–1020.

Cunningham, Mick (2008), "Influences of gender ideology and housework allocation on women's employment over the life course," *Social Science Research* (Vol. 37, No. 1, March), pp. 254–267.

Day, Arla L. and Trina C. Chamberlain (2006), "Committing to your work, spouse, and children: Implications for work-family conflict," *Journal of Vocational Behavior* (Vol. 18, No. 1, February), pp. 116–130.

De la Garza, Rudolfo O. (2004), "Latino politics," *Annual Review of Political Science* (Vol. 7, No. 1, May), pp. 91–123.

Deaux, Kay and Brenda Major (1987), "Putting gender into context: An interactive model of gender-related behavior," *Psychological Review* (Vol. 94, No. 3, July), pp. 369–389.

Deckop, John R., Carol C. Cirka, and Lynne M. Andersson (2003), "Doing unto others: The reciprocity of helping behavior in organizations," *Journal of Business Ethics* (Vol. 47, No. 2, October), pp. 101–113.

Deelstra, Janna T., Maria C. Peeters, Wilmar B. Schaufeli, *et al.* (2003), "Receiving instrumental support at work: When help is not welcome," *Journal of Applied Psychology* (Vol. 88, No. 2, April), pp. 324–331.

DeLeire, Thomas and Helen Levy (2004), "Worker sorting and the risk of death on the job," *Journal of Labor Economics* (Vol. 22, No. 4, October), pp. 925–953.

DeMato, Doris S. and Claire C. Curcio (2004), "Job satisfaction of elementary school counselors: A new look," *Professional School Counseling* (Vol. 7, No. 4, April), pp. 236–245.

DeNavas-Walt, Carmen, Bernadette D. Proctor, and Jessica C. Smith (2009), "U.S. Census Bureau: Income, poverty, and health insurance coverage, 2008," http://www.census.gov/prod/2009pubs/p60-236.pdf. Accessed December 16, 2009.

Deshpande, Satish P., Elizabeth George, and Jacob Joseph (2000), "Ethical climates and managerial success in Russian organizations," *Journal of Business Ethics* (Vol. 23, No. 2, January), pp. 211–217.

Desselle, Shane P. (2005), "Survey of certified pharmacy technicians in the United States: A quality-of-worklife study," *Journal of the American Pharmacists Association* (Vol. 45, No. 4, July/August), pp. 458–465.

DiCecio, Riccardo, Kristie M. Engemann, Michael T. Owyang, *et al.* (2008), "Changing trends in the labor force: A survey," *Review - Federal Reserve Bank of St. Louis* (Vol. 90, No. 1, January-February), pp. 47–62.

Dickerson, Niki T. (2006), "'We are a force to be reckoned with': Black and Latina women's leadership in the contemporary U.S. labor movement," *Working USA The Journal of Labor and Society* (Vol. 9, No. 3, August 25), pp. 293–313.

Dickerson, Niki T. (2007), "Black employment, segregation, and the social organization of metropolitan labor markets," *Economic Geography* (Vol. 83, No. 3, July), pp. 283–307.

Diekmann, Kristina A., Harris Sondak, and Zoe I. Barsness (2007), "Does fairness matter more to some than to others? The moderating role of workplace status on the relationship between procedural fairness perceptions and job satisfaction," *Social Justice Research* (Vol. 20, No. 2, June), pp. 161–180.

Dirks, Kurt T. and Donald L. Ferrin (2002), "Trust in leadership: Meta-analytic findings and implications for research and practice," *Journal of Applied Psychology* (Vol. 87, No. 4, July), pp. 611–628.

Dirks, Kurt T. and Daniel P. Skarlicki (2009), "The relationship between being perceived as trustworthy by coworkers and individual performance," *Journal of Management* (Vol. 35, No. 1, February), pp. 136–157.

Donohue, Susan M. and John S. Heywood (2004), "Job satisfaction and gender: An expanded specification from the NLSY," *International Journal of Manpower* (Vol. 25, No. 2, February), pp. 211–234.

Dorsey, E. Ray, David Jarjoura, and Gregory W. Rutecki (2003), "Influence of controllable lifestyle on recent trades in specialty choice by US medical students," *Journal of the American Medical Association* (Vol. 290, No. 9, September), pp. 1173–1178.

Ducharme, Lori J. and Jack K. Martin (2000), "Unrewarding work, coworker support, and job satisfaction: A test of the buffering hypothesis," *Work and Occupations* (Vol. 27, No. 2, May), pp. 223–243.

Duncan, Colin and Wendy Loretto (2004), "Never the right age? Gender and age-based discrimination in employment," *Gender, Work & Organization* (Vol. 11, No. 1, January), pp. 95–115.

Eder, Paul and Robert Eisenberger (2008), "Perceived organizational support: Reducing the negative influence of coworker withdrawal behavior," *Journal of Management* (Vol. 34, No. 1, February), pp. 55–68.

Eisenberger, Robert, Stephen Armeli, Barbara Rexwinkel, *et al.* (2001), "Reciprocation of perceived organizational support," *Journal of Applied Psychology* (Vol. 86, No. 1, January), pp. 42–51.

Enchautegui, Maria E. (1992), "Geographical differentials in the socioeconomic status of Puerto Ricans: Human capital variations and labor market characteristics," *International Migration Review* (Vol. 26, No. 4, Winter), pp. 1267–1290.

Ezeala-Harrison, Fidel (no date), "Gender earnings differential and feminization of poverty among Mississippi's African Americans," Jackson State University, Department of Economics, Finance, and General Business.

Falcao, Bruno L. S. and Rodrigo R. Soares (2007), "The demographic transition and the sexual division of labor," National Bureau of Economic Research, Working Paper 12,838.

Faubion, Clayton W., Charles D. Palmer, and Jason B. Andrew (2001), "Rural/urban differences in counselor satisfaction and extrinsic job factors," *Journal of Rehabilitation* (Vol. 67, No. 4, October/November/December), pp. 4–12.

Fernández, Raquel, Alessandra Fogli, and Claudia Olivetti (2004), "Preference formation and the rise of women's labor force participation: Evidence from WWII," National Bureau of Economic Research, Working Paper 10,589.

Ferres, Natalie, Julia Connell, and Anthony Travaglione (2004), "Co-worker trust as a social catalyst for constructive employee attitudes," *Journal of Managerial Psychology* (Vol. 19, No. 6, June), pp. 608–622.

Ferris, Gerald R., Garry Adams, Robert W. Kolodinsky, *et al.* (2002), "Perceptions of organizational politics: Theory and research directions." In *Research in Multi-level Issues. Volume 1: The Many Faces of Multi-level Issues*, edited by Francis J. Yammarino and Fred Dansereau (Oxford: JAI Press/Elsevier Science), pp. 179–254.

Fields, Dail L. (2002), *Taking the Measure of Work: A Guide to Validated Scales for Organizational Research and Diagnosis* (Thousand Oaks, CA: Sage Publications, Inc.).

Fisher, Cynthia D. (2000), "Mood and emotions while working: Missing pieces of job satisfaction?," *Journal of Organizational Behavior* (Vol. 21, Special Issue, March), pp. 185–202.

Fisher, Susan R. and Margaret A. White (2000), "Downsizing in a learning organization: Are there hidden costs?," *The Academy of Management Review* (Vol. 25, No. 1, January), pp. 224–251.

Florida Area Health Education Center Network (2009), "Pharmacist," http://flahec.org/hlthcareers/pharm.HTM. Accessed January 14, 2010.

Florida Department of Health, Office of Health Statistics and Assessment (2009a), "Florida charts community health assessment resource tool set: Florida behavioral risk factor data," http://www.floridacharts.com/CHARTS/brfss.aspx. Accessed December 9, 2009.

Florida Department of Health, Office of Health Statistics and Assessment (2009b), "Florida charts community health assessment resource tool set: Health resources availability," http://www.floridacharts.com/charts/Domain2.aspx?Domain='07'. Accessed December 18, 2009.

Florida Department of Health, Office of Health Statistics and Assessment (2009c), "Florida charts community health assessment resource tool set: Major sources of death," http://www.floridacharts.com/CHARTS/SpecReport.aspx?RepID=7226. Accessed November 17, 2009.

Florida Department of Health, Office of Health Statistics and Assessment (2009d), "Florida charts community health assessment resource tool set: Mortality atlas," http://www.floridacharts.Com/CHARTS/AtlasIntro.aspx?ID=1. Accessed November 17, 2009.

Florida Department of Health, Office of Health Statistics and Assessment (2009e), "Florida charts community health assessment resource tool set: Population characteristics," http://www. floridacharts.com/charts/CensusDataReportDisplay.aspx?indCode=0600000410&subdomain=1. Accessed November 9, 2009.

Florida Department of Health, Division of Medical Quality Assurance (2010a), "Annual report 2008–2009," http://www.doh.state.fl.us/mqa/Publications/08-09mqa-ar.pdf. Accessed January 26, 2010.

Florida Department of Health, License Verification Database (2010b), http://ww2.doh.state.fl.us/IRM00PRAES/PRASLIST.ASP?ACTION=NEXT#theBottom. Accessed January 14, 2010.

(The) Florida Legislature, Office of Economic and Demographic Research (2009a), "Demographic estimate conference–February 18, 2009," http://www.edr.state.fl.us/conferences/population/demographic.htm. Accessed November 3, 2009.

(The) Florida Legislature, Office of Economic and Demographic Research (2009b), "Florida demographic summary," http://www.edr.state.fl.us/population.htm. Accessed November 3, 2009.

(The) Florida Legislature, Office of Economic and Demographic Research (2009c), "Florida population estimates for counties and municipalities," http://www.edr.state.fl.us/population.htm. Accessed February 2, 2009.

"Florida's Population," (2009), *Econographic News* (Vol. 1A)," http://www.edr.state.fl.us/population.htm. Accessed November 5, 2009.

Fogli, Alessandra and Laura Veldkamp (2007), "Nature or nurture? Learning and female labor force dynamics," Federal Reserve Bank of Minneapolis, Research Department Staff Report 386 (February).

Franklin, John H. (2005), "The two worlds of race: A historical view," *Daedalus* (Vol. 134, No. 4, Fall), pp. 118–133.

Frey, Bruno S. and Alois Stutzer (2002a), *Happiness and Economics: How the Economy and Institutions Affect Human Well-Being* (Princeton, NJ: Princeton University Press).

Frey, Bruno S. and Alois Stutzer (2002b), "What can economists learn from happiness research?," *Journal of Economic Literature* (Vol. 40, No. 2, June), pp. 402–435.

Fritzsche, David J. (2000), "Ethical climates and the ethical dimension of decision making," *Journal of Business Ethics* (Vol. 24, No. 2, March), pp. 125–140.

Fry, Richard and B. Lindsay Lowell (2006), "The wage structure of Latino-origin groups across generations," *Industrial Relations* (Vol. 45, No. 2, April), pp. 147–168.

Gabriel, Paul E. and Susanne Schmitz (2007), "Gender differences in occupational distributions among workers," *Monthly Labor Review* (Vol. 130, No. 6, June), pp. 19–24.

Gaither, Caroline A. (1998), "An investigation of pharmacists' role stress and the work/non-work interface," *Journal of Social and Administrative Pharmacy* (Vol. 15, No. 2, June), pp. 92–103.

Gaither, Caroline A. (1999), "Career commitment: A mediator of the effects of job stress on pharmacists' work-related attitudes," *Journal of the American Pharmaceutical Association* (Vol. 39, No. 3, May/June), pp. 353–361.

Galinsky, Ellen, Stacy S. Kim, and James T. Bond (2001), *Feeling Overworked: When Work Becomes Too Much* (New York: Families and Work Institute).

Gardner, Donald G., Linn Van Dyne, and Jon L. Pierce (2004), "The effects of pay level on organization-based self-esteem and performance: A field study," *Journal of Occupational and Organizational Psychology* (Vol. 77, Part 3, September), pp. 307–322.

Gardner, Stephanie F. and Cindy D. Stowe (2007), "The impact of a gender shift on a profession: Women in pharmacy," *Forum on Public Policy* (Winter).

Gary, Debra L. (2002), "Invest in yourself—The why and wherefore of empowerment: The key to job satisfaction and professional advancement," *Nursing Forum* (Vol. 37, No. 3, July-September), pp. 33–36.

Gazioğlu, Şaziye and Aysit Tansel (2002), "Job satisfaction in Britain: Individual and job related factors," Middle East Technical University (Ankara, Turkey), ERC Working Paper in Economics 03/03.

Gegax, Tom (2006), "Relationship management: Create an enlightened work environment and reap the rewards from your employees," *Business Credit* (Vol. 108, No. 4, April), pp. 65–67.

Gershon, Sharon K., James M. Cultice, and Katherine K. Knapp (2000), "How many pharmacists are in our future? The Bureau of Health Professions projects supply to 2020," *Journal of the American Pharmaceutical Association* (Vol. 40, No. 6, November–December), pp. 757–764.

Ginther, Donna K. and Shulamit Kahn (2006), "Does science promote women? Evidence from academia 1973–2001," National Bureau of Economic Research, Working Paper 12,691.

Gitelson, Idy B., Anne C. Petersen, and Maryse H. Tobin-Richards (1982), "Adolescents' expectations of success, self-evaluations, and attributions about performance on spatial and verbal tasks," *Sex Roles* (Vol. 8, No. 4, April), pp. 411–419.

Gjerberg, Elisabeth (2003), "Women doctors in Norway: The challenging balance between career and family life," *Social Science and Medicine* (Vol. 57, No. 7, October), pp. 1327–1341.

Godfrey, Pell (2005), "Use and misuse of Likert scales," *Medical Education* (Vol. 39, No. 9, September), p. 970.

Goldin, Claudia (1990), *Understanding the Gender Gap: An Economic History of American Women* (New York: Oxford University Press).

Goldin, Claudia and Lawrence F. Katz (2002), "The power of the pill: Oral contraceptives and women's career and marriage decisions," *Journal of Political Economy* (Vol. 110, No. 4, August), pp. 730–770.

Goldin, Claudia, Lawrence F. Katz, and Ilyana Kuziemko (2006), "The homecoming of American college women: The reversal of the college gender gap," National Bureau of Economic Research, Working Paper 12,139.

Gonzalez, Libertad (2004), "Single mothers and work," *Socio-Economic Review* (Vol. 2, No. 2, Special Issue), pp. 285–313.

Gordon, Michael E. and Angelo S. Denisi (1995), "A re-examination of the relationship between union membership and job satisfaction," *Industrial and Labor Relations Review* (Vol. 48, No. 2, January), pp. 222–236.

Goris, José R., Bobby C. Vaught, and John D. Pettit, Jr. (2000), "Effects of communication direction on job performance and satisfaction: A moderated regression analysis," *The Journal of Business Communication* (Vol. 37, No. 4, October), pp. 348–368.

Gormley, Denise K. (2003), "Factors affecting job satisfaction in nurse faculty: A meta-analysis," *Journal of Nursing Education* (Vol. 42, No. 4, April), pp. 174–178.

Graefe, Deborah R. and Daniel T. Lichter (2002), "Marriage among unwed mothers: Whites, Blacks and Hispanics compared," *Perspectives on Sexual and Reproductive Health* (Vol. 34, No. 6, November–December), pp. 286–293.

Graham, Jill W. and Dennis W. Organ (1993), "Commitment and the covenantal organization," *Journal of Managerial Issues* (Vol. 5, No. 4, Winter), pp. 483–502.

Graham, John W. and Steven A. Smith (2005), "Gender differences in employment and earnings in science and engineering in the US," *Economics of Education Review* (Vol. 24, No. 3, June), pp. 341–354.

Gramling, L. G. (1973), *A History of Pharmacy in Florida* (Gainesville: Erwing Printing).

Grant-Vallone, Elisa J. and Stewart I. Donaldson (2001), "Consequences of work-family conflict on employee well-being over time," *Work and Stress* (Vol. 15, No. 3, July–September), pp. 214–226.

Green, Francis, Alan Felstead, and Brendan Burchell (2000), "Job insecurity and the difficulty of regaining employment: An empirical study of unemployment expectations," *Oxford Bulletin of Economics and Statistics* (Vol. 62, No. s1, December), pp. 855–883.

Green, T. Clifton, Narasimhan Jegadeesh, and Yue Tang (2007), "Gender and job performance: Evidence from Wall Street," National Bureau of Economic Research, Working Paper 12,897.

Greenberg, Jerald (1997), "The STEAL motive: Managing the social determinants of employee theft." In *Antisocial Behavior in Organizations*, edited by Robert Giacalone and Jerald Greenberg (Thousand Oaks, CA: Sage Publications, Inc.), pp. 85–108.

Greenwood, Jeremy, Ananth Seshadri, and Mehmet Yorukoglu (2005), "Engines of liberation," *Review of Economic Studies* (Vol. 72, No. 1, January), pp. 109–133.

Griffin, Marie L., Gaylene S. Armstrong, and John R. Hepburn (2005), "Correctional officers' perceptions of equitable treatment in the masculinized prison environment," *Criminal Justice Review* (Vol. 30, No. 2, September), pp. 189–206.

Griggs, C. M. and Kenneth T. Jones (2009), "Florida health statistic vital statistic annual report 2009," http://www.flpublichealth.com/VSBOOK/VSBOOK.aspx. Accessed November 17, 2009.

Griskevicius, Vladas, Robert B. Cialdini, and Noah J. Goldstein (2008), "Applying (and resisting) peer influence," *MIT Sloan Management Review* (Vol. 49, No. 2, Winter), pp. 84–88.

Grossi, Elizabeth L., Thomas J. Keil, and Gennaro F. Vito (1996), "Surviving 'the joint': Mitigating factors of correctional officer stress," *Journal of Crime and Justice* (Vol. 19, No. 2, October), pp. 103–120.

Gutek, Barbara A., Groff Cohen, and Anne Tsui (1996), "Reactions to perceived sex discrimination," *Human Relations* (Vol. 49, No. 6, June), pp. 791–813.

Hagan, John and Fiona Kay (2007), "Even lawyers get the blues: Gender, depression, and job satisfaction in legal practice," *Law and Society Review* (Vol. 41, No. 1, March), pp. 51–78.

Hagedorn, Linda S. and Berta V. Laden (2002), "Exploring the climate for women as community college faculty," *New Directions for Community Colleges* (Issue 118, Summer), pp. 69–78.

Hagedorn, Linda S. and Linda J. Sax (2003), "Marriage, children, and aging parents: The role of family-related factors in faculty job satisfaction," *Journal of Faculty Development* (Vol. 19, No. 2, Fall), pp. 65–76.

Hamermesh, Daniel S. (2001), "The changing distribution of job satisfaction," *The Journal of Human Resources* (Vol. 36, No. 1, Winter), pp. 1–30.

Han, Wen-Jui, Jane Waldfogel, and Jeanne Brooks-Gunn (2001), "The effects of early maternal employment on later cognitive and behavioral outcomes," *Journal of Marriage and the Family* (Vol. 63, No. 2, May), pp. 336–354.

Han, Wen-Jui, Christopher J. Ruhm, Jane Waldfogel, *et al.* (2008), "The timing of mothers' employment after childbirth," *Monthly Labor Review* (Vol. 131, No. 6, June), pp. 15–27.

Hanisch, Kathy A., Charles L. Hulin, and Mary Roznowski (1998), "The importance of individuals' repertoires of behaviors: The scientific appropriateness of studying multiple behaviors and general attitudes," *Journal of Organizational Behavior* (Vol. 19, No. 5, September), pp. 463–480.

Hardigan, Patrick C. and Manuel J. Carvajal (2007), "Job satisfaction among practicing pharmacists: A Rasch analysis," *The Internet Journal of Allied Health Sciences and Practice* (Vol. 5, No. 4, October).

Hardigan, Patrick C. and Manuel J. Carvajal (2008), "An application of the Rasch rating scale model to the analysis of job satisfaction among practicing pharmacists," *Journal of the American Pharmacists Association* (Vol. 48, No. 4, July/August), pp. 522–529.

Hardigan, Patrick C. and Stanley R. Cohen (1998), "A comparison of personality types among students enrolled in osteopathic medical, pharmacy, physical therapy, physician assistant, and occupational therapy programs," *Journal of the American Osteopathic Society* (Vol. 98, No. 11, November), pp. 637–641.

Hardigan, Patrick C., Stanley R. Cohen, and Manuel J. Carvajal (2001a), "Linking job satisfaction and career choice with personality styles: An exploratory study of practicing pharmacists," *Journal of Psychological Type* (Vol. 57), pp. 30–35.

Hardigan, Patrick C., L. Leanne Lai, and Manuel J. Carvajal (2001b), "The influence of positive and negative affectivity on reported job satisfaction among practicing pharmacists," *Journal of Pharmaceutical Marketing and Management* (Vol. 13, No. 4), pp. 57–71.

Harpaz, Itzhak and Xuanning Fu (1997), "Work centrality in Germany, Israel, Japan, and the United States," *Cross-Cultural Research* (Vol. 31, No. 3, August), pp. 171–200.

Harper, Sam, John Lynch, Scott Burris, *et al.* (2007), "Trends in the Black-White life expectancy gap in the United States, 1983-2003," *Journal of the American Medical Association* (Vol. 297, No. 11, March), pp. 1224–1232.

Harris, J. Irene, Anne M. Winskowski, and Brian E. Engdahl (2007a), "Types of workplace social support in the prediction of job satisfaction," *The Career Development Quarterly* (Vol. 56, No. 2, December), pp. 150–156.

Harris, Ranida B., Kenneth J. Harris, and Paul Harvey (2007b), "A test of competing models of the relationships among perceptions of organizational politics, perceived organizational support, and individual outcomes," *The Journal of Social Psychology* (Vol. 147, No. 6, December), pp. 631–655.

Harsanyi, John C. (1987), "Interpersonal utility comparisons." In *The New Palgrave Dictionary of Economics*, Vol. 2, edited by John Eatwell, Murray Milgate, and Peter Newman (London: Macmillan), pp. 955–958.

Hart, L. Gary, Edward Salsberg, Debra M. Phillips, *et al.* (2002), "Rural health care providers in the United States," *The Journal of Rural Health* (Vol. 18, No. 5, Supplemental), pp. S211–S232.

Hartmann, Heidi (2001), "Economic security for women and children: What will it take?" In *The Next Agenda—Blueprint for a New Progressive Movement*, edited by Robert L. Borosage and Roger Hickey (Boulder, CO: Westview Press), pp. 127–160.

Hegtvedt, Karen A. and Barry Markovsky (1994), "Justice and injustice." In *Sociological Perspectives on Social Psychology*, edited by Karen S. Cook, Gary A. Fine, and James S. House (Boston: Allyn and Bacon), pp. 257–280.

Hellerstein, Judith and David Neumark (2005), "Workplace segregation in the United States: Race, ethnicity, and skill," National Bureau of Economic Research, Working Paper 11,599.

Hellerstein, Judith, David Neumark, and Melissa McInerney (2007), "Changes in workplace segregation in the United States between 1990 and 2000: Evidence from matched employer-employee data," National Bureau of Economic Research, Working Paper 13,080.

Heneman III, Herbert G. and Timothy A. Judge (2000), "Compensation attitudes." In *Compensation in Organizations*, edited by Sara L. Rynes and Barry Gerhart (San Francisco: Jossey-Bass, Inc.), pp. 61–103.

Henry J. Kaiser Family Foundation (2009a), "Florida: Estimated underserved population living in primary care health professional shortage areas (HPSAs), as of September, 2008," http://www.statehealthfactsonline.org/profileind.jsp?ind=682&cat=8&rgn=11. Accessed December 18, 2009.

Henry J. Kaiser Family Foundation (2009b), "Florida: Health insurance coverage of the total population, states (2007-2008), U.S. (2008)," http://www.statehealthfactsonline.org/profile ind.jsp?ind=125&cat=3&rgn=11. Accessed December 16, 2009.

Henry J. Kaiser Family Foundation (2009c), "Florida: Hospitals," http://www.statehealth factsonline.org/profileind.jsp?cat=8&sub=94&rgn=11. Accessed December 18, 2009.

Henry J. Kaiser Family Foundation (2009d), "Florida: Nonfederal primary care physicians per 1,000 population, 2008," http://www.statehealthfactsonline.org/profileind.jsp?ind=690&cat=8&rgn=11. Accessed December 18, 2009.

Henry J. Kaiser Family Foundation (2009e), "Florida: Number of federally-funded federally qualified health centers, 2008," http://www.statehealthfactsonline.org/profileind.jsp?ind=424&cat=8&rgn=11. Accessed December 18, 2009.

Henry J. Kaiser Family Foundation (2009f), "Florida: Number of rural health clinics, 2009," http://www.statehealthfactsonline.org/comparetable.jsp?ind=423&cat=8&sub=98&yr=92&typ=1&sort=a. Accessed December 18, 2009.

Henry J. Kaiser Family Foundation (2009g), "Florida: Nursing facilities," http://www.statehealthfactsonline.org/profileind.jsp?cat=8&sub=97&rgn=11. Accessed December 18, 2009.

Henry J. Kaiser Family Foundation (2009h), "Florida: Percentage reporting not seeing a doctor in the past 12 months because of cost, 2008," http://www.statehealthfactsonline.org/profileind.Jsp?ind=747&cat=8&rgn11. Accessed December 17, 2009.

Hepler, Charles D. and Linda M. Strand (1990), "Opportunities and responsibilities in pharmaceutical care," *American Journal of Hospital Pharmacy* (Vol. 47, No. 3, March), pp. 533–543.

Herbst, Chris M. and Burt S. Barnow (2008), "Close to home: A simultaneous equations model of the relationship between child care accessibility and female labor force participation," *Journal of Family Economic Issues* (Vol. 29, No. 1, March), pp. 128–151.

Heron, Meloni, Donna L. Hoyert, Sherry L. Murphy, *et al.* (2009), "Deaths: Final data for 2006," *National Vital Statistics Report* (Vol. 57, No. 14, April).

Hersch, Joni (2006), "Sex discrimination in the labor market," *Foundations and Trends in Microeconomics* (Vol. 2, No. 4), pp. 281–361.

Heslop, Pauline, George D. Smith, Chris Metcalf, *et al.* (2002), "Change in job satisfaction and its association with self-reported stress, cardiovascular risk factors and mortality," *Social Science and Medicine* (Vol. 54, No. 10, May), pp. 1589–1599.

Higby, Gregory J. (1997), "American pharmacy in the twentieth century," *American Journal of Health-System Pharmacy* (Vol. 54, No. 16, August 15), pp. 1833–1836.

Hirsch, Donald (2003), *Crossroads after 50: Improving Choices in Work and Retirement* (Bristol, UK: The Policy Press).

Hochwarter, Wayne A., Gerald R. Ferris, Pamela L. Perrewe, *et al.* (2001), "A note on the nonlinearity of the age-job-satisfaction relationship," *Journal of Applied Social Psychology* (Vol. 31, No. 6, June), pp. 1223–1237.

Hojat, Mohammadreza, Joseph S. Gonnella, James B. Erdmann, *et al.* (2000), "Gender comparisons of income expectations in the USA at the beginning of medical school during the past 28 years," *Social Science and Medicine* (Vol. 50, No. 11, June), pp. 1665–1672.

Holzer, Harry and David Neumark (2000), "What does affirmative action do?," *Industrial and Labor Relations Review* (Vol. 53, No. 2, January), pp. 240–271.

Hondagneu-Sotelo, Pierrette (2001), *Doméstica: Immigrant Workers Cleaning and Caring in the Shadow of Affluence* (Berkeley: University of California Press).

Hotchkiss, Julie L. (2005), "What's up with the decline in female labor force participation?," Federal Reserve Bank of Atlanta, Working Paper No. 2005-18.

Hotchkiss, Julie L. (2006), "Changes in behavioral and characteristic determination of female labor force participation, 1975-2005," *Economic Review - Federal Reserve Bank of Atlanta* (Vol. 91, No. 2, Second Quarter), pp. 1-20.

Hotz, V. Joseph, Lixin C. Xu, Marta Tienda, *et al.* (2002), "Are there returns to the wages of young men from working while in school?," *The Review of Economics and Statistics* (Vol. 84, No. 2, May), pp. 221-236.

Howard, Ann (2002), "The new organizational reality: Downsizing, restructuring, and revitalization," *Human Resource Management* (Vol. 41, No. 3, Fall), pp. 399-402.

Hudson, Kenneth (2001), "The disposable worker," *Monthly Review* (Vol. 52, No. 11, April), pp. 43-55.

Hudson, Kenneth (2007), "The new labor market segmentation: Labor market dualism in the new economy," *Social Science Research* (Vol. 36, No. 1, March), pp. 286-312.

Hulin, Charles L. and Timothy A. Judge (2003), "Job attitudes." In *Handbook of Psychology. Volume 12: Industrial and Organizational Psychology*, edited by Walter C. Borman, Daniel R. Ilgen, Richard J. Klimonski, *et al.* (Hoboken, NJ: Wiley), pp. 255-276.

Hull, Kathleen E. (1999), "The paradox of the contented female lawyer," *Law and Society Review* (Vol. 33, No. 3, September), pp. 687-702.

Hundley, Greg (2000), "Male/female earnings differences in self-employment: The effects of marriage, children, and the household division of labor," *Industrial and Labor Relations Review* (Vol. 54, No. 1, October), pp. 95-114.

Hundley, Greg (2001a), "Why and when are the self-employed more satisfied with their work?," *Industrial Relations* (Vol. 40, No. 2, April), pp. 293-316.

Hundley, Greg (2001b), "Why women earn less than men in self-employment," *Journal of Labor Research* (Vol. 22, No. 4, Fall), pp. 817-829.

Hunt, Matthew (2004), "Race/ethnicity and beliefs about wealth and poverty," *Social Science Quarterly* (Vol. 85, No. 3, September), pp. 827-853.

Huo, Yuen J., Tom Tyler, Heather J. Smith, *et al.* (1997), *Social Justice in a Diverse Society* (Boulder, CO: Westview Press).

Iceland, John, (2003), "Why poverty remains high: The role of income growth, economic inequality, and changes in family structure, 1949-1999," *Demography* (Vol. 40, No. 3, August), pp. 499-519.

Ichino, Andrea and Enrico Moretti (2006), "Biological gender differences, absenteeism, and the earning gap," National Bureau of Economic Research, Working Paper 12,369.

Igbaria, Magid and Jack J. Baroudi (1995), "The impact of job performance evaluations on career advancement prospects: An examination of gender differences in the IS workplace," *MIS Quarterly* (Vol. 19, No. 1, March), pp. 107–123.

Igbaria, Magid and Laku Chidambaram (1997), "The impact of gender on career success of information systems professionals: A human-capital perspective," *Information Technology and People* (Vol. 10, No. 1), pp. 63–75.

Incitti, Filomena, James Rourke, Leslie L. Rourke, *et al.* (2003), "Rural women family physicians: Are they unique?," *Canadian Family Physician* (Vol. 49, No. 3, March), pp. 320–327.

Irving, P. Gregory, Daniel F. Coleman, and D. Ramona Bobocel (2005), "The moderating effect of negative affectivity in the procedural justice-job satisfaction relation," *Canadian Journal of Behavioural Science* (Vol. 37, No. 1, January), pp. 20–32.

Jacobs, Jerry A. and Kathleen Gerson (2000), "Do Americans feel overworked? Comparing ideal and actual work time." In *Work and Family: Research Informing Policy*, edited by Toby L. Parcel and Daniel B. Cornfield (Thousand Oaks, CA: Sage Publications, Inc.), pp. 71–95.

Jacobson, Christine C., Josephine C. Nguyen, and Alexa B. Kimball (2004a), "Gender and parenting significantly affect work hours of recent dermatology program graduates," *Archives of Dermatology* (Vol. 140, No. 2, February), pp. 191–196.

Jacobson, Christine C., Jack S. Resneck, Jr., and Alexa B. Kimball (2004b), "Generational differences in practice patterns of dermatologists in the United States," *Archives of Dermatology* (Vol. 140, No. 12, December), pp. 1477–1482.

James, Lawrence R., Lois A. James, and Donna K. Ashe (1990), "The meaning of organizations: The role of cognition and values." In *Organizational Climate and Culture*, edited by Benjamin Schneider (San Francisco: Jossey-Bass), pp. 40–84.

James-Burdumy, Susanne (2005), "The effect of maternal labor force participation on child development," *Journal of Labor Economics* (Vol. 23, No. 1, January), pp. 177–211.

Jamieson, Susan (2004), "Likert scales: How to (ab)use them," *Medical Education* (Vol. 38, No. 12, December), pp. 1217–1218.

Jennings, Andrea T. (2000), "Hiring Generation X," *Journal of Accountancy* (Vol. 189, No. 2, February), pp. 55–59.

Jiang, Niantao (2004), "Measurement of job satisfaction reconsidered: A structural equation modeling perspective." Paper presented at the annual meeting of the American Sociological Association (San Francisco, August 14), http://allacademic.com/meta/p110354_index.html. Accessed May 26, 2009.

Johns, Gary (2002), "The psychology of lateness, absenteeism, and turnover." In *Handbook of Industrial, Work, and Organizational Psychology. Volume 2: Organizational Psychology,* edited by Neil Anderson, Deniz S. Ones, Handan K. Sinangil, *et al.* (London: Sage Publications), pp. 232–252.

Johnson, Gloria J. and Roy W. Johnson (2000), "Perceived overqualification and dimensions of job satisfaction: A longitudinal analysis," *The Journal of Psychology* (Vol. 134, No. 5, September), pp. 537–555.

Johnson, Thomas J. (2008), "Pharmacist work force in 2020: Implications of requiring residency training for practice," *American Journal of Health-System Pharmacy* (Vol. 65, No. 2, January), pp. 166–170.

Jovic, Emily, Jean E. Wallace, and Jane Lemaire (2006), "The generation and gender shifts in medicine: An exploratory survey of internal medicine physicians," *BMC Health Services Research* (Vol. 6, No. 55, May 5).

Judge, Timothy A. and Joyce E. Bono (2001), "Relationship of core self-evaluations traits—self-esteem, generalized self-efficacy, locus of control, and emotional stability—with job satisfaction and performance: A meta-analysis," *Journal of Applied Psychology* (Vol. 86, No. 1, February), pp. 80–92.

Judge, Timothy A., Sharon K. Parker, Amy E. Colbert, *et al.* (2002), "Job satisfaction: A cross-cultural review." In *Handbook of Industrial, Work, and Organizational Psychology. Volume 2: Organizational Psychology,* edited by Neil Anderson, Deniz S. Ones, Handan K. Sinangil, *et al.* (London: Sage Publications), pp. 25–52.

Kacmar, Mikki and Robert A. Baron (1999), "Organizational politics: The state of the field, links to related processes, and an agenda for future research." In *Research in Personnel and Human Resources Management,* edited by Gerald R. Ferris, Volume 17 (Stamford, CT: JAI Press, Inc.), pp. 1–39.

Kahaleh, Abir (Abby) and Caroline A. Gaither (2005), "Effects of empowerment on pharmacists' organizational behaviors," *Journal of the American Pharmacists Association* (Vol. 45, No. 6, November/December), pp. 700–709.

Kahaleh, Abby and Caroline Gaither (2007), "The effects of work setting on pharmacists' empowerment and organizational behaviors," *Research in Social and Administrative Pharmacy* (Vol. 3, No. 2, June), pp. 199–222.

Kaiser, Lutz C. (2002), "Job satisfaction: A comparison of standard, non standard, and self-employment patterns across Europe with a special note to the gender/job satisfaction paradox," European Panel Analysis Group (Colchester, UK).

Kaiser, Lutz C. (2007), "Gender-job satisfaction differences across Europe: An indicator for labour market modernization," *International Journal of Manpower* (Vol. 28, No. 1, January), pp. 75–94.

Kalleberg, Anne L., Barbara F. Reskin, and Ken Hudson (2000), "Bad jobs in America: Standard and nonstandard employment relations and job quality in the United States," *American Sociological Review* (Vol. 65, No. 2, April), pp. 256–278.

Karl, Katherine A. and Cynthia L. Sutton (1998),"Job values in today's workforce: A comparison of public and private sector employees," *Public Personnel Management* (Vol. 27, No. 4, Winter), pp. 515–528.

Kaufman, Gayle and Peter Uhlenberg (2000), "The influence of parenthood on the work effort of married men and women," *Social Forces* (Vol. 78, No. 3, March), pp. 931–949.

Keaveny, Timothy J., Edward J. Inderrieden, and Peter G. Toumanoff (2007), "Gender differences in pay of young management professionals in the United States: A comprehensive view," *Journal of Labor Research* (Vol. XXVIII, No. 2, Spring), pp. 327–346.

Kee, Hiau J. (2006), "Glass ceiling or sticky floor? Exploring the Australian gender pay gap," *The Economic Record* (Vol. 82, No. 259, December), pp. 408–427.

Kellough, J. Edward and Katherine C. Naff (2004), "Responding to a wake-up call: An examination of federal agency diversity management programs," *Administration and Society* (Vol. 36, No. 1, March), pp. 62–90.

Kennedy, Marilyn M. (2003), "Managing different generations requires new skills, insightful leadership," *Physician Executive* (Vol. 29, No. 6, November–December), pp. 20–23.

Kenreigh, Charlotte A. and Linda T. Wagner (2006), "The pharmacist shortage: Where do we stand?," *Medscape Pharmacists* (Vol. 7, No. 1, January 13).

Kesselring, Randall G. and Dale Bremmer (2006), "Female income and the divorce decision: Evidence from micro data," *Applied Economics* (Vol. 38, No. 14, August 10), pp. 1605–1616.

Kidwell, Jr., Roland E. and Nathan Bennett (1994), "Employee reactions to electronic control systems: The role of procedural fairness," *Group & Organization Management* (Vol. 19, No. 2, June), pp. 203–218.

Kim, Sangmook (2005), "Gender differences in the job satisfaction of public employees: A study of Seoul Metropolitan Government, Korea," *Sex Roles* (Vol. 52, No. 9/10, May), pp. 667–681.

Kim, Soonhee (2002), "Participative management and job satisfaction: Lessons for management leadership," *Public Administration Review* (Vol. 62, No. 2, March/April), pp. 231–241.

Kingston, Raynard, Diana Tisnado, and David M. Carlisle (2001), "Increasing racial and ethnic diversity among physicians: An intervention to address health disparities?" In *The Right Thing to Do, the Smart Thing to Do: Enhancing Diversity in Health Professions*, edited by Brian D. Smedley *et al.* (Washington, D.C.: The National Academies Press), pp. 57–90.

Kinnier, Richard T., Ellen C. Katz, and Martha A. Berry (1991), "Successful resolutions to the career-versus-family conflict," *Journal of Counseling and Development* (Vol. 69, No. 5, May–June), pp. 439–444.

Kirk-Brown, Andrea and Debra Wallace (2004), "Predicting burnout and job satisfaction in workplace counselors: The influence of role stressors, job challenge, and organizational knowledge," *Journal of Employment Counseling* (Vol. 41, No. 1, March), pp. 29–37.

Kirkman, Bradley L. and Debra L. Shapiro (2001), "The impact of cultural values on job satisfaction and organizational commitment in self-managing work teams: The mediating role of employee resistance," *Academy of Management Journal* (Vol. 44, No. 3, June), pp. 557–569.

Kmec, Julie A. (2003), "Minority job concentration and wages," *Social Problems* (Vol. 50, No. 1, February), pp. 38–59.

Knapp, Katherine K. and James M. Cultice (2007), "New pharmacist supply projections: Lower separation rates and increased graduates boost supply estimates," *Journal of the American Pharmacists Association* (Vol. 47, No. 4, July/August), pp. 463–470.

Knapp, Katherine K. and John C. Livesey (2002), "The aggregate demand index: Measuring the balance between pharmacist supply and demand, 1999-2001," *Journal of the American Pharmaceutical Association* (Vol. 42, No. 3, May/June), pp. 391–398.

Kong, Sheldon X. (1995), "Predictors of organizational and career commitment among Illinois pharmacists," *American Journal of Health-System Pharmacy* (Vol. 52, No. 18, September), pp. 2005–2011.

Konrad, Alison M., Elizabeth Corrigall, Pamela Lieb, *et al.* (2000a), "Sex differences in job attribute preferences among managers and business students," *Group & Organization Management* (Vol. 25, No. 2, June), pp. 108–131.

Konrad, Alison M., J. Edgar Ritchie, Jr., Pamela Lieb, *et al.* (2000b), "Sex differences and similarities in job attribute preferences: A meta-analysis," *Psychological Bulletin* (Vol. 126, No. 4, July), pp. 593–641.

Kramen-Kahn, Barbara and Nancy D. Hansen (1998), "Rafting the rapids: Occupational hazards, rewards, and coping strategies of psychotherapists," *Professional Psychology: Research and Practice* (Vol. 29, No. 2, April), pp. 130–134.

Kroska, Amy (2004), "Divisions of domestic work: Revising and expanding the theoretical explanations," *Journal of Family Issues* (Vol. 25, No. 7, October), pp. 900–932.

Kulas, John T., Joanne E. McInnerney, Rachel F. DeMuth, *et al.* (2007), "Employee satisfaction and theft: Testing climate perceptions as a mediator," *The Journal of Psychology* (Vol. 141, No. 4, July), pp. 389–402.

Kumar, Shailesh, Jesse Fischer, Elizabeth Robinson, *et al.* (2007), "Burnout and job satisfaction in New Zealand psychiatrists: A national study," *International Journal of Social Psychiatry* (Vol. 53, No. 4, July), pp. 306–316.

Lambert, Eric G. (2004), "The impact of job characteristics on correctional staff members," *The Prison Journal* (Vol. 84, No. 2, June), pp. 208–227.

Lambert, Eric and Nancy Hogan (2009), "The importance of job satisfaction and organizational commitment in shaping turnover intent: A test of a causal model," *Criminal Justice Review* (Vol. 34, No. 1, March), pp. 96–118.

Lambert, Eric G. and Eugene A. Paoline III (2008), "The influence of individual, job, and organizational characteristics on correctional staff job stress, job satisfaction, and organizational commitment," *Criminal Justice Review* (Vol. 33, No. 4, December), pp. 541–564.

Lambert, Eric G., Nancy L. Hogan, and Shannon M. Barton (2001), "The impact of job satisfaction on turnover intent: A test of a structural measurement model using a national sample of workers," *The Social Science Journal* (Vol. 38, No. 2, April), pp. 233–250.

Lambert, Eric G., Calvin Edwards, Scott D. Camp, *et al.* (2005), "Here today, gone tomorrow, back again the next day: Antecedents of correctional absenteeism," *Journal of Criminal Justice* (Vol. 33, No. 2, March–April), pp. 165–175.

Landry, John T. (2004), "Downsizing in America: Reality, causes, and consequences," *Harvard Business Review* (Vol. 82, No. 2, February), p. 39.

Lang, Kevin and Michael Manove (2006), "Education and labor-market discrimination," National Bureau of Economic Research, Working Paper 12,257.

Lapane, Kate L. and Carmel M. Hughes (2006), "Job satisfaction and stress among pharmacists in the long-term care sector," *The Consultant Pharmacist* (Vol. 21, No. 4, April), pp. 287–292.

Larson, Sharon L. and Steven C. Hill (2005), "Rural-urban differences in employment-related health insurance," *The Journal of Rural Health* (Vol. 21, No. 1, Winter), pp. 21–30.

Lauerová, Jana S. and Katherine Terrell (2007), "What drives gender differences in unemployment?," *Comparative Economic Studies* (Vol. 49, No. 1, March), pp. 128–155.

Lazarus, Richard S. (1999), *Stress and Emotion: A New Synthesis* (New York: Springer Publishing Company, Inc.).

Leeth, John D. and John Ruser (2003), "Compensating wage differentials for fatal and nonfatal injury risk by gender and race," *The Journal of Risk and Uncertainty* (Vol. 27, No. 3, December), pp. 257–277.

Leggon, Cheryl B. (2006), "Women in science: Racial and ethnic differences and the differences they make," *Journal of Technology Transfer* (Vol. 31, No. 3, May), pp. 325–333.

Leonard, Thomas C. (2003), "More merciful and not less effective: Eugenics and Progressive-Era American economics," *History of Political Economy* (Vol. 35, No. 4, Winter), pp. 687–712.

Leonard, Thomas C. (2005), "Protecting family and race: The progressive case for regulating women's work," *American Journal of Economics and Sociology* (Vol. 64, No. 3, July), pp. 757–791.

Leung, Danny (2006), "The male/female earnings gap and female self-employment," *The Journal of Socio-Economics* (Vol. 35, No. 5, October), pp. 759–779.

Levy, David and Sandra Peart (2003), "Denying human homogeneity: Eugenics and the making of post-Classical economics," *Journal of the History of Economic Thought* (Vol. 25, No. 3, July), pp. 261–288.

Levy, Helen (2006), "Health insurance and the wage gap," National Bureau of Economic Research, Working Paper 11,975.

Levy, Sandra (2008), "Take this job and love it?," *Drug Topics* (Vol. 152, No. 4, March 10), pp. 34, 36–38, 40, 42.

Lewandowski, Cathleen A. (2003), "Organizational factors contributing to worker frustration: The precursor to burnout," *Journal of Sociology and Social Welfare* (Vol. 30, No. 4, December), pp. 175–185.

Lilly, Meredith B., Audrey Laporte, and Peter C. Coyte (2007), "Labor market work and home care's unpaid caregivers: A systematic review of labor force participation rates, predictors of labor market withdrawal, and hours of work," *The Milbank Quarterly* (Vol. 85, No. 4, December), pp. 641–690.

Lin, Blossom Y., Ying-Chen Yeh, and Wen-Hung Lin (2007), "The influence of job characteristics on job outcomes of pharmacists in hospital, clinic, and community pharmacies," *Journal of Medical Systems* (Vol. 31, No. 3, June), pp. 224–229.

Linacre, John L. (2002), "Optimizing rating scale category effectiveness," *Journal of Applied Measurement* (Vol. 3, No. 1, Spring), pp. 85–106.

Lindsay, Sally (2007), "Gender differences in rural and urban practice location among mid-level health care providers," *The Journal of Rural Health* (Vol. 23, No. 1, January), pp. 72–76.

Linzer, Mark, Thomas R. Konrad, Jeffrey Douglas, *et al.* (2000), "Managed care, time pressure, and physician job satisfaction: Results from the physician worklife study," *Journal of General Internal Medicine* (Vol. 15, No. 7, July), pp. 441–450.

Llorens, Jared J., Jeffrey B. Wenger, and J. Edward Kellough (2008), "Choosing public sector employment: The impact of wages on the representation of women and minorities in state bureaucracies," *Journal of Public Administration Research and Theory* (Vol. 18, No. 3, July), pp. 397–413.

LoBuono, Charlotte (2003), "Exclusive R.Ph. salary survey: Cashing in," *Drug Topics* (Vol. 147, No. 5, March 3), pp. 46–48, 54–55.

Logan, John R. and Glen Deane (2003), "Black diversity in metropolitan America," Lewis Mumford Center for Comparative Urban and Regional Research University at Albany, August 15.

Logan, Mary S. and C. Ganster (2005), "An experimental evaluation of a control intervention to alleviate job-related stress," *Journal of Management* (Vol. 31, No. 1, February), pp. 90–107.

Lombard, Karen V. (1999), "Women's rising market opportunities and increased labor force participation," *Economic Inquiry* (Vol. 37, No. 2, April), pp. 195–212.

London, Manuel, Henrik H. Larsen, and Lars N. Thisted (1999), "Relationships between feedback and self-development," *Group & Organization Management* (Vol. 24, No. 1, March), pp. 5–27.

Long, Anthea (2005), "Happily ever after? A study of job satisfaction in Australia," *The Economic Record* (Vol. 81, No. 255, December), pp. 303–321.

Loscocco, Karyn A. and Glenna D. Spitze (1991), "The organizational context of women's and men's pay satisfaction," *Social Science Quarterly* (Vol. 72, No. 1, March), pp. 3–19.

Luce, Stephanie and Mark Brenner (2006), "Women and class: What has happened in forty years?," *Monthly Review* (Vol. 58, No. 3, July–August), pp. 80–93.

Magalian, Paul (1993), "Florida Society of Hospital Pharmacists: An abbreviated history (1947–1993)." Paper presented at the 27th Annual Meeting, Seminar, and Exhibit Program of the Florida Society of Hospital Pharmacists in Orlando.

Mahrous, Sam and Dorothy Maziarz (2008), "Community pharmacist shortage: Fact or fiction?," *Pharmacy Times* (Vol. 74, No. 2, February), pp. 58–59.

Maier, Mark (1999), "On the gendered substructure of organization." In *Handbook of Gender and Work*, edited by Gary N. Powell (Thousand Oaks, CA: Sage Publications, Inc.), pp. 69–94.

Maio, Vittorio, Neil Goldfarb, and Christine Hartmann (2004), "Pharmacists' job satisfaction," *Pharmacy and Therapeutics* (Vol. 29, No. 3, June), pp. 184–190.

Malka, Ariel and Jennifer A. Chatman (2003), "Intrinsic and extrinsic work orientations as moderators of the effect of annual income on subjective well-being: A longitudinal study," *Personality and Social Psychology Bulletin* (Vol. 29, No. 6, June), pp. 737–746.

Manasse, Jr., Henri R. and Marilyn K. Speedie (2007), "Pharmacists, pharmaceuticals, and policy issues shaping the work force in pharmacy," *American Journal of Health-System Pharmacy* (Vol. 64, No. 12, June), pp. e30–e48.

Mark, Saralyn and Jhumka Gupta (2002), "Reentry into clinical practice: Challenges and strategies," *The Journal of the American Medical Association* (Vol. 288, No. 9, September 4), pp. 1091–1096.

Marsh, Kris, William A. Darity, Jr., Philip N. Cohen, *et al.* (2007), "The emerging Black middle class: Single and living alone," *Social Forces* (Vol. 86, No. 2, December), pp. 735–762.

Martin, Caren M. and Carla S. McSpadden (2008), "Dispelling the myths about medication therapy management services," *Consultant Pharmacist* (Vol. 23, No. 11, November), pp. 866–872, 875.

Martin, Kenneth E. (2000), "A rural-urban comparison of patterns of physician assistant practice," *Journal of the American Academy of Physician Assistants* (Vol. 13, No. 7, July), pp. 49–50, 56, 59, 63–66, 72.

Maslach, Christina, Wilmar B. Schaufeli, and Michael P. Leiter (2001), "Job burnout," *Annual Review of Psychology* (Vol. 52), pp. 397–422.

Mason, Patrick L. (2004), "Annual income, hourly wages, and identity among Mexican-Americans and other Latinos," *Industrial Relations* (Vol. 43, No. 4, October), pp. 817–834.

Masterson, Suzanne S., Kyle Lewis, Barry M. Goldman, *et al.* (2000), "Integrating justice and social exchange: The differing effects of fair procedures and treatment on work relationships," *Academy of Management Journal* (Vol. 43, No. 4, August), pp. 738–748.

Mathews, Audrey (1998), "Diversity: A principle of human resource management," *Public Personnel Management* (Vol. 27, No. 2, Summer), pp. 175–185.

Mathews, Deary B. (1992), "Learning styles of education majors: Are they similar to those of other students?" *SRATE Journal* (Vol. 1, No. 1, Winter), pp. 28–32.

Mau, Wei-Cheng and Amie Kopischke (2001), "Job search methods, job search outcomes, and job satisfaction of college students: A comparison of race and sex," *Journal of Employment Counseling* (Vol. 38, No. 3, September), pp. 141–149.

Maume, David J. and Rachel Sebastian (2007), "Racial composition of workgroups and job satisfaction among Whites," *The ANNALS of the American Academy of Political and Social Science* (Vol. 609, No. 1, January), pp. 85–103.

Mayer, Roger C. and James H. Davis (1999), "The effect of the performance appraisal system on trust for management: A field quasi-experiment," *Journal of Applied Psychology* (Vol. 84, No. 1, January), pp. 123–136.

Mayer, Roger C. and Mark B. Gavin (2005), "Trust in management and performance: Who minds the shop while the employees watch the boss?," *Academy of Management Journal* (Vol. 48, No. 5, October), pp. 874–888.

McCarthy, Robert and Kenneth W. Schafermeyer (eds.) (2007), *Introduction to Health Care Delivery: A Primer for Pharmacists* (Sandsbury, MA: Jones & Bartlett Publishers, Inc.).

McCleese, Carrie S. and Lillian T. Eby (2006), "Reactions to job content plateaus: Examining role ambiguity and hierarchical plateaus as moderators," *The Career Development Quarterly* (Vol. 55, No. 1, September), pp. 64–76.

McClelland, Katherine E. (1990), "The social management of ambition," *The Sociological Quarterly* (Vol. 31, No. 2, Summer), pp. 225–251.

McDuff, Elaine M. (2001), "The gender paradox in work satisfaction and the Protestant clergy," *Sociology of Religion* (Vol. 62, No. 1, Spring), pp. 1–21.

McElwain, Allyson K., Karen Korabik, and Hazel M. Rosin (2005), "An examination of gender differences in work-family conflict," *Canadian Journal of Behavioural Science* (Vol. 37, No. 4, October), pp. 283–298.

McHorney, Colleen A., John E. Ware, William Rogers, *et al.* (1992), "The validity and relative precision of MOS short- and long-form health status scales and Dartmouth COOP charts: Results from the Medical Outcomes Study," *Medical Care* (Vol. 30, No. 5 Supplemental, May), pp. MS253–MS265.

McHugh, Patrick P. (1999), "Pharmacists' attitudes regarding quality of worklife," *Journal of the American Pharmaceutical Association* (Vol. 39, No. 5, September/October), pp. 667–676.

McKinley, William, Carol M. Sanchez, and Allen G. Schick (1995), "Organizational downsizing: Constraining, cloning, learning," *Academy of Management Executive* (Vol. 9, No. 3, August), pp. 32–44.

McMurray, Julia E., Mark Linzer, Thomas R. Konrad, *et al.* (2000), "The work lives of women physicians: Results from the physician work life study," *Journal of General Internal Medicine* (Vol. 15, No. 6, June), pp. 372–380.

Mead, Holly, Lara Cartwright-Smith, Karen Jones, *et al.* (2008), "Racial and ethnic disparities in U.S. health care: A chartbook," http://www.commonwealthfund.org. Accessed December 20, 2009.

Meyer, Christine S. and Swati Mukerjee (2007), "Investigating dual labor market theory for women," *Eastern Economic Journal* (Vol. 33, No. 3, Summer), pp. 301–316.

Miles, Robert (1993), *Racism after "Race Relations"* (London: Routledge).

Milkovich, George M. and Jerry M. Newman (2004), *Compensation* (Burr Ridge, IL: Irwin McGraw-Hill).

Miller, Brian K., Matthew A. Rutherford, and Robert W. Kolodinsky (2008), "Perceptions of organizational politics: A meta-analysis of outcomes," *Journal of Business Psychology* (Vol. 22, No. 3, March), pp. 209–222.

Miller, Gerald J., Samuel J. Yeager, W. Bartley Hildreth, *et al.* (2005), "How financial managers deal with ethical stress," *Public Administration Review* (Vol. 65, No. 3, May/June), pp. 301-312.

Miller, Jeremy (2006), "Beyond cold cash—Compensation is more than just a paycheque. If you want to keep your employees happy, add a little psychic income," *CA Magazine* (Vol. 139, No. 4, May), pp. 47–48.

Mishra, Aneil K. and Gretchen M. Spreitzer (1998), "Explaining how survivors respond to downsizing: The role of trust, empowerment, justice, and work redesign," *Academy of Management Review* (Vol. 23, No. 3, July), pp. 567–588.

Mitchell, Janet B. (1984), "Why do women physicians work fewer hours than men physicians?," *Inquiry* (Vol. 21, No. 4, Winter), pp. 361–368.

Mitchell, Terence R. and Thomas W. Lee (2001), "The unfolding model of voluntary turnover and job embeddedness: Foundations for a comprehensive theory of attachment," *Research in Organizational Behavior* (Vol. 23), pp. 189–246.

Mitra, Aparna and Pooja Singh (2006), "Human capital attainment and female labor force participation—The Kerala puzzle," *Journal of Economic Issues* (Vol. XL, No. 3, September), pp. 779–798.

Moguerou, Philippe (2002), "Job satisfaction among US Ph.D. graduates: The effects of gender and employment sector," Econ WPA Labor and Demography Paper 0204002.

Mor-Barak, Michàl E., Jan A. Nissly, and Amy Levin (2001), "Antecedents to retention and turnover among child welfare, social work, and other human service employees: What can we learn from past research? A review of metanalysis," *Social Service Review* (Vol. 75, No. 4, December), pp. 625–661.

Mosisa, Abraham and Steven Hipple (2006), "Trends in labor force participation in the United States," *Monthly Labor Review* (Vol. 129, No. 10, October), pp. 35–57.

Mott, David A. (2000), "Pharmacist job turnover, length of service, and reasons for leaving, 1983-1997," *American Journal of Health-System Pharmacy* (Vol. 57, No. 10, May), pp. 975–984.

Mott, David A. (2001), "Use of labor economic theory to examine hours worked by male and female pharmacists," *Pharmaceutical Research* (Vol. 18, No. 2, February), pp. 224–233.

Mott, David A. and David H. Kreling (1994), "An internal rate of return approach to investigate pharmacist supply in the United States," *Health Economics* (Vol. 3, No. 6, November–December), pp. 373–384.

Mott, David A., David H. Kreling, and Glen G. Cain (1995), "The relationship between internal rates of return, pharmacist supply and applications and admissions: A case study in Wisconsin," *American Journal of Pharmaceutical Education* (Vol. 59, No. 1, Spring), pp. 59–66.

Mott, David A., William R. Doucette, Caroline A. Gaither, *et al.* (2002), "A ten-year trend analysis of pharmacist participation in the workforce," *American Journal of Pharmaceutical Education* (Vol. 66, No. 3, Fall), pp. 223–233.

Mott, David A., William R. Doucette, Caroline A. Gaither, *et al.* (2004), "Pharmacists' attitudes toward worklife: Results from a national survey of pharmacists," *Journal of the American Pharmacists Association* (Vol. 44, No. 3, May/June), pp. 326–336.

Mott, David A., William R. Doucette, Caroline A. Gaither, *et al.* (2006), "Pharmacist participation in the workforce: 1990, 2000, and 2004," *Journal of the American Pharmacists Association* (Vol. 46, No. 3, May/June), pp. 322–330.

Muchinsky, Paul M. and Carlyn J. Monahan (1987), "What is person-environment congruence? Supplementary versus complementary models of fit," *Journal of Vocational Behavior* (Vol. 31, No. 3, December), pp. 268–277.

Mueller, Gerrit and Erik Plug (2006), "Estimating the effect of personality on male and female earnings," *Industrial and Labor Relations Review* (Vol. 60, No. 1, October), pp. 3–22.

Muhammad, Dedrick, Attieno Davis, Meizhu Lui, *et al.* (2004), *The State of the Dream 2004: Enduring Disparities in Black and White* (Boston: United for a Fair Economy).

Murphy, Bren O. and Ted Zorn (1995), "Gendered interaction in professional relationships." In *Gendered Relationships: A Reader,* edited by Julia T. Wood (Mountain View, CA: Mayfield Publishing), pp. 213–232.

Napari, Sami (2006), "The early career gender wage gap," The London School of Economics and Political Science, Centre for Economic Performance Discussion Paper No. 738.

National Academy of Sciences, National Academy of Engineering, and Institute of Medicine of the National Academies (2007), *Beyond Bias and Barriers: Fulfilling the Potential of Women in Academic Science and Engineering* (Washington, D.C.: The National Academies Press).

National Center for Chronic Disease Prevention and Health Promotion (2007), "Chronic disease indicator: Tobacco and alcohol," http://apps.nccd.cdc.gov/cdi/Default.aspx. Accessed December 11, 2009.

National Center for Health Statistics (2009), "Health, United States, 2008 with chartbook," http://www.cdc.gov/nchs/data/hus/hus08.pdf#highlights. Accessed November 14, 2009.

Neal, Andrew and Mark A. Griffin (1999), "Developing a model of individual performance for human resource management," *Asia Pacific Journal of Human Resources* (Vol. 37, No. 2, August), pp. 44–59.

Neal, Andrew, Michael A. West, and Malcolm G. Patterson (2005), "Do organizational climate and competitive strategy moderate the relationship between human resource management and productivity?," *Journal of Management* (Vol. 31, No. 4, August), pp. 492–512.

Necowitz, Lawrence B. and Mary Roznowski (1994), "Negative affectivity and job satisfaction: Cognitive processes underlying the relationship and effects of employee behaviors," *Journal of Vocational Behavior* (Vol. 45, No. 3, December), pp. 270–294.

Nelson, Debra L. and Ronald J. Burke (2000), "Women executives: Health, stress, and success," *The Academy of Management Executive* (Vol. 14, No. 2, May), pp. 107–121.

Newstrom, John, Don Gardner, and Jon Pierce (1999), "A neglected supervisory role: Building self-esteem at work," *SuperVision* (Vol. 60, No. 2, February), pp. 9–12.

Ng, Yew-Kwang (1997), "A case for happyness, cardinalism, and interpersonal comparability," *The Economic Journal* (Vol. 107, No. 445, November), pp. 1848–1858.

Nguyen, Anh, Getinet Haile, and Jim Taylor (2005), "Ethnic and gender differences in intergenerational mobility: A study of 26-year-olds in the USA," *Scottish Journal of Political Economy* (Vol. 52, No. 4, September), pp. 544–564.

Nguyen, Bao Q. (2008), "Tomorrow's workforce: The needs for immigrant workers and strategies to retain them," *Public Personnel Management* (Vol. 37, No. 2, Summer), pp. 175–184.

Niederle, Muriel and Lise Vesterlund (2005), "Do women shy away from competition? Do men compete too much?," National Bureau of Economic Research, Working Paper 11,474.

No, Sung C., Donald Andrews, and Ashagre Yigletu (2007), "Dynamic analysis of income and independence effect of African American female labor force participation on divorce," *Atlantic Economic Journal* (Vol. 35, No. 2, June), pp. 159–171.

Nock, Steven L. (2001), "The marriages of equally dependent spouses," *Journal of Family Issues* (Vol. 22, No. 6, September), pp. 755–775.

Nolen-Hoeksema, Susan, Judith Larson, and Carla Grayson (1999), "Explaining the gender difference in depressive symptoms," *Journal of Personality and Social Psychology* (Vol. 77, No. 5, November), pp. 1061–1072.

North, Mark A. and Kenneth W. Kirk (1990), "The pharmacy supervisor and the employee pharmacist's job satisfaction," *American Pharmacy* (Vol. NS 30, No. 5, May), pp. 49–52.

O'Connell, Mary B., Eli J. Korner, Nathaniel Rickles, *et al.* (2007), "Cultural competence in health care and its implications for pharmacy, Part 1: Overview of key concepts in multicultural health care," *Pharmacotherapy* (Vol. 27, No. 7, July), pp. 1062–1079.

O'Connell, Michael L. (1991), "Toward an understanding of the psychology of careers," Harvard University, Graduate School of Education.

Oh, Yongtae, Jeffrey S. McCombs, Rebecca A. Chang, *et al.* (2002), "Pharmacist time requirements for counseling in an outpatient pharmacy," *American Journal of Health-System Pharmacy* (Vol. 59, No. 23, December), pp. 2346–2355.

O'Halloran, Patrick L. (2003), *Gender and Racial Differences: On-the-Job Training and Payment Schemes*, University of Wisconsin-Milwaukee, Ph.D. Dissertation.

Okunade, Albert A. (2006), "Determinants of full-time versus part-time job vacancies in US pharmacies," *Journal of Pharmaceutical Finance, Economics & Policy* (Vol. 15, No. 1), pp. 65–77.

Oldham, Greg R., Anne Cummings, Leann J. Mischel, *et al.* (1995), "Listen while you work? Quasi-experimental relations between personal-stereo headset use and employee work responses," *Journal of Applied Psychology* (Vol. 80, No. 5, September), pp. 547–564.

Olson, David S. and Kenneth A. Lawson (1996), "Relationship between hospital pharmacists' job satisfaction and involvement in clinical activities," *American Journal of Health-System Pharmacy* (Vol. 53, No. 2, February), pp. 281–284.

O'Neill, Bonnie S. and Mark A. Mone (1998), "Investigating equity sensitivity as a moderator of relations between self-efficacy and workplace attitudes," *Journal of Applied Psychology* (Vol. 83, No. 5, September), pp. 805–816.

O'Neill, June E. and Dave M. O'Neill (2005), "What do wage differentials tell us about labor market discrimination?," National Bureau of Economic Research, Working Paper 11,240.

Ong, Paul and R. Varisa Patraporn (2000), "Asian Americans and wealth." In *Wealth Accumulation and Communities of Color in the United States*, edited by Jessica G. Nembhard and Ngina S. Chiteji (Ann Arbor: University of Michigan Press), pp. 173–189.

Orrenius, Pia M. and Madeline Zavodny (2007), "The minimum wage and Latino workers," Federal Reserve Bank of Dallas, Working Paper 0708.

Oshagbemi, Titus (1999), "Overall job satisfaction: How good are single- versus multiple-item measures?," *Journal of Managerial Psychology* (Vol. 14, No. 5, July), pp. 388–403.

Otto, Lauren A. and Cindy Gurbey (2006), "Ethnic diversity in the nurse workforce: A literature review," *Journal of the New York State Nurses Association* (Vol. 37, No. 2, Fall-Winter), pp. 16–21.

Park, Shelly M. (1996), "Research, teaching, and service: Why shouldn't women's work count?," *Journal of Higher Education* (Vol. 67, No. 1, January/February), pp. 46–84.

Patton, Wendy and Richard Goddard (2003), "Psychological distress and burnout in Australian employment service workers: Two years on," *Journal of Employment Counseling* (Vol. 40, No. 1, March), pp. 2–16.

Pedersen, Craig A., Philip J. Schneider, and John P. Santell (2001), "ASHP national survey of pharmacy practice in hospital settings: Prescribing and transcribing 2001," *American Journal of Health-System Pharmacy* (Vol. 58, No. 23, December 1), pp. 2251–2266.

Penna, Richard P. (1990), "Pharmaceutical care-pharmacy's mission for the 1990s," *American Journal of Hospital Pharmacy* (Vol. 47, No. 3, March), pp. 543–549.

Perrewe, Pamela L. and Wayne A. Hochwarter (2001), "Can we really have it all? The attainment of work and family values," *Current Directions in Psychological Science* (Vol. 10, No. 1, February), pp. 29–33.

Perrone, Kristin M., L. Kay Webb, and Rachel H. Blalock (2005), "The effects of role congruence and role conflict on work, marital, and life satisfaction," *Journal of Career Development* (Vol. 31, No. 4, Summer), pp. 225–238.

Perry, Ronald W. and Lawrence D. Mankin (2007), "Organizational trust, trust in the chief executive and work satisfaction," *Public Personnel Management* (Vol. 36, No. 2, Summer), pp. 165–179.

Peterson, Dane K. (2002), "Deviant workplace behavior and the organization's ethical climate," *Journal of Business and Psychology* (Vol. 17, No. 1, Fall), pp. 47–61.

Pettit, Becky and Jennifer Hook (2005), "The structure of women's employment in comparative perspective," *Social Forces* (Vol. 84, No. 2, December), pp. 779–801.

Petty, Gregory C., Ernest W. Brewer, and Beth Brown (2005), "Job satisfaction among employees of a youth development organization," *Child and Youth Care Forum* (Vol. 34, No. 1, February), pp. 57–73.

Phelan, Jo (1994), "The paradox of the contented female worker: An assessment of alternative explanations," *Social Psychology Quarterly* (Vol. 57, No. 2, June), pp. 95–107.

Phillips, Susan D. and Anne R. Imhoff (1997), "Women and career development: A decade of research," *Annual Review of Psychology* (Vol. 48), pp. 31–60.

Pitts, David (2009), "Diversity management, job satisfaction, and performance: Evidence *from U.S. federal agencies," Public Administration Review* (Vol. 69, No. 2, March/April), pp. 328–338.

Poeschl, Gabrielle (2000), "Trabalho doméstico e poder familiar: Práticas, normas, e ideais," *Análise Social* (Vol. 35, No. 156), pp. 695–719.

Poeschl, Gabrielle (2003), "Représentations des différences entre les sexes et jeux de pouvoir," *Nouvelle Revue de Psychologie Sociale* (Vol. 2, No. 1), pp. 77–86.

Poeschl, Gabrielle, Cláudia Múrias, Eleonora Costa, *et al.* (2001/2002), "Representações das tarefas familiares," *Cadernos de Consulta Psicológica* (No. 17/18), pp. 161–170.

Poeschl, Gabrielle, Isabel Pinto, Cláudia Múrias, *et al.* (2006), "Representations of family practices, belief in sex differences, and sexism," *Sex Roles* (Vol. 55, No. 1/2, July), pp. 111-121.

Pogrebin, Mark, Mary Dodge, and Harold Chatman (2000), "Reflections of African-American women on their careers in urban policing: Their experiences of racial and sexual discrimination," *International Journal of the Sociology of Law* (Vol. 28, No. 4, December), pp. 311–326.

Posey, L. Michael (1997), "Productivity in consultant pharmacy: New ideas taking hold," *The Consultant Pharmacist* (Vol. 12, No. 3, March), pp. 231–245.

Posey, L. Michael (2003), *Pharmacy: An Introduction to the Profession* (Washington, D.C.: American Pharmacists Association).

Potuchek, Jean L. (1997), *Who Supports the Family? Gender and Breadwinning in Dual-Earner Marriages* (Palo Alto, CA: Stanford University Press).

Presser, Harriet B. (2003), "Race-ethnic and gender differences in nonstandard work shifts," *Work and Occupations* (Vol. 30, No. 4, November), pp. 412–439.

Preston, Anne E. (2004), *Leaving Science: Occupational Exit from Scientific Careers* (New York: Russell Sage Foundation).

Price, Cindy J. and Shaun S. Wulff (2005), "Does sex make a difference? Job satisfaction of television network news correspondents," *Women's Studies in Communication* (Vol. 28, No. 2, Fall), pp. 207-234.

Prizzia, Rose (2005), "An international perspective of privatization and women workers," *Journal of International Women's Studies* (Vol. 7, No. 1, November), pp. 55–68.

Queneau, Hervé (2006), "Changes in occupational segregation by gender and race-ethnicity in health care: Implications for policy and union practice," *Labor Studies Journal* (Vol. 31, No. 1, Spring), pp. 71–90.

Quesenberry, Jeria L., Eileen M. Trauth, and Allison J. Morgan (2006), "Understanding the 'mommy tracks': A framework for analyzing work-family balance in the IT workforce," *Information Resources Management Journal* (Vol. 19, No. 2, April-June), pp. 37–53.

Quiñones, Ana C. and Holly L. Mason (2000), "Characterizing pharmacy part-time practice," *Journal of the American Pharmaceutical Association* (Vol. 40, No. 1, January/February), pp. 17–25.

Randall, Christina S. and Charles W. Mueller (1995), "Extensions of justice theory: Justice evaluations and employees' reactions in a natural setting," *Social Psychology Quarterly* (Vol. 58, No. 3, September), pp. 178–194.

Rath, Tom and Donald O. Clifton (2004), *How Full Is Your Bucket? Positive Strategies for Work and Life* (New York: Gallup Press).

Rayle, Andrea D. (2006), "Do school counselors matter? Mattering as a moderator between job stress and job satisfaction," *Professional School Counseling* (Vol. 9, No. 3, February), pp. 206–215.

Read, Jen'nan G. and Philip N. Cohen (2007), "One size fits all? Explaining U.S.-born and immigrant women's employment across 12 ethnic groups," *Social Forces* (Vol. 85, No. 4, June), pp. 1713–1734.

Rehm, Jergun, Gerhard Gmel, Christopher T. Sempos, *et al.* (2003), "Alcohol-related morbidity and mortality," *Alcohol Research and Health* (Vol. 27, No. 1), pp. 39–51.

Reimers, Cordelia W. (2000), "Compensation for the Latino worker." In *Moving Up the Economic Ladder: Latino Workers and the Nation's Future Prosperity. State of Hispanic America, 1999,* edited by Sonia M. Perez (Washington, D.C.: National Council of La Raza), pp. 125–161.

"Report of the ASHP *Ad Hoc* Committee on Ethnic Diversity and Cultural Competency" (2005), *American Journal of Health-System Pharmacy* (Vol. 62, No. 18, September 15), pp. 1924–1930.

"Report of the ASHP Task Force on Pharmacy's Changing Demographics" (2007), *American Journal of Health-System Pharmacy* (Vol. 64, No. 12, June 15), pp. 1311–1319.

Reyes, Jessica W. (2007), "Gender gaps in income and productivity of obstetricians and gynecologists," *Obstetrics and Gynecology* (Vol. 109, No. 5, May), pp. 1031–1039.

Reynolds, Jeremy (2003), "You can't always get the hours you want: Mismatches between actual and preferred work hours in the U.S.," *Social Forces* (Vol. 81, No. 4, June), pp. 1171–1199.

Rezler, Agnes G., Robert G. Mrtek, and Henri R. Manasse, Jr. (1976), "Linking career choice to personality types: A preliminary analysis of pharmacy students," *American Journal of Pharmaceutical Education* (Vol. 41, No. 2, Summer), pp. 121–128.

Rhoades, Linda and Robert Eisenberger (2002), "Perceived organizational support: A review of the literature," *Journal of Applied Psychology* (Vol. 87, No. 4, July), pp. 698–714.

Rigby, D. (2002), "Pondering before downsizing—The disadvantages could be more than advantages when the business is losing," *Harvard Business Review Chinese Edition* (Vol. 8), pp. 18–20.

Riggins, Jennifer L. and Brandi H. Plowman (2000), "Pharmacist employment and satisfaction trends at Eli Lilly and Company," *Drug Information Journal* (Vol. 34, No. 4, October–December), pp. 1223–1229.

Rix, Sara E. (2006), "The aging of the American workforce," *Chicago-Kent Law Review* (Vol. 81, No. 2, September), pp. 593–617.

Robbins, Stephen P. (2002), *Organizational Behavior* (Upper Saddle River, NJ: Prentice-Hall).

Robinson, Bryan K. and Erica Hunter (2008), "Is mom still doing it all? Reexamining depictions of family work in popular advertising," *Journal of Family Issues* (Vol. 29, No. 4, April), pp. 465–486.

Robson, Karen and Jean E. Wallace (2001), "Gender inequalities in earnings: A study of Canadian lawyers," *The Canadian Review of Sociology and Anthropology* (Vol. 38, No. 1, February), pp. 75–95.

Rogers, Stacy J. and Paul R. Amato (2000), "Have changes in gender relations affected marital quality?," *Social Forces* (Vol. 79, No. 2, December), pp. 731–753.

Rose, Karol (1998), "Work/life flexibility: A key to maximizing productivity," *Compensation and Benefits Management* (Vol. 14, No. 4, Autumn), pp. 27–32.

Rosser, Vicki J. (2004), "Faculty members' intentions to leave: A national study on their worklife and satisfaction," *Research in Higher Education* (Vol. 45, No. 3, May), pp. 285–309.

Rosser, Vicki J. (2005), "Measuring the change in faculty perceptions over time: An examination of their worklife and satisfaction," *Research in Higher Education* (Vol. 46, No. 1, February), pp. 81–107.

Rowe, Frank A., Mark L. Waters, Mathew P. Thompson, *et al.* (1992), "Can personality-type instruments profile majors in management programs?" *Journal of Education for Business* (Vol. 68, No. 1, November–December), pp. 10–14.

Royster, Deirdre A. (2007), "What happens to potential discouraged? Masculinity norms and the contrasting institutional and labor market experiences of less affluent Black and White men," *The ANNALS of the American Academy of Political and Social Science* (Vol. 609, No. 1, January), pp. 153–180.

Ruhm, Christopher J. (2004), "Parental employment and child cognitive development," *Journal of Human Resources* (Vol. 39, No. 1, Winter), pp. 155–192.

Saltzstein, Alan L., Yuan Ting, and Grace H. Saltzstein (2001), "Work-family balance and job satisfaction: The impact of family-friendly policies on attitudes of federal government employees," *Public Administration Review* (Vol. 61, No. 4, July/August), pp. 452–467.

Schappe, Stephen P. (1998), "The influence of job satisfaction, organizational commitment, and fairness perceptions on organizational citizenship behavior," *The Journal of Psychology* (Vol. 132, No. 3, May), pp. 277–290.

Schommer, Jon C., Craig A. Pedersen, William R. Doucette, *et al.* (2002), "Community pharmacists' work activities in the United States during 2000," *Journal of the American Pharmaceutical Association* (Vol. 42, No. 3, May/June), pp. 399–406.

Schommer, Jon C., Craig A. Pedersen, Caroline A. Gaither, *et al.* (2006), "Pharmacists' desired and actual times in work activities: Evidence of gaps from the 2004 National Pharmacist Workforce Study," *Journal of the American Pharmacists Association* (Vol. 46, No. 3, May/June), pp. 340–347.

Schroder, Ralph (2008a), "Job satisfaction of employees at a Christian university," *Journal of Research on Christian Education* (Vol. 17, No. 2, July/December), pp. 225–246.

Schroder, Ralph (2008b), "Predictors of organizational commitment for faculty and administrators of a private Christian university," *Journal of Research on Christian Education* (Vol. 17, No. 1, January/June), pp. 81–97.

Seifert, Tricia A. and Paul D. Umbach (2008), "The effects of faculty demographic characteristics and disciplinary context on dimensions of job satisfaction," *Research in Higher Education* (Vol. 49, No. 4, June), pp. 357–381.

Semykina, Anastasia and Susan J. Linz (2007), "Gender differences in personality and earnings: Evidence from Russia," *Journal of Economic Psychology* (Vol. 28, No. 3, June), pp. 387–410.

Shah, Priti P. (2000), "Network destruction: The structural implications of downsizing," *Academy of Management Journal* (Vol. 43, No. 1, February), pp. 101–112.

Shauman, Kimberlee A. and Mary C. Noonan (2007), "Family migration and labor force outcomes: Sex differences in occupational context," *Social Forces* (Vol. 85, No. 4, June), pp. 1735–1764.

Sheran, Michelle (2007), "The career and family choices of women: A dynamic analysis of labor force participation, schooling, marriage, and fertility decisions," *Review of Economic Dynamics* (Vol. 10, No. 3, July), pp. 367–399.

Shields, Mark C. and Margaux T. Shields (2003), "Working with Generation X physicians," *Physician Executive* (Vol. 29, No. 6, November–December), pp. 14–18.

Shields, Michael A. and Melanie Ward (2001), "Improving nurse retention in the National Health Service in England: The impact of job satisfaction on intentions to quit," *Journal of Health Economics* (Vol. 20, No. 5, September), pp. 677–701.

Shih, Ya-Chen T. (2000), "Trends in full-time pharmacists' labor market characteristics," *Journal of the American Pharmaceutical Association* (Vol. 40, No. 1, January–February), pp. 26–35.

Sicherman, Nachum (1996), "Gender differences in departures from a large firm," *Industrial and Labor Relations Review* (Vol. 49, No. 3, April), pp. 484–505.

Sinacore, Ada L. and F. Özge Akçali (2000), "Men in families: Job satisfaction and self-esteem," *Journal of Career Development* (Vol. 27, No. 1, Fall), pp. 1-13.

Sivakumar, Alagumalai, David D. Curtis, and Njora Hungi (2005), *Applied Rasch Measurement: A Book of Exemplars* (Dordrecht, the Netherlands: Springer-Kluwer).

Sloane, Peter J. and H. Williams (2000), "Job satisfaction, comparison earnings and gender," *Labour* (Vol. 14, No. 3, September), pp. 473–502.

Smedley, Brian D., Adrienne Y. Stith, and Alan R. Nelson (eds.) (2003), *Unequal Treatment: Confronting Racial and Ethnic Disparities in Health Care* (Washington, D.C.: The National Academies Press).

Smedley, Brian D., Adrienne S. Butler, and Lonnie R. Bristow (eds.) (2004), *In the Nation's Compelling Interest: Ensuring Diversity in the Health Care Workforce* (Washington, D.C.: The National Academies Press).

Smerek, Ryan E. and Marvin Peterson (2007), "Examining Herzberg's theory: Improving job satisfaction among non-academic employees at a university," *Research in Higher Education* (Vol. 48, No. 2, March), pp. 229–250.

Smith, Ryan A. and James R. Elliott (2002), "Does ethnic concentration influence employees' access to authority? An examination of contemporary urban labor markets," *Social Forces* (Vol. 81, No. 1, September), pp. 255–279.

Smith, Stanley K. and Stefan Rayer (2009), "Population projections by age, sex, race, and Hispanic origin for Florida and its counties, 2008-2030," Bureau of Economic and Business Research, Florida Population Studies, Vol. 42, Bulletin 14.

Smith, Steven A., Stephen M. Crow, and Sandra J. Hartman (2007), "Attrition in nursing among Black and White nurses," *Journal of Nursing Management* (Vol. 15, No. 3, April), pp. 357–366.

Smola, Karen W. and Charlotte D. Sutton (2002), "Generational differences: Revisiting the generational work values for the new millenium," *Journal of Organizational Behavior* (Vol. 23, No. 4, June), pp. 363–382.

Smucker, Michael K., Warren A. Whisenant, and Paul M. Pedersen (2003), "An investigation of job satisfaction and female sports journalists," *Sex Roles* (Vol. 49, No. 7/8, October), pp. 401–407.

Sochalski, Julie (2004), "Building a home healthcare workforce to meet the quality imperative," *Journal of Health Care Quality* (Vol. 26, No. 3, May/June), pp. 19–23.

Sonnedecker, Glenn (1976), *Kremers and Urdang's History of Pharmacy* (Philadelphia: J. B. Lippincott Company).

Sørensen, Jesper B. (2007), "Organizational diversity, labor markets, and wage inequality," *The American Behavioral Scientist* (Vol. 50, No. 5, January), pp. 659–676.

Sousa-Poza, Alfonso and Andrés A. Sousa-Poza (2000a), "Taking another look at the gender/job-satisfaction paradox," *KYKLOS* (Vol. 53, Fasc. 2, May), pp. 135–152.

Sousa-Poza, Alfonso and Andrés A. Sousa-Poza (2000b), "Well-being at work: A cross-national analysis of the levels and determinants of job satisfaction," *Journal of Socio-Economics* (Vol. 29, No. 6, November), pp. 517–538.

Sousa-Poza, Alfonso and Andrés A. Sousa-Poza (2003), "Gender differences in job satisfaction in Great Britain, 1991-2000: Permanent or transitory?," *Applied Economics Letters* (Vol. 10, No. 11, September), pp. 691–694.

Southard, Glenn and Jim Lewis (2004), "Building a workplace that recognizes generational diversity," *Public Management* (Vol. 86, No. 3, April), pp. 8–12.

Spalter-Roth, Roberta and William Erskine (2005), "Beyond the fear factor: Work/family policies in academia—Resources or rewards?," *Change* (Vol. 37, No. 6, November-December), pp.18–25.

Spector, Paul E. (1997), *Job Satisfaction: Application, Assessment, Cause, and Consequences* (Thousand Oaks, CA: Sage Publications, Inc.).

Spector, Paul E., Dieter Zapf, Peter Y. Chen, *et al.* (2000), "Why negative affectivity should not be controlled in job stress research: Don't throw out the baby with the bath water," *Journal of Organizational Behavior* (Vol. 21, No. 1, February), pp. 79–95.

Spence Laschinger, Heather K., Joan Almost, and Donnalene Tuer-Hodes (2003), "Workplace empowerment and magnet hospital characteristics: Making the link," *Journal of Nursing Administration* (Vol. 33, No. 7/8, July/August), pp. 410–422.

Srinivas, Sumati (2007), "Social attitudes and the gender pay gap in the USA in recent years," *International Journal of Social Economics* (Vol. 34, No. 4, April), pp. 268–275.

Stack, Laura (2003), "Employees behaving badly: How managers can recognize and combat employee 'desk rage'—Management tools," *HR Magazine* (Vol. 48, No. 10, October), pp. 111–116.

Stephan, Paula E. and Sharon G. Levin (2005), "Leaving careers in IT: Gender differences in retention," *Journal of Technology Transfer* (Vol. 30, No. 4, October), pp. 383–396.

Stevenson, William B. and Mary C. Gilly (1991), "Information processing and problem solving: The migration of problems through formal positions and networks of ties," *Academy of Management Journal* (Vol. 34, No. 4, December), pp. 918–928.

Stewart, Karl L. and Lisa A. Felicetti (1992), "Learning styles of marketing majors," *Educational Research Quarterly* (Vol. 15, No. 2, June), pp. 15–23.

Stipek, Deborah J. (1984), "Sex differences in children's attributions for success and failure on math and spelling tests," *Sex Roles* (Vol. 11, No. 11/12, December), pp. 969–981.

Stohs, Joanne H. (1995), "Predictors of conflict over the household division of labor among women employed full-time," *Sex Roles* (Vol. 33, No. 3/4, August), pp. 257–275.

Strayhorn, Terrell L. (2008), "Influences on labor market outcomes of African American college graduates: A national study," *The Journal of Higher Education* (Vol. 79, No. 1, January/February), pp. 28–57.

Sweeney, Megan M. and Julie A. Phillips (2004), "Understanding racial differences in marital disruption: Recent trends and explanations," *Journal of Marriage and Family* (Vol. 66, No. 3, August), pp. 639–650.

Tan, Hwee H. and Augustine K. Lim (2009), "Trust in coworkers and trust in organizations," *The Journal of Psychology* (Vol. 143, No. 1, January), pp. 45–66.

Tanner, Julia, Rhonda Cockerill, Jan Barnsley, *et al.* (1999), "Gender and income in pharmacy: Human capital and gender stratification theories revisited," *British Journal of Sociology* (Vol. 50, No. 1, March), pp. 97–117.

Tansey, Timothy N., Molly K. Tschopp, Nathalie Mizelle, *et al.* (2004), "Work-related stress and the demand-control-support framework: Implications for the P x E fit model," *Journal of Rehabilitation* (Vol. 70, No. 3, July–September), pp. 34–41.

Taylor, Elizabeth A., Helen Madill, and Donald Macnab (1990), "Values, salience, and job satisfaction: Male and female occupational therapists' responses," *Occupational Therapy Journal of Research* (Vol. 10, No. 3, May–June), pp. 131–143.

Tebaldi, Edinaldo and Bruce Elmslie (2006), "Sexual orientation and labor supply," *Applied Economics* (Vol. 38, No. 5, March 20), pp. 549–562.

Teeter, David S. (2004), "Part-time pharmacists—A growing phenomenon," *U.S. Pharmacist* (Vol. 29, No. 6, June 15), pp. 77–78, 81–83.

Testa, Mark R. (2001), "Organizational commitment, job satisfaction, and effort in the service environment," *The Journal of Psychology* (Vol. 135, No. 2, March), pp. 226–236.

Tett, Robert P. and Patrick J. Murphy (2002), "Personality and situations in co-worker preference: Similarity and complementarity in worker compatibility," *Journal of Business and Psychology* (Vol. 17, No. 2, Winter), pp. 223–243.

Theodossiou, Ioannis and Efi Vasileiou (2007), "Making the risk of job loss a way of life: Does it affect job satisfaction?," *Research in Economics* (Vol. 61, No. 2, June), pp. 71–83.

Thomas, David C. and Kevin Au (2002), "The effect of cultural differences on behavioral responses to low job satisfaction," *Journal of International Business Studies* (Vol. 33, No. 2, Second Quarter), pp. 309–326.

Thomas, Li-Ping T. and Medha Talpade (1999), "Sex differences in satisfaction with pay and co-workers: Faculty and staff at a public institution of higher education," *Public Personnel Management* (Vol. 28, No. 3, Fall), pp. 345–349.

Thompson, Cheryl A. (2009), "Supply of pharmacists in work force has improved, government says," *American Journal of Health-System Pharmacy* (Vol. 66, No. 8, April 15), pp. 701–702.

Tocher, Neil, Hubert S. Feild, and William F. Giles (2006), "Valuations of compensation and benefit items by new entrants into the professional workforce: Do men and women differ?," *Journal of Employment Counseling* (Vol. 43, No. 2, June), pp. 84–96.

Toossi, Mitra (2007), "Labor force projections to 2016: More workers in their golden years," *Monthly Labor Review* (Vol. 130, No. 11, November), pp. 33–52.

Townsend, Barbara K. and Nancy LaPaglia (2000), "The community college as a workplace for women faculty members," *Initiatives* (Vol. 59, No. 4, Summer).

Trower, Cathy A. and Richard P. Chait (2002), "Faculty diversity: Too little for too long," *Harvard Magazine* (Vol. 104, No. 4, March–April), pp. 33–37, 98.

Trust for America's Health (2009), "F as in fat: How obesity policies are failing in America," http://www.rwjf.org/pr/product.jsp?id=45050. Accessed December 10, 2009.

Tsai, Philip C., Yu-Fang Chen, Liang-Chih Huang, *et al.* (2007), "A study on motivating employees' learning commitment in the post-downsizing era: Job satisfaction perspective," *Journal of World Business* (Vol. 42, No. 2, June), pp. 157–169.

Tsuya, Noriko O. and Larry L. Bumpass (2004), "Gender and housework." In *Marriage, Work and Family Life in Comparative Perspective: Japan, South Korea and the United States* (Honolulu: University of Hawaii Press), pp. 114–133.

Turner, Caroline S. (2002), "Women of color in academe: Living with multiple marginality," *Journal of Higher Education* (Vol. 73, No. 1, January/February), pp. 74–93.

Turner, Joanna, Michael Boudreaux, and Victoria Lynch (2009), "U.S. Census Bureau, Health insurance coverage paper: 2008 American Community Survey," http://www.census.gov/hhes/www/hlthins/acs08paper/index.html. Accessed September 25, 2009.

Ukens, Carol (2004), "Pharmacists stressed but satisfied with jobs, study finds," *Drug Topics* (Vol. 148, No. 12, June 21), pp. 42–43.

Ukens, Carol (2007), "Pay dirt: Pharmacist salaries are still climbing, but at a slower rate. Our exclusive survey shows who gets top dollar," *Drug Topics* (Vol. 151, No. 5, March 5), pp. 38–42.

U.S. Bureau of Health Professions, Department of Health and Human Services (2000), "The pharmacist workforce: A study of the supply and demand for pharmacists," http://bhpr.hrsa.gov/healthworforce/reports/pharmacist.htm. Accessed April 21, 2009.

U.S. Bureau of Health Professions, Department of Health and Human Services (2008), "The adequacy of pharmacy supply: 2004-2030," ftp://ftp.hrsa.gov/bhpr/workforce/pharmacy.pdf. Accessed May 13, 2009.

U.S. Bureau of Labor Statistics, Department of Labor (2009), "Ocupational outlook handbook, 2008-09 Edition," http://www.bls.gov/oco/. Accessed January 16, 2009.

U.S. Census Bureau, American Fact Finder (2000), "Census 2000 summary file 1: Sex by age," http://factfinder.census.gov/servlet/DTTable?_bm=y&-state=dt&-ds_name=DEC_2000_SF1_U_P012&-redoLog=false&-_caller=geoselect&-geo_id=NBSP&-format+&-_lang=en. Accessed May 13, 2009.

U.S. Census Bureau, Population Division (2005), "Interim state population projections, 2005," http://www.census.gov/population/projections/SummaryTabB1.pdf. Accessed January 28, 2009.

U.S. Census Bureau, Population Division (2008a), "Annual estimates of the population of metropolitan and micropolitan statistical areas: April 1, 2000 to July 1, 2008 (CBSA-EST2008-01)," http://www.census.gov/popest/metro/metro.html. Accessed November 10, 2009.

U.S. Census Bureau, Population Division (2008b), "Projections of the population by selected age groups and sex for the United States: 2010 to 2050," http://www.census.gov/population/summary tables.html. Accessed January 30, 2009.

U.S. Census Bureau, Population Estimates (2008c), "Estimates of the resident population by selected age group for the United States, states, and Puerto Rico: July 1, 2008 (SC-EST2008-01)," http://www.census.gov/popest/states/asrh/SC-EST2008-01.html. Accessed November 7, 2009.

U.S. Census Bureau (2009a), "Fact finder," http://www.factfinder.census.gov/home/saff/main.html?_lang=en. Accessed November 7, 2009.

U.S. Census Bureau (2009b), "Fact finder: American Community Survey 2008 data profile," http://www.factfinder.census.gov/servlet/DatasetMainPageServlet?_program=ACS&submenuId=data sets_2&_lang=en. Accessed November 9, 2009.

U.S. Census Bureau (2009c), "Projections of the population by selected age groups and sex for the United States: 2010 to 2050," http://www.census.gov/population/www/projections/projectionsage sex.html. Accessed November 7, 2009.

U.S. Census Bureau (2009d), "2008 population estimates program," http://www.factfinder.census.gov/home/en/official_estimates_2008.html. Accessed September 25, 2009.

U.S. Census Bureau, Small Area Health Insurance Estimates (2009e), "2006 health insurance coverage status for states by age (under 65 years), income (all income levels), and sex (both sexes)," http://smpbffl.dsd.census.gov/TheDataWeb_HotReport/servlet/HotReportEngineServlet?reportid=90d4aac94ca4506912a04df088f6a76a&emailname=saeb@census.gov&filename=sahie06_st.hrml#. Accessed September 25, 2009.

U.S. Census Bureau, USA Counties (2009f), "Resident population 65 years and over, 2008," http://censtats.census.gov/cgi-bin/usac/usatable.pl. Accessed November 7, 2009.

U.S. Department of Health and Human Services, Agency for Health Research and Quality (2009a), "National healthcare disparities report, 2008," http://www.ahrq.gov/qual/qrdr08.htm. Accessed December 1, 2009.

U.S. Department of Health and Human Services, Health Resource and Service Administration (2009b), "Shortage designations: HPSAs, MUAs and MUPs," http://bhpr.hrsa.gov/shortage/index.htm. Accessed December 18, 2009.

U.S. Office of Management and Budget (2006), "Update of statistical area definitions and guidance of their uses," OMB Bulletin 07-01," http://www.whitehouse.gov/omb/bulletins/fy2007/b07-01.pdf. Accessed November 10, 2009.

University of Florida, Bureau of Economic and Business Research (2009), "Historical census counts for Florida and its counties 1830 through 2000," http://www.bebr.ufl.edu/node/18. Accessed November 5, 2009.

University of South Florida Health (2009), "Board of Governors approves USF Doctor of Pharmacy Program," http://hscweb3.hsc.usf.edu/health/now/?p=3618. Accessed January 13, 2010.

Valentine, Sean R. (2001), "Men and women supervisors' job responsibility, job satisfaction, and employee monitoring," *Sex Roles* (Vol. 45, No. 3/4, August), pp. 179–197.

Valian, Virginia (2004), "Beyond gender schemas: Improving the advancement of women in academia," *NWSA Journal* (Vol. 16, No. 1, Spring), pp. 207–220.

Van Praag, Bernard M. (1991), "Ordinal and cardinal utility: An integration of the two dimensions of the welfare concept," *Journal of Econometrics* (Vol. 50, No. 1-2, October), pp. 69–89.

Van Voorhis, Patricia, Francis T. Cullen, Bruce G. Link, *et al.* (1991), "The impact of race and gender on correctional officers' orientation to the integrated environment," *Journal of Research in Crime and Delinquency* (Vol. 28, No. 4, November), pp. 472–500.

Vandenberghe, Christian and Michael Tremblay (2008), "The role of pay satisfaction and organizational commitment in turnover intentions: A two-sample study," *Journal of Business Psychology* (Vol. 22, No. 3, March), pp. 275–286.

Vere, James P. (2007), "'Having it all' no longer: Fertility, female labor supply, and the new life choices of generation X," *Demography* (Vol. 44, No. 4, November), pp. 821–828.

Viscusi, W. Kip (2003), "Racial differences in labor market values of a statistical life," *The Journal of Risk and Uncertainty* (Vol. 27, No. 3, December), pp. 239–256.

Voydanoff, Patricia (1988), "Work role characteristics, family structure demands, and work/family conflict," *Journal of Marriage and the Family* (Vol. 50, No. 3, August), pp. 749–761.

Wah, Louisa (2000), "Managing Gen Xers strategically," *Management Review* (Vol. 89, No. 3, March), p. 6.

Waldfogel, Jane, Wen-Jui Han, and Jeanne Brooks-Gunn (2002), "The effects of early maternal employment on child cognitive development," *Demography* (Vol. 39, No. 2, May), pp. 369–392.

Wall, Thomas P. and L. Jackson Brown (2007), "The urban and rural distribution of dentists, 2000," *The Journal of the American Dental Association* (Vol. 138, No. 7, July), pp. 1003–1011.

Wallace, Amy E. and William B. Weeks (2002), "Differences in income between male and female primary care physicians," *Journal of the American Medical Women's Association* (Vol. 57, No. 4, Fall), pp. 180–184.

Walton, Surrey M. and Judith A. Cooksey (2001), "Differences between male and female pharmacists in part-time status and employment setting," *Journal of the American Pharmaceutical Association* (Vol. 41, No. 5, September/October), pp. 703–708.

Walton, Surrey M., Judith A. Cooksey, Katherine K. Knapp, *et al.* (2004a), "Analysis of pharmacist and pharmacist-extender workforce in 1998-2000: Assessing predictors and differences across states," *Journal of the American Pharmacists Association* (Vol. 44, No. 6, November/December), pp. 673–683.

Walton, Surrey M., Gayle R. Byck, Judith A. Cooksey, *et al.* (2004b), "Assessing differences in hours worked between male and female dentists: An analysis of cross-sectional national survey data from 1979 through 1999," *Journal of the American Dental Association* (Vol. 135, No. 5, May), pp. 637–645.

Walton, Surrey M., Katherine K. Knapp, Laura Miller, *et al.* (2007), "Examination of state-level changes in the pharmacist labor market using Census data," *Journal of the American Pharmacists Association* (Vol. 47, No. 3, May/June), pp. 348–357.

Wang, Ying and Dave E. Marcotte (2007), "Golden years? The labor market effects of caring for grand-children," *Journal of Marriage and the Family* (Vol. 69, No. 5, December), pp. 1283–1296.

Washburn, Earl R. (2000), "Are you ready for Generation X?," *Physician Executive* (Vol. 26, No. 1, January–February), pp. 51–57.

Watkin, Chris (2001), "How to improve organisational climate," *People Management* (Vol. 7, No. 13, June 28), pp. 52–53.

Watrous, Kristen M., Ann H. Huffman, and Robert D. Pritchard (2006), "When coworkers and managers quit: The effects of turnover and shared values on performance," *Journal of Business and Psychology* (Vol. 21, No. 1, September), pp. 103–126.

Watson, David (2000), *Mood and Temperament* (New York: The Guilford Press).

Weaver, Sally P., Terry L. Mills, and Cindy Passmore (2001), "Job satisfaction of family practice residents," *Family Medicine* (Vol. 33, No. 9, October), pp. 678–682.

Weeks, William B. and Amy E. Wallace (2006a), "Race and gender differences in general internists' annual incomes," *Journal of General Internal Medicine* (Vol. 21, No. 11, November), pp. 1167–1171.

Weeks, William B. and Amy E. Wallace (2006b), "The influence of physician race and gender on obstetrician-gynecologists' annual incomes," *Obstetrics and Gynecology* (Vol. 108, No. 3, Part 1, September), pp. 603–611.

Weeks, William B. and Amy E. Wallace (2006c), "The influence of race and gender on family physicians' annual incomes," *Journal of the American Board of Family Medicine* (Vol. 19, No. 6, November–December), pp. 548–556.

Weeks, William B. and Amy E. Wallace (2007a), "Differences in the annual incomes of emergency physicians related to gender," *Academic Emergency Medicine* (Vol. 14, No. 5, May), pp. 434–440.

Weeks, William B. and Amy E. Wallace (2007b), "Gender differences in ophthalmologists' annual incomes," *Ophthalmology* (Vol. 114, No. 9, September), pp. 1696–1701.

Weeks, William B. and Amy E. Wallace (2007c), "The influence of provider sex on neurologists' annual incomes," *Clinical Neurology and Neurosurgery* (Vol. 109, No. 1, January), pp. 38–44.

Weeks, William B. and Amy E. Wallace (2008), "Rural-urban differences in primary care physicians' practice patterns, characteristics, and income," *The Journal of Rural Health* (Vol. 24, No. 2, Spring), pp. 161–170.

Weeks, William B., Peter J. Mahar, and Steven M. Wright (2005), "Utilization of VA and Medicare services by Medicare-eligible veterans: The impact of additional access points in a rural setting," *Journal of Health Care Management* (Vol. 50, No. 2, March–April), pp. 95–106.

Weeks, William B., Amy E. Wallace, and Todd A. Mackenzie (2007), "Gender differences in anesthesiologists' annual incomes," Anesthesiology (Vol. 106, No. 4, April), pp. 806–811.

Weinberg, Daniel H. (2007), "Earnings by gender: Evidence from Census 2000," *Monthly Labor Review* (Vol. 130, No. 7/8, July/August), pp. 26–34.

Weisbard, Phyllis H. (2003), "New reference works in women's studies," *Feminist Collections* (Vol. 24, No. 2, Winter), pp. 26–30.

West, Alan N. and William B. Weeks (2006), "Physical and mental health and access to care among nonmetropolitan veterans health administration patients younger than 65 years," *The Journal of Rural Health* (Vol. 22, No. 1, Winter), pp. 9–16.

Whelan-Berry, Karen S. and Judith R. Gordon (2000), "Strengthening human resource strategies: Insights from the experiences of midcareer professional women," *Human Resource Planning* (Vol. 23, No. 1, March), pp. 26–37.

White, David A. (1996), "It's working beautifully! Philosophical reflections on aesthetics and organization theory," *Organization* (Vol. 3, No. 3, May), pp. 195–208.

Wichert, Ines C.(2002), "Job insecurity and work intensification: The effects on health and well-being." In *Job Insecurity and Work Intensification*, edited by Brendan Burchell, David Ladipo, and Frank Wilkinson (London: Routledge), pp. 92–111.

Woods, Amelia M. and Jerie Weasmer (2002), "Maintaining job satisfaction: Engaging professionals as active practitioners," *The Clearing House* (Vol. 75, No. 4, March), pp. 186–189.

Wright, Benjamin D. and Mark H. Stone (1979), *Best Test Design: Rasch Measurement* (Chicago: MESA Press).

Wright, Thomas A., Russell Cropanzano, Philip Denney, *et al.* (2002), "When a happy worker is a productive worker: A preliminary examination of three models," *Canadian Journal of Behavioural Science* (Vol. 34, No. 3, July), pp. 146–150.

Wu, Huoying (2007), "Can the human capital approach explain life-cycle wage differentials between races and sexes?," *Economic Inquiry* (Vol. 45, No. 1, January), pp. 24–39.

Xie, Yu, James M. Raymo, Kimberly Goyette, *et al.* (2003), "Economic potential and entry into marriage and cohabitation," *Demography* (Vol. 40, No. 2, May), pp. 351–367.

Xu, Jiaquan, Kenneth D. Kochanek, and Betzaida Tejeda-Vera (2009), "Deaths: Preliminary data for 2007," *National Vital Statistics Report* (Vol. 58, No. 1, August).

Yoder, Janice D. (1991), "Rethinking tokenism: Looking beyond numbers," *Gender and Society* (Vol. 5, No. 2, June), pp. 178–192.

Yoder, Janice D. and Theodore W. McDonald (1998), "Measuring sexist discrimination in the workplace: Support for the validity of the schedule of sexist events," *Psychology of Women Quarterly* (Vol. 22, No. 3, September), pp. 487–491.

Yutzie, Janelle D., John L. Shellito, Stephen D. Helmer, *et al.* (2005), "Gender differences in general surgical careers: Results of a post-residency survey," *The American Journal of Surgery* (Vol. 190, No. 6, December), pp. 978–983.

Zhang, Liang (2005), "Advance to graduate education: The effect of college quality and undergraduate majors," *The Review of Higher Education* (Vol. 28, No. 3, Spring), pp. 313–338.

Zurmehly, Joyce (2008), "The relationship of educational preparation, autonomy, and critical thinking to nursing job satisfaction," *The Journal of Continuing Education in Nursing* (Vol. 39, No. 10, October), pp. 453–460.

Zweigenhaft, Richard L. (1994), "Negotiating multiple statuses in the corporate world: The perceptions and experiences of some Black and Jewish women with Harvard MBAs." In *Ethnic Women: A Multiple Status Reality,* edited by Vasilikie Demos and Marcia T. Segal (New York: General Hall), pp. 145–154.